NYPD

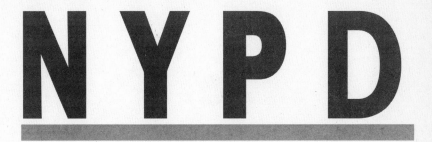

NYPD

A City and Its Police

James Lardner and Thomas Reppetto

A John Macrae / Owl Book

Henry Holt and Company   New York

Henry Holt and Company, LLC
Publishers since 1866
115 West 18th Street
New York, New York 10011

Henry Holt® is a registered trademark
of Henry Holt and Company, LLC.

Distributed in Canada by H. B. Fenn and Company Ltd.

Brief portions of this book originally appeared in
The New Yorker and *The New York Review of Books*.

Library of Congress Cataloging-in-Publication Data
Lardner, James.
   NYPD: a city and its police/James Lardner and
   Thomas Reppetto.—1st ed.
      p.   cm.
   Includes index.
   ISBN 0-8050-6737-X
   1. New York (N.Y.). Police Dept.—History.
   2. Police—New York (State)—New York.
   I. Reppetto, Thomas A.   II. Title
   HV8148.N5 N94   2000
   363.2'09747'1—dc21   00-023778

Henry Holt books are available for special promotions and
premiums. For details contact: Director, Special Markets.

First published in the United States in 2000
by Henry Holt and Company

First Owl Books Edition 2001

A John Macrae/Owl Book

Designed by Paula Russell Szafranski

Printed in the United States of America

3   5   7   9   10   8   6   4   2

"When I go to bed at night, I say a special prayer for the safety of the city. Then I say another special prayer of thanks that nothing bad happened in the police department."

—ROBERT WAGNER, MAYOR OF NEW YORK (1954–1965)

Contents

Introduction

Ghosts on Patrol

Late one summer evening, a man walked out the door of a hotel near the corner of Broadway and Forty-third Street into a hail of gunfire. The assassination of the gambler-squealer Herman Rosenthal, in July 1912, is thought to have been only the second time in New York City when a gang of killers used an automobile for their escape. It was the first and only murder for which a New York City police officer has gone to the electric chair. The cop, Lieutenant Charles Becker, who ran a much-celebrated headquarters vice squad, was accused of ordering the hit after Rosenthal went to the law with tales of police payoffs and (as he saw it) betrayal. The case filled the papers and convulsed the city right up to the grisly end, after the governor rejected the appeal for clemency made on her knees by Becker's wife. (Given the shabbiness of the evidence, a different governor might have let Becker live. Alas for the lieutenant, the man who held the office was the former district attorney who had sent him up in the first place.)

In the aftermath of Rosenthal's murder, the police commissioner was fired, the mayor dropped dead, one of the city's top political bosses was mysteriously run over by a train, and a long-established system of political control of the city's rackets came to an end, creating an opening for a dangerous new breed of crime lord. Yet the case that led to all this tumult has vanished from memory, unrecalled even by some New Yorkers who pride themselves on their knowledge of crime and local history.

Head down to the intersection of Lafayette and Kenmare Streets, in Little Italy, and you might actually find someone who has heard of Joseph Petrosino.

There's even a plaque in his memory alongside the miserable little parcel of fenced-in concrete known as Lieutenant Joseph Petrosino Square. Petrosino, you'll learn, was one of the first Italian-Americans on the NYPD and the only New York cop ever killed on foreign shores in the line of duty. The plaque skips over the more politically embarrassing details, however. You'd never know, for example, that after sending Petrosino off on a hush-hush mission to Italy in 1909, the police commissioner (a former general named Theodore Bingham) proceeded to blab about it to the press; thus, in the weeks leading up to his assassination in downtown Palermo, Petrosino's presence and purpose were well known to the very mafiosi he was there to investigate. A quarter of a million New Yorkers turned out for Petrosino's funeral. And he, too, is forgotten.

Busloads of tourists are regularly deposited at Seventy-second Street and Central Park West to gaze on the corner where John Lennon was gunned down. Chances are, their tour guides have never heard of Samuel Battle, the first African-American recruit accepted onto the NYPD. But at the beginning of his long and distinguished career, Battle frequently stood at the same intersection directing traffic. Carriage drivers would bring their passengers around to observe the "colored policeman," and local white youths would taunt him with cries of "There goes the nigger cop." Battle never responded. "They didn't know any better," he reasoned.

In fairness to the public, its amnesia on the subject of police history is hardly greater than that of the police themselves. Few of the six thousand detectives on today's NYPD would recognize the name of Inspector Thomas Byrnes, a towering figure of nineteenth-century policing who laid the foundation for modern big-city detective work. You'd be equally hard-pressed to find a cop who could identify Johnny Cordes, a real-life detective whose career was just as improbable as those of Kojak or the heroes of *NYPD Blue* or *Law and Order*. Cordes was a six-day bicycle racer and a Wall Street runner before he joined the force. Heading to work one night in March 1923, he walked into a holdup in a cigar store on Lexington Avenue near Seventieth Street. Having forgotten his gun—a habitual oversight—he was obliged to disarm the two holdup men in succession, sustaining three bullet wounds in the process. Running outside to seek help, he was shot twice more by a drunken off-duty sergeant who had mistaken Cordes for one of the robbers. His body was riddled with bullets by the time he walked into the hospital with one of the stickup men in tow. The *Times*, taking its cue from the doctors, wrote him off for dead the next morning. But Cordes survived to win the departmental medal of honor, and then to win it again—the only cop ever to do so twice—after catching a couple of kidnappers in equally wild and woolly fashion.

We could go on. And we will.

This book is a history of New York's police, from the 1820s, before the city got around to organizing them into a formal department, until the near present. Our aim is first and foremost to unearth and preserve a buried past and to show how the NYPD of today—forty thousand strong, with its high-tech war room of computer pin maps and its newfangled corporate lingo—developed out of a ragtag band of men who, in the mid-nineteenth century, slept in foul-smelling precinct dormitories for a good part of every tour of duty, smoked cigars on patrol, got their jobs through local aldermen (and lost them when the tides shifted), and often refused to investigate thefts unless rewards were offered.

Coming into being as New York rushed headlong into the industrial age, the police department was often confronted with riots and strikes, and control over the police became a matter of great importance to the city's economic elite. Police history, in other words, is a window onto the city's history; and as the nation's biggest and oldest police department—and the model on which others have patterned themselves—the NYPD's story has something to say about American urban life in general.

As often as not, the police have been a hot political topic. Just now, New Yorkers are grappling with the acquittal of four plainclothes cops in the death of Amadou Diallo, a street peddler from the West African nation of Guinea whose wallet got mistaken for a gun. Within a month of the verdict, handed down on February 25, two more unarmed black men had been shot to death, one of them an off-duty security guard wrongly suspected of being a drug dealer. Still another image in sharp focus is that of a Haitian immigrant, Abner Louima, being horribly tortured in a precinct bathroom three years ago by a Brooklyn patrolman (who later received a thirty-year prison sentence) wielding a broken broomstick. The cop had confused Louima with someone who had hit him during a sidewalk scuffle.

Mayor Rudy Giuliani is under fire for encouraging what critics regard as an over-aggressive brand of law enforcement, especially in minority neighborhoods. In fact, relations between police and minorities have been uneasy for much of the twentieth century. The twelve-year administration of Mayor Fiorello La Guardia saw two major race riots. After police killed a black man in 1942, a young Harlem minister, Adam Clayton Powell Jr., attacked the "racist police force" and "prima donna" mayor. Giuliani has tried, without great success, to get his critics to acknowledge that fatal shootings of civilians by the NYPD are at a modern low. The eleven New Yorkers killed in such incidents last year were less than one-fifth the number killed annually in the early 1970s, when the unabashedly liberal John V. Lindsay was mayor.

Does the world take a disproportionate interest in police misdeeds? It often looks that way; and strictly from a probability standpoint, a cop looking to get on TV or the front pages would be better off doing something criminal than something heroic. For all the to-do that is made over police scandals, however, the city has generally been quick to forget the bad as well as the good. In 1894, New Yorkers were transfixed by revelations of rampant crookedness and brutality. In their horror, the voters sent a mayor and a whole gang of pols packing, and with the police reins in the hands of Theodore Roosevelt—a take-charge leader if ever there was one—it looked as if the department had embarked on a decisively different course. A mere three years later, Roosevelt had vamoosed in the direction of San Juan Hill and the White House, the old crew was back in control of City Hall (amid chants of "Well, well, well, reform has gone to hell"), and the police department was in the grip of a man the reformers had tried to put behind bars—the corrupt and drunken Chief William Devery, described by the muckraking journalist Lincoln Steffens as a "magnificent villain . . . a work of art . . . a masterpiece."

In the news media, at least, the rogue cops have often come across as more compelling characters than their adversaries. Alexander "Clubber" Williams, for one, was an enormously engaging tyrant who had the wit to claim that his obviously ill gotten gains were the proceeds of real-estate speculation in Japan—an explanation almost too fantastic to disprove. (He had traveled there years earlier while working as a ship's carpenter.) Personalities aside, the dark episodes are well documented. The 1894 Lexow committee report alone required five volumes to tell the public that cops took payoffs from gamblers, madams, and saloonkeepers.

With such an abundance of data to draw on, historians naturally tend to focus on acts of wrongdoing, and police history becomes a pendular business, the profession swinging decisively back and forth between scandal and reform. But the drama of this approach is purchased at a high cost. Morally, the characters don't get accorded much in the way of middle ground. The organization, too, is either good or bad, depending on when you catch a glimpse of it. Little room is left for the acts of decency or heroism that occur under the most crooked regime; or for the haplessness and shaky judgment of a long line of reformers, of whom Roosevelt was only an early trailblazer.

From Roosevelt's day to ours, the great corruption scandals have come along every twenty years or so, with almost astronomical regularity. And each time around, the body politic seems compelled to adopt the same course. There's an investigation, followed by a trial or a round of public hearings and a call for reform. Edicts are issued, regulations promulgated, watchdog bodies created or strengthened. Time passes, the crisis fades, and . . . something like the same drama is enacted all over again.

The temptation to address police abuses with legalistic remedies is perfectly understandable. The police are a law-enforcement agency, after all, and one organized along military lines and subject to a host of rules and procedures. Underneath the bureaucratic rigmarole, however, lies a level of discretion and improvisation and just plain uncertainty that, to judge by its persistence, seems to have suited the convenience of people outside as well as inside the police profession. From the beginnings, their democratically elected masters have been reluctant to tell the police just which laws to enforce, against whom, or by what means. Whether we're talking about gambling and prostitution in the nineteenth century or the stop-and-search practices of the early twenty-first, the police have been left to sort out many of the most difficult questions for themselves. More than other municipal agencies, then, they are governed by unwritten and, in some cases, even unarticulated rules. A police station "is a great place for traditions," Steffens wrote. "There walk the ghosts of men notorious in their time," he added, "whom the town has forgotten absolutely, and the stories about them affect the manner of grip with which the policeman swings his club, or the temper in which he blackmails disorderly women."

Given the power that the police wield, the idea of their behavior being ruled, to any large extent, by hidden ideas and emotions is one that modern leaders must abhor; so they place their faith in orders, policies, and the official chain of command. Steffens expected the ghost of Teddy Roosevelt to hang over the department for a generation to come. Its failure to do so only proves what the NYPD has demonstrated time and again—that its appointed leaders are no match for what more prescient observers called its "inner life." In chronicling the affairs of this remarkable institution, we mean to zero in on that inner life—on the traditions, the fears, the lore, and all the lessons, official and unofficial, spoken and silent, that cops pass along from generation to generation, beginning with that fateful first night on patrol, when the veteran tells the rookie: "Forget everything you learned in the academy, kid."

NYPD

1

A Cry from the Bottom of the Hudson

Catching criminals and preventing crime on the streets of early-nineteenth-century New York was the work of a night watch of ordinary, moonlighting citizens and a small full-time force of constables and marshals. Watchmen were the lowly foot soldiers of policing. They walked beats, stood on fixed posts outside sentry boxes, and spent boring hours on reserve in the watchhouse. They were appointed by the alderman and assistant alderman of the ward (a neighborhood-sized municipal subdivision) and supervised by roundsmen and captains, who were part-timers themselves. Constable was also a ward office, but an elective one. Each ward had a pair of constables, who played a role akin to that of today's precinct captains. Marshals, appointed by the mayor, functioned more in the manner of detectives. While constables and marshals alike had broad police powers, the legal authority of a watchman was only that of any citizen—to make an arrest for a crime committed in his presence.

If an officer of the modern NYPD could walk in the shoes of these early forebears, he would be tempted to say they had it easy. The city was, for one thing, reassuringly finite. Its inhabitants, 123,000 strong in 1820, were concentrated at the bottom of the long narrow island of Manhattan, below Fourteenth Street, inside a crescent of docks and wharves and sailing ships with masts as high as the tallest buildings of the day. Most New Yorkers were native-born Americans and Protestants. The major ethnic division, between citizens of English and Dutch ancestry, no longer carried any sting. There were no housing projects or violent neighborhood gangs, to say nothing of such menaces as pistol-packing drug dealers. Not until the 1840s, in the frontier wars of Texas, did the Colt six-shooter win wide acceptance. In 1852, a Philadelphia gunsmith named Henry Deringer developed the Saturday night special of the nineteenth century. His competitors marketed it with an extra *r* added to the inventor's name.

Another element not yet present to disturb a police officer's peace of mind was the modern police reporter. There were newspapers—several dozen of them, including a handful of dailies. But they had a very refined idea of news. The papers were filled with ship departures and arrivals, treaty negotiations, and legislative debates over bank charter bills and the like—subject matter reflecting a readership of financiers, merchants, and close followers of politics. Local news in general got short shrift, and crime was almost invisible. A heinous offense such as a murder or embezzlement might rate a mention, but only, as a rule, when it became the subject of a legal proceeding, or, in other words, when the culprit had already been caught or hung. Little if anything was said about the unsolved case, the unapprehended suspect, or the uncontrolled disturbance—about any of the incidents with the potential to embarrass the guardians of law and order.

New Yorkers, by all reports, were reasonably satisfied with the level of public safety. "Those firebrands who would disturb the tranquillity of our city and assail the majesty of the laws comprise but a contemptible and insignificant number," Mayor De Witt Clinton declared in 1812. There were the usual sailors' haunts, of course, which attracted the predictable array of gamblers, prostitutes, and other criminal hangers-on. As late as 1817, however, an English traveler was struck by the sight of merchants leaving large stocks of goods in the streets without taking any precaution against theft.

Of all the men charged with keeping the peace in those days, the most prominent and formidable was Jacob Hays, appointed a marshal in 1798, at the age of twenty-six, and four years later named high constable of New York City—an office he continued to hold until his death in 1850, though his active career ended in the early 1840s. Hays's father ran a country store upstate and had soldiered in the revolutionary army under George Washington. The son benefited from a friendship with Aaron Burr, the political boss of the city at the beginning of the nineteenth century. Burr apparently helped engineer not only Hays's selection as high constable but the creation of the office, which was never held by anyone else.

Hays gained many admirers over the course of his long career. Short, stocky, and powerfully built, he prowled the streets attired in a black suit and a stovepipe hat with a white kerchief tied around his neck. His only weapon was a gold-tipped staff of office: he used it to break up riots by knocking the hats off the first group of combatants he reached. When they stooped to retrieve their bonnets, Hays would push them down until their bodies formed a neat pile. "Now all good citizens go home!" he would announce once he had the mob's attention; and "so well were his strength and his unflinching courage known" that these verbal directives usually sufficed, according to an account of his career published later in the century in the *New York Times*.

New Yorkers high and low tended to follow his instructions. In the 1820s, Cornelius Vanderbilt was a mere "captain"—not yet a "commodore"—illegally ferrying passengers across the Hudson River (or North River, as it was known) from New Jersey to New York City. The ferry franchise was a monopoly of the powerful Livingston family, which obtained an injunction against the interloper. Hays was assigned to enforce it. Since he had no authority in New Jersey, he had to catch Vanderbilt on the New York side of the river. The wily captain relied on spies to warn him when Hays or his men were in the vicinity. According to Vanderbilt himself, it was a personal encounter with the high constable that finally convinced him to yield. "I was mad enough to defy the whole Livingston tribe," he recalled, "but when I saw that calm smiling face with a twinkle saying in plainest words, 'If you don't obey the court's order, and obey it damn soon, I'll make you, by God,' I concluded to surrender." The surrender, however, was probably arranged. Vanderbilt's lawyers believed they had a good chance of prevailing in court, as indeed they soon did, ending the Livingston monopoly and removing an annoying obstacle from a path that would shortly lead to Vanderbilt's becoming one of the richest men in America.

The high constable was said to have a mental mug file on every rogue in the city. One day, a prosperous lawyer named R. M. Blatchford showed up at Hays's office to report the theft of a suit of clothes from a cottage that Blatchford had rented on Bleecker Street, in Greenwich Village—a bona fide village at the time. The thief had not only taken his new suit but had left in its place an old one, which Blatchford laid out for Hays's inspection. "I have reason to know this man," Hays declared. "His hair is red as blood. If you wait here for half an hour, I'll get him for you." As promised, he soon returned, ushering along the thief, who was wearing the stolen suit.

In 1820, a shipmaster named James Murray landed in New York flush with money and took a room at John Johnson's boardinghouse on Front Street. Johnson killed him and dumped the body in an alley. Out went the call for "Old Hays," as he had become known. Ordering the body removed to the watchhouse in the rotunda of City Hall, he began a canvass of the waterfront area. This turned up Johnson's name as a suspect, and Hays apprehended him on Broadway. Instead of taking him to a police facility, though, he brought the suspect into the city's most prominent church, Old Trinity, and sat him down in a pew for interrogation. God saw every act of mortal man, he began, and God would forgive, but only after confession and repentance. "Better to die by the rope than to lose one's immortal soul," he advised Johnson. The suspect chose body over soul, however, so Hays marched him over to the watchhouse, where the nude body of the dead man was reposing. Leading Johnson into the room, he stripped the sheet away and dramatically declared: "Look upon the body—have you ever seen that man before?"

"Yes, yes, I murdered him," Johnson reportedly stammered back. He recanted the confession at his trial, but reiterated it on the gallows.

In 1831, New York experienced its first recorded bank robbery, with three men stealing $200,000 in bills and Spanish doubloons from the City Bank, located on the old Dutch line of defense against Indian attacks—a boundary now known as Wall Street. Old Hays got a lead on the robbers from a servant girl who, peeking through a hotel-room keyhole, had seen them dividing up the money. Accompanied by his son, Hays raided the hotel and captured one of the gang, a man named Ed Smith, finding some of the stolen currency in a compartment of his trunk. Smith led Hays to a locksmith named Parkinson. While questioning him, Hays's attention was drawn to a jack plane that showed signs of being tampered with; he found $20,000 in stolen notes in a hollow groove of the plane. Alerted by Hays, the high constable of Philadelphia nabbed an accomplice and sent him to New York. After extracting a confession from this third suspect, Hays sent his son to Philadelphia to dig up the last bit of loot from under a big tree in Independence Square.

By the mid-1830s, however, Hays was in his sixties, and New York had begun to radiate the aura of menace and moral decay that Americans had previously—and scornfully—associated with the Old World. Even some Europeans reeled in disbelief when they visited the Five Points, the new republic's first world-class slum. Here, a few blocks up from City Hall, on spongy and noxious landfill atop what had been a pond in colonial times, tenements were nestled among saloons, dance halls, and gambling dens, which flourished under the management of Mississippi riverboat gamblers who had been driven out of their own territory. "Green groceries" displayed rotting vegetables outside and dispensed cheap liquor inside. Nearly a thousand people, half of them Irish, half black, lived in a single building—an old brewery that had been cut up into flats. Apocryphal stories held that it was the scene of a murder a night, and an adjacent path was known as Murderers' Alley.

The frontiersman and bear wrestler Davy Crockett wanted no part of New York in 1835. "I thought I would rather risque myself in an Indian fight than venture among these creatures afternight," he wrote in his diary after a brief visit. (The following year, he found himself at the Alamo, which proved to be more dangerous.)

Charles Dickens took a tour of the Five Points in January 1842, with Hays as his guide. Dickens wrote of "narrow ways . . . diverting to the right and left, and reeking everywhere with dirt and filth," "leprous houses . . . attainable only by crazy wooden stairs without," "lanes and alleys paved in mud knee-deep," and "hideous tenements which take their name from robbery and murder." Entering a house where "vapors issue forth that blind and suffocate," they made their way down to a subterranean chamber where blacks and whites "dance and game together." In this small but densely packed piece of the city, Dickens found "all that is loathsome, drooping, and decayed."

It was Mayor-turned-Governor Clinton's "Big Ditch," connecting the Great Lakes to the Hudson River, that turned the city into something more than a provincial port. With the opening of the Erie Canal, in 1825, transportation to, from, and within the new nation evolved into a hub-and-spoke system with just about everything and everybody passing through New York. Down the Hudson came wheat, coal, and timber. Up the East Coast came cotton and sugarcane. Across the Atlantic from Europe (in ships that carried American agricultural produce the other way) came silks, spices, and immigrants—many from Ireland—to do the grueling work of longshoremen, ferrymen, carters, hod carriers, ditch diggers, and railroad workers. Taking advantage of this tremendous through traffic in things and people, New York merchants set up factories to supply furniture, cast-iron stoves, ready-made clothing, and a host of other goods to the settlements of the hinterlands.

There was nothing orderly about New York's growth in the 1820s and '30s. The city took on the helter-skelter look of an oversized mining town. Buildings ate up spaces once designated as public squares. (The Common Council had "destroyed nearly all the good shaded nooks," the *New York Mirror* complained in 1840.) Public services of all kinds became a harried game of catch-up. Most streets had no sewers, and the water supply remained suspect until the opening of the Croton Reservoir in 1842. Fires were frequent and devastating. Every few years seemed to bring another cholera epidemic and a mass exodus of panicked gentry.

The first street gangs arose in the Five Points and the neighboring Bowery. One, aptly named the Forty Thieves, operated out of the Rosetta Peers green grocery as early as 1825. Another, the predominantly Irish Roach Guards, took its name from a local dive owner, Ted Roach. One night, a dissident faction of the Roach Guards was holding a meeting when somebody threw a dead rabbit in their midst; because a rabbit meant a rowdy and *dead* was an adjective connoting sharp or best, they took the name for their own. Another gang wore oversize plug hats, stuffing them with wool and leather to provide protection from brickbats and bludgeons. Soon other gangs adopted the practice, and the term *plug ugly* became a synonym for street hoodlums in general.

The Bowery, the slum to the north, was noted for its slaughterhouses, and many young men of the neighborhood worked as butcher boys—another term that became synonymous with rowdy. Here native-born "Yankees" and Irish-Americans had separate gangs, and the most spectacular clashes pitted the Yankee Bowery Boys against various contingents of Irish "b'hoys," notably the Dead Rabbits, who wore a red stripe on their trousers to set them off from the blue-striped Roach Guards. When they clashed, troops often had to be summoned to restore order.

As in most times and places when crime has been an issue, it floated in a swirl of other anxieties. An old social order was disintegrating. Longtime inhabitants did not necessarily appreciate the difference between the gang members and a new generation of clerks and mechanics who dressed in the plug-ugly manner, wore long greased curls called "soap locks," and patronized saloons, gambling joints, and oyster bars with basement antechambers featuring *tableaux vivants* of classical scenes enacted by nude women.

Clerks, laborers, and even domestics were acting uppity. With Andrew Jackson and his Democratic Party running the show in Washington, the remnants of the Knickerbocker aristocracy watched in dismay as the vote was extended to the masses of unpropertied New Yorkers and a new class of professional politician moved to the fore. On January 2, 1837, Mayor Cornelius W. Lawrence—the first mayor elected by direct vote—held an open house to usher in the new year. The guests at these affairs were expected to drop by for a glass of sherry and a bit of cake. This time, the party attracted a rougher breed of voters from the slum wards, where Lawrence had done well. Among the other offenses chronicled by the aristocratic former mayor, Philip Hone, the guests drained whiskey bottles, grabbed pieces of turkey and beef with their hands, and wiped their greasy fingers on the curtains. There was a fair amount of brawling before the mayor, with help from the police, succeeded in clearing the house and locking the doors.

By 1840, the population had risen to 300,000, and crime as well as rowdiness was a hot topic. Street robbers preyed on merchants and their messengers, who tended to carry large sums of cash. Pickpockets and sneak thieves worked the docks, the omnibus stops, and the hotels and restaurants. (Pocket watches were a choice piece of loot.) As store windows grew larger, burglars took to carrying stones or, lest they bloody their hands, glass-cutting equipment for break-ins. But while the crime rate was undoubtedly increasing, New Yorkers were also hearing more about crime, because of technological advances in the world of printing and publishing that were scarcely less important to the city's changing image than the opening of the Erie Canal.

The newspapers of the 1820s had been sold by annual subscription, at a price that worked out to about six cents an issue on average. Even if the contents had not put most people off, the cost would have. Now, like other crafts, printing was on the way to becoming an industry. With levers and rollers and steam power, the presses of the 1830s could handle thousands of sheets of paper an hour. A revolution in commerce, meanwhile, had given rise to a host of new mass-produced goods for the middle and laboring classes. Lower Broadway was a retailers' row of jewelers and watchmakers, hatters, confectioners, and dry goods stores. On Chatham Street (later renamed Park Row), a shopping boulevard that angled north and east of City Hall Park, artisans, sailors, domestic servants, and laborers and their families strolled through a raucous, multi-accented outdoor marketplace filled with "hot corn girls," secondhand clothes dealers, and pushcart peddlers selling factory-made shoe-laces and matches, among other novelties. Inspired by their example, a printer named Benjamin Day launched the *New York Sun* in September 1833. Sold for a penny an issue, it had a circulation of over nineteen thousand within a year, and news of the police courts (where, in the words of one historian, each new morning brought a fresh supply of "raggamuffins, rum heads, rogues, rioters, and runaway apprentices") swiftly emerged as one of the most popular features. By January 1836, the city had half a dozen penny papers, hawked, as Philip Hone lamented in his diary, "by a gang of troublesome, ragged boys . . . in which scandal is retailed to all who delight in it." Journalists had begun to penetrate (and write sneering stories about) the dinner parties and balls of the city's elite. To men of Hone's class and generation, the lords of the penny press were an indistinguishable mass of hooligans—until an editor more scurrilous and abhorrent than the rest emerged from the pack.

James Gordon Bennett was a small, wiry, nervous man, cross-eyed (and self-conscious about it), with a stooped posture, long silver hair, and a gray chin beard. After emigrating from Scotland in young manhood, he held a series of newspaper jobs up and down the East Coast, working for, and quarrel-ing with, some of the leading editors of the day. By the time he founded the *New York Herald*, in 1835, Bennett was through with being a hireling. "Shakespeare is the great genius of the drama," he noted, "Scott of the novel, Milton and Byron of the poem—and I mean to be the genius of the news-paper press." His paper would be "the greatest organ of social life." Why not? "Books have had their day—the temple of religion has had its day," he observed, adding that "A newspaper can send more souls to Heaven, and save more from Hell, than all the churches or chapels in New York."

Bennett used his paper to go after the perpetrators of great misdeeds, and he used it to go after people who had crossed him. Either way, the tone of high moral outrage and the rat-terrier persistence of his attacks were the same. Walt Whitman described him as a "reptile marking his path with slime wherever he goes and breathing mildew at everything fresh and fragrant." Horace Greeley, who founded the *New York Tribune* in 1841, called him an "unmitigated blockhead." ("Galvanize a large New England squash," Bennett replied, "and it would make as capable an editor as Greeley.") Yet he was a towering figure in the history of American journalism. Hugely energetic, Bennett went places the press had never been before and used language it had never used—words like *legs*, *arms*, and *pants*, for example, as applied to the female form. And nothing seemed to give him more pleasure than being denounced, as he continually was, by ministers and other preservers of decorum. "Petticoats—petticoats— petticoats—petticoats—there—you fastidious fools, vent your mawkishness on that," Bennett wrote in reply to one blast of clerical criticism.

He started out, actually, with no intention of covering crime—not the sort that took place in homes and streets, anyway. Bennett had made his reputation with a series of veil-lifting articles on the world of stock speculation. In an early declaration of the *Herald*'s purpose, he denounced the *Sun* for its frivolous police-court coverage, and especially for publishing the names of vagrants and drunks. The *Herald*, he vowed, would "exclude all such folly from our columns."

But soon enough, he realized the value of such folly. Ordinary readers were interested in the sins and missteps of ordinary people—their brawls, debauches, and drunken antics. The police courts were a bountiful source of such tales, and they came cheap. Since the police and the judiciary, at taxpayer expense, had done most of the news gathering, the reporter had only to station himself in a corner, scribbling away as suspects were brought in, one by one, to be jailed, released, warned, or held over for trial. Staying inconspicuous was a good policy, in fact, for criminal offenders were not yet accustomed to having their activities broadcast. In July 1835, the *Herald* published an account of a drunk-and-disorderly case in which the defendant appealed to the court for protection from the press. "If I did have a kick-up, that's no reason why all the city should know it," he complained.

Bennett was still getting his footing as a newspaper magnate when, on April 10, 1836, fate presented him with the hatchet murder of a courtesan, Helen Jewett. The victim (as New Yorkers learned largely through the *Herald*'s enterprise) was a poor girl from Maine, born Dorcas Doyen, who had been taken into the family of a Portland judge, only to be cast out again when he got wind of behavior—dalliances with several young men of the neighborhood—that made her a poor role model for his children. Thus was

Jewett launched on her career as a "girl in town," first in Portland, then in Boston, and finally in New York. There she was fortunate to secure a place, on Thomas Street, with Rosina Townsend, a madam who ran as orderly and refined an establishment as she could make it. Townsend was equally lucky to have Jewett, who was keenly intelligent and never made the men who paid for her company feel like customers. She accompanied them to the theater. She did their sewing. She wrote letters to them—letters filled, as Bennett commented, with "apt quotations from the Italian, French, and English poets." It was Townsend who discovered the body and, at the same time, a fire set by the killer in the hope of covering up his deed. Hearing cries of alarm, four night watchmen came running: fire was an important part of their reason for being, and with pitchers and pots of water and several of the women of the house helping, they put the fire out and sent word back to a watch station in City Hall Park, a few blocks away. More officers, including George Noble, the assistant captain of the watch, arrived. So did Dennis Brink, one of the two constables of the ward. Brink and Noble interviewed witnesses and organized a search for evidence—a search rewarded, at daybreak, by the discovery of the hatchet and a long blue cloak that had apparently served to conceal it. By late morning, they had identified a suspect and traced him to a boardinghouse on Dey Street, where they apprehended him.

The accused, Richard Robinson, was the nineteen-year-old scion of what the press, in unison, pronounced a "respectable" Connecticut family. His father farmed near New Haven and eventually served eight terms in the state legislature. Young Robinson had come to New York, like thousands of others, to make money and learn the ways of business—in his case, as a clerk in a cloth merchant's shop on Maiden Lane. The story was a rare glimpse into the world of the bordello; it was also a look at the liberated lives of a significant new class of young men. Robinson was part of a great migration of New Englanders who accounted for much of New York's population growth in the early nineteenth century, before they, in turn, were overwhelmed by the tide of Irish and Germans. Many were the surplus male children of farming families seeking to make the transition to the world of commerce. In an earlier time, they would have lived with their employers; now, with the older part of the city getting dirtier and more volatile, merchants retreated to safer and larger homes uptown, leaving their employees to dwell in boardinghouses, dine at oyster bars, and have their evenings to themselves. Robinson belonged to a set of "sporting men," many of them clerks like himself, who frequented brothels, traded tips about the women they met there, and visited them serially. The newspapers of the day were filled with tales of rustic innocents destroyed by the sinful city. Evangelical Protestant missionaries decried the waning influence of church and family on these vulnerable young men. But the much bemoaned anonymity of city life was plainly a big part of what attracted so many of them to New York in the first place.

When word of the killing reached him, Bennett did an astonishing thing: he went to the scene. The murder had occurred shortly before 3:00 A.M. Sunday. Late that afternoon, Bennett showed up at Rosina Townsend's place and, with little ado, was admitted into Jewett's room. ("He is an editor—he is on public duty," a police officer on guard duty was said to have explained.) Readers of the *Herald* were thus permitted to study the remains with Bennett as their guide.

"Here," the police officer told him. "Here is the poor creature."

The officer "half-uncovered the ghastly corpse." So ghastly, Bennett added, that he "could scarcely look at it for a second or two." A second or two was enough, however, for Bennett to take in "the perfect figure, the exquisite limbs, the fine face, the full arms, the beautiful bust"—a body as white and polished, he declared, as "the purest Parisian marble" and surpassing "in every respect the Venus de Medicis." (Bennett had evidently performed a certain amount of mental embalming work in composing these words: all traces of the hatchet blows and the fire had vanished.)

New Yorkers had never seen crime reporting like this; nor had Bennett's fellow editors. His visit to the brothel, one paper commented, was the act of a "vampire returning to a newly found graveyard . . . like any vile thing to its congenial element."

The testimony of Townsend and several of Jewett's coworkers placed Robinson in the room with her on the night of the killing. The murder weapon matched a missing hatchet used to open crates at the cloth shop on Maiden Lane where Robinson was employed. As for the cloak, the suspect denied owning such a garment until friends contradicted him; one even recalled seeing him in it earlier on the night in question. In the *Herald*, however, Robinson became a "young, amiable, and innocent youth" framed by "the police establishment, which is rotten to the heart" and the "licentious inmates of a fashionable brothel." Picking up on these themes, Robinson's slash-and-burn defense lawyer, Ogden Hoffman, zeroed in on Dennis Brink, the constable. At the trial—the O. J. Simpson case of its day—Hoffman made much of the fact that Brink lived across the street from a brothel, at 48 Leonard Street: Had he not played cards with prostitutes? Had he not adjudicated disputes between them? (No, Brink replied to both questions.)

Living across the street from a brothel was not, in fact, so very remarkable at the time. Neighborhoods had yet to become clearly identified either by class of society or by type of activity: homes, shops, factories, saloons, and, in some cases, brothels could be found on a single block. Jewett had worked for three such establishments, all in the same small area to the west of City Hall Park. The laws against prostitution, like other criminal laws, had been written in the state capital of Albany, where a strict Protestantism reigned. Constable was an elected post, and sentiment was not so one-sided in the city, especially not in Lower Manhattan, where single males formed a majority of the population. Women, of course, didn't vote. When bad publicity finally forced Rosina Townsend to close her business, she hired Brink to help oversee a streetside auction of her worldly goods; so the constable did have business dealings with a woman running a criminal enterprise. But it was common for such officials, on the side, to provide security for saloons, gambling dens, and even bordellos. Brink's only obvious slipup in the Jewett investigation was his failure to pursue a significant group of potential witnesses—the patrons of Townsend's establishment who happened to be there at the time of the murder. In the initial confusion, these men all quietly departed. But this, too, was entirely normal for the period. Brink was simply placating his constituents, while he tried to catch a killer.

The defense scenario, in any case, cast Brink as a mere accessory. Who had actually done the deed? "The deliberate setting fire to the house," Bennett argued, "has more the character of female vengeance in it than that of the heedless passion of a youth of nineteen." He did not hesitate to suggest a female. The culprit he proposed was Rosina Townsend, who, as he confided to his readers, had "the eyes of the devil."

Robinson's lawyer, Hoffman, also sought to direct suspicion her way. But the cornerstone of the defense was Hoffman's contention that the testimony of prostitutes and madams was inherently worthless—a viewpoint embraced wholeheartedly by the judge. After a three-hour summation speech that even one hostile newspaper called "as great a masterpiece of eloquence as was ever delivered at the Bar," the jury, to the dismay of most New Yorkers, took about ten minutes to find Robinson innocent. The audience—an overflow crowd of Robinson's sympathizers, some wearing soft, beret-like "Frank Rivers caps" to display their support—cheered nearly as long.

Prior to Bennett's appearance on the scene, most of the crime stories in the penny press had been brief items strung together gossip-column style. With the Jewett case, Bennett demonstrated that if a crime was bloody and disturbing enough, it could be spun out into a drama that filled columns, pages, and indeed a whole newspaper for weeks or even months on end. Robinson's trial was the first to be covered by newspapers from all over the country. Clergymen delivered sermons about it. It was talked about in shops and coffeehouses. The technology did not yet exist, of course, to permit the kind of round-the-clock, full-frontal assault on the senses that such a case might bring today; yet the *Herald* could stand tall with the news organizations of our own time when it came to the fundamentals of unearthing and communicating the most lurid aspects of a crime of horrible violence, and somehow managing to condemn and compound the horror at once. And in the police and the law-enforcement establishment, Bennett had found an easy target.

The key figures in the criminal justice system of the day were the magistrates or justices of the peace. These were petty judicial offices usually filled by men without formal legal training. The constables and marshals who served under them were largely paid on a piecework basis: a constable got thirty-seven cents for each warrant served and fifty cents for each jury summoned. That was the official compensation, anyway; victims of crime were free to supplement it, and notices were regularly posted at the police offices promising fifty or a hundred dollars for the recovery of a piece of property. Naturally enough, many officials allocated their energies accordingly. In July 1835, the *Herald* denounced a nameless group of police officers for extorting large rewards before they would return stolen property to victims of theft. The reward system, the *Herald* said, made the police "mere loafers on the public—selling their duties to the highest bidder—and only suppressing crime or catching rogues when private individuals come forward to offer money for the performance of public duties." The authorities would do nothing "without a reward," the *Herald* went on to say, "and even if they possess a clue to the mystery, still they would keep the secret intact, like a capital in trade, till public indignation has raised a sum sufficient" to arouse them. It was an arrangement that made some constables rich, and, as parallel city and state investigations found in 1840, they did not have much of a stake in preventing crime or putting criminals behind bars. "A man may have his pocket robbed of thousands of dollars, and pay half the money to some of our Justices to recover the other half back," the *Herald* noted.

The night watch, meanwhile, was looking increasingly antique. In colonial times, watch duty had been required on a rotating basis of every adult male citizen, unless he paid for a substitute. By the 1830s, it was paid work—a piece of patronage dealt out by the aldermen. Still, it remained a part-time job rather than a vocation unto itself. Members of the watch worked every other night, as a rule. While on duty, they alternated two-hour shifts, with one group posted on the streets and the other held in reserve for emergencies. In the winter, they reported for duty at 7:30 P.M., in summer at 9:00 P.M., patrolling until sunrise. They were expected to help fight fires, suppress disorder, and arrest criminals caught in the act, for a wage of $1.25 a night. The municipality equipped them with a thirty-three-inch club to protect them from evildoers, and with a wooden sentry box to shield them from the elements. Their uniform consisted of a leather helmet, which, through the process of being varnished twice a year, became as hard and heavy as iron. Members of the watch were known as "leatherheads," and the snoring leatherhead had become a popular butt of jokes and pranks. Young men out on the town would top off the evening by knocking over the whole package of box and occupant. Peer pressure had even driven the young Washington Irving, generally a well-behaved youth, to assist a group of rowdies in lassoing a box and dragging it down Broadway while the watchman inside howled for help.

Wonderfully democratic in concept, the watch was perhaps a little too democratic in practice. Party loyalty was the qualification that counted most, and sometimes the aldermen who did the hiring used the office to reward the unfortunate or infirm. Even the hardiest specimens, though, were often not in a peak state of alertness by the time they hit the streets. After a ten-hour day at his regular trade, "the jaded stevedore, teamster or mechanic could hardly be expected to display much enterprise or energy," observed the police historian Augustine Costello, writing in the 1880s. "It is safe to assume that he performed his duties in a perfunctory manner, and that 'the knights of the jimmy' and other midnight marauders did not hold him in special reverence or dread."

The 1830s seemed to bring one disaster or sensational crime after another: a cholera epidemic in 1832, an outbreak of gang warfare followed by vicious mob attacks on abolitionists in 1834. In 1835, the biggest fire in sixty years led to looting that was suppressed only by military intervention. In 1837, there were bread riots after the country fell under the grip of a terrible depression. The *Herald* tallied nineteen riots (as well as twenty-nine murders) in a ten-month period ending in February 1840. The inadequacy of the police was "notorious," declared the *Commercial Advertiser*, which had more of a reputation for accuracy. "Destructive rascality stalks at large on our streets and public places, at all times of the day and night, with none to make it afraid."

As early as 1830–31, that most astute of foreign observers, Alexis de Tocqueville, offered a suggestion. The size and demographics of American cities made them a danger to "the future security of the democratic republic of the New World," he wrote. His solution was "an armed force which, while it remains under the control of the majority of the nation . . . will be independent of the town population and able to repress its excesses."

London by now had a full-time professional force directly controlled by the national government. The London police, established in 1829 under Home Secretary Sir Robert Peel, patrolled by day as well as night; they were uniformed and highly visible; and they stressed prevention rather than investigation of crime. Whipped into shape by Colonel Charles Rowan, a Waterloo veteran who preferred to recruit his subordinate officers from former NCOs (thirteen of seventeen division superintendents were ex–sergeant majors), the London police received legal guidance from their co-commissioner, Richard Mayne, an Irish barrister, and they survived riots, parliamentary investigations, and other trials to achieve popularity with the citizenry as crime and disorder began to decrease.

In 1836, Mayor Lawrence forwarded a report to the Common Council advocating a London-style reorganization of the police. But the idea did not sit well with the committee formed to consider it. While such a force might be required "at some future period," the councillors acknowledged, "the present system, with some alterations, may be made amply sufficient for this city, for many years to come. The nature of our institutions are [*sic*] such that more reliance may be placed upon the people for aid, in case of any emergency, than in despotic governments."

But the campaign continued, and since it was not politically correct to call for a professional police force as a means of controlling riots or strikes, the crusaders focused on violent crime. Murder, for example, was something people of all classes could get excited about. With the penny press and Bennett on the case, the most sensational killings became occasions for a burst of public agitation. The decisive event came in 1841 with the death of Mary Rogers, who had set out from the boardinghouse that she ran with her mother in the heart of lower Manhattan to visit an aunt in Greenwich Village, only to turn up dead, three days later, off the shores of Hoboken, New Jersey. Her body was found floating in the Hudson, alongside what had become New Yorkers' favorite recreational area—the Elysian Fields, a complex of taverns, hotels, and parks where one contingent of young men had begun to develop the game of baseball. Rogers, who was twenty-one years old at the time of her death, had worked behind the counter of a fashionable tobacco shop on Nassau Street— the publishers' row of the day. The owner, John Anderson, had hired her to attract business, and she was said to have been admired by James Fenimore Cooper and Edgar Allan Poe, among other luminaries. Poe made her the heroine of his "Mystery of Marie Rogêt," transferring the story, as he imagined it, from New York to Paris. Bennett himself may have remembered Rogers; he was almost certainly acquainted with Anderson, who, like himself, was active in the Democratic Party club—not yet worthy of the term *machine*— known as Tammany Hall. (It had lifted the name from a similar club in Philadelphia, which had taken it from an Indian chief who signed a treaty with William Penn.)

Once more, Bennett packaged the story as a case study in official incompetence. Rogers's death—"the recent awful violation and murder of an innocent young woman," as the *Herald* put it—was an indictment of "the apathy of the great criminal judges, sitting on their own fat for a cushion bench . . . and the utter inefficiency of their police . . . leading fast to reduce this large city to a savage state of society—without law—without order—and without security of any kind." The inquiry did seem to zigzag around. Yet in fairness to the police, the law at the time permitted suspects to be held for days without being charged, and arresting first and finding evidence later was standard procedure.

There were also territorial complications: because the body had been found in New Jersey, the investigation proceeded on two tracks. The Jersey authorities, led by Justice of the Peace Gilbert Merritt, focused on a German woman, Mrs. Loss, who ran a shady tavern in the Hoboken area. On the New York side of the river, the principal investigator was Justice Robert Taylor, and he and the men under him chose to focus on the victim's sex life.

The Jewett investigation had been handled largely at the constable level, because the case seemed (to the authorities, at least) straightforward. Because Rogers's death was seen as a "mystery," the task of solving it fell to the police-court justices. Like most of his peers, though, Taylor was more cop than jurist. As a young man, he had helped defend a ship he was traveling on from a pirate attack. In 1837, Taylor had been made captain of the Third Ward night watch, and a year later he was appointed to the bench. If, in fact, the key to Rogers's death lay in her sexual history, Taylor was well prepared to lead such an investigation, for his career had frequently taken him to houses of prostitution. Much of a magistrate's work in those years involved domestic disputes, and Taylor had questioned many a brothelkeeper in his efforts to get to the bottom of a disgruntled wife's complaint against an erring husband.

In the Rogers case, he began by checking out reports of a man she had supposedly been seen with on the day of her death. The lace around her neck had been tied in a knot that, according to some accounts, indicated a seaman's training. Suspicion accordingly fell on William Kiekuck, a sailor who had lived briefly in the Rogerses' boardinghouse on Nassau Street. But Kiekuck, who said he had "never walked out with her in his life," had a well-documented and highly credible alibi. Between Sunday morning and Tuesday, when he had reboarded the U.S.S. *North Carolina* in the harbor (there to be arrested by the police), he had visited friends at a sailors' boardinghouse uptown, had gone drinking, and, both on Sunday night and again on Monday, had picked up prostitutes.

After Kiekuck's star faded, the authorities turned their attention to a wood engraver named Joseph Morse. Described by the *Tribune* as a "frequent inmate of the store of Mr. Anderson when tended by Miss Rogers," Morse had been absent from his home on the day of her disappearance, and the next morning he had fled the city after a violent quarrel with his wife. On orders from Justice Taylor, a police officer pursued Morse all the way to Boylston, Massachusetts, where he was found living under an assumed name and brought back to

New York by steamboat. ARREST OF THE SUSPECTED MURDERER, the *Tribune* proclaimed. Morse acknowledged spending the night with a woman named Mary; indeed, he had run away believing her to be the Mary Rogers whose violent death was on everyone's lips. A few days later, however, a young woman named Mary Haviland came forward to corroborate his story and declare that *she* was the Mary in question. Morse still had some issues to resolve with Mrs. Morse. Otherwise, he was off the hook.

Whatever the shortcomings of the official detective work, it certainly compared well with that of the press. The role played in Rogers's life by John Anderson, the cigar merchant, was conspicuous by its absence from all the newspapers. Anderson, as Bennett probably knew, had been Rogers's lover as well as her boss, and during her period as a "segar girl" she had disappeared once before, supposedly leaving a suicide note; the incident had been reported in the papers, as had the subsequent announcement that it had all been a great mistake—she had merely gone to see an aunt in Brooklyn. Here, surely, was a promising line of inquiry. Yet the *Herald* scarcely mentioned Anderson. Of all the statements taken by the magistrate's office after Rogers's death, his was the only one never quoted or cited. Bennett seemed almost magnetically drawn, on the other hand, to the notion that she had been abducted and killed by members of a street gang—the one theory of the case that absolved all of her intimates. At first, the *Herald* seemed convinced that a gang of black men had committed the deed, later that a gang of "butcher boys, soap-locks, and all sorts of riotous miscreants . . . armed with sticks and clubs" had taken her across the Hudson in two boats, "one with six and the other with nine desperadoes in them."

The authorities never did catch Mary Rogers's murderer. But, as time passed, it seemed increasingly unlikely that she had been murdered in the first place. In the fall of 1842, Mrs. Loss, the keeper of Nick Moore's house in Hoboken, was on her deathbed as a result of an accidental wounding. Sending for Justice Merritt, she was said to have confessed to him that Rogers had come to her with "a young physician who undertook to procure for her a premature delivery," and had died "in the hands of her physician." She had wound up in the Hudson after "a consultation . . . as to the disposal of her body." Although some devotees of the case continued to pursue other theories, the abortion story (with or without the involvement of the conveniently unidentified "young physician") rang all too true. It explained a number of things at once, including the evidence of violation and her earlier disappearance, in which a visit to an aunt had also served as a cover story. Rumors of an abortion had circulated at the time, and if the authorities were halfhearted in investigating Rogers's death, it may have been because they knew or suspected the truth. Bennett himself may have entertained suspicions along those lines. But he was not one to let considerations of fact stand in the way of a good fulmination. New York City, the *Herald* declared on August 12, 1841, "is disgraced and dishonored in the eyes of the Christian and civilized world unless one great big, one strong moral movement be made to reform and reinvigorate the administration of criminal justice, and to protect the lives and property of its inhabitants from public violence and public robbery. Who will make the first move in this truly great moral reform?"

The answer to his question was: Bennett himself. By 1841, the *Herald* had more than fifty thousand readers and could no longer afford to tilt its coverage (as it had with the Jewett case) to the tastes of sporting young men. Bennett had come around to acknowledging Robinson's probable guilt. (The failure to convict him was, in Bennett's telling, yet another proof of police ineptitude and corruption. One of the maxims of the penny press was that nobody remembered past stories.) Bennett convened a committee of public safety, placing it under the leadership of William Attree, his star police reporter, snatched away from the *Transcript*. Attree's crusading credentials were, if possible, even wobblier than his boss's. He had covered the Helen Jewett case for the *Transcript*, not bothering to mention that he had been a patron of Jewett's himself. After writing a sympathetic news story that portrayed her as a woman delivered into a life of sin by a "heartless seducer" whom she had known in Boston, Attree had written to her confessing: "What a prize the villain had who seduced you at the Boarding School. How I should liked to have been in his place."

Bennett's committee, originally created to get to the bottom of the Rogers case, gradually took on the expanded mission of pressing for a professional police department. For months on end, the *Herald* led the charge with diatribe after diatribe against a "petty officialdom" preoccupied with "petty crimes" while the "blood of Mary Rodgers [*sic*] is crying out for vengeance from the depth of the Hudson."

In 1842, public anger at the criminal justice system flared again—heated up by, among other things, the murder of Samuel Adams by John Colt, younger brother of the wealthy Colonel Samuel Colt, inventor of the revolver. In September 1841, Adams went to Colt's quarters and asked for some money due him. An altercation ensued. Later, a stench arose from a box waiting to be loaded onto a ship bound for New Orleans. In it was the body of Adams. Colt admitted to killing him with an axe but pleaded self-defense. He was convicted of murder and sentenced to hang. So far, the criminal justice system had functioned well; but in November 1842, while awaiting execution at the Tombs, Colt requested permission from the warden to marry his mistress, Carolyn Henshaw. (Completed in 1838, the jail and court complex known as the Tombs—officially, the Hall of Justice—was inspired by an ancient Egyptian mausoleum. Although it was demolished in 1896, its successors, none of which have looked at all Egyptian, have carried on the name, and all have contained a "Bridge of Sighs" connecting the prison to the scaffold or, in more recent times, to the criminal court building.)

With Colt's brother in attendance, the ceremony was performed, and the couple was allowed an hour of privacy. After the new Mrs. Colt left the prison, a fire was spotted in the adjoining courthouse. Colt took advantage of the confusion to commit suicide by stabbing himself in the chest—so, at any rate, said the officials responsible for holding him. Later, though, it came out that several prisoners had escaped during the fire. Many believed that Colt had been one of them, helped perhaps by his brother's money, and that a body had been substituted for him. These suspicions were encouraged by his bride's disappearance at about the same time, and by Sam Colt's refusal, a year later, to comment one way or the other on the matter. John Colt was widely believed to have lived the rest of his days, with his wife, on a large California estate.

That year, a city council committee issued a report decrying the level of crime and the apparent ineffectuality of the official efforts to combat it. "The property of the citizen is pilfered, almost before his eyes," the committee declared. "Dwellings and warehouses are entered with ease and apparent coolness and carelessness of detection which shows that none are safe. Thronged as our city is, men are robbed in the street. Thousands that are arrested go unpunished and the defenseless and the beautiful are ravished and murdered in the day time, and no trace of the criminal is found. The man of business, in his lawful calling at the most public corner of our city, is slaughtered in the sunshine and packed up and sent away by the most public and known channels of trade, and suspicion is hardly excited."

The inadequacy of the existing police—now consisting of 100 marshals, 16 "police officers," 108 Sunday officers (who enforced the laws of the Sabbath), and, at the ward level, 34 constables and roughly a thousand watchmen—was generally accepted. It is not clear how soon New York City officialdom, left to its own devices, would have gotten around to creating a modern police force. But municipalities were creatures of the state, so the advocates of reform took their case to the Whig governor, William H. Seward. And in 1844, at his urging, the legislature passed an act abolishing the night watch and marshals (though not the constables) and creating a unified full-time day-and-night police force of 800 men. There was a slight delay in implementing the new law, for the nativist, or Know-Nothing, party had just installed James Harper (of the publishing family) as mayor. The legislative act called for police officers, like the old night watch, to be appointed by the local aldermen. The Know-Nothings preferred to have them named by the mayor, since ward control, in parts of the city, meant giving immigrants a lot of input. There would be issues of patronage to sort out, too: the act abolished not only the mayor's marshals but a number of other municipal functionaries, such as street and dock inspectors. While the city and state dickered back and forth on these points, Mayor Harper established his own Municipal Police, or M.P.s, as they were known from the insignias they wore on their collars. But in fairly short order, the pendulum shifted back, with Democrat William Havemeyer succeeding Harper, and on May 23, 1845, the city council passed an ordinance adopting the 1844 state law, to take effect ten days later. At last the city had a police department—the child of the press, which would continue to watch over its offspring, sometimes with a harsh and unforgiving eye, and at other times with blind love.

2

"I Might as Well Carry a Club"

On a bitterly cold night in December 1847, a rookie policeman named George Washington Walling was walking a beat along Broadway near City Hall. With criminals and potential crime victims both in short supply, his gaze kept wandering to an establishment known as Buttercake Dick's, on the far side of City Hall Park. Studying its brightly lit, cream-frosted windows and imagining the warmth inside, Walling suddenly felt very sure that the city would not be harmed by his temporary absence from his post.

The place turned out to be filled with police officers who had come to the same conclusion, only sooner. Buttercake Dick himself took Walling's order as if it was the most natural thing in the world. Being new, however, Walling hurried through his cake and coffee, and returned to find the very thing he feared: his sergeant waiting for him.

"Where have you been, sir?" the sergeant asked.

"To Buttercake Dick's, sir," Walling replied, nervously but forthrightly.

"You must never do that again or your name will be sent up," said the sergeant. Seeing the young officer's dismay, he added a condition: "In *very* severe weather," Walling recalled long afterward, "if I were *very* cold, and if coffee was *very* necessary, I could wait till I saw him, ask his permission, and he would patrol my post till I returned."

Walling was a sturdily built twenty-four-year-old whose ancestors, originally from Wales and Denmark, had lived in New Jersey since the late 1600s.

His father was an engineer and surveyor who had run a general store in the county of Monmouth, twenty miles (and a world away) from New York. The son, who was big and strong and conspicuously good at sports, spent much of his youth outdoors, hunting, fishing, rowing, and sailing. As a boy, he attended village schools, clerked in his father's store, and frequently accompanied him to the city to buy supplies—a trip that took a day by packet boat. Later he worked on vessels that plied the Hudson River and Long Island Sound, and briefly on a United States revenue cutter—the forerunner of the coast guard. (During one of the big fires that plagued New York in those years, the crew stood on antilooting duty with a force of marines from the Brooklyn Navy Yard—Walling's first taste of law enforcement.) By his early twenties, the tug of urban society had overcome the call of the sea. Walling moved into the city and went into business for himself, buying produce off the riverboats and selling it at the Washington Market.

That had been his job until a few weeks earlier, in fact, when he had learned about a vacancy on the police department. A politically connected friend of his had made up his mind to resign from the force, and, as he confided while they were hunting quail in New Jersey, his alderman had encouraged him to recommend a successor. Walling, not thrilled with his life of commerce, decided that "I might as well carry a club till something better turned up."

With the endorsement of the alderman and assistant alderman and the approval of the mayor, he took the oath of office three days before Christmas. And without any further formalities (such as training), he reported to the Third Ward, which covered City Hall and the newspaper-row area where Mary Rogers and her mother had kept their boardinghouse. The stationhouse on Robinson Street was a small frame building with a stoop and a door below it that opened into a basement with cells. The forty-three officers of the command were organized into two platoons. Ordinarily, one was on street patrol while the other remained on station reserve. During a typical forty-eight hours, if there were no emergencies, an officer would patrol for a total of eighteen hours, be on reserve (and asleep, if he liked) for fourteen, and have sixteen hours to himself.

Of all the men who served as police officers in these first, formative years of the department, "Wash" Walling alone has left us a substantial personal account. And if we could reach back across time and command a single member of the force to tell his story, it would be hard to find one who saw more action.

Early in his career in the Third Ward, Walling rescued Tom Hyer— the American heavyweight boxing champion and a leading slugger for the nativist, or Know-Nothing, faction in the city's political wars—from a "howling mob" of Irishmen out to avenge his triumph over their favorite, who bore the misleading nickname "Yankee" Sullivan. In 1857, Walling, now a captain, helped quell the Dead Rabbits Riots, when the gangs of the Five Points and the Bowery decided to celebrate the Fourth of July by going to war against each other. In the Draft Riots of 1863, Walling led the police offensive against a particularly determined body of draft resisters who had set up barricades along Ninth Avenue, using carts, bricks, and wagons lashed together with telegraph wire. Later the same day, while surveying the neighborhood alone, Walling came across a mob that was preparing to break into a gun store. With no time to summon help, he clubbed the ringleader over the head, killing him. The others were too stunned to respond.

If the city seemed more violent than usual, many longtime inhabitants had a ready explanation: the Irish. They had been a visible presence since the early 1820s, some having come to build the Erie Canal and the Croton Aqueduct; others to work as carters, longshoremen, seamstresses, and domestics; still others to take up the grimiest jobs in the factories that had begun to replace the old artisan shops. But in 1846, the Irish potato famine set off the greatest migration the world had ever seen: 2.5 million people left Ireland in a single decade. Most of them went to America, and more than a million settled in the New York area, where the gentry railed against their drinking and carousing and their foreign religion, with its lax attitude toward the Sabbath. For the native-born working class, the bigger problem with the Irish was their readiness to take almost any job at any pay. Framing the threat in apocalyptic terms, the Know-Nothing Party proposed a twenty-one-year naturalization period for immigrants, a ban on Catholics in government, and the deportation of foreign-born criminals and paupers.

Of the various foreign elements capable of getting the city riled up in those years, however, nobody topped the British. Worshiped by many upper-crust New Yorkers, they were loathed by the working class, regardless of ethnicity. The Irish and anti-Irish gangs would suspend hostilities and fight side by side against a threat like, say, the great English tragedian William

Macready's attempt to play Macbeth at the Astor Place Opera House on May 7, 1849.

Stationed in one of the upper galleries that night, Walling made a valiant but unsuccessful effort to stop a Bowery hooligan named "Butt" Allen from hurling a chair at the stage. Macready had experience with thrown objects: admirers of his American rival, Edwin Forrest, had tried to unsettle him at previous stops on his U.S. tour, but usually with eggs and vegetables and the like. The chair landed "within two inches" of the actor, who, as Walling noted admiringly, "simply looked up and went on with his lines." By then, though, a number of wooden shingles had landed ominously close to his costar, Mrs. Pope, and the musicians had fled the orchestra pit. At a judiciously chosen moment in the drama, accordingly, Macready halted the show and coldly informed the management that he would never appear on a New York stage again.

But a delegation of bluebloods prevailed on him to reverse himself, and Walling was on hand for Macready's return engagement three nights later. This time, in their determination to salvage the city's reputation, the authorities had troops as well as police posted around the theater. Unfortunately, a crew of sewer-construction workers had left piles of cobblestones in the street, and they proved irresistible to the throng. When the men of the elite Seventh Regiment of the National Guard were commanded to fire into the air as a warning, anti-Macready activists assured their cohorts that the soldiers were using blanks. Emboldened, the mob pushed forward. Then the order to fire was sounded again and, according to Walling, "There was a flash," and "a deafening roar," followed by "the cries of the wounded and the groans of the dying." Twenty-two New Yorkers were killed, including a twenty-one-year-old policeman, Henry Burquist.

In the wake of the riots, it fell to Walling to find the authors of a pair of suspiciously similar flyers that had helped arouse the pro-Irish and pro-English factions against each other. He traced them to the headquarters of the Empire Club and its boss, the well-known gambler Captain Isaiah "Ike" Rynders—an advanced political thinker who, after flirting with a more primitive brand of nativism, had seen the wisdom of merging the Irish and their gangs into the political process. (He had picked up his title, and a few knife scars, in a previous career on a Mississippi riverboat.) Walling was never able to prove anything against Rynders. Encountering him outside City Hall a few months later, however, he deliberately struck up a conversation about the riots. "The man who got up those handbills ought to have been shot instead of so many innocent persons," Walling remarked.

"Well, maybe you ought to have been shot instead of me," Rynders replied, getting hot under the collar.

"I haven't accused you of it yet, Mr. Rynders," said Walling. "But if the shoe fits, you are welcome to wear it."

The luck of the draw does not explain a career as action-packed and milestone-laden as Walling's. Police work obviously agreed with him. He was a man who instinctively identified with the mission of taming an unruly city, and he was not one to calculate the odds before venturing in the direction of trouble. As a young patrolman in the Third Ward, Walling encountered six drunken young men striding down Broadway one night, shouting and cursing. Recognizing one of them as Bill Harrington, a noted tough, he confronted the horde head-on and commanded them to be quiet. "People are in bed," he pointed out.

One of the young men had the wit to ask Walling exactly what he proposed to do if, just for the sake of argument, they ignored his order. "Well, now, see here," Walling replied. "I am here to do my duty, and I shall try and arrest some of you at least if you do not go on your way quietly."

It looked like a pretty good scrap was in the making until Harrington, impressed with the young officer's coolness under fire, dramatically separated himself from his comrades. "By God, I will help you!" he proclaimed in a Kiplingesque gesture—one strong man saluting another. The rest of the group went off peaceably.

Walling had an air of authority and, at the same time, an easy manner, free of attitude, which went down well with cops and ruffians alike. He was patient and observant (his hunter's training, perhaps), and he soon acquired the who-doesn't-belong-here radar of the police profession then and now. Off duty one day, watching the boats struggle against the waves and wind near Keyport, New Jersey, where he had lived as a boy, Walling noticed a craft that didn't look like either a fishing or a trading vessel. It was February, and the seas were rough—no time for a pleasure trip, he reasoned. After the boat landed, Walling found it was carrying a load of what he took to be stolen silks. Tracing the crew to a local hotel, he recognized one of the prominent river thieves of the day, "Stuttering John" Monahan. With the help of some local oystermen he knew, Walling managed to arrest Monahan and three accomplices and bring them back to Manhattan.

En route, Walling rehearsed an argument that he was prepared to employ, if necessary, with any judge who questioned his display of initiative on jurisdictional or due-process grounds: Manhattan, he would say, was merely a stop on the most direct route to Jersey City, the legally correct place to submit an extradition request. Modern-day police officers will recognize the quality of thinking, even if the precise line of argument would no longer pass muster. The legal system was laxer about such questions in those days, and fortunately for a lawman out to score a coup, the police bureaucracy was more streamlined. Leaving his prisoners in the care of a friendly steamer captain, Walling raced to the basement apartment at City Hall that then served as police headquarters and burst in on the chief of police, George Matsell, to report his catch.

Matsell, by a happy coincidence, was closeted with a Mr. Cunard of the Cunard steamship line, listening to a tale of woe about a cargo of silks stolen from one of the company's warehouses.

"I have got them—the thieves and the property!" Walling triumphantly proclaimed.

Matsell, who served as chief of police for the first twelve years of the department's existence, exercised a powerful influence on what we would now call the culture of the organization. Prior to his appointment, he had been a police justice and one of the politically savvier participants in the campaign to give the city a serious police force. A gourmand and high liver, Matsell could drink great quantities of wine without apparent ill effect. Dining at a hotel with one of his captains as they returned from a hunting trip, he ordered two bottles of champagne—a large one and small one. The captain protested that one would be enough, since he could drink no more than half a bottle. "Never you mind, sonny," said Matsell. (He called everybody "sonny.") "The small bottle is for you, and the large one is for me."

Only three ranks—captain, assistant captain, and sergeant—stood between the top and bottom of the police hierarchy, and the chief took a personal hand in matters that a captain or inspector might delegate nowadays. One night, at a hotel owner's request, the police arrested a group of visiting

Indians for disturbing the peace; longing for fresh air and a view of the night sky, they had bedded down on the hotel roof, taking the blankets from their rooms. Matsell, who sympathized, had the charges dismissed and personally showed them around the city. The Indians, in turn, invited him to visit their wigwams in Iowa, where he eventually bought land and built a vast country retreat.

Matsell was energetic and strongly committed to the task of establishing the new department's credibility with those who counted. He called on the city's leading bankers and businessmen regularly "to discuss the affairs of the city and ask for suggestions for the improvement of the Police Department," a reporter for the *Times* wrote later, adding that "this tickled the vanity of the substantial citizens." In the spirit of "ingratiating himself with the business element," Matsell "made it a point to attend every fire, club in hand, and frequently he made the rounds at night in the business district, trying bank and shop doors." In the years of his reign, the *Times* went on to observe, "a spirit of sociability pervaded the entire force, from the doormen at the station house to the Chief," who was "free and easy with his manners" and "immensely popular with all his subordinates."

Like many popular executives, though, Matsell did not push his men too hard. Under his leadership, the much-decried reward system continued. The state had formally abolished rewards; but the department took full advantage of a loophole in the law allowing officers to accept them in special cases. Between 1845 and 1847, one detective took in rewards that came to $1,640, or about three times his annual wage. No doubt, Matsell would have unleashed a storm of protest by cracking down on this practice; he might also have drawn unwelcome attention to earnings of his own above and beyond his $1,500 annual salary.

The department was still very young, of course, and in a number of obvious ways (mostly not of Matsell's doing), it was a far cry from the strong, tightly administered force that reformers had called for. The smart blue uniforms and military deportment of London's constables left no doubt that they were officers of the crown. In Paris, the *sergents de ville* patrolled the streets with cavalry sabers swinging at their sides. New York's police officers had no uniform. Their weapon was a wooden club, and their de facto sovereign was the local alderman, who frequently doubled as a saloonkeeper.

London sought out stolid men. "A hot temper would never do, nor any vanity which would lay a man open to arts of flirtation, nor a too-innocent good nature; nor a hesitating temper of manner; nor any weakness for drink; nor any degree of stupidity," wrote Augustine Costello of the *Herald*. Nor was a constable permitted to have an "improper connection" with the people he policed. His New York counterpart, by contrast, was required to live in the ward where he worked. Besides residence, party loyalty was probably the qualification that counted most.

New Yorkers had gotten a department that reflected their conflicted feelings about police protection. A more disciplined and centralized force might have come across as a "standing army"—something that many early Americans, not just New Yorkers, had hoped to do without. Uniforms, besides the military connotations, were servant's "livery"—a symbol of the Old World class distinctions that Americans had fought a revolution against (though the immigrants who already predominated among the servant class did not object so strongly; they couldn't afford to). And yet the department was moving slowly and haltingly down the path of what we would consider professionalism. The term of appointment, originally two years (the same as an alderman's term), was increased to four in 1849. After the Astor Place Riots, the police began to get military-style instruction, and authority gradually shifted from the ward to the city level. In 1853, the police were placed under the oversight of a board of commissioners consisting of the mayor and two judges, while police tenure was made permanent, unless an officer did something to justify his removal. That was also the year Matsell overcame his officers' opposition to, as one of them put it at a protest rally, "an expensive and fantastical uniform."

Patrolman Tom Thorne, a friend of Walling's, was designated by his comrades to explain the rank and file's feelings about uniforms to the Board of Police Commissioners. Speaking for the board, a judge named Beebe told Thorne that a uniform would raise, not lower, the status of the police. Thorne, his resolve weakening, decided to purchase a uniform for himself, and he wore it to a meeting of his brother officers at Military Hall in the Bowery. On his arrival, Thorne was widely complimented on his fine-looking blue cloth coat, with its velvet collar and nine black buttons. At a strategic moment later in the proceedings, he announced that this was the very uniform they had come there to oppose. A number of officers took the opportunity to declare that, if so, they would be willing to wear it. The tide turned even more decisively when Thorne, citing Judge Beebe as his authority, pointed out that anyone who refused would be denied permanent appointment to the force. (In fact, several holdouts eventually lost their jobs.) After Thorne's superiors got wind of his contribution, they decided that he had management ability and made him a sergeant.

Many people were not impressed with the department's progress, however, and New Yorkers who had seen the great police forces of Europe tended to be especially unforgiving. London's constables, according to one traveler, were "feared and dreaded by a criminally-disposed population, not from the personal severity, moroseness or harshness of the men, (for a more mild, forbearing and respectable looking body of citizens I never saw,) but by their well-known intelligence, activity, unflinching firmness, and incorruptible honesty." In Britain and France, another chronicler observed, the police could ask bystanders for help and likely get it; in New York, such an appeal would be "received with a guffaw."

James Gerard, a rich young police buff with a particularly bad case of Anglophilia, remarked on the utter absence of rowdyism in London: if that city had any hooligans at all, he ventured, "they keep within their dens." The sidewalks of New York, by contrast, were clogged with "rowdies walking arm in arm abreast, filled with liquor and deviltry, with segars in their mouths elevated at an angle of 45 degrees and their hats cocked sideways at 30 degrees, cracking their coarse jokes, or singing their ribald songs." Anyone who came too near them or said a word against them ran a strong risk of being knocked down, if not stabbed, according to Gerard.

Chief Matsell, in the opinion of some critics, bore a large share of responsibility for the slovenly appearance and slippery integrity of his subordinates. He was often accused of taking protection money from gamblers and of steering defendants to lawyers and splitting the fees. Certainly, Matsell did not project an aura of rectitude. Under his leadership, the police seemed to get along famously with such leaders of the criminal business establishment as Madame Restell, an abortionist, and Josie Woods, who kept a high-class bordello on Eighth Street where the cheapest drink cost eight dollars.

There was an element of partisan as well as moral disapproval at work in the criticism, however. Matsell was a Democrat; otherwise, he would never have been chief of police in the first place. Indeed, Justice Robert Taylor, who had written the manual for the new force, had hoped to be put in charge of it.

But while Taylor was an interesting and capable man, he suffered from the fatal deficiency of being a Whig in a city whose political faith was Jacksonian democracy. (The Mary Rogers case, still widely remembered as an unsolved murder, was another troublesome item on Taylor's résumé.)

The alderman who had originally sponsored Walling's appointment to the force was a Whig and a close associate of Horace Greeley's; Greeley loathed Matsell and lambasted him frequently in the pages of the *Tribune*. But Walling himself, within a year, went to headquarters to join a team of detectives working directly under the chief's supervision. The move cost him his job, temporarily. In 1849, his backers refused to reappoint him. But he simply moved to a different ward—the politically more convivial Eighteenth—and was soon invited to join the force anew.

In crude career terms, there was much to be said for an alliance with Matsell. Walling was an exceedingly capable investigator; as a detective (not a formal rank in those days, just a designation), he nailed the notorious river pirates Nicholas Howlett and William Saul after they murdered the watchman of a ship they had been plundering in August 1852. Their hanging, according to Walling, "had a wholesome effect for a time upon this sort of villainy." Walling was ambitious without being annoying about it, and detective work was already the way to get ahead in the police world, despite a great deal of pompous rhetoric about the importance of the patrol force and the prevention of crime. (Because prevention was "the most important object in view," Justice Taylor had written, instructing the force with phrases borrowed from London's police manuals, "your exertions must be constantly used to accomplish that end," and "the absence of crime will be considered the best proof of the efficiency of the police.")

In the memoirs that Walling published after the end of his thirty-eight-year career, he skips over many things, including his marriages (there were two) and children (one of them became a police officer). He is maddeningly circumspect about departmental politics and the strings he may have had to pull at various stages of his career. But when it comes to certain larger truths of the police world, Walling presents a picture that is a good deal fuller and more credible than the commentaries of more no-holds-barred observers.

Critics paint a portrait of rampant, police-protected vice, and of gangs and hooligans running amok. Walling alludes often, in a general way, to the financial and political relationships that kept the police from enforcing the law against certain criminal interests. But, as his recollections make clear, graft was routine and widely accepted; the notion of separating public duty from private business was far from firmly established as a concept, and many of the laws that the police enforced erratically or not at all had been enacted by what New Yorkers were inclined to regard as a bunch of hayseeds in the state capital of Albany. In any case, Walling reminds us, there was plenty of crime that the police were free to attack, and they had a strong legal position from which to do so. According to the laws of search and seizure at the time, a police officer could stop and examine pretty much anyone carrying a package, especially at night. If the contents proved to be stolen, there was no "exclusionary rule" to forbid the admission at a trial of unlawfully seized evidence. Prisoners could be detained for up to five days before being arraigned; then, if a justice or magistrate saw fit, he could authorize the police to continue holding the suspect while they "worked up" the case. It was up to a precinct captain to decide whether to let a prisoner see a lawyer, and there were no Miranda rules about interrogation. "There is no shilly shallying by a New York police officer," Walling noted. "He doesn't consider himself half patrolman and half Supreme Court judge."

During his stint as a headquarters detective, Walling and three colleagues received an urgent briefing from Matsell one day about a rash of store burglaries. Matsell would have to "jump off the dock," he told them, if the break-ins, occurring on successive Saturday nights along Maiden Lane and John Street, were not solved. In the most recent case, the thieves had taken some cutlery and three pairs of fancy suspenders. Scouring the premises, the detectives discovered a button from a new style of sack coat. Since no employee or customer had lost a button of that sort, they figured that it had been torn off the coat or fallen out of the pocket of one the thieves. For several weeks, Walling and the other officers rousted the usual thieves' haunts without finding such a button. Then, while patrolling near the Chatham Theater one night, Walling's partner, Shadbolt, spotted three young men he knew to be thieves. Walling followed them up to the gallery and took a seat nearby while Shadbolt hung back so as not to alert them. One of the men, Walling noted, was wearing a sack coat with a button of a slightly different pattern from the others. When the performance ended at midnight, Walling tailed the suspects to a lodging house on Duane Street. At 5:00 A.M., he and two other detectives pounded on the door of their room. A sleepy figure opened it a crack, and Walling and his partners pushed their way in. In a search of the premises, they found three pairs of suspenders of the same type taken in the burglary. The men were arrested and taken to Chief Matsell's office.

Walling was sure they had the thieves, but since the suspenders carried no markings to link them to the burglarized store, he and Shadbolt decided to employ the 1850 version of good cop, bad cop. Walling left the suspects with Matsell and went away for a few minutes; during his absence, Shadbolt walked in, supposedly hoping to see the chief on unrelated business. Feigning surprise at the sight of the three men, he inquired about their trouble. Walling reappeared and, expressing outrage that another detective had dared to interfere in his case, removed the prisoners to a hallway. Then he walked away, and when Shadbolt passed by again, the prisoners called to him. Shadbolt expressed great reluctance to get involved: he was in danger of losing his job, he said, but he would speak to the three men briefly. If they confessed, he told them, they stood to gain a shorter sentence. They followed his advice, implicating a fence on Centre Street. When Walling and his partner searched the place, they found the proceeds of a number of burglaries. Both the thieves and the fence ended up in state prison.

By European standards, New York's police were a motley crew. Smoking cigars on duty was common practice, as was spitting tobacco juice. Citizens frequently had to make payoffs for stolen property to be returned. Yet if the police didn't get the same automatic respect as their British and French peers, many officers took the attitude that respect was something each man had to establish for himself. And though there were no hiring standards to speak of, an able and well-intentioned person could nevertheless be hired—we have Walling's own example as proof of that. In the course of his narrative, we also meet Shadbolt, Thorne, and other officers who upset the stereotype of the 1850s policeman as a drunk and a wastrel. In addition, the ranks of headquarters detectives in those years included William Bell, who dutifully inspected the city's pawnshops and (according to a diary that begins in September 1850) familiarized himself with the city's burglars, pickpockets, and petty thieves—men with names like "Dick the Blower," "Bristol" Bill, and "One-Eyed Thompson." When Bell spotted a suspected criminal, he would "pipe" him—tail him to see what he was up to. Or he would stop him and see if the suspect was carrying stolen goods or burglary tools. On national holidays, Bell and other detectives would be out looking for "knucks," or pickpockets.

In his diary, Bell describes the damage wrought by a runaway steer on Broadway and by a pool of stagnant sewage in which several people drowned. He tells us about doing guard duty for Daniel Webster, among other VIPs. He recalls being asked to assist an old man who had walked seventy miles down to New York City from his home in the Catskills, accompanied by a grandson, in an attempt to secure a veteran's pension. Bell made them comfortable and took up a collection to send them home. Chief Matsell contributed the largest amount—one dollar. Bell tried to convince the superintendent of the Erie Railroad to transport the pair for free, but "the man had a heart about as big as a louse," Bell writes. Eventually, he arranged with a stagecoach clerk to take the old man and his grandson home for a nominal sum.

Those who thought that the city was going to rack and ruin in the early 1850s had seen nothing yet. In 1854, New York elected a new mayor, Fernando Wood—first of the big-city political bosses who would flourish in America over the next hundred years. Born in Philadelphia in 1812, Wood came to New York with his family and went into the liquor and cigar business as a young man. In 1840, he was elected to Congress with Tammany Hall backing. After losing his first race for mayor, in 1850, he was careful to obtain the backing of Ike Rynders and other eminences of organized crime the next time around.

Wood was a charmer. Early in his reign he mounted a number of high-profile initiatives that helped him gain the backing of William Astor, former mayors Harper and Havemeyer, business tycoon Peter Cooper, and even Horace Greeley. Responding to growing complaints about the carriage and omnibus traffic on the nation's most famous shopping boulevard, he created a "Broadway squad" of tall, handsome officers who stood ready to help nervous citizens (especially young female ones) make the difficult crossing. By this time, the rowdy volunteer fire companies, which sometimes fought each other instead of the fire, had become great magnets of local political pride. (The city would not have a professional fire department until 1865.) Inspired by their example, Wood instituted an annual police parade, which remained a great civic event for the next seventy-five years. The dashing mayor personally led the police in closing saloons on Sunday and chasing prostitutes from the streets.

But his more serious innovations had to do with getting votes and collecting graft. He was the first city leader to appreciate the full value of the police in both these areas and to efficiently organize them to serve the interests of the political machine. In the 1852 primary, gangs had seized ballot boxes and barred entrance to the polls while the cops did nothing. Control of the police was estimated to be worth 10,000 votes in a mayoral election, at a time when fewer than 100,000 votes were cast.

Wood was not subtle. While his predecessors had tried to maintain a certain veneer of respectability, he openly ran city government to benefit himself and his Tammany Hall cohorts. It was also in this period that the police department's possibilities as a vessel of political patronage came to be fully appreciated. In an administration that relied on saloonkeepers, gangs, and "shoulder-hitters" to manage elections, it was only natural for the police to draw on the same general pool of talent. Under Wood, the force took in men who were described as "five foot nothing" with names like "English Bill" and "Dutch Pete." Mike Murray, a saloon brawler, was appointed directly from civilian life as captain of the First District.

In May 1855, the murder of the nativist slugger Bill "the Butcher" Poole firmed up the impression of many New Yorkers that the thugs and the police were becoming difficult to distinguish. The fatal shot lingered in Poole's chest for eleven days, giving him plenty of time to dream up the last words that solidified his martyrdom: "I die a true American." The shot had been fired by Lewis Baker, a recently dismissed policeman who, in the words of the judge at one of the three trials in which Baker was unsuccessfully prosecuted, had "a most unaccountable passion for disorderly scenes and associates." In making his escape, first to New Jersey and later, by ship, across the Atlantic, Baker received extensive help from several friends who remained on the force. Only after Poole's followers raised a huge ruckus (and offered the city the free use of a fast boat to chase him down) did the authorities evince any interest in pursuing the suspect. They caught him, finally—and abducted him—off the Canary Islands.

It was during Wood's reign, too, that the police department began to take on an Irish flavor. He was the first mayor to mobilize the immigrant vote on a grand scale; newly arrived aliens would report to the courts with Tammany

Hall–stamped notes that read, "Please naturalize the bearer." In 1855, responding to an inquiry by the Board of Aldermen, Matsell reported that almost 17 percent of the department's officers were Irish-born (compared to 28.2 percent of the city). Many of the aldermen thought he was understating. But that was the least of Matsell's troubles, for it had come out during the probe that he himself had been born abroad—in Liverpool, England, in 1806, rather than, as he had claimed, in New York in 1811. Put on trial for alienage (or holding office while not a citizen), Matsell was acquitted on a technicality: he was a citizen by virtue of his father's naturalization. By now, however, his closeness to Fernando Wood had become a bigger burden.

In 1856, public opinion turned sharply against Wood after an election campaign in which he won a second term with the conspicuous help of the Dead Rabbits as well as the police. The following January, the newly elected governor of New York, John King—a Republican—proposed an ingenious measure designed to pull the rug out from under Wood and his associates. The state would create a metropolitan police district to include New York City, Kings County (Brooklyn), Westchester County, and Richmond County (Staten Island). Of course, the real target of the legislation was New York City and its 750,000 residents: Westchester and Richmond counties were rural, and the policing of Brooklyn's 250,000 inhabitants had not yet become a problem. Patrol districts would be called precincts and would no longer be coterminous with wards. The legislation also shifted the mayoral election to December, cutting Wood's second term in half.

The governor's move presented Walling with a difficult decision. Wood, with Matsell's support, resolved to defy Albany by maintaining the police force as it was and refusing to turn over its equipment or real estate: any officer who recognized the authority of the usurpers, he warned, would be fired. Walling, now the captain of the Eighteenth Precinct, owed much to Matsell, and there is every reason to think he considered him a friend. His collection of police memorabilia included a baton ornamented with silver, which the chief had given him on August 13, 1850, along with a note expressing "the gratification I experienced on witnessing your noble conduct on the Fifth of August inst., on the occasion of the burning . . . of the five-story building . . . at No. 40 Spruce street, when you toiled with your own hands, and imperiled your own life to extricate a fellow being from a mass of rubbish in which he was buried." The baton was "not intrinsically valuable," Matsell wrote, "yet it will serve as a memento of the noble act that called forth the praise of all who witnessed it."

Walling was not a puritanical sort. He cut corners when he had to. In his mind, however, Wood and his gang had gone too far. (Walling, in his autobiography, recalls participating in a "laughable" vice crackdown in 1856—one of the "spasmodic efforts" with which Wood sought to improve "his reputation among certain classes in the community.") In any event, he joined with 300 of the 1,100 officers and 7 of the 22 captains—about a quarter of the force—in going over to the newly created Metropolitans and taking up arms, pretty much literally, against his former comrades.

"Here is just the man we want," one of the commissioners of the new department declared when Walling entered its headquarters on White Street. They were looking for someone to execute an arrest warrant against Fernando Wood. The charge was obstruction of governmental administration. Cleaning the streets was a police duty, and Wood had forcibly ejected a new street commissioner named by the state. The mayor, it was rumored, had already sold this lucrative post for $50,000. Walling volunteered to take the warrant. How many men would he need? "None."

Walking past hundreds of Municipal Police officers stationed outside City Hall, he strode into the mayor's anteroom and requested an interview. After a few minutes, he was admitted into Wood's presence.

"Well, sir, what will you have?" the mayor asked coldly.

Walling explained his mission.

"I will not submit to arrest, or go with you, or concede that you are an officer at all," Wood told him.

"Well, sir," Walling replied, "as we don't agree on that point, I shall be obliged to do as I always did when I served warrants under your authority; I shall have to take you out forcibly if you resist."

"I will not be taken!" the mayor insisted. "You may consider that resistance if you please."

"No, sir, that is not resistance," said Walling. "That is only refusal."

The mayor struck his office bell and a Municipal captain rushed in with several officers, who seized Walling and forcibly ejected him from the office. He was not put out of the building, however, and when a newly hired Municipal cop sought to chivy him along, other Municipals, well acquainted with Walling, shouted, "Let go of him! He's all right."

Walling returned to the judge who had issued the warrant. The judge summoned the sheriff, and he, in turn, asked for legal counsel. While these worthies were moving toward a decision, fifty Metropolitan policemen marched to City Hall to execute a separate warrant—this one for assault against the same would-be street commissioner. On the steps of City Hall, the Metropolitans were met and attacked by hundreds of club-swinging Municipals.

"Mr. Mayor, the Metropolitans came and we beat them off," Matsell reported, sticking his head in Wood's door. Unwilling to push their luck too far, Walling and his party withdrew from City Hall; but just as they did, the Seventh Regiment of the National Guard came marching down Broadway with drums and bugles blaring, en route to a ship that would take the troops to Boston for a patriotic celebration. The Seventh—the same unit that had fired on the rioters in Astor Place eight years earlier—was well trained and predominantly composed of native-born Protestants. Halting the procession, the Metropolitan police commissioners called on the National Guard commander, General Sanford, for assistance. He ordered the regiment to fix bayonets and deploy for action.

"Well, our game is up," Matsell muttered, watching from a window. This time, Walling and Sanford entered City Hall together, and the general read the warrants to the mayor, who, bowing to superior force, at last submitted to arrest. (Later on, a number of Metropolitan officers sued him personally and were awarded damages for injuries they had suffered in the riot. Wood passed the bill on to the taxpayers.)

For the next several weeks, New York was subject to the spectacle of two rival police forces patrolling the streets and vying for custody of police buildings. In some instances, one force would arrest a prisoner, and the other would try to release him. The street gangs found this a stimulating state of affairs. During a two-day battle between the Dead Rabbits and the Bowery Boys, eight people were killed and a hundred injured. In an attempt to stop the fighting, Ike Rynders was beaten up, and he promptly demanded that the police commissioners call for the National Guard. They did, and General Sanford's troops saved the day again. Eventually, the state's highest court ruled in favor of the Metropolitans, and the Municipal force was disbanded. At the next election, Wood was defeated.

It was a bad year all around. A major financial panic in August plunged the nation into a depression. Thousands of people were thrown out of work. In the Five Points area alone, as many as ten thousand were fed by charity in a single day. The homeless camped outside City Hall Park, and when a group of them attempted to seize the building, a force of three hundred policemen was assigned to guard it. Marines and soldiers, meanwhile, patrolled outside the federal buildings in the financial district. Crime soared. Six citizens were shot during a twenty-four-hour period in November of 1857.

By now, some cops had been carrying firearms on an informal basis for several years. With the state takeover, this became official department policy, though some captains initially urged their men to ignore it. Immediately, there was trouble. In July, disorders broke out following an attempt to enforce Sunday closing laws on German beer joints. An innocent German man walking with his wife was said to have been shot to death by police. In November, a patrolman named Cairnes, having arrested an Irish longshoreman known as Sailor Jack on a disorderly conduct charge, was escorting him to jail when, according to the officer, the prisoner attacked him. Cairnes fired three times, killing the longshoreman with his third shot. Another officer arrested Cairnes, exclaiming, "Why did you do that? There was plenty of help around." With the Irish community in a fury, Cairnes was charged with murder by a coroner's jury of ordinary citizens and committed to the Tombs. Eventually, a grand jury of more substantial citizens refused to indict him. Thus, the year witnessed New York's first two controversial police shooting incidents, complete with charges of ethnic discrimination. From then on, policemen making arrests would caution the suspects: "No skipping, I'm fixed."

In 1858, Walling was placed in charge of the city's twenty-four-man detective force, in addition to his duties as commander of the City Hall precinct. His rough-and-ready methods, including the preventive detention of all known pickpockets during parades and national holidays, would raise a furor today. They were entirely routine then. In the mid–nineteenth century, the city's criminal justice system retained much of the flavor of the eighteenth. Executions were still popular public spectacles. In 1860, the hanging of the river pirate Al Hicks took on the trappings of a civic event. The ceremony was presided over by that pillar of law and order United States Marshal Ike Rynders. A few minutes before nine in the morning, he went to the Tombs wearing a ceremonial sword borrowed from the sheriff and read the death warrant. Hicks was then escorted out into the street, where he and Marshal

Rynders bowed in response to an ovation from a crowd of thousands. Next, a fife-and-drum corps marched down Centre Street, followed by several carriages drawn by black horses and driven by coachmen clad in black from head to toe. Marshal Rynders took his place in the front seat of the first carriage while his deputies placed the prisoner in the back seat. At a signal from Rynders, the musicians struck up a funeral march and the carriages rolled along the streets through cheering crowds to Canal Street, where a steamboat waited to take them to Bedloe Island (now the site of the Statue of Liberty). As the steamboat passed an ocean liner, Rynders brought the shackled Hicks to the rail and, with his sword in one hand and a voice trumpet in the other, announced the purpose of the cruise to the liners' passengers. Upon arrival at the island, the prisoner passed through lines of marines, and a detachment of soldiers escorted him to the scene of his execution while their regimental band played another dirge. The island was surrounded by hundreds of boats, including excursion craft decorated with flags and bunting, among whom hawkers were peddling hot corn and candy to the passengers. As Hicks stepped onto the platform, Rynders and other officials shook hands with him. After the execution, the steamer carried his corpse back to Manhattan. Before he was cold in his grave at Calvary Cemetery, his body had been stolen and sold to medical students.

With the outbreak of the Civil War, New York's police force became, in effect, a national police force. The United States Secret Service was not formed until 1865. The general superintendent of the Metropolitans, John Kennedy, was an active Republican politician—rough, forceful, and autocratic. When friends came to him for favors, he would jump up and berate them, shouting, "And you call yourself an honest man and honorable citizen and have the assurance to come in here and ask me to let you commit a breach of the law! Get out! Get out at once!" Kennedy worked vigorously to support the Union cause. Even before Fort Sumter was fired on, he issued orders forbidding arms shipments from New York to the South and investigated reported threats to assassinate president-elect Lincoln. Together, Kennedy and Walling journeyed to Washington, D.C., to consult with high Republican politicians. Their preliminary soundings indicated that Baltimore would be the likely trouble spot, and Walling assigned two detectives to look over the situation. They worked their way into the confidence of rebel sympathizers, even joining a local volunteer company sworn to fight for the South.

During the war, the police received federal funds to recruit five regiments of infantry and four companies of cavalry for the Union army. In 1862, the secretary of war designated the Metropolitan Police as provost marshals, allowing them to arrest deserters and citizens guilty of making "disloyal" statements. New York detectives ranged as far afield as Ohio to arrest Southern sympathizers. The following year, the police became full-fledged soldiers in what can fairly be considered one of the significant battles of the war.

It was precipitated by the enactment of a draft law—the country's first—which took effect in July 1863. Not only was conscription repugnant to Anglo-American tradition, but the law contained a discriminatory provision that permitted anyone drafted to be excused upon payment of $300 dollars, a sum that no working man could easily raise.

There was considerable antiwar sentiment in New York. To the Irish, the abolition of slavery raised the specter of more low-wage workers competing for scarce jobs. (In 1853, black workers armed with revolvers had been hired as scabs after Irish laborers struck against the Erie Railroad, seeking a salary of $1.25 a day and a limit of ten hours.) Fernando Wood, who had returned as mayor in 1859, declared secession "a fixed and certain fact" and suggested that New York emulate the South's example by establishing a free city. (This would be like the front doorstep setting up housekeeping on its own, Lincoln commented.) Other outspoken proponents of peace were Governor Horatio Seymour and the leader of the city council, Tammany boss William Marcy Tweed, ex-foreman of the famous "Big Six" volunteer fire company. The three submerged their mutual dislike in passionate attacks on Lincoln and the Republicans. Addressing a mass meeting on the draft law days before it was scheduled to take effect, Seymour asked a predominantly Irish crowd to remember that "the bloody, treasonable and revolutionary doctrine of public necessity can be proclaimed by a mob as well as by government."

In early July, as provost marshals went about taking names to register people for the draft, the state militia was dispatched to Gettysburg to help stem Lee's invasion of the North, leaving the defense of the city largely in the hands of the police. During the registration process there were signs of the trouble to come. One provost marshal, army captain Joel Erhardt (later a New York City police commissioner), was threatened with a lead pipe while attempting to take the names of some construction workers at Liberty Street and Broadway. He had to draw a gun to clear his retreat.

On Saturday, July 11, the first drawings were held in two districts. Large police detachments were on hand, and despite much muttering there was no trouble. A Rubicon had been crossed, Kennedy declared optimistically. But the next day, Sunday, was the usual day of rest for working people—a time when saloons were full and beer and liquor flowed freely. It was also a day on which the papers printed a list of the twelve hundred men whose names had just been drawn. They included members of a prominent company of volunteer firemen, the Black Joke, who had expected to be exempt.

On Monday, July 13, drawings were to be held at the provost marshal's offices at Twenty-ninth Street and Broadway and at Forty-sixth Street and Third Avenue. The first was carried out in the presence of a sixty-nine-man police detail and continued peaceably until noon, when the proceedings were adjourned. At Forty-sixth and Third, it was a different story. A large and unruly crowd was present when the drawings started at 10:15. After approximately twenty minutes, the crowd began blocking horse-drawn streetcars on Third Avenue. As the passengers alighted, the mob swelled. Sixty police officers had been deployed there, but they were no match for the rioters and had to retreat. After they left, the mob burned the draft office.

Superintendent Kennedy, unaware of all this, was heading into the storm. At seven in the morning, he received a warning of possible trouble: the street contractor's workmen in the Nineteenth Ward, which encompassed Forty-sixth and Third, had not reported to work. Kennedy ordered the details strengthened at the provost marshals' offices and telegraphed to all precincts to recall men who had gone off duty at the 6:00 A.M. shift change. At ten he started uptown, alone and unarmed, to assess the situation. Traveling by horse-drawn cart in civilian clothes, he visited Twenty-ninth Street and Broadway and an armory at Thirty-fifth Street and Seventh Avenue being held by police. From there, he headed east toward Forty-sixth and Third. As he drew near, Kennedy spotted smoke from the fires, and his way was blocked by masses of protesters. Dismounting, he started walking through the crowd, at first without being molested. Then came a cry of "There's Kennedy. Kill him." Now the mob attacked. Kennedy, who was sixty at the time, was struck repeatedly, and after briefly escaping, was caught again, beaten some more, and eventually dumped into a small pond. He struggled out, only to be assaulted yet once more. He was back on his feet—"a mass of gore," according to one account—when he recognized John Eagan, a local Irish leader, and called to him for help. Rushing in, Eagan kept the mob back while others hustled Kennedy onto a passing feed wagon, which transported him down to police headquarters. He arrived unconscious, and so badly mauled that the president of the police board, Thomas Acton, at first didn't recognize his own superintendent. (Amazingly, Kennedy was back to work on Thursday; he remained in office until 1870.)

Acton was twenty years younger than Kennedy and another strong supporter of the war. "Holding the views of the first Napoleon respecting mobs, he did not believe in speechmaking to them," Augustine Costello observed. "His addresses were to be locust clubs and grape-shot." With Acton in charge, the police reserves were ordered to report to headquarters and the river police to secure federal troops and arms from the harbor forts. Acton remained at his post without sleeping from 6:00 A.M. Monday until 2:00 A.M. Friday. During that interval, he received and answered over four thousand telegrams. The police telegraph system was flooded with reports of trouble around the city. Rioters, recognizing the telegraph's value as an intelligence and rapid-response tool, tore down poles and cut wires. Throughout the riot, the superintendent of telegraphy and his staff (often moving about in disguise) were busy rerouting lines and putting up poles, though several times they were attacked by policemen who mistook them for rioters out to sabotage the system. Tom Thorne, in command of the Twenty-sixth Precinct—the City Hall police—had five of his men in civilian dress mixing with the crowd and monitoring its plans.

At first, the police moved toward the trouble spots in numbers that were far too small to contend with mobs of hundreds or thousands. Sergeant Ellison of the Eighth Precinct, en route with thirteen men from Twenty-ninth and Broadway to Forty-sixth and Third, was captured and beaten before being rescued by other policemen. Sergeant "Fighting Mack" McCredie of the Fifteenth Precinct arrived at Forty-third and Third with fourteen men and gathered up others from various scattered commands for a total of forty-four. He then fought his way through to the provost marshal's office at Forty-sixth Street but was surrounded by masses of rioters and routed. McCredie himself was struck on the arm with an iron bar and had to hide in a nearby house, where a young German woman concealed him in a mattress from pursuing mobs. Officer Bennett of the Fifteenth was beaten, stripped to his underwear, and hauled to the morgue. Only his wife, who had been summoned to view the body, noticed that Bennett was breathing. He eventually recovered. Officer Kiernan, advancing with his comrades from the Fifteenth, was beaten into unconsciousness and saved from death when Mrs. John Eagan, the wife of Superintendent Kennedy's rescuer, prostrated herself over his body. An Officer Travis of the Fifteenth Precinct was transported to St. Luke's Hospital. After seizing a pistol from a rioter, he had been knocked to the ground, beaten to a jelly, and stripped naked.

Mobs moved on a gun factory at Twenty-first Street and Second Avenue. Just in the nick of time, Sergeant Burdick and thirty-two men of the Broadway squad managed to fight their way into the factory, where they helped themselves to some of the four thousand stored carbines. The undaunted rioters battered down the door. The first man through was shot in the head. Still the mob pressed on, until the police were compelled to evacuate. Over the next two days the factory was recaptured, lost again, recaptured, and burned down. Another mob of thousands began marching toward police headquarters and the financial district. Instead of waiting for it to arrive, Inspector Dan Carpenter took two hundred policemen to meet them at Broadway and Houston Street. The cops charged with clubs swinging, and in ten minutes the mob was routed, their flags and banners captured.

George Walling commanded the Twentieth Precinct, at 212 West Thirty-fifth Street, which covered a tough section of the West Side known as Hell's Kitchen. On Sunday, he was sufficiently concerned to remain in the station overnight. On his way to headquarters Monday morning, he heard reports of rioting and immediately started on a dead run back to his station, nearly two miles away. Leaving only a small detachment to guard the building, Walling gathered up his men, commandeered a fleet of stagecoaches, and reported to headquarters.

One of their first missions was to protect the newspaper offices, including Greeley's *Tribune*; the newspapers were special targets because of their support for the war, and arms brought from the harbor forts were distributed to their employees. On the first day, the police beat off attacks against the *Tribune* building on Park Row. Later, Greeley himself was trapped in a restaurant and had to hide behind a woman's skirts. Next, Walling's men were ordered to guard City Hall. In the middle of the night, one of his officers reported seeing a rough-looking fellow peering through the window. Walling slipped out a side door, came up behind the man, and grabbed him by the collar. It turned out to be his brother, Leonard, who had come to help. He was sworn in and given a club.

On Tuesday, Walling led a hundred men up Broadway, supported by a company of soldiers. At Forty-fifth Street and Fifth Avenue, they were confronted by a mob of two thousand. "Kill every man who has a club," Walling ordered in a voice loud enough for all the rioters to hear. "Double-quick. Charge!" They took no prisoners, leaving the rioters where they fell.

On Wednesday, Walling was assigned to escort a group of black men from the Arsenal on the West Side to the Twentieth Precinct. On Ninth Avenue, a mob had begun erecting barricades "after the Parisian fashion," as one chronicler put it. In what became known as the Battle of the Barricades, Walling and his men, supported by a company of infantry, marched up the avenue, clearing the barricades and exchanging shots with the rioters.

After reaching his precinct, Walling went out by himself to take stock. He spotted a group of rioters trying to break into a hardware store that he knew to carry a large inventory of guns. With "a scientific twirl of his locust," Costello wrote, Walling laid the ringleader "prostrate in the gutter." A physician was summoned. After looking the victim over, he announced, "He doesn't want a doctor, he needs an undertaker." That night, Walling and his men responded to a report that a black church was being attacked on Twenty-seventh Street. They found it occupied by rioters inside and out, and "no sooner was our presence made known," Walling recalled, "than we were greeted with a sharp fusillade from pistols, muskets, shotguns, etc. My men returned the fire with their revolvers." One of the rioters had taken up a position on the roof, straddling the church's ridgepole, and was hacking away at the timbers with an axe. "The outline of his form stood out boldly against the sky, and he was in full view of the crowd," according to Walling. A police officer fired a shot, and the man plunged to his death. Then "a howl of rage" went up from the rioters, who attacked the police "in a savage and determined manner." But "we also set to work with a will," Walling said, "clubbing our opponents most unmercifully."

Although police officers carried firearms now, clubs were the principal weapon employed in the riots. And many officers were grateful for the decision to replace the old-fashioned rosewood clubs—which "splintered and broke as fast as the heads they were used on," according to one chronicler—with locustwood, which was lighter and more flexible, and "sonorous," emitting "a sound like a bell."

The riots had started out as a protest against the draft. As they continued, blacks were more and more often the main targets. They were attacked everywhere mobs found them. Twenty families were besieged in their homes at Baxter and Leonard Streets before being rescued by the police. At Roosevelt Street and New Bowery, blacks had to jump from the rooftops of burning buildings. One man was hanged at Thirty-second Street and Fifth Avenue. Others fled to Brooklyn in boats.

After a mob hanged a crippled man, a sixteen-year-old butcher boy dragged the body through the streets while the crowd cheered. The police drillmaster led a large detachment of officers in marching over to Clarkson Street, where they recovered the body of a black man who had been hanged and set on fire. In another ghastly episode, rioters torched the Coloured Orphan Asylum, on Fifth Avenue between Forty-third and Forty-fourth Streets. One little girl was burned to death, and more than two hundred children were evacuated to the Twentieth Precinct. "Almost crazed with terror," Walling recalled, they made the trip on foot, "the small upon the backs of the larger." The children remained at the precinct, under the care of Walling's men, for a week. About seven hundred other blacks had taken refuge at police headquarters.

The police and troops showed no mercy, nor did the rioters. An army colonel, himself a local Irishman, fired artillery at a mob and then, unwisely, went home, where he was caught and tortured to death. The East Thirty-fifth Street police station was nearby, but the precinct cops were besieged. Bread was smuggled in by the two small sons of a woman who was running a local bakery while her husband was away at war; she herself gave a gun to a policeman who needed one. Neighborhood toughs who knew about her husband's support for the Union threatened to burn down the store and the living quarters above; still, she managed to save herself by paying ten dollars to a local gang leader. For three days, the neighborhood was controlled by mobs, until the Seventh Regiment broke through. One group of rioters, in an attempt to prevent the landing of marines from Brooklyn Navy Yard, stormed the Fulton Ferry; they were routed by the police. Others took advantage of the turmoil to engage in looting; police drove looters from Brooks Brothers and Lord & Taylor, among other stores. Brooklyn, though, remained calm throughout, and most of the police stationed there were sent into New York City as reinforcements.

By the fifth day, the city was secured, although troops remained for another month. The number of riot deaths was originally put in the hundreds, and later estimates ranged into the thousands. Modern-day researchers, by contrast, have placed the toll at around a hundred. While the higher estimates were probably exaggerated, nineteenth-century authorities were not good at keeping records, even of policemen killed in the line of duty. Very probably, a significant number of rioters killed by police and troops never made it into the official tally. (Their families might have been reluctant to reveal the cause of their deaths, for fear of official retaliation.)

Were the riots planned? There were claims of Southern agents stirring up discontent. A knife-wielding man who led a mob attack on the police met his death when he fell against an iron railing and one of the pickets pierced his throat. A search was said to have disclosed an expensive vest, trousers, and shirt under his dirty outer overalls. Other commentators pointed to the cutting of rail and telegraph lines as evidence of a directing force. After the fighting, police search parties ranged through the Five Points and the Bowery, recovering thousands of dollars' worth of stolen goods. Merchandise worth $10,000 was returned to Brooks Brothers alone. Whatever the original motives behind a riot, Walling commented, thieves take advantage and "idle persons, with no interests at stake . . . amalgamate with the thieves for the purpose of sharing the plunder. . . . People should understand this."

In the postwar years, draft rioters (or New Yorkers willing to acknowledge themselves as such) became increasingly difficult to find. In fact, sentiment began shifting almost immediately as the Confederate army retreated southward and the Union's ultimate triumph became clear. The police came in for widespread praise, even though half of them were Catholics and three-quarters were Democrats. "When the streets of the City of New York ran with blood," declared one upstate Republican, ". . . but for the fact that . . . the control of its police was in loyal hands, in all human probability, what was a mere mob . . . employed in riot, arson and blood-shed, would have been a revolution, and we should have had to fight with the elements of rebellion here upon our own soil, as well as in the South."

3

The Finest

New York, like other nineteenth-century municipalities, did not have many people on the public payroll, and the police, as the city's largest workforce, got saddled with a number of non–law enforcement tasks. They ran the election machinery, supervised the cleaning of streets, and provided temporary shelter for the homeless at precinct stationhouses. In recognition of this function, the poor sometimes spoke of the precinct buildings, which had green lights at their entrances (in imitation of the green lamps carried by the watchmen of old), as "green light hotels." The police themselves referred to the shelters, generally located in the basement, as lodging houses; Peter Conlin, the police chief at the time of the decision to end the practice in 1896, described them as havens for the "lazy, dissipated, filthy, vermin-covered, disease-breeding and disease-scattering scum of the city's population."

In 1870, a twenty-one-year-old immigrant from Denmark, Jacob Riis, arrived in the great republic seeking a new life. Riis was bright and energetic, but jobs were scarce and his funds soon ran out. A mongrel dog had latched on to him, and the two spent many a night sleeping in the doorway of Barnum's clothing store on the edge of the Bowery, where Riis was often prodded awake by cops and told to move on. One very cold night, he decided to take shelter in the Church Street stationhouse, leaving his dog outside. He had heard tales of theft in the lodging houses, so he put his gold locket in a bag and tied it up. While he slept, another lodger cut the string and stole the locket.

50

Weeping, Riis ran to the desk sergeant to complain that he had been robbed. The sergeant, a burly German, had formed an unfavorable opinion of Riis from some overheard remarks of his that were favorable to the French side in the then-unfolding Franco-Prussian War. He waved Riis off, remarking that he had surely stolen the locket in the first place. When Riis persisted, the sergeant threatened to arrest him. Eventually he told the doorman to remove Riis from the premises. This functionary, a combination turnkey and janitor, was in the process of kicking Riis down the stoop when the dog grasped his leg in its teeth. Letting Riis go, the doorman seized the dog and beat its brains out on the stone steps. Riis, crazed with fury, began hurling stones at the station. Perhaps to save him from further trouble, two cops who had witnessed the encounter dragged him away and deposited him at a ferry landing. Wisely, Riis boarded a boat for New Jersey, vowing never to return to New York.

In the city he left behind, the banks and exchanges of the prewar era had blossomed into the great financial entity known as Wall Street, and a handful of men had become fabulously rich. During the war, Commodore Vanderbilt had had the presence of mind to unload most of his shipping empire and, though already in his seventies, to begin buying commuter rail lines and stretching and amalgamating them into the first national railroad, the New York Central. New York was also the headquarters of Jay Gould, who in 1869 nearly managed to corner the nation's gold market using money embezzled from investors in the Erie Railroad—the so-called Scarlet Woman of Wall Street. And the city was home to the dour Gould's more colorful henchman, Colonel Jim Fisk, a former circus roustabout who used a portion of his Erie loot to build an opera house and buy a militia regiment.

Jay Cooke, who had made a fortune by convincing people that millions of immigrants were about to swarm into the Minnesota and Dakota lands surrounding his Northern Pacific Railway right of way, was actually a Philadelphian—but enough of a presence in New York for the collapse of his firm, on September 13, 1873, to be a major seismic event in the local economy. In the wake of Black Thursday, as the date became known, scores of banks, brokerages, and insurance companies went bust and tens of thousands of New Yorkers lost their jobs, in most cases without the niceties of notice or severance pay. Shantytowns soon sprang up across the West Side of

Manhattan. When winter came, bedraggled citizens lined up for shelter at the almshouses and police stations.

Some of the economically dispossessed hooked up with a growing community of radicals, loosely described by the press of the day as "communists." The term and the dread associated with it were products of the Paris Commune—a revolutionary government that rose from the ashes of the Franco-Prussian War and the defeat of Emperor Napoleon III. The "communards," as the Parisian rebels were called, were not actual communists—Karl Marx himself denounced them for murdering the archbishop of Paris when, he said, they should have been dynamiting the Bank of France. And their triumph was short-lived: within months, a conservative national government had seized control and killed thousands of the rebels, mostly after they surrendered.

But the propertied classes were frightened—in America as well as Europe. In New York, the fear was made more immediate by the sudden appearance of a large and vocal community of transplanted European radicals, including refugees from the commune and members of Karl Marx's International Working Men's Association, the First International, although the latter crossed the ocean partly to avoid being taken over by Russian anarchists. Some of the newcomers made common cause with native-born agitators, adopting Tompkins Square Park as a roosting place. For the next hundred years and more, the square—named for a New York governor who had been James Monroe's vice president—assumed the function of London's Hyde Park as a place for radicals to make speeches and hold protest meetings. The *Times*, surveying the local political landscape, found conditions disturbingly similar to those in Paris and anguished about the potential influence of "communist leaders and 'philosophers' and reformers" upon "the seething, ignorant, passionate, half-criminal class" who "hate and envy the rich." Among those who worried about such things, there was widespread skepticism about the police as a line of defense, now that the force was back under the city's control.

This was the doing, in 1870, of William Marcy Tweed, the grand sachem of Tammany Hall. Tweed had moved up rapidly, becoming an alderman at twenty-eight and a congressman at twenty-nine. Winning overnight admission to the bar, he was paid hefty sums for his legal services to the Erie Railroad by Jay Gould and Jim Fisk. As Boss Tweed, he installed his puppet, former district attorney A. Oakey Hall, in the mayor's office, while another lieutenant, John T. "Toots" Hoffman, occupied the governor's mansion in Albany.

Democrats also controlled the legislature, producing the votes necessary to win passage of the "Tweed Charter," which, among its other provisions, ended a thirteen-year interval of state dominion over the police of New York and Brooklyn.

No sooner had the charter been enacted than doubts began to be expressed about the ability and desire of the police to manage disorder. Nor were those doubts put to rest by the force's handling of the annual Orange Parade of 1870, commemorating the Battle of the Boyne—a sacred day for Ulster's Irish Protestants. Under the Metropolitan Police, these parades had gone off without incident. This time the marchers came to blows with Catholic laborers, setting off two days of violence, during which five people died and a hundred were injured.

In their next test, the cops did better. In May 1871, Irish quarry workers from the Yorkville section of the Upper East Side struck for higher wages. Armed with clubs and axes, they paraded down the avenues, pausing at a number of work sites to recruit more men for their protest. At First Avenue and Forty-seventh Street, just a few blocks from the intersection where the draft riot had broken out eight years earlier, a crowd of two thousand, largely composed of women and children, gathered to cheer the marchers. Police Captain John Gunner, an Englishman who had been a roundsman during the 1863 riot, arrived with a company of officers and dispersed the marchers and onlookers without violence. The next day, the strikers gathered in Central Park and decided to parade on the West Side.

Tweed had re-created the old Democratic Party alliance between businessmen and workers, and the quarrymen were an important element of his constituency. Tammany's police superintendent, James Kelso, was a street-wary cop who had spent his career at headquarters, mostly in clerical posts. Recognizing his own limitations, however, Kelso wisely left field command to the man the press called "the hero of the draft riots"—Inspector George Walling—who lined the streets with police, ordered detectives to infiltrate the crowds, posted men to guard the telegraph lines, and took the precaution of closing down the saloons. The protesters marched and eventually returned to Central Park without serious incident. Over the next few days, Walling played a clever game, anticipating the so-called New York strategy of disorder control that would emerge in the twentieth century: patience, containment, and a heavy deployment of manpower. He allowed the strikers to remain in Central

Park while maintaining tight control over the streets and continuing to keep the saloons shut. With this policy, he avoided complaints from responsible citizens that mobs were allowed to rampage, yet prevented the strikers from fueling their anger with liquor even as he gave them some breathing space. Within two weeks, the strike collapsed. The shovelmen resumed their work at the old pay rates, though the rockmen refused to do so.

Although the city had regained control of its law-enforcement apparatus, the Tweed Ring understood the need to exercise that power with care. The state government might no longer be a threat, but the federal government was. The Republican administration in Washington still maintained its military occupation of the former Confederacy, and in more than one election year, President Grant sent troops to New York City to assist U.S. marshals in combating vote fraud.

In 1871, Superintendent Kelso issued an order banning that year's Orange Parade as a threat to public safety. If they allowed the parade to take place, Tweed and his associates feared, there would be a riot, and that, in turn, would give Grant a reason to seize the city. But a torrent of complaints poured forth, and on the day before the great procession, Protestant businessmen lined up outside the produce exchange to sign a petition denouncing Kelso's order, while the *Times* condemned City Hall for what was termed a cowardly surrender to the threats of a Catholic mob. After hurried deliberations with Tweed and other city leaders, Governor Hoffman, who had presidential ambitions and couldn't afford to have his antimob fortitude questioned, authorized the parade to go ahead after all.

The results were grave. On the afternoon of July 12, a large force of police and national guardsmen were massed near the start of the march at Twenty-ninth Street and Eighth Avenue. Despite their presence, stones and other missiles were thrown from housetops, striking some of the guardsmen. A shot was heard. Some claimed that it came from a corner window on Twenty-fourth Street. According to other accounts, it was the accidental discharge of a soldier's rifle. Either way, a phalanx of guardsmen responded by opening fire, killing thirty-seven people and wounding sixty-seven. George Walling decried the guard's actions as "reckless" and widely trumpeted the fact that Colonel Fisk, at the first shot, jumped off his horse and fled to New Jersey, discarding his uniform along the way.

By now, the press had already raised questions about some $10 million spent on purported repairs, furniture, and fixtures for a new courthouse—a building that, according to the law authorizing its construction, was not to have cost more than $250,000, contents included. Ten days after the blood-bath, the *Times*, with the help of a disgruntled insider, began publishing a series of articles documenting a byzantine set of kickback arrangements. By the end of 1871, Mayor Hall had been indicted (he later exiled himself to Europe) and Boss Tweed's rule had been broken. (Tweed himself would soon be behind bars.) But the 1870s brought a succession of further—and increas-ingly economic—protests; and while Tweed himself was no longer around, the ability of the police to manage social unrest continued to be a source of con-cern to many in the ruling elite.

In Europe, the police of the great cities were controlled by the national government and the cops themselves were peasants in uniform. "We like to get them straight from the plough," a London police commissioner explained. Farm laborers tended not to identify with urban workers, and lest they develop more sympathy over time, London's police were quartered in special housing, where their social contacts were largely with their peers. Everywhere except England, superior officers were drawn from the educated classes, just as in the army.

In American cities, by contrast, cops were homegrown. They came from working-class neighborhoods and went on living there after they joined the force. Their top officers were men who had come up from the beat, and many were immigrants. A survey in the mid-1880s found that out of approximately three thousand police officers of all ranks and grades, a third had come over from Ireland. So, too, had the parents of many native-born cops.

In January 1874, a coalition of East Side radicals scheduled a rally at Tompkins Square to demand public-works projects to create employment. William Havemeyer, the mayor who had presided over the creation of the municipal police three decades earlier, was back in office. In a burst of nostal-gia he appointed George Matsell, now sixty-seven and out of headquarters for sixteen years, as superintendent. Matsell was well past it, however, and Havemeyer's own attitude toward working-class unrest was conflicted. At first, to the ill-concealed dismay of his friends in the business community, he promised to address the rally; then he decided not to let it take place. Many people came anyway, and scores were injured in a mounted-police charge. A few months later, Havemeyer kicked Matsell up to the Board of Police

Commissioners, appointing the able Inspector George Walling as police superintendent.

But the greatest and most memorable of the era's disorders came in the summer of 1877, after railroad workers struck in West Virginia and then across the country. In Baltimore, the state militia proved incapable of taming the strikers, and ten people were killed before federal troops claimed control. In Pittsburgh, there were twenty-five deaths, and a mob drove the state troops out of town, burning millions of dollars' worth of property before the regulars were finally dispatched. In Chicago, troops and police killed twenty rioters. Reminded of secession and 1861, a number of prominent citizens urged President Hayes to follow Lincoln's example by calling out a hundred thousand militiamen to suppress the rebellion.

In New York, the trouble started on the waterfront. The longshoremen of the Pennsylvania Railroad had seen their hourly wages drop from twenty cents to fifteen over the previous four years. In June, after the railroad cut their wages to thirteen and a half cents, they struck. Many of them gathered in McHugh's saloon on Battery Place, while fifty cops nervously patrolled nearby. The railroad ordered its shipping clerks to replace the longshoremen. The clerks' own wages had fallen to ten cents an hour, so they were not particularly pleased with their new assignment. But when the first man to complain was fired, the rest did as they were told. Eventually, the longshoremen went back to work for fourteen cents.

As economic conditions worsened, large numbers of the idle and distressed gathered nightly in Battery Park, among other places. Even at the best of times, summer was hard on the poor in New York City. The tenements were swelteringly hot, and the sun shining down on the amalgam of dirt and horse droppings in the streets made for a pungent smell and a high rate of infectious disease. A thousand babies a week would die in the slums, the *New York Times* predicted that July. In better neighborhoods, those who could afford it left town for places like the Adirondacks or Atlantic City rather than deal with the heat and the possibility of riots.

The United States Army was small and heavily concentrated in the West, where Custer had been massacred a year earlier. In New York, Assistant U.S. Treasurer Thomas Hillhouse, responsible for roughly a $100 million dollars stored in the customshouse and subtreasury, telegraphed a warning to his superiors not to "draw too heavily on the few small detachments of U.S.

troops in the harbor forts for service elsewhere." Conditions reminded Hill-house of the Draft Riots: the city, he noted in a letter to his boss, the secretary of the treasury, "is filled with the most inflammable materials for a riot, if an opportunity should occur." When the decision makers in Washington ignored him, transferring the harbor garrisons out of the city, Hillhouse pleaded with them to send at least one or two companies back. At a cabinet meeting, the president's advisers debated the wisdom of the secretary of the navy's offer to furnish a warship with heavy guns to "clear the streets around the Custom House." The streets were too crooked for that, the secretary of the treasury objected. "The big guns will straighten them out," the secretary of state declared.

Galvanized by the great strike, a coalition of East Side radicals asked the authorities for permission to hold a mass meeting in Tompkins Square Park. William H. Vanderbilt, Cornelius's son, appealed to the mayor, Smith Ely, to follow the example of his predecessor, Havemeyer, by withholding a permit. While far from eager to see such a gathering, Mayor Ely did not feel he had the legal right (or perhaps the political elbow room) to prevent it.

By seven-thirty on the appointed night, some five thousand New Yorkers had assembled around stands set up for speakers of English, German, and French—the two latter groups often more fearful of each other than of the police. The police department, for its part, had sent a three-hundred-man detail under Inspector William Murray, a rising star of the force, and Captain Thomas Byrnes, of the Mercer Street precinct. (Sixteen years earlier almost to the day, Murray and Byrnes had fought together at Bull Run.) In reserve nearby was Inspector Thomas Thorne with another four hundred officers on foot and horseback, and telegraph lines had been strung between police precincts and National Guard armories, where four regiments were on alert. As the meeting began, a calcium light at the corner of the square suddenly expired with a fizzing sound like the hiss of a bomb. A nervous murmur went through the crowd, and all eyes turned toward the police, massed in the shadows around the park. John Swinton of the *New York Sun*, presiding at the English speakers' stand, had trouble claiming the podium from a drunken Irishman. When Swinton finally spoke, reading his notes by candlelight, he solemnly noted the "eight thousand rifles over [our] heads and twelve hundred clubs drawn." He went on to denounce the railroad bosses in general and Jay Gould in particular. The mood was lighter at the German stand, where steins of beer were passed up to the speakers. Justus Schwab, a saloonkeeper whose place on First Avenue was a hangout for European radicals, ended his address with "three cheers for the striking men of America who are defending their right to live."

Around nine-fifteen, the crowd started to leave the park. But about three hundred "roughs," as the *Times* dubbed them, gathered at Eighth Street and Avenue A and began marching toward First Avenue. Moving his forces quickly into place to block the street, Inspector Murray ordered the marchers to disperse. They ignored him. At Murray's unhesitating command, the police charged with batons flying.

Murray and Byrnes played a frontline role, and both got hit by bricks. But there was no ambiguity about the outcome. "It was the most glorious sight I ever saw the way the police broke and drove that crowd," Abram Duryea, a member of the Board of Police Commissioners, recalled later. By the time the battle ended, the ability of the municipal police to control a mob was evident to all. Even the *Times*, while highly critical of the participants, could not help noting that the cops "used clubs more freely than necessary," landing some of their blows upon respectable neighborhood residents who were not part of the crowd. When word of the events at Tompkins Square flashed across the country, the heart went out of the railroad strike, which soon collapsed.

The dependability of the police in these situations was partly a matter of leadership. Tough young street kids in volunteer fire companies at the time of secession, Murray and Byrnes had joined the New York "Fire Zouaves" to be part of the great adventure. Styling themselves after several French infantry units in Algeria, the New York Zouaves wore fezes, short jackets, and baggy Arab trousers, and they marched at a fast clip. The regiment's commander was E. Elmer Ellsworth, a close friend of Abraham Lincoln's and an associate in his Springfield law office. After organizing a Zouave drill team in Chicago shortly before the war, Ellsworth took them all over the northern states giving demonstrations. He and his men achieved the kind of celebrity that now accrues to a quarterback and his team who have won the Super Bowl. The Ellsworth Zouaves, as they came to be known, were one of the first regiments to arrive in Washington, where they acquired a reputation for rowdiness, though their experience came in handy when a shop next to the Willard Hotel caught fire. Their dashing colonel played on the White House lawn with the president's sons, who worshiped him. Thirsting for glory, Ellsworth didn't have to wait long for an opportunity. A Confederate flag flying across the Potomac in Alexandria, Virginia, could be seen from the White House, to the president's great distress. Ellsworth, accompanied by a reporter from Greeley's *Tribune*, marched his regiment across the river to end the affront. Observing the rebel banner on a hotel flagpole, he drew his sword, raced up the stairs, and cut it down, only to be intercepted by the proprietor, who blasted him with a shotgun. The killer himself was immediately shot and, for good measure, bayoneted by the Zouaves. Ellsworth's body lay in state at the White House, and the whole Union went into mourning. In postwar northern legend, particularly among the veterans, men like Ellsworth, who had acted decisively, were heroes, while those who had temporized with rebels were scorned.

But in their strong aversion to public disorder and their lack of sympathy with radicals and disgruntled workers, the police commanders of the era were not that far out of step with the rank and file. Cops might have come from the working class, but they were on their way toward becoming a class of their own. Given an order to charge, said Joel Erhardt, who served on the Board of Police Commissioners in the 1870s, they "know nothing but duty, and ties of friendship, of kindred, of religion, count as nothing to stay their progress in enforcing the law—they are irresistible." Had the police faltered during the troubles of the 1870s, the state might have moved to retake control of the force permanently. (This had already happened in St. Louis and Baltimore, after major riots against Union troops at the beginning of the Civil War.) If so, other cities might well have done the same, and America's urban police departments, like those of Europe, would have been independent of municipal politics.

In the prewar years, the force had attracted a goodly number of skilled workers. No more. The cops of the late nineteenth century came largely from the ranks of teamsters, dock laborers, and streetcar men. For most of them, however—and for their families—appointment to the force represented a step up in the world. In the 1880s, a patrolman made $1,200 a year, which was about twice the wage of the average worker. An extra benefit luring many to the force was retirement after twenty or twenty-five years (the period shifted back and forth) with half pay. Very few workers of the time had any pension plan, much less one so generous.

Being a police officer carried a certain status in the blue-collar world, particularly among immigrants, for it signified acceptance of the "foreigner" as an American of such trustworthiness that he could be allowed to bear arms and exercise authority on behalf of the state. Appointment to the force also meant that someone was well connected, since a candidate needed political sponsorship. In the first place, five persons had to certify from personal knowledge to his sobriety, industry, and good conduct—and they had better be the kind of people that Tammany Hall approved of. With the enactment of the first civil-service rules in 1884, applicants had to submit to examination by a board consisting of the inspector of detectives, the chief of the fire department, and the secretary of the Board of Police Commissioners. The final requirement, often, was a payment of roughly $250—a quarter of a year's pay—to a local politician. (In 1894, the president of the Board of Police Commissioners admitted to a state legislative committee that 85 percent of his appointments were made on Tammany's recommendation.)

Recruits attended a school of instruction for one month, where they received training in military drill; became familiar with about 700 rules of patrol duty, 250 general orders, some criminal law, and the sanitary code; and heard five lectures by a surgeon from the Society for First Aid. The real training, though, came after the recruit reported to his assigned precinct. Because of the reserve system, a nineteenth-century cop spent many hours in the station section room or dormitory—the police equivalent of an army barracks, where veterans tell rookies how to behave and the loudest and toughest dominate. The dormitories were the municipal equivalent of a flophouse. Typically, they could accommodate about forty men in beds spaced less than two feet apart. Officers coming off patrol hung their clothes, wet or dry, on the wall. There were no showers, and a couple of narrow windows supplied what there was in the way of ventilation. Over the aroma of the cops and their clothing hung a steady cloud of pipe and cigar smoke.

To sleep soundly in such a setting, you had to adjust not only to the smell but to the sound of drunks shouting and singing in the cells below. All too soon, you had to bear with the wake-up call of the station doorman, usually a hulking brute, who would burst in shouting, "Get up, you bums," or some other summons that he found humorous. (Doormen were not full-fledged cops until 1898, when the legislature merged them into the ranks.) In winter, the room was likely to be overheated, and if the desk sergeant sounded three bells—an emergency—the men often had to go directly from a hothouse into freezing weather. In the summer, the dormitories baked. It was an environment friendlier to pneumonia and tuberculosis germs than to humans.

Recruits were subject to a fraternity-lodge-style initiation. From the first day, the old-timers would test a new man's mettle with a vigorous series of hazing exercises. Being doused with a bucket of water while in bed was common. The severity of the treatment, though, depended on the victim: Irish-born cops held sway in most stations, so a rookie born on the old sod—assuming, of course, he was a Catholic—started with an advantage. An American-born "narrowback," on the other hand, was in for it. Germans benefited from a reputation for being tough—it wasn't considered wise to antagonize a former butcher's apprentice who had carried sides of beef for years, lest he flatten one of his tormentors. (Germans were referred to as "Dutchmen." Many cops, owing to their hazy familiarity with the map of continental Europe, applied the term to pretty much anyone born east of France.) Members of other ethnic groups were presumed unfit for the job until they proved otherwise. The hazing process came to a climax with "party night," when the rookie was tied to his bed and other cops danced around and painted his skin—Irish green was the favorite color. The final rituals included a solemn oath never to reveal departmental secrets. The worst name an Irishman could bestow was that of informer. To be even suspected of it made a cop a pariah. A veteran advising a rookie about how to get along on the job would tell him to express no opinions on religion or politics, take his hazing like a man, never "peach" on his comrades, and—the key to acceptance—rush forward with club swinging, no questions asked, to back up another cop who was in trouble.

Under the two-platoon system, duty hours were complicated, and a patrolman often met himself coming and going. On Sunday night he might begin a patrol at midnight that would end at 6:00 A.M. Monday morning. Then he'd be allowed to go home until 6:00 P.M., return to the precinct to patrol until midnight, and be sent home again. On Tuesday, he would patrol from 8:00 A.M. until 1:00 P.M., have reserve duty till midnight, and go back on the street. At 6:00 A.M. Wednesday, he would be allowed to go home for another twelve hours, and was expected back at the precinct at 6:00 P.M. to patrol until midnight. Then he'd be on reserve until 6:00 A.M. Thursday, out for two hours on the "dog watch," back on reserve till 1:00 P.M., put on patrol till 6:00 P.M., and on reserve again until midnight, when he would start a new four-day cycle: a total of thirty-six hours on patrol and twenty-eight on reserve over the four days. The brother of a sergeant from upstate wrote to inquire about joining the force. Stay home, he was told, the work is too hard.

A platoon was commanded by a sergeant and divided into two sections, each overseen by a roundsman (so named because he made the rounds checking on patrolmen). As first-line supervisors, the roundsmen set the standards for their men. After roll call at the precinct, the patrolman went directly to a designated "relieving point" on his beat, where he met the man going off duty. He was expected to remain on post unless police duty or the call of nature required him to leave, in either case noting the incident in his memo book. If a roundsman could not locate a patrolman after a thorough canvass, he was supposed to whistle or rap his club loudly three times—in the center and at both ends of the post. When that failed, the roundsman, if he was a strict sort, ordered the patrolman on an adjacent post to fill the gap or filled it himself, and gave the errant cop a "dido," or disciplinary charge. A cop generally stayed alert till he got his "see"—till he met the roundsman, that is, and exchanged salutes. Then he could relax, unless the roundsman was one of those annoying ones who made a practice of doubling back.

Patrolmen had a less formal system for communicating a roundsman's whereabouts. A patrolman would signal to the man on the next post by extending his arm in the direction the roundsman had last been seen heading. Both arms spread horizontal meant "I don't know where he is." As a last resort, he could drop his club on the pavement to warn a colleague of the roundsman's approach. (Police officers had three types of clubs, a twenty-six-inch-long nightstick, a shorter daystick, or billy club, and a ceremonial rosewood baton. Because of its greater length, the preferred instrument for riot duty was the nightstick, which was made of locustwood.) While fifteen complaints a year was par for most precinct roundsmen, headquarters roundsmen, or "shooflys," were constantly "looking for meat." ("Shoofly Don't Bother Me" was a popular song of the 1860s. In the police world, however, the term was sometimes spelled *shoefly* because an errant cop's shoes would "fly away" when he sighted the roundsman.) A cop who went into a "coop," such as the backroom of a store, to smoke or get warm tried to make sure it had two exits in case a boss appeared at one of them. If a patrolman off his post heard that the roundsman had been looking for him, there were standard tricks for avoiding a dido; one was to borrow a horse and carriage from a friendly hackman, take it to the precinct, and claim he had found it straying. This might work in the instance, but it angered the roundsman, and from then on the cop had better watch his back. Roundsmen, too, had to watch their backs. A notably strict one was John H. McCullagh, from County Tyrone, Ireland, who joined the force in 1864 and was assigned to the Twentieth Precinct under Captain Walling. Even many veteran cops shunned assignment to Hell's Kitchen, where tough gangs preyed upon the railroads passing through their territory. But Walling gave the rookie a post there, and early on he pursued three boxcar thieves, knocked them out, threw them into a wheelbarrow, and took them to the police station. Soon the young officer developed a reputation for fearlessness much like Walling's own as a rookie. When McCullagh was promoted to roundsmen and assigned to the Twelfth Precinct, Walling requested that he be returned to his command. There a rogue cop, notorious for leaving his post and frequenting saloons, threatened to kill any roundsman who reported him. McCullagh did just that, and Walling backed him up—the cop was fired. Later, while McCullagh was on duty at the corner of Thirty-seventh Street and Ninth Avenue, the dismissed policeman shot and wounded him severely. The former officer was sent to Sing Sing for five years.

In 1885, the commissioners sitting as a trial board heard 2,570 charges against officers of all grades for violation of the rules. Typical complaints were being off post or talking while on duty. In practice, cops spent a lot of time gabbing with citizens, so a roundsman who issued such a complaint was either a hard case or had it in for the patrolman. Sixteen officers were dismissed that year, mainly for intoxication; since drinking on duty was common, they were probably hopeless drunks or in bad with their superiors. If a break-in occurred on a cop's post and he didn't at least know about it before the store owner did, he could be charged with neglect of duty. Usually, though, the officer could escape punishment with a plausible claim of having been tied up on police business at the opposite end of his beat. In the remaining cases, 1,620 men were fined a total of nearly $10,000, 317 were reprimanded, and 517 were found not guilty. (The rest were yet to be disposed of.) Eighty percent of the time, in other words, the officer was found guilty.

The nature of a patrolman's work depended on the precinct he was assigned to. The Bronx and the northern end of Manhattan were largely rural areas containing city dumps where goats fed. Older cops liked these precincts—collectively known as Goatsville—because they were quiet. The posts tended to be large, and some were patrolled on horseback. A rookie who knew how to ride, therefore, stood a good chance of being sent uptown regardless of his own preferences; if he was, his training-school buddies would commiserate with him, for, as everyone understood, Goatsville offered few if any opportunities for "sugar," or graft. From that standpoint, the old badlands of the Five Points and the Bowery remained choice assignments. The most lucrative area of all, though, was the Tenderloin, which stretched from Seventh Avenue on the west to Fourth (now Park) on the east, taking in most of the cross streets in the twenties and thirties (Sixth Avenue was its backbone). Here a patrolman would have no trouble about free meals and beer and could even expect the occasional tip.

The roughest beats were called "battle rows" because of the gangs or combative citizens to be found there. As captain of the Eighteenth Precinct, George Walling had organized a strong-arm squad of a half dozen plainclothes officers to slug on sight members of the troublesome Honeymoon Gang. "By dint of a few hard licks judiciously administered, the district was 'cleared,' " he recalled in his memoirs. So frequently did his men use their clubs that a local physician got rich treating injured prisoners on contract to the city: patching a cut brought him a dollar, and a broken head was worth five. One of the worst battle rows was on Twenty-second Street between Second and Third Avenues, where there were tenements occupied by English on one side and Irish on the other, and fights constantly broke out between them. Walling solved that problem too, with his strong-arm squad.

It took a special breed of cop to handle such a beat—someone like Alexander "Clubber" Williams. Born in Canada in 1839, Williams spent a number of years at sea as a ship's carpenter before joining the force in 1866. Tall, muscular, and bullet-headed, he started out in a Brooklyn precinct but found his way onto the Broadway squad two years later. Within two days after his arrival in the new assignment, according to legend, he picked a fight with a pair of local toughs, clubbed them, and pitched them through the plate-glass window of a saloon for an encore. When a half dozen of their buddies emerged, they too were supposedly beaten unconscious. For the next four years, he was said to have averaged a fight a day. In 1872, he was made captain of the tough Gashouse precinct in the East Twenties. There he acquired a city-wide reputation and his nickname, based on his oft-stated belief that "there is more law in the end of a policeman's night stick than a Supreme Court decision." While escorting a group of reporters on a stroll around the Gashouse area, Williams paused to remove his expensive watch and hang it on a nearby lamppost. Though the act was reputedly observed by a score of potential thieves, he cavalierly led the party of reporters around the block and, when they returned, pointed to the untouched watch as marvelous proof of the fear that he inspired. In 1876, he was transferred to the West Twenty-ninth Street station, in charge of an area then known as Satan's Circus. Its name changed, though, after Williams told a reporter, "All my life I have never had anything but chuck steak. Now I'm gonna get me some tenderloin."

If a cop sought promotion, he was expected to pay for it. Tammany Hall had worked out a fee schedule: an officer promoted to roundsman might be charged $300; a roundsman to sergeant, $1,600; a sergeant to captain, $12,000 to $15,000. These requirements could be modified in special cases. If you belonged to a Tammany club, you could pay some of your dues by selling tickets for dances and picnics to the gamblers and divekeepers in your precinct. A politician might waive the necessary payments for someone he liked. Police Commissioner William "Baldy" Smith, who had been a general in the Civil War, was partial to ex-soldiers. Timothy Creedon, a wounded veteran of twenty-three Civil War battles, was promoted to roundsman and sergeant without paying. Twice, he took the captain's exam and scored well without being promoted. Creedon was well liked by the pols. Even if he had won the war single-handedly, though, they would not have given him a captaincy for free. Precinct commands were bonanzas, and there were plenty of people ready to stake a claim. As a special accommodation, Creedon was permitted to borrow the money from saloonkeepers and other friends, and repay it from the extra income associated with his new post. But there was a last-minute hitch. Creedon was supposed to purchase his rank for a rock-bottom price of $12,000, but another aspirant had offered $15,000. So Creedon's backers raised another $3,000. Then they learned that he was going to the First Precinct in the Wall Street financial district—the city's richest neighborhood, but one of the poorest for police graft. Bordellos, which operated on the same block as churches in other parts of the city, were not permitted anywhere near the temples of finance. Calculating that it would take forever to get their money back, Creedon's friends backed off. Finally, Tammany consented to send him to a more active precinct, and the deal was consummated.

By taking graft, cops in effect "licensed" joints and made them obey some informal rules. But the police were hardly in a position to suppress vice. With the city divided between the immigrant majority and a significant Protestant elite, they had to play an elaborate game of make-believe, enforcing the law enough to satisfy the minority but not so much as to alienate the majority. "Never get between the people and their beer" was a Tammany maxim.

It was an attitude that sometimes drew criticism from influential citizens. Others, in their fear of radicals and riots, were willing to overlook such lapses. "Men who have surrendered their citizenship to Tammany might do worse with it," William Allen White, a liberal Republican, observed at the turn of the century. "In all their ignorance, and greed and mendacity they might use that citizenship. If the time ever comes when they do . . . heaven protect wealth and social order in New York City! Take away the steel hoops of Tammany from the social dynamite, and let it go kicking around under the feet of any cheap agitators, and then look out for the fireworks. . . . With all the mold of feudalism which Tammany preserves," White went on, "the Tammany-made citizen is more trustworthy than the red anarchists would make. . . . For Tammany preaches contentment, it tolerates no Jeremiahs."

Tammany kept the trolleys running. The streetcar lines, owned by enormously powerful traction barons who had acquired their franchises through political clout, were vital to the city's commerce. When the trolley workers walked off the job, as they often did, it was standard practice to replace them with scabs. The striking workers were mostly Irishmen from the same neighborhoods (and even the same families) as cops; yet it fell to the police to protect the trolley lines and head off any attempts to block the tracks or drag the scabs off the cars. Theodore Dreiser, in his novel *Sister Carrie*, describes a streetcar strike in Brooklyn in which the fallen George Hurstwood is reduced to looking for work as a scab motorman.

"What are you looking for?" a police officer asks him.

"I want to see if I can get a place," Hurstwood replies.

"The offices are up those steps," says the bluecoat, whose face is "a very neutral thing to contemplate," for "in his heart of hearts," Dreiser writes, he sympathizes with the strikers and can't abide the scabs, yet "in his heart of hearts, also," he feels the dignity of his office and the call of a higher duty.

In other situations as well—not just political protests—the police attitude was to preempt trouble by striking the first blow. The job, cops reasoned, was dangerous; indeed, it was probably a good deal rougher than it has been portrayed. The cops of the nineteenth century had neither cars nor radios. The first call boxes were installed in the Bronx in the '80s, making it possible for an officer to contact the precinct and summon assistance. Manhattan did not have call boxes until early in the twentieth century, and not until the '90s were horse-drawn patrol wagons available to rush reserves out to assist an officer in trouble and bring in a prisoner. Normally, a cop summoned help by rapping his club on the pavement and hoping his fellows on adjoining beats would hear. Locustwood was noted for the ringing sound it made and was preferable to blowing a whistle. But since the signal might go unheard, a wise cop cultivated friends among the local residents. That way, he would have people to talk to when he was feeling bored or lonely, and he could hope to get some assistance in time of need.

Few people carried guns in the gaslight era, and the weapons they did carry were notably unreliable. (That, of course, cut both ways. Police revolvers could also misfire; hence the maxim that "clubs are more trustworthy than leaden balls.") But a surprisingly large number of cops, proportionately, were killed in the line of duty in the nineteenth century—including many not reflected in departmental records. According to the official tally, twenty men— among them one member of the Brooklyn force, an independent entity from 1870–98—lost their lives between the founding of the department in 1845 and the end of the century. (Of these, eighteen died as a result of criminal homicide, the others from drowning and a horse accident.) But for reasons that are not entirely clear, a substantial number of other slain officers were not listed as such.* If the police were slipshod in recording the deaths of their own comrades, the homicide figures for the general population may also have been less than strictly reliable. According to scholars who have studied New York City crime, the annual murder rate per 100,000 citizens was in the single digits until the Draft Riots, except for the troubled year of 1857, when it reached 12.7. Afterward, it fluctuated between 4 and 8 per 100,000 until the end of the '70s; for the rest of the century, it remained between 3 and 6. (At its

---

*The NYPD has a Roll of Honor that is meant to include every officer killed in the line of duty. There appear to be many omissions, however. Officially, the first policeman killed was Patrolman James Cahill— shot to death by a burglar in 1854. In our research, we came across reports of two officers murdered a month apart in 1851. Two retired members of the force, Sergeant Mike Bosak and Detective John Reilly, have conducted an extensive inquiry into this matter. According to the data gathered by Bosak and Reilly, there may be thirty or more additional cases before 1900. There is also evidence of similar problems, on a smaller scale, with the twentieth-century record.

twentieth-century height, in 1990, the murder rate reached 30 per 100,000.) Some nineteenth-century criminal homicides, however, were not recorded properly or brought to official attention in the first place. Manhattan was surrounded by rivers, all within easy walking distance. The waterfront was the domain of violent gangs who preyed on the unwary and one another. It was no trick to drop a body into the water or, if need be, to find a hackman to transport a corpse to the waterfront from another location. Properly weighted, the victim might never be found; and even a corpse floating in the river could be listed as a suicide or accident if the authorities didn't have a suspect. In the same spirit, a body found in the streets, particularly in the Bowery or the Five Points, was likely to go down as a natural death if there were no obvious bullet or stab wounds. Coroners were patronage appointees, and some could be bribed to turn a murder into a suicide, a justifiable homicide, or an accident. The police were even more cavalier about recording other kinds of crime.

Of course, murders and riots were a rarity. Most policemen spent their careers on uniformed street patrol, where their daily concerns were with far less spectacular and dangerous matters, such as keeping their beats clear of drunks, rowdies, and loiterers. In doing so, they had to make on-the-spot decisions. Some were easy: a boisterous drunk urinating in front of a church would be hauled off to the precinct forthwith, and the next day a magistrate would sentence him to serve ninety days on Blackwells (now Roosevelt) Island. But a group of older teens or young men hanging out on the corner in their own neighborhood was a tougher call. In crowded tenement districts, virtually the only place for young people to socialize was in the streets. So a cop would do a quick assessment of the loiterers' character and act accordingly. Were they good kids? Or were they members of a gang likely to disturb neighbors with loud horseplay, make insulting remarks to females, rob or assault passing strangers, or break into the corner store? The force had been founded at a time of widespread fear of street rowdies; the police of the late nineteenth century were close enough to those days to believe that unchecked public disorder led to serious crime and general public discomfort. An important calculation for a cop was what "they"—a vague term encompassing department superiors, city government, and society—expected of him. These expectations were not always spelled out in formal policies and orders; better guidance often came from the criticism or backing that a cop received after the fact.

Many chroniclers of the period depict constant battling between gang members and police. But if the cops of the day had been as free and easy about clubbing people as Alexander Williams claimed to be, they would have been widely loathed, and Tammany Hall would have been deluged with complaints. Cornelius Willemse, a Dutch-born sailor who joined the force in 1899, portrayed himself as something of a latter-day Williams; yet he recalled making a distinction between men who had jobs—who were allowed to hang out on a corner—and unemployed "loafers," who weren't. One of the most enduring stereotypes of urban life is the beat cop banging his club on the feet of a sleeping hobo as a signal for him to move along. While this sort of thing happened often enough, many cops were capable of more sensitivity; the well-known chronicler of vagrant life Josiah Flynt described the police as "friends of beggars," adding that he had "seldom met a hobo who was angry with a NY bull." By the 1880s, the New York police were commonly referred to by the name Mayor Havemeyer and Chief Matsell are both credited with bestowing on them, "the Finest," and the annual police parades drew thousands of cheering citizens. And all this is to say nothing of the beloved patrolman, who, in nostalgic Hollywood re-creations of this era, would be portrayed as a burly man with the map of Ireland on his face, a cheery "good marnin' " to the adults, and plenty of fatherly advice for any kid who might be tempted by gang life. It was a role Pat O'Brien and Lloyd Nolan later played to perfection, and the cop often ended up married to the sweet neighborhood colleen played by Ann Sheridan or Dorothy McGuire.

The love of the people for their beat patrolman, though, could also be overdrawn; cops changed shifts frequently, and the citizenry periodically relocated. On May 1, the traditional moving day, it sometimes seemed as though half of the city was going or coming. The citizens who came into the most frequent contact with the beat patrolman were local businessmen and people who hung out on the streets. The businesspeople saw the cop as a protector but resented his petty shakedowns and the myriad of municipal regulations that he could enforce against them if they failed to pay. The opinion of corner lads often underwent a change: in their teen years, as tough kids, they saw the bluecoats as "lousy coppers." In middle age, they were more likely to wax nostalgic about "good old Officer Kelly," and call for another chorus of "The Sidewalks of New York."

Williams's own claims are dubious; he lived to be seventy-eight—an achievement for a man who supposedly engaged in a fight a day for four years (a Williams legend recycled in many books). And while Williams was certainly an extreme case, other cops probably also overstated their own brutality. But the exaggeration is illuminating in itself. If cops had the sense to keep fairly quiet about graft, there was little need for discretion when it came to violence. Even many social reformers, following de Tocqueville's thesis, accepted the need for a police department willing to crack heads on a fairly frequent basis. As Henry George put it, "Let the policeman's club be thrown down or wrested from him, and the fountains of the great deep are opened, and quicker than ever before chaos comes again. Strong as it may seem, our civilization is evolving destructive forces. Not desert and forest, but city and slums and country roadsides are nursing the barbarians who may be to the new what Hun and Vandal were to the old."

Clubber Williams wore his nickname as well as his club in the open. Nevertheless, *Harper's Monthly*, in 1887, made him out a hero in a lengthy article celebrating the professionalism of New York's police department. Williams was a renowned figure—"I've been around so long even the car horses nod to me," he said—and his baton, in the *Harper's* telling, became a latter-day Excalibur. It "enjoys the reputation among the roughs of being as hard, ready, and rough as themselves, and is certainly a notable instrument," the author, Richard Wheatley, observed. "Its owner is one of the most venomously hated, frequently tried, and most valuable of police officers." He dubbed the police in general "Knights of the Club"—approvingly. An officer's entrance into the force was described as his "investiture with all the rights and responsibilities of the baton."

It was in the second generation of the police department, the post-1870 municipal period, that the ethos of the force was established, not by manuals of procedure but in the accumulated experiences of its members, passed on in the section room from veteran to rookie. Cops saw themselves as beholden to corrupt ward politicians who expected them to turn a blind eye to protected vice, though many officers did not hesitate to call on those same politicians to advance their own interests. For a cop's career to flourish, in fact, he needed a sponsor; this was a given. (In the twentieth century, the preferred term would be "rabbi." A rabbi could be a politician, a businessmen, or a gangster. To the amusement of outsiders, a cop might even speak of a Monsignor Murphy as his "rabbi.")

Otherwise, civilians could not be trusted. However loudly they might cheer a police parade, at heart they neither understood nor sympathized with the police. Many cops had a dim opinion of their own commanders, viewing them as indifferent if not actually hostile and oppressive. Only another cop could be relied upon for support. And if he failed to provide it, he would be cast out of the brotherhood, because the job was always dangerous, whether you were alone on the beat facing down a gang of toughs or massed with two hundred of your comrades charging a mob. The police department, in some ways, mirrored the Irish homeland of many of its members. Both cultures stressed hostility to the overlords and hatred of informers. In these years, the roots were planted of what came to be called "the blue wall of silence." Coexisting with this attitude, however, was the Irish sense of humor and innate sympathy with the underdog. These ordinary men faced danger with courage and cheer and, despite their toughness, engaged in many acts of kindness.

Police use of force was accepted as a fact of life, even by some of those on the receiving end. Jacob Riis was at the scene of a fire in midtown Manhattan one day as police tried to hold back a group of bystanders. Riis was now a reporter for the *Tribune*, having long since broken his vow to stay out of New York. As he watched, an older man in an ulster coat, his head buried deep in his collar and a cigar sticking out of his mouth, emerged from a nearby hotel and walked toward the fire. Suddenly a policeman grabbed him by the collar, swung him about, and gave him a resounding whack across the back with his club. "What's the matter with you?" the cop shouted. "Don't you see the fire lines? Chase yourself out of here, and be quick about it." Meekly, the man retreated. Riis strolled over and casually asked the cop if he was aware of the identity of his victim. He didn't know, he said—or care. Riis calmly dropped the bomb. It was Ulysses S. Grant, who, following his presidency, had settled in New York. Riis supposed that the cop didn't sleep for a week. Disgrace, dismissal, even jail loomed ahead in his imagination. But the axe never fell. Perhaps Grant did not expect too much from Americans in uniform; perhaps he considered the officer's actions justified. As the *Harper's* article observed, "the ideal policeman is only an ideal. The actual is but an approximation to the imaginary archetype because he is only a man under all the limitations of the commonplace American citizen." Grant, in any case, did not lodge a complaint.

4

The Great Detective

On a sunny Sunday morning in October 1878, a short, thin, middle-aged man with a gray beard and a frenzied look on his face bolted out the side door of the Manhattan Savings Bank onto Bleecker Street and, turning the corner, ran down Broadway. He was barefoot and had a pair of handcuffs dangling from his wrists, firming up the impression of some churchbound pedestrians that the man was probably an escaped lunatic.

"The bank's been robbed!" he exclaimed, after bursting in on the startled occupants of a basement barbershop. The lunatic was the bank janitor, Louis Werckle. The way he told the story, half a dozen men wearing black masks and wielding revolvers had broken into his family living quarters in the bank at about 6:00 A.M. After tying up the Werckle household, including his wife and mother-in-law, the robbers had spent more than two hours looting the vault. They had made off with a stupendous sum for the time—somewhere between $2 million and $3 million, according to preliminary estimates. After their departure, Werckle had managed to free himself and run for help.

In the swarm of inquisitive people who showed up at the bank that morning was a husky man, nearly six feet tall, with a flowing mustache and a bearing that denoted power and self-confidence. Neatly dressed in a low derby and a cutaway coat, he might have been a successful businessman. In fact, he was the captain of the local precinct, Thomas Byrnes, and the robbery would be a pivotal moment in his long and mostly glorious career. Byrnes had emigrated from famine-ridden Ireland as a boy of six, arriving in New York with his parents in the late 1840s—at the height of the Know-Nothing era, when prospects for Irish Catholics were poor. Raised in the Gashouse District, Byrnes left school early, apprenticed as a gas-pipe fitter, and joined one of the rowdy volunteer fire companies. In 1861, when the Civil War broke out, he could have stayed home, as most young Irishmen did. Instead, he enlisted in the Union army in time to fight in the First Battle of Bull Run and, as he laughingly recollected, to eventually take flight with the rest of his regiment. Mustered out of the army at the end of 1863, Byrnes joined the Metropolitan Police, his fitness for appointment demonstrated by his war service. He spent five years as a patrolman in the Fifteenth Precinct, which encompassed the black section of Greenwich Village and the mansions of the old aristocracy on lower Fifth Avenue.

Even as a patrolman, Byrnes excelled in the investigation of crime. In one early case, a house on Madison Avenue had been entered, a safe unlocked, and money and jewels taken. Byrnes found the only apparent clue: a piece of scarlet ribbon caught between the sides of the safe and the inner drawer. Scrutinizing the dozen or more female servants employed in the house, he determined that one of them was partial to ribbons of the same shade. Some time later, when she gave notice to her employer, Byrnes decided to shadow her. After following her on a streetcar downtown, he saw her enter a small tenement house. There Byrnes and two other officers found her in the company of a couple of well-known burglars. The threesome broke down and confessed. In 1868, Byrnes was made a roundsman, a year later a sergeant, and in 1870, when the Metropolitans were replaced by the Municipals, a captain. (With the establishment of the Metropolitan force in 1857, the rank of lieutenant, which had existed for a few years, was abolished, not to be restored until the twentieth century.) In the next eight years, he rotated in command of several precincts and the Broadway squad.

The police department scarcely had a detective bureau at the time. The small squad of headquarters detectives was a rudimentary appendage to the force, and precinct captains could override them if they chose. Byrnes had already made a name for himself by breaking the Van Tine Silk company burglary case and by capturing Paul Law, the son of an ex-governor of Maryland, who had shot four men in New York City. He was not going to let a case as big as the Manhattan Savings Bank job slip from his grasp.

The new wealth and mobility of post–Civil War New York gave rise to a class of professional criminals as venturesome as the robber barons of the business world. New York, the economic capital of the nation—easily reached by steamer from Europe or train from anywhere in the United States—offered pickings for every type of crook, ranging from skilled burglars and polished confidence men who fleeced socialites and bank presidents to corner toughs. The con men, or bunco artists, were fashionably dressed and well spoken. (The term had a dual origin: it stemmed, on the one hand, from a card game called banco and, on the other, from a slang expression for phony talk, *buncombe*.) They stayed at the finest hotels, dined at the best restaurants, traveled first-class, and mingled with leaders of commerce and finance. Franklin J. Moses, the former governor of South Carolina and son of a distinguished judge, was involved in hundreds of swindles. Hugh Courtenay (originally Clinton), the son of a groundskeeper on the estate of an English earl, was one of a number of phony noblemen who preyed on the gullibility of affluent Americans. He posed as Lord Courtenay, a British naval officer, or as Sir Harry Vane, an officer of "Her Majesty's lights." Women loved to cut the buttons off his uniforms as keepsakes, and wealthy men were happy to loan him money. When they inquired about delays in repayment, he blamed his "idiot banker." Then he disappeared.

A few notches down were the characters who fleeced rubes with gold bricks and the peddlers of "green goods," or counterfeit money. The typical brick was triple-gold-plated lead with a slug of solid gold in the center. Often, the con man would use a phony assayer as a partner. In the "green goods" swindle, the victim was sold a package of genuine money, which was exchanged for a bundle of worthless sheets of paper or a bag filled with sawdust. Usually, the suckers' names were obtained from lists of subscribers to lotteries or gift-book companies. A pale version of the con man was the bunco steerer; generally a young man of good family in need of money to pay off his debts or maintain his social position, he would lead his compatriots to gambling joints and get a cut of their losses.

Other common thieves were pickpockets, or "dips" (*knucks* had become archaic), who infested urban crowds, typically operating in gangs of four or five. One man was the "tool" who actually lifted the wallet of the victim, while the others jostled him and stood by to block pursuit or accept the handoff of the wallet from the tool. Among the well-known gangs were the Sheeny Mob, led by "General" Abe Greenthal, which operated nationally, and the Dutch Mob, which worked the Lower East Side for many years. Their tactic was to stage a fight that would attract a crowd, whose pockets would then be picked.

At the bottom of the professional criminal hierarchy were the bold but unskilled who relied on muscle and daring. One of their strategies was to lie in wait for a bank messenger (or anyone else carrying a large sum), slug him, jump in a waiting horse and cart, and make a getaway. The practice had begun before the Civil War, when young men would ride up to butcher shops, seize a carcass, and throw it onto their wagons. After the war, they switched to robbing people.

As he sized up the Manhattan Savings Bank job, Byrnes discerned the work of a crew of big-time "yeggs"—a term that had originated from the name of a famous safecracker and, in a strict sense, referred only to burglars, though it was also commonly used for robbers and other categories of heist men. (Legally, an act of theft became a robbery if force or intimidation was used; nonviolent breaking and entering was burglary. But these terms, too, were often used interchangeably.) Among the obvious suspects were the Miles Gang, led by George Miles and Max Shinburn, and the Patchen Avenue Gang, a Brooklyn outfit led by Billy Porter and Johnny Irving. But the most likely suspects were the Leslie Gang, whose brain was George Leonidas Leslie, aka George Howard, Western George, and other monikers. Prominent among Leslie's associates was Jimmy Hope, who had started out by robbing the paymaster's safe at the Philadelphia Navy Yard and, along with Jimmy Brady, had pulled off a burglary in Delaware for which they received forty lashes and twenty years. The Delaware prisons were not strong enough to hold them, however, and they had escaped to New York. The gang also included Abe Coakley, John "Red" Leary, "Worcester" Sam Parris, "Banjo" Pete Emerson (a former minstrel man), and the notorious Tom "Shang" Draper, a dive owner, suspected murderer, and all-round thug.

Leslie came from an unusual background for a yegg. He was not a product of a New York street gang but a brewery owner's son from Cincinnati, where he was reputed to have graduated from college before heading east. In appearance, he was a short, clean-cut, robust man, always well dressed, with a taste for the arts. He possessed a considerable knowledge of mechanical engineering and architectural drawing, which he put to good use in sketching the layouts of banks. While he sometimes went on robberies himself, he was best known in the underworld as a "putter up"—a man who planned jobs or reviewed the plans of others. Around 1870, he made his headquarters in Philadelphia, where he led a double life as a respectable citizen and a robber. In the former capacity, he married his landlady's fifteen-year-old daughter, telling her that his frequent absences and furtive habits were due to his work as a detective for the federal Internal Revenue Service.

His friendship with Josh Taggart, a Philadelphia cop with the modern-sounding title of chief of operational intelligence, enabled Leslie to avoid arrest for crimes in Pennsylvania, Delaware, and New Jersey. In time, though, he and Taggart had a falling-out over money and the cops grabbed him and another yegg for a Philadelphia store burglary. Realizing that he could not square the rap, Leslie jumped bail and settled down with his bride in Brooklyn, where he resumed his career. So successful was he that he earned the nicknames King of the Bank Robbers and the Napoleon of Crime. Among the more spectacular jobs pulled off by the Leslie Gang was a bank robbery in Northampton, Massachusetts, in January 1876. Working with an outside lock expert, the gang broke into the cashier's house, bound his wife and children, and took him to the bank, where he was forced to unlock vaults containing $1.5 million in bonds and cash. The outside expert eventually talked, and some members of the gang, including Shang Draper, were arrested. Forcing a bank officer to open the vault was, in fact, a common yegg tactic, but small-town bankers could be stubborn. In February 1878, a cashier in Dexter, Maine, refused to reveal the combination of the safe even under torture. Maddened by his refusal to cooperate, Worcester Sam locked the man in the vault, where he died.

Leslie himself had an ironclad alibi in the Manhattan Savings Bank job. He had been murdered a few months earlier by confederates. But Leslie had planned the crime for three years, obtaining financing from New York's top fence, 250-pound Frederika "Mother" (or "Marm") Mandelbaum, who with her husband, son, and two daughters operated from a dry goods and haberdashery store on the Lower East Side. Typically, the stolen goods would be "planted" at another location and Marm would send a subordinate to look them over. It was understood she had first choice from any robbery or burglary, her favorite items being silk, gold, and silverware. If she agreed to take the goods, all labels, tags, and private marks had to be removed before delivery. Whatever Marm did not want went to "Traveling Mike" Grady, who also bought a share of Leslie's caper. Marm ran a lucrative sideline in stolen bonds and maintained connections with a number of Wall Street brokers. In addition to providing financing for jobs from New York to San Francisco, she was there with her money and powerful connections if one of her boys got in trouble. Marm was, in effect, banker and fixer for the top criminals in New York and the nation. How did a Jewish woman obtain such power in an underworld composed largely of Christian men? Like any other successful power broker, she was a first-rate judge of people, and her ethics, among her own kind, were above reproach.

Though Leslie rated the bank easy—a "pudding," in the vernacular of the day—there were logistical difficulties. The gang couldn't use explosives to crack the safes within the vault because the people living in the adjoining residences would hear the blast, and the cracking of plateglass windows along Broadway would alert the beat cops. Through an intermediary, Leslie made contact with a watchman named Patrick Shevlin, who permitted the robbers to hold practice drills after bank hours in order to determine just which tools they would need. For protection, they enlisted the help of a crooked New York cop, John Nugent, on sick leave from the Eighteenth Precinct.

In May 1878, in the midst of planning the job, Leslie disappeared. Worried, Marm Mandelbaum made inquiries. In June, a New York City mounted cop patrolling on the sparsely populated Yonkers-Bronx border discovered a partly decomposed body with a pearl-handled pistol alongside it. A small newspaper story reported the incident as a possible suicide. But Marm sent her husband up to inspect the body, which, as she feared, turned out to be Leslie's. And it was not suicide but murder. Seized in Brooklyn, Leslie had been taken for a ride to the far end of town by one of the best-known getaway cart men of the day. According to underworld rumor, Leslie had been fooling with a woman named Babe, another yegg's sister, or with Shang Draper's girlfriend or, in still another version, with Draper's wife. Others said Leslie had been indiscreet in his conversations with the police about the cashier's murder in Maine. The knowledgeable agreed that the killing had been a gang decision—a punishment for squealing—and Draper had been the triggerman.*

With Leslie out of the picture, Jimmy Hope took over the gang. In October, when the job went down, he and his twenty-two-year-old son Johnny attacked the safes. A new recruit, Bill Kelly, was left to guard the janitor while Abe Coakley, Officer Nugent, and Pete Emerson acted as lookouts and removed the loot. The job took longer than expected, though, and, under time pressure, the men bypassed several other safes containing even more spectacular sums of money. Had they stuck around for a mere ten minutes more, the take would have been twice as great. There was one moment of panic. A police officer patrolling his beat walked past the bank window and observed Coakley inside. The clever yegg, however, began dusting a desk and nodded casually to the officer, who, taking Coakley for a janitor, went on his way. More serious difficulties arose afterward. Most of the $2.75 million stolen was worthless to the gang: only $12,000 was in cash and $250,000 in negotiable bonds; the rest consisted of registered bonds that could not be passed. Still, a quarter of a million was not bad, and the thieves had only to lie low until they could fence the loot.

A criminal who made the proper arrangements with cops, lawyers, and politicians did not have to worry too much about the law in those days. In 1870, Max Shinburn roamed freely about New York City while wanted on a warrant for a Vermont bank job. When the Vermont authorities became increasingly frustrated by the unwillingness of the New York police to arrest him, they delivered the warrant to Inspector George Walling, known as a straight shooter. He, in turn, went to the police superintendent to ask whether he should serve it personally or hand it to someone else. "Keep it and serve it—if you can," the superintendent replied. Walling couldn't: tipped off by other cops, Shinburn fled to Canada.

In the Manhattan Savings Bank case, Byrnes zeroed in on the watchman,

---

*Many books have dealt with the Manhattan Savings Bank job. Reading a number of them, you might never guess that Leslie was dead at the time. In this as in other matters, a succession of authors have followed the lead of Herbert Asbury's delightful, and utterly unreliable, *Gangs of New York*. Asbury not only has Leslie taking an active part in the robbery but involves him in a series of subsequent crimes. In Asbury's account, Leslie's murder is deferred until June 1884. Accounts of his actual death can be found in *The New York Times* of June 5–10, 1878.

Shevlin. Not being a professional yegg, he was unlikely to stand up under interrogation, and Byrnes taunted him with the fact that he had gotten peanuts out of the job—only $10,000, while the others had struck it rich. Shevlin blew up. In fact, he said, he had received a mere $1,200, despite a promise of $250,000. Shevlin's confession led Byrnes to the Hopes, Kelly, and a bartender who had helped dispose of some of the goods. Coakley and Emerson were caught in Philadelphia trying to fence stolen bonds. Officer Nugent made the mistake of going, as a spectator, to the trial of Johnny Hope and Kelly, where he was recognized and arrested.

That, at any rate, was how Byrnes told the story to the newspapers and how they, in turn, gave it out to the world. George Walling, who disliked Byrnes, suggested that Nugent had given the game away by indiscreet barroom boasting. Lending credence to this theory is the fact of Nugent's eventual acquittal. While Nugent was said to have bribed a juror, he could have walked free in return for squealing to his fellow cops; if so, Shevlin's supposed role might have served as a useful cover. Still another theory was laid out by Julian Hawthorne, the novelist son of Nathaniel, in one of several books supposedly based on inside information from Byrnes. In his account, "Traveling Mike" Grady was cast as the mastermind, and his lover, a society woman, was also implicated. Since Grady was never arrested or tried for the crime, he, too, could have tipped off the authorities.

The police force as a whole was not faring very well in this period. The Manhattan Savings Bank job was just one of three "crimes of the century," as all were described, that rocked the city in the 1870s. The first was the July 1874 kidnapping of four-year-old Charley Ross from the Germantown section of Philadelphia by two men driving a horse-drawn wagon. Kidnapping was rare in nineteenth-century America, and the tender age of the victim sent a shiver down the spine of parents across the country. The case had the same impact in the 1870s as the Lindbergh kidnapping in the 1930s. His abduction became a New York police matter when Captain Henry Hedden of the Thirteenth Precinct received a tip identifying the culprits as William Mosher and Joseph Douglas, old-time New York yeggs of sufficient stature to fence goods with Marm Mandelbaum. They were fugitives at the time, having broken out of jail, where they were serving sentences for burglary. Mosher's brother, also an ex-convict, told police that the two had asked him to help them abduct Commodore Vanderbilt's grandson. Mosher's handwriting turned out to match that on the Ross ransom letter, and he and Douglas were known to travel around the country in a wagon, selling moth preventative. Mosher had a brother-in-law named William Westerveldt, a discharged New York City police officer with an unsavory reputation. George Walling, recently elevated to the post of superintendent, personally asked Westerveldt for help—a bad idea, he later admitted. Under the cover of aiding the police, Westerveldt apparently sent messages that helped Mosher and Douglas elude capture for many months.

The case was not solved until December, when two men broke into a judge's summer home in the semirural Bay Ridge section of Brooklyn, over-looking the Narrows. Alerted by a silent alarm, the judge, his sons, grand-son, and servants emerged from an adjacent house with guns blazing, and the two burglars were fatally wounded. They were Mosher and Douglas. The latter, before his death, confessed to his part in the kidnapping but professed to be ignorant of the boy's whereabouts. Later, Charley Ross's older brother identified the suspects. The detectives working on the case eventually con-cluded that Westerveldt had been in on the kidnapping all along; when the heat grew intense, it was theorized, he had drowned the child in the East River. The ex-cop was convicted on a conspiracy charge and sentenced to seven years.

In November 1878, less than two weeks after the Manhattan Savings Bank burglary, the body of Alexander T. Stewart, one of the country's richest and most unpopular men, was snatched from his grave in the churchyard of St. Marks on the Bowery. In the 1840s, Stewart had built the country's first department store on Broadway between Chambers and Reade Streets; twenty years later, he had opened an even bigger emporium on Broadway between Ninth and Tenth. Covering a whole city block, it had ornate bathrooms, a blaring organ, and six steam-powered elevators. Once again, the police depart-ment acquiesced in the selection of an unsavory intermediary. In this case, it was General Patrick H. Jones, a lawyer and former New York City postmaster, who claimed to have been contacted by an old Civil War comrade wishing to return the body for $250,000. The Stewart family's lawyer refused to pay a penny, but Jones was encouraged to continue his correspondence with the robbers; more than two years passed before he prevailed on Stewart's widow to fork over $20,000. The deal was consummated on a deserted country lane in the farming region of what is now Westchester County. Stewart's remains were reburied, this time in an alarm-equipped vault in Garden City, Long Island. The case was never solved.

Against this background, Byrnes's success seemed almost magical. In 1880 he was promoted to inspector and placed in command of the Detective Bureau. Over the next twelve years, he shaped not just New York's Detective Bureau but the template for detective work as it would come be to organized and practiced in every modern American metropolis. Until Byrnes came along, the work of detectives wasn't so different from that of patrolmen, and it was generally considered a secondary police function. But the mobile criminals of the postwar era were not going to be controlled by uniformed cops—that seemed clear. The way to catch them was through intelligence—information acquired from criminals and informants.

Under Byrnes, intelligence gathering became an organized enterprise. Adhering to an 1866 regulation that had gone unenforced in the past, Byrnes had his detectives keep regular diaries detailing their work. He initiated the practice of photographing suspects and using the photographs as a means of identification. Information of all kinds began to be maintained and filed systematically. Byrnes's photograph and record department, under Sergeant Thomas Adams, had portraits of seven thousand criminals. There was also a rogues' gallery; in the prewar years, it had consisted of busts of a few hundred top crooks; now photographs took the place of the busts. Fifty copies were made of each photo, with the history of the person printed on the back. One copy would be dispatched to each of the city's thirty-four precincts, where it was entered into the record book. The remainder were given to detectives or exchanged with police authorities in other cities. (Byrnes used the rogues' gallery material as the basis for a book, *Professional Criminals of America*—an invaluable who's who of the new underworld.)

Byrnes was also ahead of his time in appreciating the power of statistics, both as an investigative tool and as a means of silencing critics. In the four years prior to his taking command, he let it be known, the detective force had made 1,943 arrests, resulting in sentences totaling 505 years. Over the next four years, his men made 3,324 arrests, resulting in sentences totaling 2,488 years. (Until the 1930s, it remained common to use the years-sentenced figure as a gauge of detective efficiency. With the adoption of the FBI Uniform Crime Reporting System, the practice was discontinued in favor of the percentage of crimes cleared by arrest, without reference to the outcome in court.)

Byrnes moved quickly to develop relationships with the business elite, especially with Wall Street and the stock exchange, the citadel of American financial power. On the very day of his appointment, he opened an office at 17 Wall. So pleased were the bankers with this attention that they gave Byrnes's men quarters in the exchange itself and hooked up a direct telephone line from there to every financial house in the district. As a result, a detective could be summoned to any such firm in less than five minutes. Before he established the substation, millions had been stolen from the district by professional thieves, according to Byrnes; afterward, "not even a ten cent stamp." He announced a "deadline"—a police-declared boundary at Fulton Street just north of the financial district—and forbade any criminal to cross it. Enforcing this arrangement became the specialty of Detectives George Radford and John J. Dunn, who would become better known as "Wall Street Johnny." They simply arrested any "suspicious individual" they found in the prohibited area. If he couldn't explain his presence to their satisfaction, he spent the night in jail.

Detective work began to branch off, informally, into specialties. Sergeant Tim Golden, the dean of Byrnes's staff, had been a detective in the Sixth Precinct before the Civil War, arresting a goodly number of murderers and street thugs. After the war, he operated out of headquarters, concentrating on financial crimes. In 1879, he followed a forger named J. R. Robinson, who had stolen $286,000 in Pennsylvania, to England, Spain, Portugal, then Peru, Argentina, and finally Brazil, where he nailed his man and got him extradited to the United States. Since the case had not originated in New York, we can surmise that Golden was working for the reward. But despite all his globe hopping, Robinson escaped conviction. The case, in the elliptical account of Augustine Costello, writing in the *Herald*, was "compromised." Sergeants Frank Cosgrove and George Lanthier specialized in servicing the elite or, as it was called, "the upper tendom" (the richest and most prominent ten thousand people in New York), frequently turning out in evening clothes to guard society affairs. Sergeant William Frink spent most of his time on con games, jewel theft, and other high-level crimes; one of his triumphs was the arrest of former governor Moses.

Detectives did not spend all their time, though, in top hat and tails or in international pursuit of master con artists. One day, Detective George Dilks and his partner, Tully, spotted the yegg Jimmy Brady, a suspect in the theft of some bonds, in earnest conversation with Traveling Mike Grady, Marm Mandelbaum's colleague. As the detectives approached, Brady took off. While Tully grabbed Grady, who offered no resistance, Dilks went after Brady. During the chase, Brady opened fire and Dilks returned it, wounding Brady in the leg. Desperate, Brady dove through a plateglass window with Dilks right behind him. Sent off to Sing Sing, he eventually escaped, only to resurface a few years later in a pursuit in which he shot an officer from the Broadway squad. This time he got seventeen and a half years.

This preoccupation with the financial community and its needs was, on one level, mere realpolitik. Byrnes, much like George Matsell, knew that the opinion of this tiny slice of the population could be decisive in determining the perception of his success. But he was also building an independent power base that would help the Detective Bureau emerge as a separate fiefdom. Byrnes's Wall Street connections effectively placed him beyond the control of Walling or the commissioners. He was also in a position to defy district leaders when they tried to intervene on behalf of some yegg or gang punk.

Under Byrnes, detectives became men of great prestige. Known as "the immortals" by a press that took to calling Byrnes "the great detective," they were ranked as the equivalent of sergeants—that is, just below captains. They were paid $1,600 a year, which was a third more than a patrolman's salary; and, among other sources of supplemental income, they periodically served as guides for so-called elephant hunters—society matrons, English lords, and other big shots who longed to go slumming in the badlands. Naturally, the detective who took them around to the dives and pointed out the exotic characters was entitled to a generous tip. Byrnes himself was able to become wealthy through his Wall Street ties, and without resorting to the typical methods of police enrichment. Why doff one's hat to petty racketeers and politicians? Byrnes had no less a financial expert than Jay Gould personally overseeing a nest egg of railroad stocks for him. In 1888, Byrnes received the title of chief inspector, making him in theory the number two man on the force, though he had no authority beyond the Detective Bureau. By the 1890s, his salary was $5,000 per year, yet he had a net worth of $350,000 (or about $6 million to $8 million in today's money). And no one was ever able to prove he had done anything illegal to get it.

Soon the rich and famous were seeking audiences with him. "I will have it for you in forty-eight hours," Byrnes would say to a wealthy citizen whose watch had been stolen. Forty-eight hours later on the dot, the watch would be delivered by a detective, "compliments of the Inspector." Even the young reporter Lincoln Steffens received this treatment after his paycheck was lifted by a "dip" on a trolley car in 1892. Julian Hawthorne depicted Byrnes as an omniscient crime fighter whose detectives "shadowed" criminals around town and brought back information to the master. In Hawthorne's books (taken "from the casebook of Inspector Byrnes"), he came across as a brilliant psychologist who knew just which interrogative technique would work with which suspect. Byrnes himself fostered the notion that his success resulted from the tight surveillance that his men kept over the underworld. Augustine Costello of the *Herald*, now run by James Gordon Bennett Jr., described a walk he had taken with Byrnes: spotting a criminal named Sam, Byrnes called him over and ordered him to report to headquarters the next day. To Costello's protest that the man would surely flee the city, Byrnes replied, "Look there." Costello looked. He saw Sam turn a corner. Moments later, a man in a long overcoat approached, stood still for a brief second, then saluted the inspector. With a low chuckle, Byrnes returned the salute, and the mysterious figure in the flowing ulster rapidly disappeared in the same direction as Sam.

The reality was messier. Detectives might shadow people from time to time; more often, they bullied them or cut deals with them. Informants, willing and unwilling, were their main stock in trade. There was no honor among thieves—that was basic detective doctrine. Sooner or later, everybody "peached" if it was to his advantage. While the best informants were criminals themselves, hack drivers were also valued sources, particularly the "night hawks" with their broken-down carriages and horses who worked the late hours ferrying customers to bordellos and gambling joints. Such men could be pressured, too, for they were often mixed up in the rolling of drunks or in the transport of stolen property or even, on occasion, of dead bodies.

In the case of Steffens's paycheck, all the inspector needed was the number of the trolley line on which the theft had occurred. His men knew which pickpockets worked which routes, and they had only to tell the dip that the victim was a special friend of the inspector's. One of Byrnes's successors told the presumably apocryphal but not entirely far-fetched story of a prominent citizen whose watch had been stolen while he was crossing the Brooklyn Bridge. Byrnes allegedly called in his best detective, gave him the serial number, and ordered the watch recovered and brought back to his office in twenty-four hours. At the appointed time, the detective returned, crestfallen. "Chief," he explained, "I made every thief in town show me all the watches he stole on Brooklyn Bridge the other day, and none has that serial number."

The use of physical force seems to have played a large, if rarely mentioned, role in Byrnes's mode of detective work. George B. McClellan Jr., who held several city posts during Byrnes's later years and eventually became the city's mayor, recalled seeing suspects stand in front of Byrnes while he fired questions at them. If the right answers were not forthcoming, according to McClellan, Byrnes knocked them down, and kept on doing so until they talked. Lincoln Steffens, another Byrnes skeptic, described him as "a man who would buy you or beat you, as you might choose, but get you he would."

Criminals picked up for routine questioning, or as suspects in big cases, were brought to the inspector's inner sanctum, where a thick, soft carpet muffled the noise of footsteps and the lower window panes were rendered opaque with white paint. Byrnes could sit motionless for long periods of time, his ever present cigar in hand, while his piercing eyes fixed on the suspect. Even before the questioning began, Byrnes would unnerve a suspect by showing him around the "museum," with its pictures of captured criminals and exhibits of their confiscated tools. Instead of directly asking about the crime, he might start out by talking about home and mother. A criminal's thoughts, Byrnes understood, inevitably revolve around his crime, and given the opportunity he would often blurt out his guilt. In a case involving the murder of a liquor store owner, the suspects were members of a vicious street gang called the Whyos. When his men brought in the leader, Mike McGloin, along with two of McGloin's partners, Byrnes ordered the confederates put in the sweatbox, an airless room where they were given the third degree, and he sat McGloin at the window of his office. As the suspect watched, a door banged below and one of his friends was led across the courtyard. Fifteen minutes later the door banged again and the second prisoner was led out. "Squealed, both," Byrnes muttered. They had not, but McGloin broke down and confessed. The night before his execution, his bravado returned. He invited Byrnes to attend his wake and "have a devil of a time."

In 1883, Byrnes succeeded in having the precinct detectives, or "wardmen," put under his command, but the captains protested: precinct detectives not only collected graft for their captain but could investigate crimes in which the victim was someone the captain wanted to accommodate. Tammany district leaders also opposed the move, and two years later the wardmen were returned to precinct control.

The Detective Bureau was less adept in complex murder investigations. Many killings, of course, were the result of disputes among the poor, who were usually immigrants, and these cases had a way of almost solving themselves. Drunken husbands who beat their wives to death were usually still on the scene when the police arrived, while fatal barroom brawls tended to occur in front of witnesses, some of them friendly to the victim and ready to identify the assailant. The more puzzling cases were not Byrnes's forte, despite his carefully cultivated reputation as a cerebral detective.

In April 1892, a bordello owner named Anna Sutherland fell gravely ill and died of a cerebral hemorrhage. Her will, written two years earlier, left her fortune to the man she had married at that time, Robert Buchanan, a Greenwich Village physician twenty years younger than his wife. Some of the late Mrs. Buchanan's friends were convinced that the doctor had murdered her, but the police ignored them. They got a better hearing from Isaac Deforest "Ike" White, a reporter for the *New York World*, who learned of incautious statements that Buchanan had made about the resemblance between death by apoplexy, on the one hand, and death by morphine poisoning, on the other. If a medication known as atrophine were administered together with morphine, the doctor was heard to say, it would prevent the pupils from dilating—normally the tip-off to morphine poisoning. White published a story, and the district attorney opened an investigation.

Byrnes had been bested by a reporter, but he was quick to adapt. He told Detective Arthur Carey to follow Buchanan and conduct the surveillance openly, so he would realize he was being watched. Meanwhile, the body was exhumed and autopsied, revealing evidence of a large dose of morphine. Taking the stand in his defense, Buchanan said so many contradictory things that the jury found him guilty. He went to the electric chair, which the state had recently adopted in place of the rope.

Ike White was often an annoyance to Byrnes, perhaps most of all in the investigation of an explosion that killed two men in the office of the financier Russell Sage, a close friend and professional associate of Jay Gould's, and even less popular. Sage dressed like a tramp and ate sparingly unless someone else was picking up the tab. Once a little girl in the Midwest wrote and asked him to pay for a glass eye to replace the real eye she had lost. Sage ignored the request until a *New York Sun* writer threatened to blast him in print. Even then, Sage contributed only three dollars, allowing the writer to make up the difference. In December 1891, he was conducting business at his office in the Arcade Building at Rector Street and Broadway when a young man arrived asking to see him. Normally, unexpected visitors were turned away. Men like Sage were accustomed to receiving threatening notes demanding money. Such matters usually received attention from Byrnes personally. (At the time, both Gould and Sage were under threat from a crazy dentist.)

When the red-bearded visitor spoke of a letter of introduction from John D. Rockefeller, Sage let him in the door and read the letter. Unless the young man received a million and a half dollars immediately, the note declared, he would set off a bomb in a briefcase he was holding. Sage asked the man to wait while he saw off a previous visitor. What happened next became the subject of considerable legal dispute. According to one account, however, Sage pushed the innocent visitor between him and the bomber. There was an explosion, in any case, and the bomber, the visitor, and one of Sage's employees were killed. Byrnes, accompanied by his protégé, a tall, good-looking young sergeant named George McClusky—a man with such a swaggering manner that his colleagues nicknamed him "Chesty George"—arrived shortly after the precinct cops. The ubiquitous Ike White was also on hand. The police failed to secure the crime scene, and the first suspect they seized trying to leave the office was Sage's brother-in-law, who served as his chief clerk. With Byrnes supervising, a fireman unearthed a red-bearded head from the debris. The head was identified as that of the bomber. The inspector's only reaction was to shift his unlit cigar from one side of his mouth to the other.

This was before the age of fingerprinting. In order to identify the suspect, Byrnes had the head put on exhibit in the window of a nearby undertaker's parlor. But when the newspapers ran stories about "the head in Duffy's window," the area was thronged with curiosity seekers, and Wall Street expressed its disapproval. Forced to take the head off display, Byrnes got nowhere with the case. White, meanwhile, had picked up a distinctive trouser button at the scene. Eventually he traced it to a tailor's shop near Harvard Yard in Cambridge, Massachusetts. Through the tailor, he located the parents of the mysterious young man. Their last communication from their son, White learned, had been a letter announcing that he would soon come into a large sum of money—or be dead. The case had been solved but, to Byrnes's embarrassment, by a reporter.

Not until the late 1890s did two of the younger men he had brought into the bureau, Jim McCafferty and Arthur Carey, team up to become the first ersatz homicide unit. One went on to be chief of detectives; the other became the longtime head of the homicide squad officially established in 1907. Unlike the more swashbuckling "immortals" or Byrnes himself, who was good at striking fear into the hearts of yeggs, McCafferty and Carey were quiet, patient men, suited to the detailed work of investigating murders.

Byrnes, although he presented a cool demeanor, could be rash. In the late 1880s, while Jack the Ripper was terrorizing London, Byrnes publicly dared him to come to New York. Soon enough, an old prostitute known as Shakespeare, who claimed to have been an actress and went about spouting lines from the bard, was cut up Ripper-style in a waterfront resort. Byrnes arrested a man named Frenchie for the crime. Underworld gossip, however, maintained that it was a Ripper murder and that Frenchie had been framed to preserve Byrnes's honor. The killer was almost certainly not the London Ripper. He was probably not Frenchie either, though, because Byrnes was instrumental in securing his release from prison a few years later.

George Walling was one of many police officers of the day who viewed Byrnes with distrust. Despite his own experience as a detective, Walling was a proponent of what might be termed the "patrol school" of crime fighting, which put the emphasis on crime prevention through a visible uniformed presence and vigorous efforts to maintain order. In the early 1880s, when Walling was superintendent and Byrnes the chief of detectives, the two were openly hostile. Walling, who remained a country boy by temperament, was suspicious of fast-talking New Yorkers like Byrnes. "I have rarely found that the one whose deductions were very rapid was a safe man," he commented in his memoirs. "The rapid generalizer turns out usually to be one who shapes his facts to his theories. . . . I have rather liked the hesitating man, the officer who doubted the correctness of his own theories, providing he constructed any. The cock-sure man, I have always found, made a mess of his business."

Walling derided Byrnes's operation as a "star chamber," emphasizing revenge and restitution rather than prevention. Byrnes and his men, to hear Walling tell it, were public-relations geniuses who made themselves the heroes of every case, no matter how much or little they had to do with its solution. As an illustration of the method, he cited the case of a bank forger whose arrest, according to the newspapers, had been the work of "certain detectives" who had been "shadowing the unfortunate criminal for weeks." In truth, the bank itself had caught the forger when he came in attempting to pass a second bad check; Byrnes's office hadn't even been aware of the crime until then. If a case wasn't broken, Byrnes and his men would not speak of it at all, leaving the public, according to Walling, "in blissful ignorance" of Byrnes's failures.

Many prominent New Yorkers, however, took an almost reverent view of Byrnes's efforts against professional criminals. Even an observer as skeptical as Jacob Riis, the great journalist and social critic of late-nineteenth-century New York, saw Byrnes as a giant who "broke up the old gang of crooks, and drove those whom he did not put in jail over the sea to ply their trade in Europe." In his own day, Byrnes kept his legend at high gloss, and hardly anyone spoke ill of him—certainly not the men who served under him. His disciples would run the Detective Bureau for another generation, and his influence would hang over the department for many years after that.

5

"Down with the Police"

T his, then, is a corrupt world, and Christianity is the antiseptic that is to be
rubbed into it in order to arrest the process of decay." From a broad
plateau of scriptural generality, the Reverend Charles H. Parkhurst made
a remarkably swift descent into the sinful particulars. "In its municipal
life, our city is rotten," he told worshipers at the Madison Square Presbyterian Church on a Sunday morning in February 1892, and "every effort to
make men respectable, honest, temperate, and sexually clean is a direct blow
between the eyes of the mayor and his whole gang of drunken and lecherous
subordinates."

Like many crusaders against vice and corruption in the nation's largest city,
Parkhurst was not a native New Yorker. A tall, slender, gray-bearded man of
forty-nine, he had moved to the city twelve years earlier, leaving a Congrega-
tionalist pulpit in Massachusetts. His new base of operations, the Madison
Square Presbyterian Church, had a reputation for social activism that appealed
to Parkhurst. And his choice of vice as a topic of concern had surely been
influenced by the church's location: Madison Square, at Twenty-fourth Street
and Madison Avenue, marked the southern boundary of the Tenderloin
District, so the minister was reminded daily of the world's wickedness. Two
years earlier, he had accepted an invitation to join a number of other leading
clergymen, as well as businessmen, lawyers, and civic leaders, as a member of
the Society for the Prevention of Crime. In 1891, Parkhurst had agreed to
become its president—with a condition. Members of the society, as he put it

90

later, had to stop "occupying ourselves with cutting off the tops and apply ourselves to taking up the roots."

Parkhurst was not a preacher given to sonorous tones or wild flailings of the arms. His voice was flat as he read his text. But he had a stern gaze and an intense demeanor that underscored the harshness of his admonitions. New Yorkers, he said, "ought to understand that crime in this city is entrenched in our municipal administration, and what ought to be a bulwark against crime is a stronghold in its defense. . . . I should not be surprised," he added, "if in every building in this town in which gambling or prostitution or the illicit sale of liquor is carried on, immunity is secured to it by police taxation." The mayor, the district attorney, and the police were "stultifying our entire municipal life, making New York a very hotbed of knavery, debauchery, and bestiality."

Thanks to the presence of a reporter from the *New York World*, Parkhurst's words reached a wide audience. But some of the newspapers denounced his sermon even as they eagerly reported on it. The *Sun* went as far as to suggest that the reverend's intemperate remarks made him unfit to hold such an influential position. Mayor Hugh Grant took another tack, publicly challenging Parkhurst to prove his charges. The socially prominent district attorney, DeLancey Nicoll, described Parkhurst's tirade as "the coarsest and most vindictive utterance from the pulpit that I ever heard," and summoned him before a grand jury. Accompanied by the crime prevention society's lawyer, Frank Moss, the minister dutifully appeared. When pressed, though, he could offer no evidence to support his accusations of rampant immorality and paid protection. In the presentment that the jurors handed down, they declared that the charges had no basis in fact, and the presiding judge congratulated them on their good judgment.

There were powerful echoes of the city's past in Parkhurst's jeremiad. Matthew Simpson, a Methodist bishop, had sounded a similar warning in the 1860s and '70s. The Reverend Henry Ward Beecher—the most prominent American clergyman of his time—had done the same, even using New York City detectives to collect some of his information. In the eyes of many citizens, however, Beecher's authority had been seriously undermined by revelations of affairs with his friends' wives.

The previous president of the society, the Reverend Howard Crosby, had also spoken out against vice and corruption; and some people felt that he, too, had gone overboard. Crosby had been less willing to attack Tammany Hall or the city's elected officials; he had blamed German and Irish immigrants for lowering the city's morality. New Yorkers did "not wish our political atmosphere to smell of either whiskey or beer," Crosby said. "We have institutions that we cherish as our own distinctively. They're American, not European, and we do not intend to surrender them to arrogant and impudent foreigners who abuse our hospitality by their insulting effrontery."

Elected officials, too, had taken up the cause. But not for long, as a rule. The state assembly was roused to conduct investigations of municipal corruption in 1875 and 1884. Both inquiries stopped short of implicating anybody in particular. The second one, directed by a young legislator named Teddy Roosevelt, ran aground when a fellow assemblyman from upstate, as vociferous against the sins of the flesh as any of his neighbors, decided to sample the wares of a New York courtesan and fell into a vice-squad trap. To save him from exposure, his colleagues soft-pedaled the section of their report dealing with the police.

In 1886, New Yorkers elected a mayor with notions of combating vice and graft. Abraham Hewitt, a millionaire businessman and the son-in-law of one of New York's most distinguished citizens, Peter Cooper, was one of those vaguely reformist scions of wealth and breeding who were periodically embraced by Tammany Hall, usually when it was seeking to prevent the election of someone even more threatening. (In that year's three-way contest, both of the other candidates fit that description: they were Roosevelt, a Republican, and the socialist "single-taxer" Henry George, running on a workingman's ticket.) Soon after his election, Hewitt summoned then–police superintendent William Murray to his home for a conference. Vice, the mayor-elect pointed out, had reached scandalous proportions, and "obviously, such conditions prevailed because of police graft." Murray, cool under fire, conceded the point. The surprised Hewitt asked if the illegal places could be closed. "Certainly—it is only necessary to give the order," Murray replied, as if teaching the ABCs to a child. Hewitt asked why they existed at all. Murray advised him to put that question to some of his political friends. "If the order goes out," Murray noted, "you will be attacking the men who were your best supporters in the last election and who put you in the mayor's chair." Hewitt boldly asked about Murray's own personal wealth. Unfazed, the superintendent admitted that while his salary as an inspector had been $3,500 a year, he was worth about $300,000—at least $6 million in today's dollars. And what of the other police commanders? Most of them, Murray told Hewitt, had probably made similar fortunes. Looking on the bright side, Hewitt said: "If you're worth $300,000, you can afford to be honest."

The new mayor ordered the police to furnish him with lists of dives, and, as a check, he hired a private detective to draw up an independent list. As it turned out, the police list contained many omissions, and Hewitt had to personally write in the names of the missing establishments. Under his orders, the police undertook a halfhearted cleanup. But it had no lasting effect—these crackdowns never did. They came when the heat was on, and they were an accepted part of life for cops and vice operators alike.

Mayor Grant and District Attorney Nicoll were pleased with themselves for hauling Parkhurst before a grand jury and exposing him to ridicule. In doing so, however, they had stiffened the pastor's resolve. True, Parkhurst had not been thinking about legal standards of proof when he drafted his sermon. Now he began to ask himself how he might gather the kind of evidence that couldn't be laughed out of court—not, at least, out of the court of public opinion.

The task was, in one sense, far from daunting, for corruption and vice were omnipresent. The Tenderloin was studded with celebrated resorts like Richard Canfield's Madison Square Club, an elegant gambling establishment housed in a four-story brownstone on Twenty-sixth Street just west of Fifth Avenue. Canfield operated quietly even as he paid off handsomely. He presented himself as a Harvard graduate; his actual alma mater was the county jail in Providence, Rhode Island, where he had done six months for running a gambling joint. After his move to New York, however, Canfield catered to an upper-crust clientele. Downtown were the American Mabille, at Bleecker and Broadway, and Billy McGlory's Amory Hall on Hester Street. The Mabille was run by Theodore "The" Allen, who had pretensions to religious piety, while McGlory, a graduate of a Five Points gang, was notorious for rolling drunken customers. The Haymarket, in the heart of the Tenderloin, had as many as five hundred ladies waiting to entertain visitors in its private rooms. A man could easily spend a hundred dollars buying champagne for the woman of his choice. Robbing a john on the premises was a violation of house rules. If a "trimmer" stole from a patron after taking him elsewhere and the john complained to the police, the culprit was forced to return the money and was subsequently banished. The rules also forbade cheek-to-cheek dancing and daring steps like the fox-trot. Nevertheless, the financier and bon vivant "Diamond Jim" Brady made a practice of leaving his jewelry at home when he took out-of-town clients there. On East Twenty-ninth Street, a row of brothels known as the Seven Sisters required customers to wear evening dress.

Dance halls and brothels were known tourist attractions for certain classes of society, including a slice of high society. For a generous tip, anyone could receive a personal tour of the hot spots from one of Inspector Thomas Byrnes's headquarters detectives. At the time of Parkhurst's sermon, a popular song was on everyone's lips. It told the story of a rube out on the town who wandered onto the Bowery.

> On the night that I struck New York,
> I went out for a quiet walk;
> Folks who are "on to" the city say,
> Better by far that I took Broadway;
> But I was out to enjoy the sights,
> There was the Bow'ry ablaze with lights;
> I had one of the devil's own nights!
> I'll never go there anymore.

Chorus:

> The Bow'ry, the Bow'ry!
> They say such things and they do strange things on the Bow'ry!
> The Bow'ry! I'll never go there anymore!

Many police officers personally disapproved of prostitution. Captain Bill Devery of the Eldridge Street precinct on the Lower East Side was strolling about in civilian clothes one day when he was solicited by some prostitutes leaning out of a window. He summoned the bordello owner to his office and tore into him, shouting, "You son of a bitch, that is you, is it? Well, if them women cows of yours call me up again, I will take you by the neck and throw you out of the window." Devery's attitude toward prostitutes was shared by many of his fellow Irish Catholics. Some families had lost a daughter or other relative to the Tenderloin or the streets; the girls' pictures were ritualistically turned toward the wall in shame. Some cops at least made a show of rejecting "whore money." Inspector Tom McAvoy would say to his collector, "If any of that money is from prostitution, I don't want it." The wardman would then dutifully assure him it was not, though some of it was. (Since McAvoy later became a Tammany district leader, it is hard to believe he didn't know better.) Devery, however, was more practical. A few days after his temper tantrum, his wardman called on the bordello owner and told him that, in addition to the $500 initiation fee and $50 a month he paid, he would have to come up with an extra $10 a month as punishment for annoying the captain.

The police were on the take, to be sure. But a policeman could reasonably tell himself there wasn't much he could do about gambling and prostitution, even if he had a mind to. To actually enforce the law against a protected establishment was to risk a transfer to Goatsville. Even superior officers could be called on the carpet for such a transgression. Captain Max Schmittberger, given command of a precinct in the West Fifties after serving as Clubber Williams's wardman, was warned not to interfere with the brothel operated by Georgeanna Hastings. Her clientele included millionaires, judges, and high city officials. Schmittberger heeded the advice but sent an officer to warn another madam, Sadie West, to be more considerate of neighbors who complained about her noisy house. Commissioner James Martin soon summoned the captain to his office and instructed him to send the officer back to Mrs. West with an apology for having disturbed her.

Not even the superintendent had the ready power to check such abuses. The precinct captains reported to district inspectors, and captains and inspectors alike aimed mainly to please members of the Board of Police Commissioners and Tammany district leaders. During George Walling's eleven years as superintendent, he was forced to kowtow to the politicians. Anything else, he understood, would cost him his job.

Mere compliance was not enough to save Walling, however—not after Richard Croker assumed control of Tammany Hall in 1885. Croker came to America from Ireland as a child, grew up in the Gashouse District, and joined the Fourth Street Tunnel Gang. A short but powerfully built young man, he became a noted Election Day slugger, and in 1874 a man dying from a bullet wound after a political brawl named Croker as his killer. (At the time, Croker also served as a city coroner responsible for investigating homicides. Although he was acquitted of murder, the incident haunted his career for years.) After persuading the legislature to pass a law allowing the commissioners to retire an officer at age sixty, he forced out Walling, a Republican, and replaced him with the more accommodating Inspector William Murray, a Democrat—and still remembered as the "man who stopped the march of communism" in Tompkins Square in 1877.

The legal system, too, did little to spur cops toward vigorous enforcement of the law. Even in the face of overwhelming evidence of guilt, a defendant with the right lawyer or political connections was likely to escape punishment. In the last third of the nineteenth century, New York's top criminal law firm was the team of Howe and Hummel. Over their careers, they defended more than a thousand people charged with homicide—in 1873, their clients included twenty-three of the twenty-five prisoners being held in the Tombs on murder or manslaughter charges. William Howe, an English-born ex-convict, started the firm in 1862. Abe Hummel, a small, spare man known as "Little Abe," joined as an office boy the next year, read law under Howe, and in 1869 was made a partner. The senior partner, Howe, was a large, flamboyant man, the voice of the duo. His usual attire was a purple waistcoat, checked trousers, and jewelry galore. His organlike tones boomed out in lengthy orations to the jury, sometimes delivered on his knees and always accompanied by tears, earning him the nickname "the Weeper." Hummel, the legal eagle of the two, always dressed in somber black. From its office on Centre Street, across from the Tombs, the firm functioned as house counsel to divekeepers, madams, and gamblers, as well as top professional criminals. Mother Mandelbaum kept them on a $5,000-a-year retainer. Clients as diverse as the Whyo Gang and the abortion queen Madame Restell called on them. They were retained by heavyweight champion John L. Sullivan, actresses Lillian Russell and Lillie Langtry, and showman P. T. Barnum.

Though Hummel possessed some legal skills, the firm exemplified the maxim that it was better for a lawyer to know the judge than the law. In a three-year period, supreme court justice Albert Cardozo (to this day, the court of general felony jurisdiction in New York State is called the supreme court) released two hundred of Howe and Hummel's clients in exchange for bribes. Cardozo would eventually resign with impeachment looming. His colleague Justice George Barnard sat on the bench sipping from a brandy bottle, and sometimes held court in the home of the actress Josie Mansfield (the onetime mistress of Jim Fisk, who had been killed by a rival for her affections), since he couldn't bear to tear himself away from her company. More than a million dollars in cash and bonds were found among Barnard's effects after his death.

On the people's side—in New York, cases are presented by district attorneys on behalf of the people of New York, not the state—the ethical tone was scarcely more elevated. Assistant D.A.s dressed like gentlemen with tall silk hats, frock coats, and high stiff collars. They smoked big black cigars, got their jobs through political sponsors, and kicked back 10 percent of their salary to Tammany. They would often go easy on defendants with the right political connection: "He is a boy from the neighborhood" was a phrase used by ward heelers to alert the judge that the young defendant before him came from a family with some claim to Tammany preference. Only when a crime attracted major attention did countervailing forces such as press and public opinion intervene, leading to some measure of justice.

All this was widely known—and, at the same time, not known. Many New Yorkers had only a dim idea what actually went on in places like the Haymarket. Others knew but could not afford to admit they knew; and once the truth was thrown in their face, the feelings of their more prudish peers required them to press for remedial action. Still others—the editors of *Harper's*, for example—viewed the Tenderloin with disdain but were reluctant to attack the police, who kept the city from descending into anarchy.

The owners of the Tenderloin's dives did not usually pay off beat cops, though they might hand them some change now and then. (So, occasionally, would a visitor who drank too much and got into a fight or other troubles.) The "heavy sugar" went to the captain by way of his wardman, or collector, who would keep a portion (usually 20 percent) for himself. Clubber Williams commanded the Tenderloin precinct for all but two of the years between 1876 and 1887, when a captain's official salary was $2,750. Yet in 1894, Williams acknowledged a net worth in excess of $300,000.

Stories of graft dogged Williams throughout his career. As far back as 1874, George Walling had summoned him before a departmental trial board to answer a bordello owner's claim that she had given him a pistol, a pair of slippers, and a gold-headed cane, among other presents. Williams had been brought up on charges several hundred times, winning some of the cases, paying fines to settle others. Yet even he saw the need for some discretion—about graft, if not brutality. His legendary "get me some tenderloin" comment had been published in the *Herald* by Augustine Costello. Williams apparently didn't care for that bit of publicity. His words had been misunderstood, he said later. He had really just been talking about steak.*

In 1885, Costello published a history of the police department by arrangement with the commissioners. It was a glowing portrait of gods and heroes, and Costello planned for most of the profits to go to the police pension fund. At an advanced stage of the undertaking, however—and for reasons never made fully clear—the department withdrew its support; the book was just starting to be a success, said Costello. When asked about it later, he noted that, coincidentally, Byrnes's guide to the world of professional crime had been "in embryo" at the time. In any case, Costello transferred his literary allegiance to the fire department, writing a similarly worshipful book about that organization, under the same sort of charitable arrangement. This time he had a letter of endorsement from the fire commissioners, and he gave copies of it to a number of agents for use in selling advertisements and "subscriptions." Then, to Costello's surprise, his fire department sponsorship was also withdrawn and two of his sales agents arrested. His protest led to a confrontation with Clubber Williams at headquarters. Now an inspector in charge of the Lower East Side precincts, Williams was "in one of his hectoring and bullying moods," Costello recalled later, "and as soon as he saw me he caught me by the throat and threw me against the wall, and gave me a jab of the club." When Costello was finally allowed to leave, around midnight, two detectives took him downtown by elevated train to the First Precinct. On its front steps, Costello saw two figures come out of the darkness, and he was sent rolling into the gutter. As he tried to protect himself with his umbrella, his assailants kicked him. Although Costello emerged "covered with blood and mud and dirt," he kept the story pretty much to himself for five years.

Indeed, there were excellent arguments against making a fuss over police wrongdoing. But the Reverend Parkhurst was oblivious to them. Determined to escape from his state of embarrassment, Parkhurst set out to acquire the evidence to support his charges. He decided to gather it himself by going on a tour of the dives. Feeling the need for a witness to second his accounts, though, he asked a young parishioner named John Langdon Irving—so clean-

---

*In another version of the Tenderloin's naming, the lawyer Abe Hummel gets credit. Running into Hummel soon after his transfer, Williams was said to have kidded him about eating beefsteak for lunch every day; "That's a pretty good piece of tenderloin *you* were just handed," Hummel supposedly replied.

cut that he was nicknamed "Sunshine"—to accompany him. Since neither knew much about vice, Parkhurst enlisted the additional services of a freelance detective, Charles Gardner, who agreed to work for a fee of six dollars a night plus expenses.

Gardner, who had once been a railroad detective, was at home in the dives. And Parkhurst himself, for all his seeming ignorance, was not entirely the naive clergyman that he and his opponents liked to portray. He was, at any rate, well aware of the success of the ambitious zealot Anthony Comstock, head of a rival civic group known as the Society for the Prevention of Vice. Comstock, exercising quasi-governmental authority conferred by the post office, had by now arrested thousands of people for obscenity while seizing literature he deemed pornographic. He was alleged to have pressured the Department of the Interior to fire a poet he disapproved of, Walt Whitman, and he had boasted of driving Madame Restell, the abortionist, to suicide.

On a Saturday evening in March 1892, the odd trio of Parkhurst, Irving, and Gardner set out for a night on the town. The staid minister, told by Gardner to dress appropriately, nonetheless showed up in a suit in which the detective sniffed "the aroma of the pulpit." Gardner toned his pupil down with a dirty shirt, a pair of checked black-and-white trousers, a sailor's jacket, a red flannel tie, and a battered slouch hat. Their first stop was an East Side waterfront saloon on Cherry Street run by Tom Summers, who doubled as a fence for stolen goods. Parkhurst gulped a shot of Cherry Hill whiskey and, according to Gardner, "looked as though he had swallowed a whole political parade—torch lights and all." Next, they cruised past sailors' dives on Water Street, where three prostitutes pulled them indoors. After some conversation, the trio left. On succeeding nights they visited Chinese opium dens and "tight houses"—a name that referred to the skimpy outfits worn by the resident women. At each stop, Parkhurst kept saying, "Show me something worse."

On Third Street, they stopped at a house run by a woman known as Scotch Ann. The inmates seemed to be attractive young girls, but their falsetto voices puzzled the minister. When Gardner explained the situation, Parkhurst fled. "Why, I would not stay here for all the money in the world!" he proclaimed. One night the trio bumped into one of Parkhurst's Amherst College classmates. The man, who had been drinking, indiscreetly mentioned the minister's name. The bartender ordered them out of the place and threw their money after them. Later, at Hattie Adams's bordello, a few blocks from the Madison Square church, Gardner arranged to have a nude "dance of nature" performed by five girls who were paid three dollars each. Then it was time for a game of leapfrog, with naked girls jumping over Gardner. The work soon became tiresome, though, and Gardner arranged for additional private detectives to visit other dives.

On March 13, a stream of reporters filed into the Madison Square Presbyterian Church to hear Parkhurst spell out the lurid details of his quest. This time, he had names, dates, and addresses, as well as a bundle of sworn affidavits describing his adventures and the findings of his investigators. Parkhurst was derided for immersing himself in a milieu that he professed to abhor. Howe and Hummel, acting as attorneys for Hattie Adams, denounced him as a "liar," a "poltroon," and "a lecher in ministerial broadcloth." By attending orgies, even as a mere observer, they argued, he had been a party to the crime.

Many people, including some fellow clergymen, expressed shock that a minister could fall so low as to visit saloons and bordellos. When the leapfrog episode became known, it gave rise to a song that would be heard for years in New York's honky-tonks.

Dr. Parkhurst on the floor
Playing leapfrog with a whore
Ta-ra-ra-boom-de-ay,
Ta-ra-ra-boom-de-ay.

The ditty endured, even though it was Gardner who had been the frog while Parkhurst sat quietly sipping his beer. But the exposé moved forward with inexorable force. A new grand jury was convened to hear Parkhurst's charges. As a result, four of the women he had charged with keeping brothels were arrested. The jury also handed down a general presentment against the police, who were "good at preventing gross crimes," the jurors concluded, "but weak at suppressing disorderly houses, gambling places and excise [liquor] law breakers." Superintendent Murray resigned, citing ill health, and his job went to Inspector Byrnes. He, in turn, ordered a series of show raids and, with his usual statistical élan, reported the closing of 444 houses of ill fame during his first seven months in office. On a single day, Byrnes transferred half the department's captains and inspectors to new commands—another shopworn technique (though why a captain on the take in one precinct was expected to be honest in another was never explained). Parkhurst, meanwhile, enjoyed the limelight and picked up public support because he looked like a winner. He organized a "vigilance league," which put up money to hire an army of private detectives to gather information. He made frequent appearances before the grand jury, accusing police captains and inspectors of neglect of duty while charging that many judges had bought their seats on the bench. He boldly adopted the slogan "Down with the police"—an expression heretofore heard almost exclusively from soapbox orators in Tompkins Square, where it had been likely to be answered with a cop's nightstick.

All else having failed, the police began to get rough with their critics, though they should have realized that Parkhurst would not bow to intimidation. Byrnes's men arrested the detective, Gardner, for allegedly extorting money from keepers of houses of prostitution. He was found guilty and sentenced to two years, but his lawyers persuaded the court of appeals to overturn the conviction. The divorced Gardner then shocked Parkhurst by getting remarried in a risqué ceremony at the Statue of Liberty. To the minister's relief, he left town shortly afterward and never returned.

Cruder tactics were employed by Captain Devery in his Lower East Side precinct, where Clubber Williams was district inspector. "There is a lot of silk-stocking people coming from uptown to bulldoze you people," Devery warned the dive owners, "and if they open their mouths you stand them on their heads." He even tossed one complaining minister out of the station. After Parkhurst's investigators testified at the local Essex Market court against the owners of disorderly houses in the neighborhood, a Tammany ward heeler threatened to "demolish" his lawyer Frank Moss's face and organized a mob of five hundred people to pursue Parkhurst's investigators down the street when they left the courthouse. According to Moss, the detectives were about to draw their guns but held off, so as not to give critics any help in their efforts to discredit the cause of reform. Some of Devery's precinct cops witnessed the whole affair and stood by laughing. Finally, a detachment of police from the adjoining precinct came running up and drove off the mob. The reinforcements may well have been sent by Superintendent Byrnes, who often had the sense to undermine the foolish actions of his brethren. In November 1892, when federal marshals were assigned to monitor polling places to prevent fraud by Tammany, Commissioner Martin ordered cops to arrest them. Byrnes, recalling the Grant administration's outrage over similar stunts in the 1870s, countermanded the order.

But even Byrnes was becoming rattled by the critics. Addressing a meeting of headquarters brass, he lapsed into the Gashouse slang of his youth: "Gentlemen . . . did not I command you last Monday on this very spot in this same office to enforce to the letter the laws regulating the saloons in this city—and to close them one and all at the legally fixed hours for closing? . . . Well, and what I want to know now is: did youse did it?"

After two years of Parkhurst's crusading, an influential parishioner of his decided that the time had come to act. This was former United States senator Thomas Collier Platt, the boss of the state Republican Party, who operated out of the lobby of the Fifth Avenue Hotel, across the square from Parkhurst's church—more precisely, from the "amen corner" of the lobby, so named because Platt's lieutenants supposedly said "amen" to every statement the boss uttered. Platt was on the outs with Richard Croker, and he was eager to use Parkhurst to teach Tammany a lesson about what happens when the politicians of one party refuse to share their patronage with those of the other. Platt pushed through the appointment of a joint investigative committee headed by an ally, state Senator Clarence Lexow. Now that it looked like there would be a real probe, Croker promptly left for Europe, and some dive owners decamped to places like Canada and Chicago.

Lexow himself proved to be a cipher, though his name firmly attached itself to the scandal and even, for a time, entered the local political vocabulary as a verb meaning "to mount a serious corruption probe." The investigation was largely managed by the committee's chief counsel, John W. Goff, who had been Parkhurst's insistent choice for the job. Goff was tall, bearded, humorless, and widely disliked. Later, on the bench, he would be called "the cruelest, the most sadistic judge we have had in New York in this century" by one of the lawyers unfortunate enough to appear before him. He was an Irish Catholic immigrant and ardent supporter of revolutionary movements against Britain; among his projects was the arming of an American expedition to free some Irish rebel prisoners. But he was bitterly anti-Tammany.

In March 1894, the Lexow committee opened hearings in the "Tweed" courthouse; the symbolism was not lost on observers. The inquiry focused heavily at first on allegations of police-assisted vote fraud. Platt and his allies hoped to anger the public and embarrass Tammany sufficiently to ensure a Republican victory in the next city election. (Meanwhile, they laid plans to create a permanent Republican majority in the city by merging Democratic Manhattan and Republican Brooklyn into Greater New York.) But Parkhurst and Goff were not about to let the investigation be channeled into these narrow partisan purposes. They wanted blood, not patronage.

Goff and his staff sought out two kinds of witnesses. One was the hard case: obviously crooked but unapologetic cops like Devery and Williams could be used to show the arrogance of Tammany; they were dummies for Goff and Moss, who had signed on as an assistant counsel, to beat on. The other kind of witness was the squealer, the man who would readily confess in exchange for leniency. Such turncoats were usually handled by another assistant counsel, William Travers Jerome, the liveliest and cleverest of the three inquisitors. (His cousin Jennie was the wife of Lord Randolph Churchill and the mother of Winston.) The word went out among the dive owners: Cooperate and you will be all right; refuse and you will suffer the consequences. Under Jerome's guidance, a parade of gamblers, brothel madams, and saloonkeepers took the stand to admit to paying off the police. Harry Hill, whose downtown establishment had once been as famous as the Haymarket—though now long out of business—testified about a precinct commander named Murphy who had milked him dry with requests for money and had drunk gallon upon gallon of the house champagne.

The most sought-after witnesses, of course, were police officers who would admit to the payoff system. One of the committee's first targets was Captain Max Schmittberger. He was a likely candidate, not being bred of the Irish code of silence. Schmittberger's parents had brought him over from Germany at the age of four. Tall, handsome, clean-cut, and likable, he had gotten on the force without paying off because a politician considered him physically ideal for the Broadway squad. Schmittberger was then transferred to a beat in the "colored quarter" of the west Tenderloin, where he was introduced to graft. He claimed not to like it but went along regardless. He accommodated himself to the practice so thoroughly, in fact, that he was made a wardman and eventually rose to captain. In July 1894, when the committee approached him, Schmittberger claimed to be ill with "brain fever." As the investigation rolled on, however, he realized which way the wind was blowing, especially after seeing another captain sentenced to three years and nine months in prison for accepting a gift of a $6 basket of fruit. Schmittberger himself, charged with accepting a $500 "New Year's gift" from a businessman, decided to strike a deal. At the outset of the negotiations, committee counsels assured him that he was merely a pawn: he could expect to be treated leniently if he delivered the kind of testimony that they were looking for.

Thus reassured, Maxie peached, cataloging not only his own sins but those of a number of fellow officers, notably Williams, his former boss. (Byrnes, on the other hand, received a clean bill of moral health from Schmittberger, to the great annoyance of Parkhurst and the committee staff, who suspected some secret machinations on the part of the great detective. Parkhurst, however, eventually became a champion of Schmittberger's.) The next target was Captain Timothy Creedon, the Civil War hero. When first called to the witness stand, he denied buying his promotion. But the investigators had sized him up as an innately honest man who would not be able to live with such a whopping lie. They were right; after thinking about it overnight, Creedon returned in the morning and admitted to purchasing his captaincy for $15,000. Grateful for the speedy confession, Goff gently led the remorseful witness through his testimony, even giving his fellow Irishman a rationale for his previous misstatement. Creedon said that he did not wish to be an informer, and Goff sympathetically added, "That is your nature, a distinct feature of your race. . . . The word informer carries a terrible significance there."

Clubber Williams, as expected, was defiant. Had anyone else ever been charged with so much corruption, he was asked. "If so, I have not heard of it," he replied.

At another point in Williams's testimony, Goff expressed reluctance to get into a personal quarrel with the witness.

"You better not, either," Williams shot back.

Although he seemed to revel in his reputation for violence, Williams went to extreme lengths to absolve himself of the charge of grafting. He claimed that his wealth—including a seventeen-room house and a yacht—was the result of a lucky piece of real estate speculation, dating from his long-ago days as a sailor in, of all places, Japan. According to an affidavit from the Japanese consul, it had been illegal for foreigners to own property at the time. But Williams could not be dislodged from his story.

Byrnes had been incautious in comments to the press, referring to the

Lexow committee and its agents as "blackmailers" who, by paying people to commit acts of entrapment, "fomented" the evils they professed to expose. Byrnes also fell into a pattern common to many leaders facing corruption probes: he treated the cooperative witnesses mercilessly, suspending Captain Creedon, for example, after his payoff admissions. But when the committee suggested that Creedon's punishment might be seen as an attempt to intimidate other witnesses, Byrnes insisted that such a result was the furthest thing from his mind: he hoped that everyone would testify fully and truthfully.

The committee looked on Creedon "more as the victim of a bad system than as a bad man himself," a state senator told Byrnes.

"Well, that is the way I look upon Captain Creedon as a man, too," he replied.

As to his own activities, however, Byrnes was a brilliantly obscure and wily witness throughout a long appearance before the committee. His wealth, he said, had been garnered through investments recommended by Jay Gould and other well-heeled friends. Thankful to Byrnes for his assistance at the time of a kidnapping threat against Gould, the financier had supposedly given him stock tips that resulted in a net profit of $273,000. Perhaps Byrnes's Wall Street acquaintances spoke up for him, or perhaps he was able to reach out to Goff through their common friends in the various Irish societies; in any case, the committee did not attempt to dispute his story. Byrnes thanked the Lexow committee for its work and expressed regret that he had not previously enjoyed so much outside support in his anticorruption efforts. Ever the statistics fiend, he managed to point out that during his long service as head of the Detective Bureau, he and his men had put away criminals for a cumulative ten thousand years.

When the investigation began to threaten Republican as well as Democratic leaders, Platt called the hearings to a halt. Parkhurst, in a fury, equated Platt to the self-exiled Croker—sleazy politicians both of them, he implied. This piece of impudence was too much for the Republicans. Platt, a longtime parishioner of Parkhurst's, transferred his enrollment to the Marble Collegiate Church. Senator Lexow now denounced Parkhurst. "This man considers himself the uncrowned king of New York," he snarled.

In fact, that was a fairly apt description of Parkhurst's position at the time. The fallout from his crusade led to the formation of a "fusion," or multiparty, ticket that proceeded to elect William J. Strong, a banker and an independent

Republican, as mayor by a plurality of forty-five thousand in November 1894. Parkhurst celebrated by hanging three United States flags outside his home. In time, John Goff received an important judgeship, Frank Moss became president of the Board of Police Commissioners, and William Travers Jerome was elected district attorney. The Parkhurst crusade's successful formula would often be imitated over the next hundred years: arouse moral indignation against the cops; form an investigative body; cultivate key journalists; target a few individuals; cut deals with the rogues to tell all; and demolish the incumbents at the polls.

Not all the imitators succeeded, though, and some New Yorkers would be puzzled by the widely differing outcomes of these probes. One line of explanation focuses on specific actors and events—on, for example, Parkhurst, Platt, and Goff. The Lexow inquiry would never have achieved such results, it can be argued, if Parkhurst had not had the gumption to go out and document his accusations, if his agenda had not meshed (however briefly) with that of Platt and the Republicans; or if the chief counsel had not been someone as driven and knowledgeable as Goff. And yet a look over the long arc of history suggests a less personality-driven view of these great upwellings of outrage: the times must be right, and when they are, the actors will appear.

By the last decade of the nineteenth century, public patience with the established political and economic order had worn thin. In the "elegant '80s," most men worked twelve hours a day, six days a week, for an average weekly wage of ten dollars. Shopgirls earned less than half that, usually only three or four dollars, and some ended up working as prostitutes to make ends meet. The '90s marked the dawn of the Progressive Era, when the middle class, comfortable in their neat brownstones and red-brick townhouses, began to develop a social conscience. Almost for the first time, it seemed, the well-off took notice of how ordinary people lived, particularly the mass of immigrants in the tenements or flats. (Flats were considered a step above tenements because they had a janitor and a locked front door.)

There were individual agents of change in this story as well, of course— Jacob Riis, to name one. While his main employment had been as a police reporter for the *New York Sun*, Riis's passion was chronicling the plight of the underprivileged. When he wasn't covering trunk murders and jewel heists, he wrote about slum life. His 1890 book *How the Other Half Lives* had a profound influence on the sensibilities of affluent New Yorkers. But it was influential, in part, because there was more receptivity to such a message: the public mood was shifting.

And so, too, with graft. The rapaciousness of many public officials (not just police bosses) had reached new heights in the '80s. The vice joints operated with unprecedented openness. The Tivoli, down the street from the Haymarket, was notorious for robbing customers. Yet complaints to the police fell on deaf ears until one night when a Tammany state senator was victimized and, after making a fuss, tossed out of the place. It was promptly padlocked. In 1912, 1930, 1950, 1970, and 1992, the same elements—people, events, and public opinion—would converge again, and the Lexow story would be repeated, to the great good fortune of the probers and the great misfortune of the probed.

6

The Glorious Retreat

The nerve center of the city in the late nineteenth century was a square, compact, marble-faced building at 300 Mulberry Street, nestled among the slums of the Lower East Side. Here, at police headquarters, word was received of all serious crimes, accidents, and disasters. Conveniently, a good deal of trouble took place in the immediate neighborhood. The Mabille was nearby, as was the Florence Saloon, where the young Clubber Williams had supposedly thrown a couple of toughs through a plateglass window. For police officers with a fondness for gambling, there was a joint on the same block as headquarters itself.

Since its construction in the 1860s, the building had taken on a deep mustard color—the effect of accumulated soot. Other than the shifting appearance of the walls, however, change was exceedingly rare at 300 Mulberry until the morning of May 6, 1895, when a reform-minded new Board of Police Commissioners, led by thirty-six-year-old Teddy Roosevelt, moved in. If there was a moment in the Lexow drama when it looked as if somebody was going to seize the reigns of history, this was it.

The newspapers, generous in the space they devoted to the police, had apartments, or "shacks," from which their reporters could keep a close watch on the doings at headquarters. Jacob Riis popped out of his shack at 303 Mulberry in time to see Roosevelt running down Mulberry Street at full tilt after a triumphal march uptown from City Hall, where he and the three other commissioners had been sworn in. Riis alerted his fellow reporters, and

Roosevelt, an exceedingly press-conscious man, invited them to follow him inside. He was particularly attentive to Riis and his young colleague Lincoln Steffens—a sign that these long-outspoken critics of the department would now be close to the throne. Roosevelt made it known that he would appoint a young woman named Minnie Kelly as his personal secretary. Her appearance in a close-fitting gown caused a stir. Up until then, the only women at headquarters had been cleaning ladies or the buxom police matrons charged with supervising the lost children's room.

When the reformist city administration took office in January, its supporters—who ran the gamut from moral crusaders like Parkhurst to practical politicians like Boss Platt—could reasonably hope that it marked the beginning of a permanent shift in power. By uncovering the thorough corruption of the police department under Tammany misrule, the Lexow inquiry had convinced the electorate to, in the slogan of the time, "turn the rascals out." At the instigation of Boss Platt, in 1896, the state legislature would approve the merger of Brooklyn and Queens with Manhattan, Staten Island, and the Bronx into a "greater New York City." The idea had been discussed for thirty years. It appealed to civic boosters who wanted New York to remain the most populous American city, rather than be overtaken by the up-and-coming Chicago. Initially, the Republican Party had been hesitant to put Brooklyn, which often voted for the GOP, under Tammany rule. Now that a Republican had been elected mayor, though, the party could reasonably hope to remain in charge of the city's politics for years to come. And in Roosevelt himself, it seemed, the reformers had a winner. But while his dramatic capture of headquarters reflected some of the same bravado that would mark his charge up San Juan Hill three years later, the police bureaucracy proved to be a much more formidable adversary than the enfeebled forces of imperial Spain.

From the moment of the reform victory in November 1894, Roosevelt's friends began pushing him for appointment to the Board of Police Commissioners. He was restless in his post as a member of the U.S. Civil Service Commission in Washington, D.C. The bulk of his career had been spent immersed in the politics of New York City and State. Only a year out of Harvard, in 1881, he had been elected to the state assembly from the silk-stocking district, and he had been chosen just a year after that as the party's minority leader. Roosevelt was a born-and-bred aristocrat, and he dressed and talked in the upper-class style of the day. He favored a pair of eyeglasses with a gold chain over his ears, a cutaway coat with tails that almost reached the top of his shoes, a gold-headed cane, and a silk hat. He used expressions—such as "dee-lighted"—that struck the city pols as bizarre, causing them to ask one another, "Who's the dude?" Roosevelt, for his part, was similarly put off by his urban political antagonists, especially by the Irish Democrats, whom he once described as "a stupid, sodden, vicious lot, most of them being equally deficient in brains and virtue." One of these sorry characters, "Big John" McManus—an ex-prizefighter—proposed to toss "that damn dude" in a blanket. The "dude" retorted in a most ungentlemanly way that should McManus attempt to do so, he would kick him in the balls.

In the aftermath of the Lexow investigation, the legislature had provided for a bipartisan board of four police commissioners. The other Republican besides Roosevelt was Colonel Fred Grant, eldest son of former President Ulysses Grant. The Democrats were Avery Andrews, a West Point graduate who had left the service to practice law, and Andrew Parker, a clever former assistant district attorney who represented a non-Tammany faction of the party. At its first meeting, the board unanimously elected Roosevelt president. Legally, however, his authority was no greater than that of his peers. Parker was put in charge of the detective branch; Andrews was given responsibility for the trial room where errant cops were disciplined; and the rather ineffective Grant was left to deal with supplies and repair—a duty that involved inspecting the department's stationhouses and other property. (In the army, such a post might have been called "inspector of latrines.") It was an unpromising arrangement. Roosevelt was not the type to share power, and after years of mismanagement and scandal, the police department needed a stronger hand than any committee could provide.

The most pressing matter immediately before the commissioners was filling the department's top jobs. The first to fall was Clubber Williams, inspector in charge of the first district. Though he strutted around with apparent unconcern about his future, Williams was easily prodded into submitting his retirement papers, and the press snidely suggested that he would now be free to supervise his Japanese real estate. The next year, he offered himself as a Republican candidate for the state senate from his old East Side inspection district. Picturing himself a hero in the badlands, Williams was surprised when the Tammany voters rejected him.

Getting rid of Williams was an obvious move; the next one was less so. Mayor Strong, perhaps on the advice of friends on Wall Street, suggested that Thomas Byrnes, still on the job five months into the new administration, be retained. That idea also appealed to Jacob Riis, a longtime Byrnes admirer. But it was repugnant to the Parkhurst wing of the reform movement, and the autocratic-leaning Roosevelt had no stomach for a collaboration with anyone as strong and tough as Byrnes. As Roosevelt told his friend Henry Cabot Lodge, "I think I shall move against Byrnes at once, I thoroughly distrust him, and cannot do any thorough work while he remains." Byrnes, always a realist, submitted his resignation, and on May 27 he walked out of head-quarters with his head held high. But his departure provoked widespread alarm among bankers and other prominent New Yorkers. "Who will protect us now?" they asked. (A decade later, in 1906, Wall Street made one last effort on Byrnes's behalf. Thomas Fortune Ryan, a transit tycoon and a leading fund-raiser for the Democratic Party, asked Mayor McClellan to give Byrnes a chance to run the department again and, incidentally, "clear his name." The mayor refused. Parkhurst and the reformers, he explained, would never stand for it.)

The new chief of police (the legislature had changed the title from superin-tendent) was Inspector Peter Conlin. A career cop, Conlin was a smooth talker, after the fashion of his half-brother, the noted actor William Florence; no "youses" or "dems" ever slipped from his mouth. Conlin had been a cap-tain in a prominent Union regiment, the Irish "Fighting Sixty-ninth," and he cut a dashing figure on horseback—a useful quality for the annual police parade. When it came to matters of substance, however, he was a careerist who would not get in Roosevelt's way.

Then came the problem of Max Schmittberger. After singing like a canary to the Lexow committee, Schmittberger had become the pet of the reformers, particularly Lincoln Steffens, who saw him as a naive dupe. Even Parkhurst found him charming, buying into the reformed-sinner theory. Swayed by their recommendations, Roosevelt agreed to bring Schmittberger back from Goatsville and put him in command of an Upper West Side precinct, where Commissioner Parker arranged for him to be given an in-tegrity test. Some wiretappers, crooks who got racing results in time to place bets on the winner, were sent to bribe him. Schmittberger beat them up so badly that they landed in the hospital. "Attaboy," was Roosevelt's one-word comment. Commissioner Parker merely remarked that Schmittberger should wear gloves, and the "Big Dutchman" soon emerged as the reform administration's favorite "broom," assigned to precincts that were deemed to need a wholesale cleaning.

A month after the new board took over, the department was scheduled to stage its annual parade. Roosevelt canceled the festivities, officially explaining that he considered them inappropriate so soon after the Lexow investigation. A parade might also have been risky from a public relations standpoint, since no one knew how the cops or citizens would behave. Maybe the crowds would boo the men in blue or pelt them with ripe fruit, precipitating a baton charge. On the other hand, Tammany had a knack for turning out people, so Roosevelt and his fellow commissioners themselves might have gotten a going-over. Roosevelt could reasonably imagine such an affair developing into a riot.

Determined to affix his brand on the department without delay, he commenced a series of late-night tours to assess the state of policing, making sure he was accompanied by friendly reporters. The first was on June 7, 1895, when Roosevelt and Jacob Riis prowled through the East Twenties and Thirties well after 2:00 A.M. They found several patrolmen gossiping with citizens and one sitting asleep on a butter tub in the middle of the sidewalk, snoring away. Others could not be found at all. Not a single roundsman or sergeant could be located; only one officer appeared to be patrolling.

At four in the morning, Roosevelt stormed into the local precinct and demanded to know the whereabouts of the roundsmen. He ordered the sergeant of the reserves to be awakened so he could look for a patrolman named Mahoney, whom they had been unable to find. Before the sergeant could act, Roosevelt rushed out himself and found the officer talking with Roundsman White and a couple of citizens in front of a saloon at Forty-second Street and Third Avenue. Dispensing with the introductions, Roosevelt asked him to explain what he was doing. "Why, I'm standing, of course," Patrolman Mahoney replied. Roosevelt identified himself and ordered Mahoney, White, and every other officer who had been deemed missing to report to 300 Mulberry Street at 9:30 in the morning. When they arrived, they all received warnings; one more such infraction, Roosevelt said, and they could expect to face charges and possible dismissal.

A week later, having tried out his act with his close friend Riis, Roosevelt invited Richard Harding Davis, the king of American journalism, to accompany him on another such tour, this time in the Fourteenth Street area and the Tenderloin. Davis was a highly paid, world-famous writer who had covered wars, revolutions, and presidential elections. He dressed like a gentleman and was welcome in the haunts of society. He was also known to run with a fast Broadway crowd that included the architect Stanford White, infamous for having a chorus girl on each arm. In addition to Davis, Roosevelt was accompanied by Avery Andrews, one of the rare Democrats who admired the board's president. This time they found cops patrolling, with the exception of one Officer William Rath, who was ensconced in a Third Avenue oyster bar. When Roosevelt inquired why he was not on his post, Rath replied, "What the hell is it to you?" Even the counterman took umbrage, telling the commissioner and his cohorts, "You got a good nerve coming in here and interfering with an officer." The commissioner decided that the time had come to identify himself.

But Rath figured he was dealing with a crank. "Yes, you are," he replied. "You're Grover Cleveland an' Mayor Strong all in a bunch, you are. Move on now or—"

Suddenly, the counterman's memory was jogged. "Shut up, Bill, it's his nibs, sure," he exclaimed. "Don't you spot the glasses?"

Roosevelt found another cop deep in conversation with a lady of the streets. Angry about being interrupted, the officer sought his companion's advice about whether he should "fan"—that is, club—his inquisitor. When Roosevelt introduced himself, the astounded bluecoat went racing off into the night. After Roosevelt broke all the roundsmen in the Twenty-sixth Precinct back to patrolmen, the word was out that cops should be on their posts lest they run into "Haroun Al Roosevelt," as the press dubbed him, on one of his "midnight rambles."

Roosevelt's swashbuckling approach won widespread acclaim. The curtain had gone up in "a new epoch," according to the *Sun*. "We have a real Police Commissioner," the *World* rhapsodized. "His teeth are big and white, his eyes are small and piercing, his voice is rasping. He makes our policemen feel as the little froggies did when the stork came to rule over them." In generations to come, new commissioners would win more such applause with midnight rambles of their own. But the tactic had a downside. Making cops look like fools was not a way to win their trust, and expanding the inspections unit by one part-time shoofly, however highly placed, was not going to produce general obedience. Holding line commanders accountable for their officers might have been a more effective, if less theatrical, means of enforcing discipline.

At headquarters, the departure of the old guard gave the new group an opportunity to settle scores. For fifteen years, the brass had resented the power of Thomas Byrnes; now the path was clear for an attack on his Detective Bureau. The new man in charge was acting captain Steve O'Brien. He had served under the old master, making a name for himself as the scourge of the Fourth Ward waterfront gang, but O'Brien claimed not to favor Byrnes's methods. In practice, though, crooks were still required to report in regularly at headquarters. When Chief Conlin proposed cutting down on the use of stool pigeons, Commissioner Parker, functioning as the real chief of detectives, objected. As a former assistant district attorney, he understood that turncoats were the lifeblood of criminal investigation. Roosevelt, who considered detective work ungentlemanly, was not interested. The informant system remained in place.

The next Byrnes staple to be questioned was the Wall Street boundary. A detective pulled in a career criminal and at the Tombs court explained that he had been arrested for crossing the "deadline." The magistrate ruled that a deadline was illegal and dismissed the charges. Chief Conlin, questioned about the matter by a reporter, showed some flair for headquarters double-speak: there had never been a deadline, he insisted, adding that the police would not enforce it anymore. The board also approved Conlin's proposal to abolish the darlings of the shopping public—the Broadway squad. The attacks on the Detective Bureau and the department's "grenadier guards" would become typical of the way reformers, or new brooms, operated, denigrating the elite units created by the administrations that had come before them.

Under Roosevelt's leadership, the department took important steps in the area of training and recruiting. In general, the force was poorly educated; one candidate for a police job identified County Cork as one of the thirteen original colonies. Now the board adopted a rule permitting applicants to reside anywhere in New York State—a move designed to bring in better-educated, native-born candidates (who were also more likely to be Republicans). Over the two years of Roosevelt's regime, seventeen hundred cops were hired, four times as many as in the previous two years, and eight hundred were from outside the city; Tammanyites disparagingly referred to them as "bushwhackers."

Police officers had been armed with revolvers for forty years. But they carried a ragtag arsenal of weapons, which some cops kept unloaded. Now, the board insisted, every officer would be issued a .32-caliber revolver with a four-inch barrel, and trained in its proper use. Sergeant William Petty, an expert marksman, became the chief firearms instructor. Classes took place in the basement of the Eighth Regiment Armory at Ninety-fourth Street and Park Avenue. Petty accurately forecast that few cops would be able to "hit a barn door." But a few weeks would be sufficient, he predicted, to "turn out a company of twenty that will shoot the cotton out of anything in New York." In fact, many cops had never fired a revolver, even at a target. (Some had never carried one.) Two of the early graduates of the new program, Patrolmen Patrick Reid and Daniel Ryan—plainclothesmen assigned to the Morrisania precinct in the Bronx—soon surprised a couple of would-be burglars outside a house at 156th Street and Prospect Avenue. There was a footrace. The suspects shot at the officers, hitting Ryan's hat and Reid's coat. They fired back. Ryan missed, but Reid hit one of the suspects in the neck, killing him.

Jacob Riis used his clout to do something about the "lodger" problem or, as he put it, "to avenge" his dog—the little dog beaten to death by a cop twenty-five years earlier. Riis convinced Roosevelt to ban the practice and establish a shelter system. Chief Conlin, who supported the move, pointed out that "the huddling like cattle of a large number of drunken, dirty, and oftentimes diseased wretches, contaminates the air breathed by patrolmen in the same building." (Today's shelters are not without problems, of course, and the effect of Roosevelt's order, as a practical matter, was to encourage the police to arrest the homeless for vagrancy, which often resulted in their being sent to jail.)

Roosevelt frequently took over the trial-room proceedings from Commissioner Avery. His bark tended to be worse than his bite, and some of his rulings were downright strange. Lincoln Steffens wrote in his memoirs that he could never figure out how Roosevelt decided a case. Sometimes, it seemed, he would let a Tammany politician guide his decisions; on other days, he would resent the importuning of a Republican stalwart. He was a sucker for emotional pleas, rarely taking the trouble to ascertain how much of a basis there was for them in fact. One patrolman, facing charges that seemed sure to result in dismissal, showed up for his trial with eleven children, introduced each by name, and sorrowfully told Roosevelt of his wife's recent death. After receiving a lenient sentence, he returned the children to their real parents.

Roosevelt took a hard line, by contrast, with police applicants who had worked in liquor establishments. One, Cornelius Willemse, pleaded his case in person, arguing that he had done no more than serve lunch at the Bowery's Eagle Hotel and had never drunk there himself. (He didn't mention the fact that the place was a house of assignation and his work involved acting as an occasional bouncer.) Roosevelt was unmoved.

Making sure that cops patrolled their posts, obtaining higher-caliber recruits, training them in firearms, tightening discipline, reigning in the Detective Bureau, and even abolishing the Broadway squad—most people understood these moves and approved of them. What set off a political storm was Roosevelt's stance on the liquor question. For an astute politician who was not a Puritan, Roosevelt took a surprisingly uncompromising position on enforcing the excise laws, which required the closing of saloons at 1:00 A.M. and on Sundays. He knew such measures would be bitterly resisted by the Irish and Germans; he undoubtedly knew that the latter—a large community stretching along the East Side from the Bowery downtown to Yorkville uptown—tended to vote Republican. Very probably, there was heavy pressure from Parkhurst and other Protestant leaders not to equivocate about the Sabbath. Perhaps Roosevelt, who never lost sight of the big political picture, calculated that such a policy would make a favorable impression outside the city even as it cost him support inside. In any case, his public stand was absolutist: the law was the law, and cops were expected to enforce it on pain of disciplinary action. In practice, most captains raided just enough places to give an impression of following orders; but that was sufficient (as the captains probably understood) to create a tremendous upwelling of popular sentiment against Roosevelt and reform.

A few patrolmen failed to understand the careful balancing act in which their superiors were engaged. One warm Sunday evening in June, a rookie named Eddie Bourke was walking his beat in Chatham Square when he noticed the saloon of a Tammany politician, Pat "King" Callahan, going full blast. Bourke walked in and told Callahan he was under arrest. The saloonkeeper figured the rookie was joking; realizing he wasn't, he slugged him.

Bourke returned the blow with his nightstick and the "King" was hauled off to the precinct. A few days later, when the case was called, the Tombs courtroom was filled with Tammany politicians expecting the charges to be dismissed and Bourke to be pilloried. But Lincoln Steffens alerted Roosevelt, who raced from police headquarters to the courthouse. Noting the commissioner's presence, the judge decided that Callahan should be held for trial. At the next meeting of the police board, Patrolman Bourke was promoted to roundsman—a signal from Roosevelt that cops who carried out his reform policies with zeal would be rewarded.

In September, the United Societies for Liberal Sunday Laws staged a protest parade through Yorkville. Roosevelt was even given an invitation to come uptown and review the procession. Never one to refuse a challenge, he accepted, arriving unannounced at Eighty-sixth Street and taking his place on the reviewing stand. There was a shout of *"Wo ist Herr Roosevelt?"* To which he replied, *"Hier bin ich."* Then he watched as a coffin labeled "Teddyism" was carried past, along with banners protesting "Roosevelt's Russian Rule" and proclaiming "Send the Police Czar to Russia." A float depicting a "Million-aire's Club" showed society types gulping champagne; one of the figures was a caricature of the commissioner, with comically large teeth and round-framed spectacles. In the elections of 1895, the German vote went 80 percent Democratic, and the Republicans were routed. In Albany, legislative leaders decided that enough was enough and began to create a set of legal subterfuges to help bars dodge the excise laws. Under the Raines law, for example, a liquor establishment with hotel facilities became exempt from early and Sunday closings. Many taverns put a bed in some tiny nook or cranny in order to qualify. Having gone to this trouble, some of the tavernkeepers took to renting the beds out for quick assignations.

In 1896, Roosevelt felt comfortable enough with the changes he had brought about to allow the annual police parade to take place. The parade, a tradition that dated back to Fernando Wood's heyday in the 1850s, mimicked the lavish and formal military reviews of European capitals and gave Tammany a chance to bask in its glory. The entire force, with the exception of those actually on duty, assembled at the foot of Broadway, decked out in full regalia. With superior officers at the fore, the cops marched uptown past a formal reviewing stand in Madison Square, where they exchanged salutes with the Board of Police Commissioners. It might have been a public-relations triumph once again, except for the participation of two spectral figures from the Lexow investigation: the "good" crook, Captain Max Schmittberger, and the "bad" crook, Captain William Devery. After refusing to cooperate with the Lexow committee, the latter had been indicted in a case involving blackmail as well as graft. He had survived that accusation and another extortion charge to win reinstatement. Shortly before the parade, Devery was restored to police duty by court order. Nevertheless, Roosevelt ruled that he would not be allowed to participate. Schmittberger, on the other hand, was to have an honored place in the procession.

On the afternoon of the parade, Roosevelt stood with the mayor and his fellow commissioners on the reviewing stand near Twenty-third Street, across the park from the Reverend Parkhurst's church. With them was a living symbol of the old Republican Metropolitan Force, Thomas Acton, who had helped put down the Draft Riot as head of the police board thirty-three years earlier. Band music in the distance signaled the approach of the paraders. An advance guard on bicycles and horses cleared the way for Chief Peter Conlin, who, mounted on a noble steed, looked like the heroic soldier of old. Conlin, who was about to retire, rode up to the reviewing stand and, in proper military style, swung his horse around and positioned himself to receive salutes from the five oncoming battalions of bluecoats.

A murmur began to run through the crowd—a tittering that quickly turned into a gasp. Captain Devery was marching. Conlin, without telling the commissioners, had given him permission. There were scattered boos as Devery reached the reviewing stand, but they were drowned out by a tumultuous roar of approval from the crowd, heavily composed of Tammany stalwarts. Roosevelt and his fellow commissioners pointedly declined to applaud and then, after a few more police units had passed, watched in embarrassment as Max Schmittberger came up Broadway. A few supporters of reform raised a cheer, but the masses drowned them out with hisses, boos, and shouts of "Squealer!"

The parade was a dark episode for the commissioner. Roosevelt's surprise at the welcomes accorded Devery and Schmittberger was emblematic of his failure to understand what policemen thought and felt. Over the years, he gained the affection of everyone from cowboys to coal miners; but he never seemed to inspire much loyalty among New York cops. Six months later, some of them tried to catch him in a compromising situation. In December, one of

P. T. Barnum's nephews decided to throw a bachelor party for his brother in a private room at Louis Sherry's fashionable Fifth Avenue restaurant. There were several dancing girls, and the featured attraction was Little Egypt, who had wowed the 1893 Chicago World's Fair. Abruptly, a squad of cops led by a captain burst in. According to the word around the department afterward, they had expected to find Commissioner Roosevelt present, though his intimates attested that he never attended such affairs. In any case, after a brief look around, the raiders left without making any arrests.

When he heard about the plot from Riis, Roosevelt was aghast. "What!" he exclaimed. "And I at home with my babies!"

His blustery style had also alienated his fellow commissioners Grant and Parker, and even the agreeable Chief Conlin found him grating. The meetings of the commissioners became marked by constant bickering and an inability to agree on points large and small. In one heated argument, Roosevelt sneeringly accused the city controller of being too cowardly to meet him man to man. The controller was a fencing champion, and the newspapers plunged into a fever of excited speculation about the upcoming duel, though nothing came of it. Editorialists began to remark on Roosevelt's unfortunate combativeness. One paper suggested that he needed a war to suit his talents. In a letter to his sister, Roosevelt complained that the entire city had seemingly turned against him.

After repeated clashes, he demanded that Parker be removed from the board. Mayor Strong obligingly ordered an administrative trial. Roosevelt engaged lawyer Elihu Root to prosecute the case. (Root, a prominent Republican and one of New York's leading lawyers, was frequently retained by cops in lawsuits against the department and had a good deal of influence in police affairs at the time.) Although Commissioner Grant and Chief Conlin testified for Parker, Roosevelt prevailed. But the governor refused to approve the finding, so Parker was not dismissed after all.

Roosevelt had considered the job something of a token in the first place. Now, bored and frustrated (and aware that his head could roll at any time), he sought a graceful exit from Mulberry Street. The presidential election of 1896 gave him his opportunity. William McKinley, the governor of Ohio, had not been his choice for the Republican nomination; Roosevelt offered to campaign for him anyway. He stumped throughout the Northeast and Midwest, riling up audiences with furious assaults on the Democrats.

The Democratic candidate, William Jennings Bryan, decided to open his campaign with a mass rally at Madison Square Garden in mid-August. To men of Roosevelt's background, Bryan was a dangerous radical, not just another political opponent to be bested. Fear of a Democratic victory probably drove Roosevelt to do what he could to undermine Bryan's rally at the Garden. The New York police force, the largest and most experienced in the country, should have had no trouble handling the event. But Roosevelt assigned an inadequate detail under the command of a Republican inspector. The affair quickly got out of order, and cops stationed at the Garden's doors turned away many legitimate ticket holders while letting thousands of gate-crashers through unchallenged. Roosevelt was severely criticized, even by the friendly press. A week later, when McKinley supporters held their own rally at the Garden, there were enough cops on hand to ensure that things went smoothly.

After the election, Roosevelt lobbied hard to be appointed assistant secretary of the navy, canvassing prominent Republicans and even pledging to support Boss Platt in his bid—later successful—to return to the United States Senate. In April 1897, when the coveted appointment came through, Andrew Parker called Roosevelt's escape from Mulberry Street "a glorious retreat." A more prescient observer, Bram Stoker, the author of *Dracula*, wrote in his diary, "Must be president someday. A man you can't cajole, can't frighten, can't buy."

Roosevelt's impact on the force was much debated among his contemporaries. Some, like Steffens, thought the noble memory of the "square commissioner" would continue to inspire the next generation of cops, many of them hired on Roosevelt's watch. To others, his overzealous enforcement of the liquor laws showed that reformers were too impractical to hold on to power. For a time, the reformers retained their influence, with Parkhurst's man, Frank Moss, replacing Roosevelt as president of the Board of Police Commissioners, and Inspector John McCullagh succeeding Conlin as chief of police. But in November 1897, the voters of the newly consolidated New York restored Tammany to power by a wide margin. Democratic Party stalwarts snake-danced triumphantly through the streets, shouting, "Well, well, well, reform has gone to hell."

With the figurehead Robert Van Wyck as mayor, the frontline leadership effectively passed to state senator "Big Tim" Sullivan, a tall, broad-shouldered Irishman who had been born in a Five Points tenement in 1863. Sullivan was another saloonkeeper-politician, who, in his twenties, had joined others of his ilk in the state legislature. There he made his name by leading the fight against a bill pushed by Inspector Byrnes—to authorize the arrest of known criminals on sight. (It was a de facto extension of the Wall Street deadline to the city limits.) When Byrnes blasted Sullivan for giving aid and comfort to criminals and allegedly attempting to bribe a detective to fix a case, Sullivan retaliated by introducing legislation to take away policemen's clubs.

Sullivan had a big heart and considerable charm. As a ten-year-old boy, he had arrived at school without shoes one day, and a kindly female teacher bought him a pair. After he had earned some money and influence, he began to commemorate the incident by distributing thousands of pairs of free shoes to the needy every year. His feelings for that benevolent teacher helped transform him into a committed feminist in the state senate—a body that generally took a dim view of women's rights. With greater than usual zeal, Sullivan doled out the traditional Tammany holiday dinners and buckets of coal to heat tenement flats. He had a hand in prizefights and the Broadway theater, among other enterprises. He even served a term in Congress, but the job bored him; perhaps his greatest distinction on Capitol Hill was winning the congressional pinochle championship.

McCullagh was allowed to stay on as chief for a while. But when Patrolman Matthew McConnell raided a joint run by a well-connected gambler, Sullivan demanded the offending cop's head. For refusing to oblige, McCullagh was replaced by the notorious William Devery, just in time for him to lead the 1898 police parade. To rub in his amazing rehabilitation, Devery barred Maxie Schmittberger from participating. (McCullagh eventually went off to be chief of police of newly liberated Havana.)

Parkhurst was outraged by Devery's appointment. "I know him as a man knows a serpent, by studying the trail where a serpent has crawled past," he told reporters. "Devery's precinct was a moral cesspool. . . . The Lexow investigation had its direct origin in the damnably vicious condition of the precinct that was captained by a man who has just been made the responsible head of the biggest police force in America." But Devery was oblivious to the old crusader's tongue-lashing. A Byrnes favorite, Captain "Chesty George" McClusky, took charge of the Detective Bureau, and gambling throughout Manhattan fell under the control of a syndicate consisting of Tim Sullivan, Frank Farrell, and Devery himself. In 1900, according to the *Times*, payoffs to the police and politicians from the borough's gamblers added up to about $3 million—$60 million in today's currency. When Captain Herlihy made the mistake of raiding a protected gambling den, Devery ordered his transfer to the far reaches of the Bronx.

Devery was an informal administrator. He ran the force mostly from in front of a saloon on Ninth Avenue, where he would hold court until two or three in the morning. Sometimes he would go on a prolonged drunk, riding around town in a hack throwing handfuls of silver at sidewalk crowds. As many had predicted, though, Tammany soon fell out with the Brooklyn machine over the distribution of graft. The Brooklyn borough commander, a relative of Boss Hugh McLaughlin, was transferred to semirural Queens. Inspector Kane, a mere sergeant three years earlier, was dispatched to Brooklyn from Manhattan to show the hicks how things were supposed to be done. In 1900, the legislature again formed a committee to investigate city government, under the chairmanship of Assemblyman Mazet, with Frank Moss as chief counsel. This time, the public was not particularly moved by revelations of police-protected vice; they had heard that tune too recently. But the investigation revealed a piece of corruption that struck many New Yorkers as far weightier than anything to do with liquor or cards. Tammany had given a monopoly on the sale of ice to the American Ice Company, which had taken advantage of its position to do away with the custom of selling five-cent chunks. Now people had to buy hundred-pound cakes for sixty cents—a sum that many found unaffordable. In the days before refrigeration, ice was needed to keep children's milk from spoiling, and the number of infant deaths rose sharply.

Mayor Van Wyck, according to the Mazet committee, had acquired $500,000 worth of American Ice Company stock, and he was unable to prove that he had paid for any of it. Moss got the normally prudent Croker to admit he was "always working for my pocket." Though the investigation stirred far less public outcry and interest than had that of the Lexow committee, it led to a fundamental change in police governance. In 1900, Governor Roosevelt (as he now was) pushed through a bill, drafted by his friend Root, creating a single police commissioner—a move that Republicans expected to undermine the power of the noxious Chief Devery. (The term of office was set at five years. To this day, all new terms begin at five-year intervals from the original date of appointment, February 22, 1901. If the commissioner leaves before his term expires, his successor fills out the unexpired portion. There is no limit on the number of terms a commissioner may serve.) But Tammany was nothing if not resourceful, and in February 1901 the mayor named a National Guard colonel, Mike Murphy, as commissioner. Murphy, in turn, appointed Devery as his first deputy, permitting him to maintain his domination over the force.

The disciplinary hearings that he presided over became occasions of great hilarity among reporters. Brought up on charges of recklessly firing his gun in the streets, one patrolman was fined thirty days' pay for, in Devery's words, "not hittin' nobody." Another cop, accused of kissing a girl on duty, was found guilty—not for the act, which Devery admitted to having committed himself many times, but for being careless enough to get caught. When McClusky's men collared a group of well-connected swindlers, Devery removed his chief of detectives, explaining that he had "gotten too chesty."

It was an election year, and a revived "fusion" party nominated Seth Low, the president of Columbia University (and a former Republican mayor of Brooklyn). Joining him on the ticket, as the candidate for district attorney of New York County (i.e., Manhattan, since there had been no consolidation of district attorneys or courts), was William Travers Jerome. Jerome had been languishing as a lower court judge, though, as such, he constituted a one-man Lexow committee. He would summon police captains to his courtroom, grill them about gambling and prostitution, and personally lead raiding parties, using search warrants issued against that fixture of jurisprudence John Doe. After his raiders had chopped down the door of a gambling joint to gain entrance, Jerome would leap on the crap table, produce a Bible, swear the witnesses, and hold court.

Because Low himself was an uninspiring candidate (dubbed "the human turnip" by one contemporary pol), the election devolved into a shouting match between Devery and Jerome. The latter characterized the former as "head of the city's pimps, procurers and madams." Devery suggested that Jerome be locked up on Ward's Island, where the city had its principal mental institution at the time. The race became a rerun of 1894, with the fusion party victorious. Devery resigned from the police force. A loyal Tammanyite, he expected to be given an important post in the organization. But like Williams, he found that crooked former police commanders had little future in politics. When he ran for district leader, Tammany sent sluggers into the district, and twenty of them piled onto a man they mistook for him. Though Devery won the election,

Tammany refused to recognize the results, causing the enraged ex-chief to denounce the bosses as vociferously as he had once condemned the reformers. Lincoln Steffens, among others, praised Devery in his new incarnation as crusader. But he was to have greater success in business than in politics. With Farrell, the city's gambling overlord, Devery purchased a baseball franchise in the American League, and together they installed a team that was first called the Highlanders, later the Yankees.

While New York City was descending back into its pre-Parkhurst morass, Teddy Roosevelt was zooming up the political ladder. As soon as the Spanish-American War was declared in 1898, he resigned as assistant secretary of the navy to become lieutenant colonel of the First U.S. Volunteer Cavalry—the so-called Rough Riders, commanded by Colonel Leonard Wood. When Wood moved up to brigadier general, Roosevelt took over the unit. In Cuba, the Rough Riders were one of several regiments that charged on foot up Kettle Hill to fight the battle that became known as San Juan Hill. Contrary to myth, they attacked neither on horseback nor by themselves; but the public was not much interested in these fine points. In the fall, with victory in hand, the triumphant Roosevelt became the Republican candidate for governor of New York, winning in a landslide. Two years later, to get rid of him, Boss Platt engineered his elevation to the inconsequential post of vice president. Less than a year after that, Roosevelt was president, courtesy of an assassin's bullet. The only man ever to make the leap from police headquarters to the White House was, by common consent, one of the more effective leaders in American history. Perhaps he had become a more skillful executive in the intervening years. Or perhaps his unhappy reign on Mulberry Street said more about the institution than the man. The police job had gotten the better of Roosevelt. Running the country was, comparatively speaking, a breeze.

7

"So Many Races Up Against You"

On a hot night in the late summer of 1903, half a dozen gangsters crossed from the Five Points into the Bowery to hold up a card game. This would have been a dangerous move half a century earlier, and it still was. But the drama had a fresh cast of characters: the Five Points, once the domain of the Irish Dead Rabbits and Whyos, was now controlled by a gang of Italians led by Paul Kelly, born Paulo Vaccarelli. Their adversaries were a group of Jewish thugs called the Eastmans, after their leader, Edward "Monk" Eastman, originally Osterman. The card game (known as stuss—a Jewish variation of faro) operated under Monk Eastman's personal protection, and he received a cut of the take. Shortly after eleven, a half dozen Eastmans spotted the Five Pointers on Rivington Street and opened fire, killing one of them. After the invaders returned the shots, both sides sought cover behind the pillars of the Allen Street arch of the Second Avenue Elevated. Runners left and returned with reinforcements. A small band of cops attempted to intervene but beat a hasty retreat, chased by bullets. By midnight, a hundred men had joined the fray. More police appeared, only to be driven off by gunfire again. It took reserves from several precincts and a gun-blazing charge down Rivington Street to finally disperse the gangsters. They left three dead, seven wounded, and a score of their comrades, Monk Eastman included, in police custody.

It was a modest incident compared to the two-day war between the Dead Rabbits and the Bowery Boys in July 1857, when eight people were killed and the National Guard had to be called out. But New Yorkers had higher expectations of their police now, and gangs weren't supposed to be so brazen. There was a huge public outcry, which came at a bad moment for Tammany Hall. The city was about to have a mayoral election, in which Tammany aimed to unseat the reform mayor, Seth Low. The political patron of both gangs was Tammany's most powerful district leader (and czar of organized crime), state senator "Big Tim" Sullivan. Unlike many Irish bosses, Sullivan got on well with the new immigrants from southern and eastern Europe. When the occasion required, he could don the yarmulke or dance the tarantella as if he were born to it. After the Allen Street shoot-out, Sullivan and his lieutenant, Tom Foley, warned Kelly and Eastman that any more such incidents would mean an end to their political protection.

The city administration, equally embarrassed, unleashed Inspector Max Schmittberger. Under Devery, who had run the force for four years, Schmittberger had been subjected to many slights, including exclusion from the annual police parade. Now Devery was out and Schmittberger was in, even if many of his police peers scorned him. As the commanding officer of the district that embraced the Bowery and the Five Points, he received an infusion of manpower and got carte blanche to bring the gangs in line.

At the turn of the century, the perceptions of New Yorkers regarding the identity of the "dangerous classes" underwent a change. Now it was the city's half million Italians and three-quarter million Jews who were seen as the font of criminality. There were still Irish gangs around, particularly on the West Side of Manhattan. Hell's Kitchen, where the young men of the neighborhood often made their entrance into a life of crime by stealing from the cars of the New York Central Railroad, had become the territory of the Gophers, who had a reputation for dropping bricks on the heads of patrolling cops. Downtown, around the West Village, were the Hudson Dusters, so called for their cocaine sniffing. But the Irish had advanced in the world. In 1880, William Grace of the shipping family had been elected mayor. In the last two decades of the century, the most prominent figures in the police department were Superintendent William Murray and Chief Inspector Thomas Byrnes. Germans, the other major immigrant group of the nineteenth century, had never seemed particularly menacing, except when they drank beer on Sunday. By the dawn of the twentieth century, the Irish and the Germans were as fearful of the newcomers as the nativists had once been of them. The stories of O. Henry, the great chronicler of early-twentieth-century New York, are filled with such phrases as "guineas always carry knives" and "I have many times told you those Dagoes would do you up."

At the time of the Allen Street "massacre," Schmittberger was struggling with another big case. One morning in April, a woman had noticed a barrel in a courtyard off Eleventh Street near Avenue D. Curious, she peered in, found a mutilated body, and went screaming for the police. The victim had been stabbed, slashed repeatedly, and his genitals had been removed and stuffed into his mouth. A barrel murder was the modus operandi of the Mafia, and the condition of the body suggested the motive. Their victims were usually weighted down and dropped in the river or put in a barrel and shipped to another city. If it was an informer, though, he would likely be mutilated and left in a conspicuous place as a warning to others.

In New York City, there were two Little Italys: one in East Harlem, and a larger one anchored around Mulberry Street downtown. Some of the residents of both communities had been affiliated with criminal organizations in the old country, including the Mafia of Sicily—a name that would become shorthand for all Italian-American organized crime. Whenever the northern-dominated Italian government cracked down on banditry, as it did in the 1890s, placing Sicily under martial law for two years, mafiosi fled to the United States, where they loomed large in the counterfeiting business, drawing the attention of both the NYPD and the United States Secret Service. In 1888, Antonio Flaccomio was stabbed to death by Carlo Quarteraro after the victim left a St. Marks Place restaurant where he had been with a man who had given information to the police about counterfeiters. Inspector Byrnes described the killers as forgers, counterfeiters, and assassins from Palermo. Murder was just a pastime for them, he asserted. The suspect fled back to Italy disguised as a priest, and the killing went down as New York's first Mafia murder. (As early as 1857, though, police officer Eugene Anderson was beaten to death by Mike Cancemi, whom the *New York Times* described years later as a "Mafia leader.")

The most influential figure in the Sicilian underworld of New York was Ignazio Saietta, known as "Lupo the Wolf," who came to the United States in 1899 after murdering a man in his hometown. Lupo and his partner, Giuseppe Morello, had their hands in drug smuggling and ran a counterfeit-money factory in the Catskills as well as a "murder factory" in a stable on East 107th Street. The chief of the U.S. Secret Service, William Flynn, credited the gang with sixty killings in all. When the names of Lupo and Morello were mentioned in Little Italy, people crossed themselves.

Often the press confused the Mafia with the Black Hand, which was more a method of operation than an organization. Around the turn of the century, Italian-American criminals would target certain of their countrymen with extortion letters containing the symbol of a black hand bordered by knives and skulls. (The Black Hand was originally the name of a group of Spanish anarchists and later of the Serbian nationalist organization responsible for killing Archduke Francis Ferdinand at Sarajevo in 1914.) Italians were not welcome in the police department. Unlike the Irish, they spoke the language awkwardly, if at all, and they tended to be unfamiliar with Anglo-American customs and governmental arrangements. It took Clubber Williams, of all people, to appreciate the talents of the first Italian-American to make it big on the force. Giuseppe "Joe" Petrosino, who was born in 1860 near Salerno in southern Italy, arrived in New York with his family at the age of thirteen. At eighteen, he became a "white wing," or city street sweeper, and quickly rose to a foreman's job. In 1879, Williams was put in command of the sanitation department, and Petrosino, who had come to admire cops while shining shoes outside police headquarters as a boy, managed to impress him with his drill-sergeant-style of bossing his crew around. Like Williams, the powerfully built Petrosino took no backtalk. When Williams returned to precinct duty, he used the young Italian as an informer, and in 1883, he had him appointed to the regular force, even though Petrosino was just five feet three—four inches below the required height.

His superiors always liked Petrosino, who was hardworking and deferential. But he had a swarthy complexion and spoke English with a strong accent, and he was not overly popular with his mostly Irish colleagues in the Lower East Side precinct to which he was first assigned. As Italian crime grew, however, Petrosino's value rose like that of a hot stock. In 1890, the department made him a detective, principally to investigate crimes involving his countrymen. His knowledge of the language and culture gave him an advantage over non-Italian detectives: many of them did not understand, for example, that Italians preferred to live among their own "paisanos"—people from their town or section of Italy. Thus, if a suspect was from Calabria, the place to look for him was among other Calabrians.

At first, Petrosino's results couldn't have been much worse if his name had been Murphy and he had been born in Tipperary. Merely to talk to a cop went against the grain for many immigrants; even if they didn't object personally, they had to consider the risk of ending up in a barrel with their throats cut. The usual response of a stabbing victim, when cops came asking questions, was "Fix heem myself." In the southern dialect, Petrosino's name meant "parsley." "I have some nice parsley—see the beautiful parsley," street characters would cry, seeing him approach. It was the equivalent of "Cheese it, the cops."

But Petrosino eventually won the confidence of some of his countrymen. In his investigative tactics, he blended the tried-and-true with the unorthodox. Sometimes he appeared as a New York detective, in a dark suit, a Prince Albert coat, a high black derby, and elevated shoes (the hat and shoes to make him look taller), banging on doors and throwing suspects up against a wall. At other times he would wander around disguised as an Italian peasant just off the boat, so people could talk to him without attracting suspicion. Theodore Roosevelt was impressed enough in 1895 to make Petrosino a detective sergeant with a roving commission. Counterfeiting, extortion, murder—any crime was within his province, as long as Italians were involved. The brass had only to glimpse the slightest Italian angle to a case, and the cry rang out: "Send for the dago!"

By the turn of the century, Petrosino was one of New York's best-known detectives and was frequently the subject of flattering stories in the English-language papers, which he would tip off when he was about to do something noteworthy. The Italian-American papers were not so enamored of him, by and large, and the wiseguys circulated a rumor that he had become a cop because, being a non-Sicilian, he was ineligible for the Mafia. On the evidence of his behavior toward criminals, however, Petrosino truly disliked them: "He knocked out more teeth than a dentist," an alderman said of his methods. Until well into middle age, Petrosino had no social life, choosing to live in a two-room apartment in an Irish section away from Little Italy, where his only relaxation was playing the violin. (He liked to pretend that he had been educated as a musician in the old country.) In 1900, a Tuscan-born anarchist, Gaetano Brescia, left Paterson, New Jersey, for Italy and wound up assassinating King Umberto I. Petrosino was assigned to look into the activities of

Italian anarchists in New York. The following year, William McKinley was assassinated, and Petrosino told the papers that he had warned the authorities of an anarchist plot against the president.

The Eleventh Street murder case was assigned to Petrosino, working with the homicide sleuths Arthur Carey and Jim McCafferty. The first thing they did was trace the barrel, which contained sawdust and the mark "W&T 233." It turned out that Wallace & Thompson, a firm of confectioners, had shipped it to an Italian café on Elizabeth Street—a place known as a rendezvous for counterfeiters. Petrosino and his fellow detectives managed to match the sawdust from the floor with the sawdust from the barrel. A U.S. Secret Service agent, Larry Richey, had been running a surveillance on an unknown man—dubbed "the newcomer"—who had been seen conversing with members of the Lupo-Morello gang. Richey and his fellow agents had tailed him to the same Elizabeth Street restaurant, and from there to Morello's saloon on Prince Street. Then he had disappeared.

The Secret Service heard rumbles that "the newcomer" had been involved with an imprisoned counterfeiter named Giuseppe De Priemo. Petrosino journeyed to Sing Sing, where De Priemo identified a picture of the murder victim as his brother-in-law, but would say no more. From other squeals, Petrosino heard that the prisoner had sent his brother-in-law, whose name was Benditto Madonia, to collect money owed him by Joe Morello in connection with a counterfeiting deal. When Morello refused to pay, the brother-in-law unwisely threatened to go to the police. Just as the detectives suspected, he was killed as a potential informer. About this time, a Lupo-Morello associate named Tomas "the Ox" Petto came into a windfall of money, which he and his girlfriend began spending all over Little Italy. The detectives decided that it was time to haul in the entire crew. When they raided the Prince Street saloon "the Ox" pulled a stiletto. The cops knocked him cold, confiscating a second knife, a pistol, and a pawn ticket. Morello, Lupo, and others, including a mafioso recently arrived from Sicily who bore the title of Don Vito Cascio Ferro, went along quietly. Petto's pawn ticket was for a watch that had belonged to the man in the barrel. While the gang was out on bail, Petto and Don Vito fled New York, and the case ground to a halt. Two years later, after De Priemo was released from prison, Petto—or Tomas Carillo, as he was then known—was murdered on his doorstep in a town in Pennsylvania. Don Vito, after a year in New Orleans, returned to Sicily and rose higher in the Mafia.

Petrosino won further acclaim for a Black Hand case involving his friend Enrico Caruso. The great tenor's first reaction to an extortion note demanding $5,000 was to pay off—the amount was small for a man of his income. Petrosino convinced him that he would only be letting himself in for more of the same. With Caruso's consent, a detective impersonated him, depositing a brown paper bag of money at the designated location. Petrosino and three other detectives, staked out in the vicinity, nailed the man who came to collect the money. Public attention to the case presented the judiciary with a chance to send a message to Black Handers, so the extortionist got ten years. "When murder and blackmail are in the air," the *Times* rhapsodized, "and the men folks are white-faced but searing and the women folk are saying litanies to the Blessed Mother that their dark-haired cherub children may be saved from the Black Hand kidnappers, a telephone call comes to Police Headquarters in Mulberry Street for Petrosino, and all Little Italy looks to the Italian detective for protection."

The flood of foreign criminals made some police officers nostalgic for the Byrnes era, when, as one detective put it, there were "not so many different races up against you." The department adapted to the new situation, and in January 1905 Commissioner William McAdoo formed a five-man "Italian squad," with Petrosino in charge. The unit was made up of some uncommon detectives. Joe DeGilio, who was five foot six with gray hair and spectacles, frequently masqueraded as an inspector for the Board of Health. One of the most effective members was not actually Italian: Maurice Bonsoil was of French-Irish descent, but he had grown up on the East Side and spoke fluent Sicilian. In contrast, Detective Hugh Cassidy, who had an Irish name, had been born Ugo Cassidi. At the outset, the squad suffered a small embarrassment. Petrosino had established a safe house on Waverly Place, not far from Little Italy. The furtive comings and goings of so many Italians were noted by the beat cops, who reported the place, pegging it as a hideout for anarchists or Black Handers. A police raid followed. So as not to give the safe house away, the squad allowed themselves to be hauled off in a patrol wagon. When they were out of the neighborhood, Petrosino identified himself to an angry police captain.

Paul Kelly, leader of the Five Pointers, was not a mafioso, although he had made certain accommodations. Kelly, who had acquired his Irish moniker as a boxer, was a short, slim, well-dressed, gentlemanly type. One night, a woman on a police-escorted elephant hunt was taken by a central office detective to Kelly's headquarters, the New Brighton Dance Hall Saloon on Great Jones Street, to catch a glimpse of the vicious gangster she had read about so often. The detective sat her down at a table with a clean-cut young man, who conversed with her for a half hour on the subject of art. Though she found him charming, she complained afterward that she had gone there to meet Paul Kelly, not another uptown slummer. The detective informed her that the man she had been talking to was none other.

Kelly's great rival, Monk Eastman, had made his reputation as a teenage bouncer at the Paradise dance hall, where, by his own testimony, he'd never hit a lady without first removing his brass knuckles. Eastman had a broken nose, cauliflower ears, a short thick neck, and a body scarred from head to toe, and he liked to emphasize his oddly ferocious appearance by wearing a derby hat several sizes too small. In his speech, dress, and general demeanor, he set a tone for a generation of toughs who would live on in Bowery Boys movies. Monk was a great animal fancier. At one time, he owned more than a hundred cats and five hundred pigeons, and he even tried his hand at running a pet store, on Broome Street. The business failed, however, largely because the ferocious gangster could rarely bear to part with any of his beloved animals. Sometimes he functioned as a one-man anticruelty society, saying, "I'll beat up any guy dat gits gay wit' a kit or a boyd in my neck of de woods."

After the Allen Street affair, tension smoldered on the East Side. To cool things down, Eastman and Kelly agreed to stage a private fight in a Bronx barn. It ended in a draw—a result that did nothing to improve the mood in either camp. It was Eastman who brought the situation to a climax. In the wee hours of a morning in February 1904, he and a fellow hoodlum were heading home from a slugging for hire. Passing through the Tenderloin, they noticed an intoxicated young man in top hat and tails stumbling along the street, followed by two burly characters. Taking the threesome for two thugs about to rob a rich drunk, Eastman decided to strike first. The thugs turned out to be Pinkerton detectives guarding the wayward offspring of a wealthy family; they opened fire and the surprised Eastman fled, running into a policeman, who clubbed him unconscious. He woke up in the lockup at the Thirtieth Street station. Plenty of money was offered to fix the case—even Paul Kelly promised to kick in $10,000—but it was no deal. Monk had been warned. To compound matters, the aristocratic George B. McClellan Jr. had been elected mayor, backed by Tammany Hall in one of its periodic image-polishing phases. Eastman spent the next five years in Sing Sing.

The following year Kelly was the target of an assassination attempt at his headquarters at the New Brighton. After taking a bullet through his coat sleeve, he dove under the table and came up on the other side with a pair of pistols blazing. Someone switched out the lights, and for five minutes gun flashes lit the darkness. When the police arrived, one of the assailants lay dead under a picture of Big Tim Sullivan. Kelly, wounded three times, had been carried away to a hideout in East Harlem to convalesce. Although the police eventually arrested him, prosecutors never brought him to trial, unable to dispute his claim of self-defense. Unlike Monk Eastman, Kelly knew when to fold his hand. He closed the New Brighton and began to draw away from the Five Points in favor of East Harlem, where he came to terms with the Lupo-Morello gang and eventually became a high official of the longshoremen's union.

After the departure of Monk Eastman, his followers split into factions, and in time the most powerful group fell under the leadership of "Big Jack" Zelig, born William Alberts. Zelig began his criminal career at fourteen as a pickpocket in the Bowery. He was a thin-faced boy with big brown eyes capable of producing copious tears whenever he was arrested. Victims generally declined to prosecute, and even after Zelig grew into manhood, he carried on with the same basic strategy, arranging, in encounters with the courts, for a pitiful-looking girl to plead, "Don't send my husband, the father of my baby, to jail." This worked with some judges. Not, however, with John Goff, who had the girl thrown out of the courtroom and Zelig sent to jail. Big Jack eventually dropped the pretense, emerging as the leader of a vicious gang of hired killers.

The East Side was a hotbed of gambling activity at the time, and it was not difficult for a young strong arm to find employment protecting gangsters from rivals or collecting debts from welshers. The spawning ground of many of the gamblers was Tim Sullivan's Hesper Club on Second Avenue between Fifth and Sixth Streets. One of the regulars was Bridgey Webber, who had begun his career by kidnapping pedigreed dogs for ransom (history does not record

Monk Eastman's opinion of this) and later expanded from gambling to dealing drugs. Two other stalwart members of the club were Herman Rosenthal,
its president (a special protégé of Big Tim's) and "Bald Jack" Rose, born Jacob
Rosenzweig, an albino who had been left without eyebrows, eyelashes, or a
hair on his head by a childhood illness.

By now, the police ranks included a respectable sprinkling of Jews—men
like Otto Raphael, who had been encouraged to join by Teddy Roosevelt after
rescuing some people from a fire. In 1902, there were 140 Jewish officers; ten
years later, the number had risen to nearly 600, including two captains. But
headquarters did not form a unit of Jewish detectives like the "Italian squad"
to combat crimes by their countrymen, and no Jewish Petrosino emerged.*
Instead, the department searched the ranks and found an ethnic specialist in
the person of that all-around man Max Schmittberger.

Lincoln Steffens took it on himself to give Schmittberger lessons in dealing
with Jews. They could be sharp and aggressive, he explained, but you had to
understand what they were up against: the poverty, the discrimination, the
sense of being apart. "Be patient with them," Steffens advised. "Be considerate. When they come to you, listen to them and try to settle their quarrels
without a fight or an arrest."

Indeed, with Jews and other Lower East Siders, Schmittberger developed
into a kind of judge or godfather. Men and women would run after him, ges-
ticulating wildly as they scrambled for an opportunity to seek his advice,
secure his protection, or gain official forgiveness for petty offenses. After brief
thought, the inspector would render a decision. In one block, he might advise
against a divorce or in favor of taking back a wayward girl. In another, he
would settle a zoning question by allowing a vendor of ice cream to push his
stand two or three inches out on the sidewalk. In a third, he would promise
special police vigilance for the first appearance of a new rabbi at the synagogue

---

* In 1912, however, a private Jewish secret service, the Bureau of Investigation, was created as part of the
communal organization known as the Kehillah. It was directed by the "Jewish Parkhurst," Rabbi Judah
Magnus, and its chief investigator was private detective Abe Shoenfeld, who, like Petrosino, wandered about
the East Side in disguise. When he or one of his men entered a Jewish gambling joint, the regulars would
say "Zechs" (a nickname for the Kehillah), and the racketeers would fall silent. Bureau of Investigation
detectives kept index cards providing the name, age, birthplace, nationality, and type of racket of the criminal under surveillance; the address of his business; his hangout; and a number of other facts. They turned
the information over to the police, who, when they raided a brothel or gambling den, had a complete history of the place and every man therein. The bureau's lawyer would also be present, "with legal books at
the ready."

on the upcoming Sabbath. To the poor of the Lower East Side, where the population density rivaled that of Bombay, the cops were, as the great sociologist Max Weber put it, "the representatives of God on earth."

During Schmittberger's tenure, the heart of the Lower East Side's still-strong German community was the Weiss Garten (or "White Garden"), an area adjacent to Tompkins Square and enclosed by white fences. It was the spiritual center of the larger neighborhood known since 1840 as Kleindeutschland ("Little Germany"). One of the highlights of the community social calendar was a picnic that St. Mark's Evangelical Lutheran Church held every year on the North Shore of Long Island. On a Wednesday morning in June 1904, 1,350 people, mostly children accompanied by mothers, aunts, and grandmothers, boarded a three-decker side-paneled steamer, the *General Slocum*, at Third Street. The vessel proceeded upriver, with a band playing on the deck. Shortly after departure, a fire broke out in the hold and the crew failed to report it to the captain. Then, as the ship cruised off the Upper East Side, it burst into flames. Thousands watched from the shore. For some reason, the captain, instead of heading for one of the many nearby wharves in the East 100s, pressed on through the treacherous Hell Gate currents toward North Brother Island a couple of miles ahead, intending to beach the vessel. The *Slocum* plowed directly into a brisk wind, sending great walls of oil-fed flames whipping from stacks to stern.

Some passengers were incinerated where they stood; others jumped overboard and perished in the swift currents. Headquarters flashed an order to all commands to turn out the reserves. At the East Eighty-eighth Street station, Officer Thomas Skelly scrambled into a police wagon with his buddy Tom Cooney and two dozen other patrolmen and headed north along the Manhattan shoreline. Ship traffic all along the river stopped, and small boats pitched in to assist the police. Skelly and Cooney boarded a tugboat. As it neared the burning ship, Cooney dove into the water, where he single-handedly rescued ten people by swimming back again and again with hysterical survivors clutching him around the neck. When the tug was filled, it pulled away; only then did Skelly realize that Cooney was missing. Frantically, the cops searched the boat and then the waters strewn with bodies and burning debris. Cooney was nowhere to be found. Later that afternoon, his body was pulled out of the river along with hundreds of others.

Police boats from the Harbor Unit bore the brunt of the rescue work.

Officer Edward Mulrooney, a former pilot on Hudson River barges, pulled his launch alongside the *Slocum* and helped rescue survivors. Later, he took twenty-nine dead bodies out of the hold. After three days' duty without sleep, he went home and was sick in bed for several days. Nearly a thousand corpses were brought to the Twenty-sixth Street pier in Manhattan, where relatives lined up for blocks to identify them. Inspector Schmittberger took charge, going from group to group to comfort the victims' families. With the loss of so many children, life went out of the White Garden, and most of the residents departed within a few years. Some survivors of the disaster committed suicide. Old Kleindeutschland died and was reborn uptown in Yorkville. New Yorkers of that generation never forgot the *Slocum* disaster or the heroism and devotion to duty of the NYPD. (The captain, crippled and blinded in the disaster, spent several years in Sing Sing before being pardoned by President Taft. In Tompkins Square stands a small monument to "earth's purest children, young and fair.")

At the turn of the century, Chinatown was a small neighborhood centered around Chatham Square in the area of Doyers, Pell, and Mott Streets. It served as the Tenderloin for Chinese-Americans scattered throughout the metropolitan area. There they could play fan-tan, visit a bordello, or obtain an opium pipe. The neighborhood also developed into an exotic tourist trap. Day and night, touring cars cruised through midtown offering round-trips to Chinatown for a dollar or two, with Caucasian "lobbygows" as guides. (The term connoted an aide-de-camp or, less flatteringly, a flunky; in the slang of the day, "I'm not your lobbygow" was a common response to an unwelcome request.) The area was a cop's paradise: after just a year in command of the precinct, it was said, a captain could retire rich. Gambling games and opium dens paid off—to the cops as well as the heads of the various Chinese associations known as "tongs." Their activities also proved lucrative to a coterie of Caucasian lawyers and politicians. Around 1899, the Hip Sings challenged the On Leongs for control of Chinatown's gambling, and the "tong wars" began. Chief among the Hip Sing gangsters was Mock Duck, who wore a suit of chain mail and carried two guns and a hatchet. Chinese gunmen, who tended to judge the value of a firearm by its size, had a fondness for .45-caliber revolvers, which were huge and unwieldy. Some tong shooters, like Mock Duck, had a habit of closing their eyes when they fired, so their ratio of kills to shots was low. But they enjoyed an advantage over the police: firecracker explosions were such a regular occurrence in Chinatown that the noise of shots fired did not always get a prompt response. Tourists grew to expect a tong battle with every trip to Chinatown. To accommodate them, the lobby-gows would arrange for someone dressed up as a hatchet man to chase a supposed victim on cue.

Since the Chinese never cooperated with the American criminal justice system, cops could take their money with impunity. Still, the tongs knew a thing or two about political manipulation. Mock Duck, who styled himself "Colonel," once went to Reverend Parkhurst's crime prevention society and furnished Frank Moss with the addresses of the On Leong gambling spots. Under pressure from Moss, the police staged a series of raids. So pleased was "Colonel" Duck that he hung a portrait of Moss in a place of honor at Hip Sing headquarters.

In the racial climate of the times, the appointment of an Asian to the NYPD was unthinkable, although the "mayor" of Chinatown, Tom Lee, head of the Hip Sings, got himself named a New York County deputy sheriff as a piece of political patronage. Not having any Chinese in the ranks, the department assigned an Irishman, Sergeant Dan Costigan, to clean up the area. In 1904, Commissioner McAdoo put Costigan in charge of a special eight-man Chinatown vice squad. Costigan had been a cop for fifteen years, and he had a strong aversion to gambling and vice—an attitude of no help to him, professionally, up to now. Given his head, he soon had Chinatown reeling. His squad mounted raid after raid, while turning down a fortune in bribes. Costigan's fellow cops and the press dubbed him "Honest Dan." He was so bad for local business that even the lobbygows, with the tourist trade falling off, cursed his name. The Chinatown establishment eventually convinced the city government to declare victory and make this splendid officer available for challenging assignments elsewhere in the city. Having gotten the bit between his teeth, however, Honest Dan would not let go; for the next fifteen years, he remained the department's best-known untouchable and the bane of crooked cops.

Although blacks had been living in Manhattan for two centuries, there were no black officers on the force in that borough. In the late nineteenth century, blacks began moving north and west from the Five Points. Many settled in Greenwich Village, where the violent street at night was tiny Minetta Lane. Cataloging its denizens, Frank Moss listed "No Toe Charlie," "Black Cat," and

"Blood Thirsty," who was a big man with a rolling eye and scarred neck. But Italian immigrants were moving into the area by now. Finding them too violent and too foreign in their ways, particularly in their inability to speak English, blacks began to depart for neighborhoods west of the Tenderloin, although the Village retained a significant black population into the new century. Others moved to a neighborhood in the West Sixties, whose black-white clashes led it to become known, after the Spanish-American War, as San Juan Hill. Between the two West Side black enclaves was Irish Hell's Kitchen.

In the midst of a prolonged heat wave in August 1900, a precinct plainclothesman, Robert Thorpe, attempted to arrest a black woman, May Enoch, at Forty-first Street and Eighth Avenue in the west Tenderloin. Her common-law husband, Arthur Harris, objected, and, according to the police account, stabbed the detective three times with a knife. The next day, Officer Thorpe died. He lived in the area, and, as was the custom of the time, his wake was held at his home. While it was in progress, a black man came by Thorpe's house, passing several dozen cops who were gathered outside. Two white women screamed that he had a gun, and he was beaten senseless and dragged off to the stationhouse. Soon, white toughs from the Kitchen began congregating. By some accounts, there were more than ten thousand of them stretching for a mile up and down Eighth Avenue, and they rampaged through the west Tenderloin, pursuing and beating blacks at random. One victim fled into the Marlborough Hotel, running straight through a banquet honoring the chief of the fire department. Other whites invaded San Juan Hill and battled with local residents. The police responded in force, but they intervened, in most cases, on behalf of the attackers. From the victims' perspective, indeed, some white citizens seemed more helpful than the cops. One woman single-handedly shamed a crowd that had pounced on two black newsboys; a Salvation Army captain sheltered a black man who had been chased from Times Square to Bryant Park. One of the victims of the rioting was rescued from the mob and put on a trolley by a police officer—only to be yanked off by a second officer, who began beating him with a club to cries of "Shame" from passengers. Cops fired their revolvers at windows, claiming that objects had been thrown at them from above. Most of the people arrested were black. It was "a sad commentary," one magistrate said later, that only one of the prisoners before him, a small boy, was white.

Chief Devery, assuming direct command, cleared the streets with a club-swinging charge, and the *Herald* characterized the whole affair as a "police riot." The *Tribune* attributed its severity to "the unskillful and treacherous conduct of the police," blaming their actions, in turn, on subservience to Tammany Hall. A group of reform Democrats denounced Devery as "a ruffian." One black group attributed the police response to the fact that many members of the force had been recruited from the "coarsest and most ignorant individuals of the Irish race."

The department's appalling performance was probably due more to its leadership than to the character of the rank and file. In riot situations, cops worked under the direct supervision of their ranking officers. Thirty-seven years earlier, under the Metropolitan board, the police had vigorously protected blacks from Irish draft rioters. In 1900, the protests caused Mayor Van Wyck to order an investigation by the Board of Police Commissioners. At the outset of the inquiry, the board president expressed his opinion that if someone had been hit by a policeman's billy or nightstick, it was "proof that he was where he had no business to be." Not surprisingly, the police were exonerated, although another probe, led by Frank Moss, condemned them. Perhaps the department meant to express a small measure of doubt about its role when it omitted Detective Thorpe's name from the official roll of officers killed in the line of duty.

Brooklyn had frequently been controlled by Republicans, who, as the party of Abraham Lincoln, automatically got the black vote. The Brooklyn police had, accordingly, accepted a few black officers in the years before consolidation. The first, Wiley Overton, hired in 1891, was assigned to the Adams Street precinct, where he patrolled the colored section around Hudson Avenue and Navy Street. Shunned by his colleagues, he left after little more than one year. In 1892, Moses Cobb and John Lee joined the Brooklyn force. With the creation of Greater New York in 1898, they were merged into the NYPD.

But the department's principal "Negro expert" was its everybody expert, Max Schmittberger. At first, Steffens recalled, he lacked finesse: mothers would frighten their children with the warning "Cap'n Max'll come and ketch you." Schmittberger would enter a colored dance hall and people would begin running out doors and diving out windows. Later, according to Steffens's implausible but no doubt sincere account, Schmittberger became "beloved by the colored people."

Sam Battle, the first black to make it onto the consolidated NYPD, was a tall, powerfully built twenty-eight-year-old porter who had grown up in North Carolina. Moving north as a teenager, he settled in Brooklyn. By 1910, Battle was married, living on West 136th Street in Harlem, and working as an assistant chief redcap at Grand Central Station. Although it was a good job with (he recalled) great tips, Battle decided to follow in the footsteps of his brother-in-law, Moses Cobb. He took the police exam and placed high. But the examining physician rejected him for "heart trouble." This was a familiar finding among the small number of blacks who had attempted to join the force. Cobb, among others, had taken the precaution of getting a private physical exam in advance. Now Battle went to one of the city's leading heart specialists, who agreed to examine him at a fraction of his regular fee and declared him fit. Under pressure from black politicians as well as leaders of Battle's church and other Harlem eminences, the department had him reexamined and, in 1911, deemed him acceptable.

By now, reserve duty had dwindled to just one eight-hour tour every three days. But that was enough to pose a problem: where would a Negro cop sleep? Not, it soon emerged, with any of the white officers of the Sixty-eighth Street station in the San Juan Hill area—his first assignment. They gave Battle the silent treatment, exiling him, at reserve time, to the station flag loft, where he slept alone. Like the tong hatchet men, the city's first colored policeman became a novelty item on guided tours of the city. "There goes the nigger cop," street kids would sometimes shout. Battle would not respond "because they didn't know any better," he said later.

Battle enjoyed a good scrap, and San Juan Hill held no terrors for him. One night, the reserves were called out to deal with a racial confrontation. Dressing quickly, Battle did not wait for the patrol wagon to take him. Instead, with a few other cops, he ran toward the scene. Racing down Amsterdam Avenue past a firehouse, he heard a fireman say, "There goes Battle, he's in the lead!" At the sight of white cops beating up black residents, he told himself, "Here's my chance to get even." So Battle began clubbing white hoodlums. But he always made a point of rushing to the aid of cops in trouble, and his full-speed-ahead style, along with his great size, gradually won him favor, even from white officers who continued to shun him socially. Superior officers liked Battle, as they had liked Petrosino, because he was hardworking and conscientious.

After a couple of years on the job, Battle was put on election duty one day at the East Eighty-eighth Street precinct. (Cops were not permitted to work in their own precincts at election time, lest they turn their backs on fraud by the local politicians.) After a long and exhausting tour of duty, he entered the strange precinct and decided to lie down on a bunk—something he had never done before. Half-asleep, he heard his fellow officers from the Sixty-eighth Street station talking about him. They had always wondered how Battle had gotten onto the force. Some had speculated about the possible influence of the Vanderbilt family, which owned Grand Central Station. Battle had been shrewd enough not to refute that rumor. Listening, he was not surprised to hear the name Vanderbilt coupled with his. The gist of the conversation, though, was that, however he had secured his appointment, the other cops liked him and felt bad about how he had been treated. From that night on, they began to greet him with a friendly "Hello, Sam." But Battle wasn't overly pleased: the use of his first name smacked too much of "boy."

It was not just the rank and file in those years who had trouble viewing an African-American as fit company. Police Commissioner William McAdoo was a former congressman and assistant secretary of the navy. (He is sometimes confused with William Gibbs McAdoo, secretary of the treasury in the administration of his father-in-law, Woodrow Wilson.) Yet he wrote about the "Tenderloin Negro" as "an overdressed, flashy bejeweled loafer, gambler, and in many instances a general criminal," adding, "They never work and they go heavily armed." When blacks got drunk, according to McAdoo, "murder came easy to them, and an officer could take for granted that the man to be arrested had a revolver in one pocket, a razor in the other, and possibly a blackjack, and he would use them all with murderous intent." As commissioner, McAdoo took strong exception to "black-and-tan" clubs, where the races commingled.

His successor as police commissioner, General Theodore Bingham, was even more outspoken about ethnic groups—and about a wider assortment of them. In the September 1908 edition of the prestigious *North American Review*, Bingham asserted that at least 85 percent of New York's criminals were "of exotic origin," as he put it. Jews, he wrote, constituted 50 percent, and Italians 20 percent of the criminal population. Jews went into crime because they were unfit for hard labor, Bingham explained, while Italians were a "riffraff of desperate scoundrels, ex-convicts and jailbirds." In response to protests by Jewish leaders and prodding from Mayor McClellan, Bingham issued a public apology; but it was a measured one. His purpose, he said, had been "not to enter upon a scientific inquiry into the race or religion of those charged with criminality but solely to make a plea for a secret service fund in order that criminality might be more effectively dealt with than is now possible."

To overcome the criticism while demonstrating his mettle against "exotic" foreigners, the commissioner turned to the reliable Joe Petrosino. In 1906, Bingham had expanded the Italian squad to twenty-five men, renaming it the Italian Legion and appointing Petrosino commander, with the rank of lieutenant. The following year, Petrosino married a thirty-seven-year-old widow and moved to a four-room apartment. He continued to make news in 1908, by capturing Enrico "Big Henry" Erricino, a leader of the Neapolitan secret society the Camorra, who had fled from Naples to New York after committing a double murder. Before he made the collar, Petrosino had the presence of mind to call some friends at the *Times*, which sent a reporter. In recognition of his services, the Italian authorities presented Petrosino with a watch, although, generally, they may not have been too upset about the departure of criminals from their jurisdiction. In any case, the flow was steady, leading Congress, in 1907, to pass a law intended to strike a blow against these unwanted immigrants. The statute allowed for deportation, within three years of arrival, of any alien found to have concealed a criminal record. And since Italian criminal records were in Italy, a federal consultant proposed that American detectives go there to investigate.

When this idea reached Commissioner Bingham's desk, his response was unhesitating: send Petrosino. The detective himself was not eager to make the journey, for his wife was expecting, and he realized that he might be coolly received in parts of his homeland. "South of Rome, everyone is Mafia," one of Petrosino's colleagues remarked at the time. To compound matters, Petrosino was on sick leave, having been ill for an extended period. Without enthusiasm, he departed in February 1909, carrying a list of two thousand names.

The mission was supposed to be secret. Yet even on the ship going over, Petrosino drew suspicious glances; and by the time he arrived, Bingham, perhaps in a bid for favorable publicity, had revealed the plan to the *New York Herald*, whose story appeared in the Paris edition of the paper as well and was soon picked up by the Italian press. Petrosino carried letters in which the United States government appealed to the Italian government for cooperation. But he was badly out of his element at the higher levels of international policing. Following general European practice, the Italian police had an elite corps of officers, recruited and trained separately from their subordinates. Petrosino was a simple southern Italian who spoke in dialect; had he become a cop in his native country, he could never have risen above sergeant. On his mission to Italy, he would be confronting well-educated men of social standing, with *Excellency* and *Cavalieri* before their names. It was an impossible social gulf to bridge. Petrosino had left Italy as a child thirty-five years earlier, and Washington had not seen fit to brief him on the political nuances of the mission—or, indeed, on the most basic political realities. Arriving in Rome, Petrosino met with an aide to Prime Minister Giovanni Giolitti and took the aide to be the prime minister himself, who, incidentally, had significant political support from Mafia sources. The aide arranged for Petrosino to meet with the head of the Italian police, who was outwardly cordial and issued a letter requesting other Italian officials to cooperate. Privately, however, he was not impressed with the American. He offered a bodyguard. Petrosino refused. The same thing happened when Petrosino met the police commissioner of Palermo, Sicily.

Petrosino's mission required someone of higher rank as well as social standing. In command of all the city's detectives was deputy commissioner Arthur Woods, a product of Groton, Harvard, and postgraduate study in a German university. As an English instructor at Groton, he had taught Teddy Roosevelt's children. (Through the White House connection, he had obtained a government post before taking a job as a reporter on the *New York Sun*.) Bingham, Roosevelt's man, had appointed Woods a deputy commissioner in 1907. To prepare for his new post, Woods had traveled to Europe to study Continental police methods. Sleuthing fascinated him, and he frequently went out with Arthur Carey and other detectives to work on cases personally. He also began to be received in society. (A few years later, as police commissioner, Woods would marry J. P. Morgan's granddaughter.) Had he accompanied Petrosino—which would no doubt have appealed to his love of action—the Italian government, recognizing the international embarrassment that would result from the murder of a prominent American and a friend of the president's, might have taken steps to ensure their safety, whether requested to or not.

It is not clear just what Petrosino did in Sicily, though he apparently met with a number of informants, or people claiming to be such. Certainly, there were Sicilians then in residence who had something to lose if Petrosino actually gathered any intelligence. Six years earlier, he had worked with Schmittberger on the barrel-murder case. A suspect, Don Vito Cascio Ferro, had fled New York after his arrest; he was in Sicily now, and could possibly be extradited to New York. On March 12, while waiting for a trolley near a statue of Garibaldi in downtown Palermo, Petrosino was shot to death. The shots were fired by two paid gunmen, according to the American consul; others said that Don Vito had committed the murder personally. Many years later, serving a life sentence in one of Mussolini's prisons after his breakup of the Mafia, Don Vito was reported to have confessed to the deed: Petrosino, he explained, was an honorable man and deserved to be killed by another honorable man rather than by mere hirelings. In New York City, 250,000 spectators turned out to view the detective's funeral cortege, and flags were flown at half-mast.

The Secret Service sent its star agent, Larry Richey (né Ricci), into Little Italy after Petrosino's death. As a result, the Lupo-Morello counterfeiting gang was broken—the two principals received sentences of twenty-five and thirty years, respectively—and barrel murders became less common. Richey later served as secretary, or chief of staff, to President Herbert Hoover.

Without Petrosino's leadership, the Italian squad petered out, and its functions devolved to a unit specializing in Black Hand crimes. Then a new Petrosino emerged in the person of "Big Mike" Fiaschetti, who as a rookie in 1908 had been recruited by the master. In 1918, the NYPD restored the Italian squad, assigning Fiaschetti as commanding officer. Headquarters' memory was short, however. In 1921, there was almost a repeat of the Petrosino murder. Fiaschetti was ordered to go to Naples on a hunt for a fugitive from the United States in the territory of the Camorra. If the NYPD had forgotten the events of 1909, the Italian government had not. It assigned detectives to trail Fiaschetti, who, like Petrosino, preferred to operate alone. The Roman-born detective moved about the Neapolitan underworld in the guise of an Italian criminal, Don Pasquale. Soon he lost his shadows and came across information about the identity of the trigger man in the Petrosino killing, although, according to his intelligence, it was not Don Vito. Fiaschetti extended his mission, hoping to pursue the lead. But when he showed up at a gathering of Camorra leaders, he heard the startling news that the famous Fiaschetti, head of the New York Italian squad, was in Italy in disguise to penetrate the underworld. In his presence, Camorra leaders expressed their determination to obtain a description of Fiaschetti and "hunt this policeman by the blood of the Madonna." Wisely, Don Pasquale disappeared. With the help of the Italian police, he picked up the fugitive he had been seeking in the first place and left Italy posthaste.

The Italian underworld was unable to get rid of Fiaschetti. An American lawyer-politician had better success the following year. When he stormed into Fiaschetti's office during an interrogation, the detective warned him not to interfere and threatened to kick him off the premises if he persisted. "You wouldn't dare," Fiaschetti was told. He dared. As a result, the Italian squad was disbanded and Big Mike pushed into early retirement. In the 1930s, as part of a drive against racketeering in the produce industry, Mayor La Guardia brought him back, as a deputy commissioner in the Department of Markets.

8

"Just a Little Lieutenant"

I n October 1896, Patrolman Charles Becker arrested a streetwalker and landed in trouble. The complaint against him was a novel one. Prostitution was undoubtedly the woman's livelihood. Becker stood accused merely of fabricating his testimony. While he claimed to have observed her in the act of solicitation, a witness insisted that she had been doing no such thing. "Whatever her character, the arrest was an outrage," the witness told reporters. "The policeman flatly lied."

It was a fine point. Even with Teddy Roosevelt running the show, such a complaint would probably have been dismissed out of hand if the witness—Becker's accuser—had been just anybody. But he was the young author Stephen Crane, who had catapulted to fame a year earlier with his great novel of the Civil War, *The Red Badge of Courage*. Crane had met Roosevelt socially, and he apparently expected the commissioners to share his own sense of outrage.

To hear the arrested woman, Dora Clark, tell it, she had been targeted for harassment after rebuffing the advances of a member of Becker's unit—a dark-complexioned cop named Rosenberg: She didn't go out with colored men, she had told him. Virtually all the cops in Becker's precinct attended his disciplinary hearing, which was the longest in the department's history. It ran as late as it did, until nearly three in the morning, because of the aggressive defense strategy of Becker's lawyer, who succeeded in putting Crane rather than Becker on trial. Crane had encountered Clark (and Becker) while gathering information for a series of newspaper articles on the denizens of the Tenderloin. The lawyer devoted much of his energies to showing, or implying, that Crane was a pimp and an opium addict, thus giving him a less elevated motive for his nighttime meanderings.

The commissioners eventually came to the strained conclusion that Becker had made an honest mistake. Roosevelt himself showed up at the stationhouse to congratulate Becker on his exoneration. While he was at it, though, Roosevelt addressed a few gently admonishing words to the assembled officers about the need to be considerate of the rights of all New Yorkers, including "unfortunate women." How seriously they took this appeal is unclear. Certainly, Crane saw little evidence of increased solicitude. By the end of the year, he had decided to abandon the city after a series of unpleasant run-ins with the police. He had intended to write a series of stories about cops in addition to his Tenderloin sketches. Now he dropped that project, becoming a war correspondent in Cuba and in Crete, where the Turks and Greeks were embroiled. Much like Roosevelt, Crane came to prefer the simple dangers of a shooting war to the vexations of dealing with New York City cops.

Most police-reform sentiment in this period focused on graft and the lax enforcement of the laws against gambling, prostitution, and the sale of liquor on Sunday. Yet in the chorus of criticism, a line of counterpoint was audible. The police were beginning to be criticized for overzealousness as well as corruption. The Lexow committee had devoted a whole day of its hearings to a series of witnesses who claimed to have been beaten by New York City cops. Some bore the evidence of their experiences in the form of welts, scars, cracked ribs, or broken noses. More than ninety cops were made to stand, visible to all, and listen to the grisly tales of their alleged victims. The testimony caused such a stir that Thomas Byrnes, the superintendent at the time, ordered the force to stop carrying clubs.

Roosevelt was quick to countermand that decision. "The nightsticks are in," he declared, adding, "They ought never to have been taken away." Roosevelt and his colleagues were determined not to have the "moral tone" of the police be improved at the expense of their "fighting efficiency," since, as he sought to explain later, "We did not possess a particle of that maudlin sympathy for the criminal, disorderly, and lawless classes which is such a particularly unhealthy sign of social development."

Cornelius Willemse's first attempt to become a New York City cop had been stymied by Roosevelt's refusal to hire anyone who had worked in a liquor-dispensing establishment. Willemse had to wait three more years before he succeeded in getting onto the force, with the sponsorship of a Tammany district leader. Eventually he became known as one of the rougher cops of the first quarter of the twentieth century. But by his own account—a self-serving one, to be sure—he was merely following an unwritten code. It was spelled out for him (according to Willemse's memoir, *Behind the Green Lights*) soon after his appointment, when he arrested two thugs for beating a man and robbing him of seven dollars and his wristwatch.

Taking a long look at the victim and then at the accused assailants, Willemse's sergeant asked him how long he had been on the force.

"A couple of months, sir," he replied.

"I thought so," said the sergeant. "Look at the condition of this poor fellow," he said, pointing to the victim. "And not a mark on these two bums," he added, indicating the assailants. The sergeant pushed a button, summoning two veteran cops from a back room. He told them to take the suspects outside "and show the rookie how to bring them in right."

The instruction consisted of a few minutes' work with their nightsticks. When it was done, Willemse submitted his prisoners for reexamination, and the sergeant pronounced himself satisfied. "Now let me tell you something," he added. "They may beat you in court, the complainant may not show up, they may jump their bail, politicians may interfere . . . but this"—the bruises—"they've got, and make no damned mistake about it."

Beating up criminals as a form of preemptive justice would remain common police practice for years to come. Even in the mid-1930s, the police commissioner in the administration of a famously liberal mayor, Fiorello La Guardia, would publicly excoriate a group of detectives for arresting a smartly dressed young hoodlum without giving him a proper thrashing. But the commissioner's remarks would set off a storm of protest, and even at the beginning of the century these attitudes were beginning to collide with post-Lexow morality.

In June 1907, Brooklyn detectives picked up a seventeen-year-old boy named George Duffy, on "suspicion." Duffy was photographed, held overnight, and released the next morning after a brief court hearing. Five months later, cops hauled him in for "obstructing a sidewalk." Once again, the charges were quickly dismissed. In September 1908, young Duffy was arrested for robbery and assault but released yet again when the victim failed to make an identification. All this was routine procedure: in the unending police effort to keep young punks in line, such practices enjoyed wide public support—often even from the parents of the victims, who, at least according to myth, would give the kid a whack of their own. But Duffy's father apparently wasn't one of those parents. Instead of whacking the boy, he took his side, seeking to have his picture removed from the rogues' gallery. In this effort, he gained the support of a Brooklyn supreme court justice, William Gaynor, who wrote an irate letter to Police Commissioner Theodore Bingham, opening an acrimonious correspondence between them.

Gaynor, a relentless critic of the police, had started out as a lawyer in Flatbush, defending drunks, liquor dealers, and, somewhat incongruously, a local temperance group. Elected to the court in 1893, he didn't just take up for young punks like Duffy; to the dismay of law-enforcement officials and religious reformers, Gaynor also championed the rights of gamblers and brothelkeepers. In one attention-getting case, he overturned a lower-court decision—by Judge John Goff—against a wardman who had failed to arrest the keeper of a house of ill fame. "So long as the house on my block is so decorous and orderly in the windows and on the stoops that I am not able to see a single thing wrong with it," Gaynor wrote, "I am willing to go by and leave it alone and I want the police to do the same." The law, Gaynor observed, "does not commit the supreme folly" of making the police "the custodians or guardians of the private morals of the community."

Attending a Saint Patrick's Day gathering at Delmonico's, Police Commissioner William McAdoo made Gaynor the target of a scornful speech. Things had reached such a pass, McAdoo said, that the owners of vice joints targeted by the police had only to seek out "a well-known firm of lawyers" (Gaynor's former partners) who, "bundle of papers" in hand, would head over to Gaynor's courtroom, where the judge "instantly grants the writs, denounces the police commissioner, shrieks for personal liberty, talks about Russian despotism, and threatens the Governor if the police commissioner is not removed at once."

It has never been easy to be a New York City police officer. But it has rarely been as hard as it was in the first decade of the twentieth century. By now, police reform was no longer just a spasmodic impulse; it had become an industry—the seemingly permanent livelihood of an interlocking directorate of citizen activists and advocacy groups. Exposing, or decrying, police misdeeds was also an accepted way to get ahead in the prosecutorial and journalism fraternities, where, as one policeman complained to McAdoo, "thieves, ex-convicts, prostitutes, procurers [and] disorderly housekeepers" were "received with open arms" and "coddled and talked softly to," if only they came bearing tales that reflected ill on the police.

The reform groups enjoyed the backing of some of the richest and most influential New Yorkers of the day, and the flow of revelations kept the issue in the public eye. In an era of manifold social ills—sweatshops, child labor, the exploitation of immigrants, the buying of politicians—it frequently appeared, as the journalist Andy Logan has written, "that the most hideous sin of all in the minds of many Americans . . . was the greasing of the palms of city policemen by prostitutes, gamblers, and other small-time local criminals."

To cops, on the other hand, grafting was the normal state of affairs in all walks of life. "But why do you men take this dirty money?" Frank Moss once asked a veteran police captain.

"Wouldn't we be fools if we didn't?" replied the captain, adding that "everybody in New York works his job, even the ministers."

"Do you believe that?" said Moss.

"I know it," the captain declared.

But the money was "so dirty," Moss persisted.

"We fumigate it," said the captain. "It's clean after we get it."

The civil libertarian and the moral crusader were, of course, coming from different places. To the still-active Reverend Charles H. Parkhurst, Gaynor was an apologist for the city's most depraved criminals; to Gaynor, Parkhurst was a self-righteous busybody. Among cops with the duty of combating prostitution and gambling, the work did not seem to leave much room for such niceties as an actual observation of the crime. Some cops detected a certain hollowness in the rhetoric of both groups. During the periodic vice crackdowns, it was understood, in any case, that civil liberties became a secondary concern. Yet Parkhurst and his allies had, however unwittingly, created the climate in which Gaynor's brand of criticism began to resonate. And it wasn't all hollow. There was hypocrisy, to be sure, but there was change in the air as well.

In June 1909, the Duffy furor arose anew when the police picked him up on a vagrancy charge. He was, by their lights, a known criminal out on the street and unable to give a satisfactory account of himself. This time, Gaynor complained directly to Mayor McClellan, adding that if *he* were mayor, such a thing would never be permitted to happen. McClellan ordered an investigation, which led to a sixty-page report raking the police department over the coals. The mayor told his police commissioner, Theodore Bingham, to fire a number of the high-ranking officers involved. When Bingham refused, McClellan fired *him* instead. Deputy Commissioner Arthur Woods resigned in protest.

McClellan, now finishing up his second term, had entered office with Tammany Hall's support, but like many other politicians of an independent disposition, he craved more independence than the party bosses would give him. So he began laying plans to break with Tammany and form an alliance with the Brooklyn machine. Tammany boss Charles Murphy and Big Tim Sullivan suspected that an untethered Mayor McClellan would be entirely too attentive to the likes of the Reverend Parkhurst—an odious prospect. Yet with antipolice sentiment running high, it behooved Tammany to establish its own police-reform bona fides. Thus it was that, in one of the odder political moments in the city's history, the Manhattan bosses cut a deal with the Brooklyn machine to back, of all people, Judge Gaynor; and this irascible loner, a man in his early sixties who had seemed destined to end his years on the bench, became mayor of New York—possibly the most eccentric figure ever to occupy that post and certainly the one with the most intense and deeply cherished feelings against the police.

For most of its history, New York City had been confined to the lower portion of the island of Manhattan. The city that elected Gaynor mayor in November 1909 sprawled across Brooklyn and Queens (between them, a substantial swath of western Long Island) and, with the rapidly filling Bronx, had a beachhead on the mainland. Swelled by a continued flow of immigrants, now largely from eastern and southern Europe, the population was approaching five million. The police ranks had expanded from four thousand in 1897, Roosevelt's last year as president of the police board, to ten thousand.

With the opening of the Great Bridge across the East River in 1883, many people left the crowded slums of lower Manhattan for the cleaner and more spacious city of Brooklyn. By the turn of the century, it had its own extensive slum districts. On its sprawling crazy quilt of streets, the speeding trolleys earned Brooklynites the nickname "Trolley Dodgers"—an abbreviated version of which would, in time, become the name of a baseball team. The Brooklyn political bosses were proving themselves equal to Tammany, whose expansion they blocked with the slogan "The tiger shall not cross the bridge." Even after consolidation, Brooklyn cops were regarded by "New York" (Manhattan) cops as hicks. But because of Brooklyn's size and political importance, headquarters often treated the borough as a semiautonomous barony.

In 1895, automobiles appeared on the streets of New York. (Diamond Jim Brady owned the first one, a Woods electric brougham.) Although they were just rich men's toys at the time, Roosevelt had had the foresight to insist that their operators be licensed by the police department (thus giving rise to that enduring police line "Lemme see your license"). He also created a traffic squad of four officers on bicycles. In 1899, the city recorded its first automobile fatality when a passenger stepped off a Central Park West streetcar into the path of a limousine. In 1904, Commissioner McAdoo sent a captain to Europe to study how the British and Continental police dealt with the problem of automobile traffic. The findings led McAdoo to form a traffic bureau; but police enforcement still faced considerable opposition among the "automobilists." Seeking an injunction against the new regulations, lawyers for the auto owners had the good sense to take their plea to Justice Gaynor in Brooklyn. In a ruling eventually overturned by the state Court of Appeals, Gaynor swallowed their argument whole. The regulation of traffic, he agreed, was an illegal curtailment of individual liberties.

In 1905, headquarters moved from 300 Mulberry Street to a more ample and elegant gray stone building a few blocks south at 240 Centre Street. There, from 1906 on, the commissioner arrived in a chauffeured touring car, though, in the cautious police department, his horse-drawn buggy was kept on reserve. By 1910, the department had a five-hundred-man traffic bureau deployed on foot, bicycle, and horseback, and even Gaynor no longer doubted the need for such a unit. But when it came to other areas of law-enforcement policy, Gaynor the mayor picked up where Gaynor the judge had left off.

Involving himself in matters that later mayors would consider beneath them, Gaynor instructed policemen to stay out of saloons and enjoined them from moonlighting as enforcers for employers in strikes. He halted the practice of warrantless raids. The police, he declared proudly, ticking off his early achievements, "do not club boys and defenseless people in this town . . . nor break into houses without warrants, either." Citizens were encouraged to visit the new mayor personally if they had complaints against the police. One New Yorker who took Gaynor up on the offer was Owney "the Killer" Madden, leader of the Gopher gang in Hell's Kitchen. The police had gone to Madden's hangout to investigate a loud-noise complaint. Pounding on the door, they had been met by gunfire from one of the windows. Eventually they had entered by another window and subdued the gangsters with their clubs. Madden, still a minor, was given a lecture by the judge and released on bond. Not satisfied to have gotten off easy, the young hoodlum decided to lodge a protest with Mayor Gaynor, who sympathized sufficiently to issue a general order prohibiting policemen from using their clubs except in defense of their lives.

Around the same time, a Brooklyn patrolman received a five-day suspension for clubbing a burglar who had resisted arrest. Such cases were having a demoralizing effect on the police, critics charged. "It sometimes seems that we are not trying the crooks, but the policemen who appear against them," one judge declared. "It is now nearly two years," he added, "since I've had a pickpocket before me for trial. . . . Apparently the police are afraid to do their duty."

Most New Yorkers probably didn't care about the treatment meted out to someone like Madden. (As young as he was, he had already earned his nickname. Four years later, he would be sent up for murder, to emerge as one of the gang lords of the 1920s.) Gaynor was also out of step with public opinion in some of his other decisions, such as discontinuing the regular police lineups of arrested thugs and destroying their rogues' gallery photos and criminal histories. Yet at the beginning of his term, there was a widespread readiness to forgive the particulars of Gaynor's policies as expressions of an independent and courageous mind. He was an ornery man—but people liked him for it. Every morning, Gaynor would walk the three and a half miles from home to work, and with his Vandyke beard and the high silk hat that he wore even on his daily crossings of the Brooklyn Bridge, he became a familiar and respected figure. When New Yorkers waved, he would merely grunt and nod. Still, they went on waving. Gaynor was the preeminent antipolitician of his day, renowned and even admired for his witty candor. "Now that the election is over, nobody has any immediate reason for lying," he remarked early in his term. During his brief initial surge of popularity, there was even talk of him as a Democratic candidate for president in 1912.

Ten months after his election, Gaynor decided that he needed a rest and booked passage to Europe on a transatlantic liner. On the morning of his departure, a small crowd of well-wishers gathered at the Hoboken Pier across the Hudson River. Standing on the promenade deck, the mayor was acknowledging the cheers with his usual grunts when a man lunged forward, gun in hand, and shot him. On his way to the hospital, with the bullet lodged just under his right ear, Gaynor told an aide to prepare a statement of farewell to the people. Three weeks earlier, the gunman had been discharged for incompetence from his job as a watchman for the New York City Department of Docks and had written the mayor petitioning for reinstatement. When the cops searched him, they found in his pocket a crumpled letter from Gaynor's secretary. The mayor, it said, could do nothing for him.

Against expectations, including his own, Gaynor recovered, although the bullet remained in his head, interfering with his speech, so that his normally harsh voice became even more grating. Some felt he was never the same afterward. But if so, the bullet may not have been the only explanation. In dealing with vice, Gaynor was coming up against urban realities that didn't square with the idealized picture he had presented in some of his judicial opinions: Simply put, vice and violence had become inseparably entwined.

One of the forces responsible was the automobile. As Lower East Side gangsters and gamblers branched out into the Tenderloin, they brought with them the rougher methods of the Bowery, including the employment of sluggers—hired through such contractors as Big Jack Zelig—to beat or kill troublesome rivals. Cars not only helped underworld business magnates get around to their various outposts but made it easier for them to carry rifles and other weapons with them. When it became necessary to use these tools, a car provided a means of quick escape.

In April 1910, the city recorded its first automobile-related murder when a gang leader named Spanish Louie was hit by rifle fire from a passing Pierce-Arrow on Second Avenue. Although no arrests were made, the authorities eventually identified, among the occupants of this pioneering getaway car, three of Big Jack Zelig's main operatives: "Gyp the Blood" (Harry Horowitz), "Lefty Louie" (Louis Rosenberg), and "Whitey Lewis" (Jacob Siedenshiner). Gyp the Blood had begun as a bouncer in the Monk Eastman mold and Lefty Louie as a pickpocket, while Whitey Lewis had made his reputation with a blackjack. Another suspect, Boob Walker, was a close associate of the gambling magnate

Bridgey Webber, who was known to have employed the same crew of enforcers on other occasions. Mayor Gaynor's policies were posited on the gentlemanly behavior of a previous generation of gamblers. The new crowd did things differently. And if the mayor was behind the times, the man he eventually chose as his police commissioner was even more seriously out of touch.

Thanks to the single-commissioner law, enacted in 1900, the NYPD now had the the clear command structure for which Roosevelt, among others, had longed. Or so it appeared. The legislation replaced the city's four-member board with a police commissioner who served a five-year term and could be removed only for cause (either by the mayor or by the governor). The commissioner could choose his own deputies, name his own precinct and borough commanders, and scatter to the four corners of the city those cops, of whatever rank, who didn't enjoy his trust. He could bring formal charges against cops who broke the rules, as he interpreted them; he could even dismiss an officer from the force, though such an action had to stand up in court if the cop sued to get his job back.

Statutorily, the commissioner had vast authority. Practically, though, he served at the pleasure of the mayor, and his deputies were often selected by "the Hall" (City or Tammany, with input from Brooklyn and, in later years, the Bronx). When told to leave, he did so; wise commissioners understood, as foolish ones discovered, that the mayor could slash their budgets, publicly embarrass them, and even put them on trial for offenses real or imagined. The force recognized the reality long before the reformers did. If it didn't like a particular commissioner, it waited him out. When Frank Moss asked a captain to define the kind of commissioner the brass liked, he replied, "A nice, honest gentleman who does not know he is alive. He makes a good front . . . while the insiders do the business behind his back."

With Roosevelt's image burnished by the luster of his presidency (1901–9), many hoped that a new, unfettered TR would come along and set the police department right for good. Instead, the single-commissioner law produced a parade of top-hatted gentlemen who sat at Teddy's old desk barely long enough to locate the bathroom. It was not hard for a mayor to appoint an outsider who reeked of integrity—a soldier, a judge, or a blueblood—and, if things went bad, to replace him with yet another such figure. The police commissioners of the first decade of the twentieth century included John Partridge, a militia colonel and distinguished engineer, and General Francis

Greene, who had finished first in the West Point class of 1870 and served in the Philippines during the Spanish-American War. General Theodore Bingham, Mayor McClellan's commissioner, had been the superintendent of grounds of Washington, D.C., and a military aide to President Roosevelt. The old superintendent or chief-of-police position, meanwhile, had been renamed chief inspector. It had little turnover. Only two men held the post from 1901 to 1917.

Rhinelander Waldo, the eighth commissioner to pass through headquarters in ten years—and by general consent the most hapless—was a thirty-four-year-old former army captain who had been Gaynor's fire commissioner. His mother's family, the Rhinelanders, traced their origins to the earliest days of the Dutch settlement, and Waldo was connected by blood and marriage to many descendants of the Knickerbocker elite. He was a clean and energetic young man with the manner of an earnest cadet—cartoonists often drew him in a Boy Scout uniform. His career to date had been marked more by enthusiasm than by accomplishment, however. After graduating from West Point in 1901, he had been dispatched to the Philippines, where he had fought against rebels and Moro tribesmen. After the creation of the Philippine Constabulary, a militarized police force, Waldo was assigned to it with a rank of captain and went off with 250 men into the jungles and swamps in pursuit of bandits. Tired of soldiering, he returned to New York City in 1905. The following year, he was named a deputy police commissioner under General Bingham. In 1907, he quit to head the police force for the Catskill water system. His subsequent post as fire commissioner gave him the opportunity to rush to blazes, give orders, and get his picture in the paper. Waldo fancied himself an authority on international policing, and leather-bound editions of books on the subject adorned his apartment at the Ritz-Carlton. Upon taking over as police commissioner, he announced that he intended to make the New York Police Department a replica of Scotland Yard.

He was Gaynor's third police commissioner, replacing a former judicial colleague, Judge Joseph Cropsey of Brooklyn. The mayor, with his strong convictions about law enforcement, had had difficulty finding someone who could carry out his policies to his satisfaction. But the fast shuffle of Gaynor's police commissioners also reflected a growing awareness, on the part of the public and of the mayor himself, that vice and violence were getting out of hand.

The police had been ordered to ignore vice establishments that were out-wardly orderly. To reduce the danger of police shakedowns of after-hours liquor establishments, officers were told not even to enter such places; if they suspected a problem, they were to file an affidavit with the district attorney, who could then secure a warrant. The ever attentive Reverend Parkhurst raised a logical objection: if a cop would take a payoff not to "pull" a dive on the spot, why couldn't he equally well be bribed not to file an affidavit?

In fairness to Mayor Gaynor, his ideas on these matters were subtle and complex. By the time they had filtered down to the streets, though, the mes-sage was a good deal simpler: to the vice cops, it meant free-flowing graft. To the gamblers and gangsters, it meant a wide-open town; even Big Tim Sullivan found their behavior alarming. In 1911, the legislature rushed through a law that still carries his name, making it a felony punishable by seven years' imprisonment to carry a gun without a permit. Now, at least, the police had some leverage against hoodlums. Some of them, like Zelig, took the precau-tion of having their pockets sewn shut so that a cop or a rival gangster could not plant a gun on them.

Grappling with some of the same problems more than half a century later, police commissioner Patrick V. Murphy would all but make gambling legal by ordering an end to most enforcement of the laws against it. But when Rhinelander Waldo took over as commissioner in 1911, the city was far from ready for such a drastic step. What was needed, plainly, was a crackdown—even Mayor Gaynor had come around to that view. So Waldo did the tradi-tional thing: he ordered raids. And to run one of several headquarters squads that were set up to carry out the new program, he chose a cop renowned for his ruthlessness: Charles Becker, now a forty-year-old lieutenant working the desk at the Madison Street stationhouse.

Waldo had already made a number of key personnel decisions. For dep-uty commissioner in charge of the Detective Bureau, he picked George Dougherty, who, before his appointment, had run the New York office of the Pinkerton detective agency. Assisting him was the central office detective inspector, Edward Hughes. Both men were later accused of graft. Another Waldo appointee, the secretary of the department—chief of staff to the commissioner, in effect—was a former *New York World* reporter, Winfield Sheehan, who would go on to be a major Hollywood producer. Sheehan had a side job as a member of Tim Sullivan's gambling commission. Becker's appointment, then, was far from the only indication of Waldo's deficiencies as a judge of character. Still, Becker was an extreme case.

The son of German immigrants, he had grown up on a farm upstate, working as a baker's assistant and Bowery beer-garden bouncer before joining the force in 1893. Although he and Clubber Williams overlapped only briefly, Becker became a staunch defender of his, and, like Williams, he collected more than his share of complaints from citizens. A respectable New Jersey matron who asked him for directions claimed that when she didn't understand his answer and asked him to repeat it, he arrested her on a drunk charge. Another time, Becker and his partner shot at a suspected burglar, killed an innocent bystander, and tried to cover up by claiming that the dead man was the burglar. Becker's first wife died of pneumonia shortly after their marriage. (Years later, with his career at a low ebb, people would suggest, without supplying any evidence, that he had drowned her in a bathtub.) His second wife divorced him and married his brother. In 1905, he married again, and this time it took. Becker and his third wife, Helen, a public-school teacher of handicapped children, were often seen together holding hands.

A bond with Clubber Williams meant conflict with Max Schmittberger, who had ratted on him. In 1901, Becker found himself under Schmittberger's command, and soon enough Max had him transferred elsewhere. Becker retaliated by claiming that he had been punished for arresting saloonkeepers friendly with the captain. (He eventually withdrew the accusation, but it added to his reputation as a wild man.) Becker was the kind of cop viewed with suspicion by reform and machine administrations alike; it took him ten years to advance to roundsman, and his record was such that, in 1905, Commissioner McAdoo refused to make him a sergeant. The next year, though, with McAdoo gone, a new deputy commissioner picked Becker for a special shoofly squad to check up on the commander of the Third District—who was none other than Max Schmittberger. Becker's squad proceeded to go on a raiding rampage, gaining him a reputation as someone who, in the words of one fellow cop, "would raid his own crippled grandmother if he thought it would make him look good at headquarters." The objective, which Becker more than met, was to bust enough gambling joints and brothels to suggest that Schmittberger had been derelict. Schmittberger was put on departmental trial, although with the reformers rallying to his support, he won acquittal. In 1909, he was named chief inspector.

Despite that reversal, Becker had made a positive impression on Rhinelander Waldo, the deputy police commissioner who had chosen him for the assignment. Accordingly, Becker was promoted to sergeant and then, after the department returned to its pre–Civil War hierarchy by abolishing the rank of roundsman, to lieutenant along with all the other sergeants. When Waldo returned to the force as police commissioner, Becker's career took off once again. At first, he was placed in command of a squad charged with going after gangsters and gunmen. In October 1911, pleased with Becker's work, Waldo gave him the added duty of suppressing gambling.

Becker was a formidable-looking man with huge arms and a fierce visage—"picturesque as a wolf," in Stephen Crane's words. Herbert Bayard Swope of the *World* was another journalist who had an opportunity to study him at close range. "His eyes are brown and look straight at you," Swope wrote. "He is dark in hair and skin. His nose is big and straight . . . jutting out uncompromisingly over a long upper lip, a mouth like the cut of a knife, and a chin that sticks out squarely at the end of a jaw that looks like a granite block."

In his eighteen-year career, Becker had never been handed such a fat opportunity. He wasted no time making the proper arrangements with Bald Jack Rose, a leading gambler and fixer, who would later claim that in ten months he and his lieutenants had collected $640,000 ($10 million today) for Becker; he, in turn, passed a share of the money on to Dougherty, Hughes, Sheehan, and local commanders in the Tenderloin. The motivation for Rose's generosity was fairly straightforward: either you met the price that Becker set or he raided your place and chopped it to pieces. "It was money or the ax," one city official explained at the time.

The newly powerful and affluent Becker now moved in circles far above those of a police lieutenant. He was a Broadway regular, often stopping in at fashionable nightspots with his pal Bat Masterson, sports editor of the *Morning Telegraph*, who would regale the crowd with tales of his days as a Western lawman. The $2,200-a-year cop sometimes rode around in a chauffeured limousine, courtesy of a rich friend, and reporters eagerly sought him out. He retained the services of a sort of press agent, one Charles Plitt, who helped fill the newspapers with the exploits of Becker's strong-arm squad. Soon Becker was in a position to put down $9,000 in cash for a two-story Tudor house in the Bronx.

Some of this newfound prosperity was the result of a fortuitous encounter that took place on New Year's Eve at the annual Elks Club ball. There, Becker, who was off-duty and accompanied by his wife, met Herman Rosenthal, one of the second-tier members of the Lower East Side gambling fraternity. Rosenthal had fallen on hard times, but, like any other businessman with financial problems, he emphasized the positive, which was his readiness to pay Becker generously for protection. According to Rosenthal's later recollection, the two men developed a strong and sudden mutual affection. Rosenthal would claim that Becker kissed him that night; Becker would deny it. Such details aside, it seems clear that with Bald Jack Rose's encouragement, they reached a financial accommodation. And the highly emotional Rosenthal plainly expected more from the relationship than he got.

Among the Lower East Side crowd were a few gamblers noted for their talkativeness as well as their violence. Having made their deals with the law, these "holler guys," as they were known, felt free to complain whenever they received anything less than top-drawer service. Unsurprisingly, they were not popular with the police. Inspector Sweeney of the Sixth District, up in Harlem, refused to take Jewish money unless it had been laundered by intermediaries. Lieutenant Becker was not so fastidious. But, as he explained to Rosenthal, he was in a delicate position. There were limits to the amount of protection he could offer. He had superiors to worry about. They, in turn, had to answer to the mayor, the D.A., and the various reform groups. Every now and again, citizens known as "kickers" would write City Hall or police headquarters with specific information about gambling joints and houses of prostitution. In such situations, the police had to do *something*.

Most gamblers understood these realities and put up with raids or even the occasional inconvenience of being shut down for a spell. Rosenthal, despite his professions of love for Lieutenant Becker, was a holler guy. Prior to their association, in fact, he and several other discontented gamblers had gone to see Mayor Gaynor. The mayor, of course, had invited New Yorkers to come in with tales of their mistreatment by the police; Rosenthal's delegation got no sympathy from him, however. They were "the worst gang of men I had ever seen," he said later. They were asking him for help, moreover, in carrying on an illegal activity—that struck even Gaynor as a bit much. But then, no one had ever accused Rosenthal of being discreet. On another occasion, Inspector Cornelius Hayes, who was responsible for a large piece of midtown

Manhattan, raised Rosenthal's hackles by implying that he ran a "crooked wheel" at his place on West Forty-fifth Street. "That's a lie!" Rosenthal was said to have exclaimed in response. "I got straight faro tables and two honest wheels in my house." On the basis of their exchange, Hayes secured a warrant, and Rosenthal's establishment was raided and shut down—only four days after he had opened it.

"The trouble with Herman is that he don't know the rules," one old-time gambler told the *Evening Post* when Rosenthal's difficulties worsened. "The rules are, pay your license money, . . . lay low, and play like gentlemen. When you get a hint, take it and close down."

Rosenthal was already on the outs with many of his fellow gamblers and with several midtown police commanders. His relationship with Becker soon went sour, too. In March, Charles Plitt, Becker's press agent, shot and killed a man while accompanying the police on a raid. Plitt was charged with murder. Becker raised a defense fund by putting a special assessment on the gamblers. Rosenthal refused to contribute.

Becker knew how to deal with "hard givers." Rosenthal got the axe, of course—his Forty-fifth Street place, which he had just managed to reopen, was raided and shut down once more, and this time Becker had a patrolman stationed outside to scare away patrons. Putting a cop in front of a raided gambling house was a common practice, but usually it was just for show. "This is a gambling house and likely to be raided any minute," the officer would tell an arriving customer. "If you go in, you are knowingly entering an unlawful resort, and what I tell you may be used against you." This was how strangers would be greeted, at any rate; with regulars, the cop would skip the song and dance and say, "Good evening, sir. A fine night, indeed." For the cop, it meant ten dollars a night, an occasional bottle of good liquor from the house, and a cigar (sometimes with a bill wrapped around it) from the customers as they went in. At Rosenthal's establishment, though, even the regulars got the rough treatment, making him angrier—so angry that he locked his police guard inside the building one day. His next step was to file a lawsuit against Inspector Hayes and his subordinate, Captain William Day, commander of the West Forty-seventh Street precinct—the two men officially responsible for stationing the officer at his place.

Sorting out such situations was one of the tasks of Tim Sullivan's gambling commission. Normally, Sullivan and his aides would have moved in to discipline Becker and Rosenthal. By now, however, Big Tim was mentally unbalanced, apparently from the effects of venereal disease. So Rosenthal was on his own and he could think of no recourse but to make an even bigger holler. He had already been to the mayor. Now he went to Herbert Bayard Swope at the *World*. Swope, in turn, took Rosenthal to see the Manhattan district attorney, Charles Whitman.

In the long lineage of muckraking journalists and crusading prosecutors, few have played the game more artfully than these two, although it took some prodding from Swope to make Whitman see the full potential of the case. Swope was a dandy who would turn up at an East Side murder in white tie and tails, after the fashion of his role model, Richard Harding Davis, the leading gentleman-journalist of the day. After coming to New York from St. Louis eleven years earlier, at the age of nineteen, Swope had spent a good deal of his young adulthood hanging around the crap tables and racetracks. Whitman, a minister's son from New Hampshire, had had a plodding legal career until 1907, when, as a compromise choice for the generally low-profile job of president of the city's board of magistrates, he had taken a page from William Travers Jerome's book by roaming the city and raiding after-hours joints. Elected to his current office at the same time Gaynor won his, Whitman would be cited by U.S. Supreme Court Justice Felix Frankfurter as the prototype of "the politically minded D.A.—one of the great curses of America."

In Herman Rosenthal, Whitman had trouble seeing beyond the obvious: his incoherence, his boasting, his mental instability. Swope, by contrast, was willing to invest the kind of time it took to clean up Rosenthal's account and supply a story line that people could follow. And while Rosenthal was initially inclined not to mention Lieutenant Becker by name, Swope convinced him that he wouldn't get the kind of attention he craved if he held a detail of that kind back.

Like Whitman, Swope's superiors at the *World* were reluctant to make Rosenthal the linchpin of a major exposé. Swope insisted that his friend the D.A. intended to investigate, but the editors wanted confirmation. So Swope rushed up to Newport, Rhode Island, where Whitman was staying with some swells of his acquaintance. In the face of Swope's badgering, Whitman agreed to state for the record that he planned to interview Rosenthal again. His luke-warm endorsement was enough to win over Swope's editors, and the *World* went with his story, which filled most of the first two pages of the paper on Sunday, July 14, 1912.

The article focused squarely on Lieutenant Becker. It described the New Year's Eve meeting where, according to Rosenthal, Becker had introduced him to three members of the gambling squad, saying, "This is my best pal and do anything he wants you to do." Before things had gone sour between them, Becker and Rosenthal had met frequently, according to the latter, either at the Elks Club or at the Lafayette Street Turkish Baths. Becker had bragged about "getting hold of a lot of money" in his new job. He was even said to have sought and obtained a 20 percent interest in the Forty-fifth Street place, putting up $1,500 for it.

The night after Swope's sensational story appeared, Rosenthal showed up at the Metropole Hotel on West Forty-third Street. Something was in the works—that much seemed clear to everyone present, including Rosenthal. But while his peers shied away from him, and some even left the premises rather than linger in his company, Rosenthal appeared to be more excited than worried. He left the Metropole briefly to buy the evening papers, including seven copies of the *World*, which featured a follow-up story on his revelations.

"What about *that* for a headline?" Rosenthal said, proudly displaying the paper to the few buddies of his who remained.

Shortly before 2:00 A.M., a man stepped into the Metropole and spoke the last words that Rosenthal would ever hear: "Can you come outside a minute, Herman?" He went willingly, taking the papers with him and leaving a dollar on the table to cover eighty cents' worth of drinks.

Rosenthal was shot four times at close range—in the neck, in the nose, and twice in the side of his head. He fell to the sidewalk, bleeding profusely, and some of the newspapers landed on top of him, "so that he seemed to lie in a grotesque shroud of early editions," as Andy Logan put it in her account of the affair. The gunmen—four or five in all—fled in a 1909 Packard. An off-duty detective named Billy Files, a onetime sparring partner of former heavyweight champion Jim Corbett's, was sitting in the Metropole at the time and, hearing the shots, drew his gun and ran outside. Meanwhile, a group of nearby beat cops commandeered a taxi and gave chase, but they lost the fugitive vehicle.

Rosenthal's body attracted a crowd of "street walkers, gamblers, soft-treading gentry of ill-chosen professions," according to one newspaper account. "Chorus girls and their rattle-brained escorts joke[d] heartlessly."

"Hello, Herman," said one of his gambling compatriots, peering down at the remains. "*Good-bye,* Herman."

The news traveled fast. "Ye gods," was Rhinelander Waldo's reaction when reached around 2:30 A.M. at the Ritz-Carlton. Despite his shock, Waldo apparently saw no need to rouse himself. Such distasteful matters were for his line commanders to handle, leaving Waldo free to concentrate on more important duties, such as a police chiefs' conference in Toronto, where, a few days earlier, he had presented a paper entitled "How to Wipe Out Police Graft."

District Attorney Whitman's first instinct was similar, at least in Swope's telling. Whitman thought the case could wait until morning.

"No, you've got to come right now," Swope insisted.

"But I'm in bed," Whitman protested. "I've got my pajamas on."

He got dressed and went anyway, after Swope fetched him personally and shamed him into it.

Becker, alerted by a reporter for the *Sun,* rushed to the Sixteenth Precinct stationhouse, on West Forty-seventh Street, where Rosenthal's body had been moved, in accordance with standard police practice. Becker apparently hoped to take a hand in the investigation. But by the time he arrived, he found Whitman seated at the captain's desk. The D.A. glared at him accusingly, and Becker made a quick exit.

He found the street teeming with newspapermen, to whom he asserted his innocence in characteristically grandiloquent fashion. "It ought to be needless for me to say," he declared, "—and I think I ought not to be asked to say— what you newspapermen know to be the fact that I know absolutely nothing about the crime—who perpetrated it, what the motive was, or what was to be gained by it. I want to say now that I have said this much—and perhaps I am violating a rule of the department by so saying—that it was to my best and only advantage that Rosenthal should have been permitted to live for many years. I bear this man no malice. He set himself up as my enemy. I have explained every move I made with this man to the satisfaction of my superiors." Indeed, Becker had been gathering up what he called "documentary legal evidence" with which he hoped soon to prove the falseness of the charges against him.

Whitman had been slow off the mark, but he soon made the most of a case that, in speeches to excited reform groups, he would call "a challenge to our very civilization." In a statement issued hours before the killing, Whitman had described Rosenthal contemptuously, as an unreliable witness who wasn't worth putting in front of a grand jury. That, however, was the living Herman Rosenthal. Now that he was dead, the D.A. saw him in a more respectful light. "Rosenthal," he said, "had in his hands the proof—or the close equivalent— of the alliance between the police and crime. Just as he was preparing to come to my home with additional information, just as the situation shaped up most dangerously for the police involved, he was killed, and with him dies his evidence."

As Whitman now saw things, the killing of Herman Rosenthal exposed the crookedness of the police from top to bottom. Even the cops who had chased the taxi had not made a real effort, Whitman claimed, implying that the beat men in Times Square had known what was going to happen. The police had produced several slightly bollixed renderings of the plate number on the get-away vehicle. These mistakes, in Whitman's mind, proved that they had made "little more than a pretense of pursuing the killers." The D.A. even had Files, the off-duty detective, brought up on charges of neglect of duty, deeming his mere presence in the Metropole as suspicious, though when the shots went off, the ex-boxer was at a table absorbed in conversation with a young lady. (No one who has studied the case has found any evidence that Files or the beat cops knew of a murder plot.)

With Swope at his side promising "all the help in the world," Whitman mapped out a long-term battle plan—a strategy for breaking the case and, at the same time, cracking down on gambling and prostitution. Seeking and obtaining the financial backing of a group of rich businessmen, Whitman leased a suite at the Waldorf (then at Thirty-fourth Street and Fifth Avenue) as the headquarters for his vast probe. Later, wealthy backers would provide another $200,000, enabling him to use private detectives to assist in the investigation, since the cops could plainly not be trusted. The getaway car's license was soon traced, and the shooters were identified as Gyp the Blood, Whitey Lewis, Lefty Louie, and "Dago" Frank Cirofici. In custody, they quickly confessed, naming the men who had hired them: Bald Jack Rose and the dognapper and drug dealer Bridgey Webber. When they, in turn, were arrested, it became apparent that they were what Whitman needed—witnesses who could link Becker to the murder. Rose and Webber both cut deals for immunity. They, too, of course, had motives for wanting to get rid of Rosenthal. Webber ran a gambling joint on the same block of West Forty-fifth Street. Rosenthal was competition, and with his loud ways he was making it impossible for other gamblers to operate, even the more discreet ones. With a straight face, Rose told the D.A. that Becker had threatened to plant a gun on him if he didn't arrange the murder. His story was thin stuff, but the prosecution built a case around it. Becker was transferred to a Bronx precinct—a sign that the department was going to "let him splash," or, in other words, not back him up. A few days later, while working the desk, he was taken into custody by detectives from the D.A.'s office, charged with murder, and sent to the Tombs.

Gaynor and Waldo were completely unhinged by now. Even before the Rosenthal killing, the newspapers had been holding Waldo up to ridicule; he had sued three of them for libel. When Gaynor issued a statement criticizing Becker for having sat down to dinner with a man like Rosenthal, the press made it look as though he was accusing the lieutenant of a mere social faux pas. The mayor tried to minimize Becker's importance, referring to him as "just a little lieutenant." Echoing his old enemy Theodore Bingham, Gaynor characterized the murderers and their victim as "degenerate foreigners," by which he seemed to mean Jews. Prominent Jewish leaders protested that the vices of the Tenderloin, until recent years "proverbially unknown among our people," were the result of "the moral and political degeneracy of the city."

Angry at his elite critics, Gaynor ordered Waldo to crack down on the after-hours night spots along the Great White Way. The strong-arm squads obligingly began to throw society people in evening dress headfirst into the street. They stopped when Whitman and Richard Harding Davis, caught drinking at a fashionable establishment known as Healey's, led a group of well-heeled uptown types in organized resistance and brought charges against the inspector who had ordered the raid. After that, Gaynor threw in the towel.

If Becker had come right out and admitted his grafting, he might have won more respect for his denial of murder. It was far from clear who decided that Rosenthal should be killed rather than merely beaten up or sent out of town.

A few years later, evidence would surface that strongly suggested that his execution had been an impromptu decision by Webber and Rose or the hit men themselves. But Becker staked out a claim of near-total innocence. Perhaps he could not bring himself to admit anything else to his wife; at any rate, she stuck by him throughout, even to the point of telling reporters that her penny-pinching ways had allowed them to save up the money for the down payment on their bungalow in the Bronx.

Becker must surely have felt that the game was tilted against him when his trial was assigned to Judge John Goff. Whitman, for his part, delegated the day-to-day business of prosecuting Becker to Frank Moss, the Reverend Parkhurst's former counsel. Becker was represented by an old-time New York criminal lawyer of Irish revolutionary sympathies who had won an acquittal in London for a Fenian accused of plotting to kill Queen Victoria. Helen Becker, who was Irish, apparently picked him on the theory that he would know how to soften up Judge Goff. She was obviously not acquainted with New York's cruelest judge, who consistently ruled for the prosecution, sometimes even before being asked to. It couldn't have helped Becker, either, to have retired Inspector Clubber Williams in the courtroom daily, lending his support. To compound matters, the jury that convicted Becker was drawn not from his peers but from a panel of affluent citizens—the type found on reform committees. Just before the trial opened, Big Jack Zelig was shot to death on a streetcar for reasons unrelated to the Becker case, though Whitman implied publicly that Becker's friends had rubbed out a key witness.

Briefly it appeared that Becker might escape the death penalty. After Goff handed down the mandatory death sentence, the defendant hired a new team of lawyers, and they convinced the Court of Appeals to reverse the verdict, citing, among other problems, prejudicial behavior by the judge. In May 1914, Becker was tried a second time, now before a more restrained jurist, the aristocratic Samuel Seabury, and with the famously eloquent William Bourke Cockran (oratorical role model to Winston Churchill, among others) arguing his case. Once again, however, he was convicted and sentenced to die in the electric chair. Even at this late stage, Becker might have saved his life by confessing and naming names; but a man in the mold of Clubber Williams was not likely to break down, nor was he encouraged to do so by Tammany's Cockran.

In the midst of the furor, Tim Sullivan, too ill to take his place in the state senate, was elected to a less demanding berth in Congress. Even this proved too taxing for Sullivan, who was soon committed to private care in the Bronx. Then, in August 1913, he escaped from his keepers and was run over by a freight train—or so it was claimed. Sullivan lay in the Bellevue morgue for ten days, unidentified, until a policeman recognized him and went screaming through the wards shouting, "It's Big Tim! Lord God, it's Big Tim."

Mayor Gaynor had not been renominated by Tammany, although he was offered a ballot line by a citizens' committee. A month after Sullivan's death, he died on an ocean liner while taking a short vacation. The acting mayor who succeeded him dismissed Commissioner Waldo, on the grounds that Waldo had been willing to sacrifice the interests of the department to "satisfy his pique." (Claiming he had resigned, Waldo sued to change the official city record, but a court ruled that it lacked the power to do so. He served as a colonel in World War I and afterward dabbled in politics, switching from the Democratic Party to the Republican. He died in 1927 at the age of fifty.)

Becker's wife pressed for clemency to the very end, finally pleading on her knees to the governor. It cannot have been easy for her, since the governor, newly elected, was Charles Whitman. Indeed, he had campaigned for the office as the man who had nailed her husband. Mrs. Becker nevertheless went through with her appeal, which Whitman denied. The way was then clear for Becker to become the first (and, to date, last) New York City cop to be put to death by the state.

At this point, things went less smoothly. The execution team, apparently failing to reckon with Becker's considerable bulk, set the voltage too low. Twice the switch was pulled, the body heaved, sparks flew, and Becker's heart was found to be beating still. Each time, he was duly strapped in again, until, on the third try, his life finally expired. His coffin carried a silver plate inscribed, at his wife's instructions: "Charles Becker. Murdered July 30, 1915, by Governor Whitman." Only the threat of prosecution for criminal libel by the governor dissuaded her from placing the same words on his tombstone.

9

The NYPD Goes to War

On Saturday night, July 29, 1916, the sky was clear, the temperature in the sixties, the streets crowded. Only the rich went away for weekends in those days; to many New Yorkers, however, the city felt like a fine place to be. At Ebbets Field, more than twenty thousand people turned out to watch the Dodgers beat the Cincinnati Reds, whose new manager, Christy Mathewson, had been the idol of New York when he pitched for the Giants. The Giants were in town, too, with thirty thousand fans filling the Polo Grounds to see them beat Pittsburgh. In midtown, bars, dance halls, nickelodeons, and theaters were doing a lively business. Fanny Brice was starring in the Ziegfeld Follies at the New Amsterdam, on Forty-second Street. One group was conspicuously absent. That summer, the world's first major polio epidemic had hit New York City, and most of the victims were children. Trolleys refused to carry them, theaters would not admit them, and wise parents kept them at home. (By October, when the epidemic had run its course, some nine thousand cases had been recorded, more than a quarter of them fatal.) Much of the commercial entertainment had an adult orientation, in any case. Couples went to dance halls and men to gambling joints and bordellos, which operated more discreetly now. Another reform administration was in power at City Hall, and from the Bronx to Brooklyn, the Becker case still cast a powerful spell over the police. The next day would be the first anniversary of his execution.

A big streetcar strike was in progress. On Friday, some of the five thousand strikers had attacked a group of scabs hired to replace them. When police moved in, there were clashes. A car carrying Chief Inspector Max Schmittberger and a deputy commissioner was surrounded by strikers; in the ensuing melee, a trolley struck their vehicle. That same day, a mob of two hundred Wobblies (members of the Industrial Workers of the World, or IWW), led by the Irish revolutionary labor leader Jim Larkin, had wrecked the offices of the Italian-American newspaper *Il Progresso* because the editor would not run a column urging freedom for a group of jailed radicals. The Wobblies beat several cops, including a detective captain who raced to the scene.

In France, there was numbing slaughter, and no obvious progress for either side. If the war had a clear winner at this stage, it was the United States, with its economy booming on the strength of Allied war orders. Every day, ships left New York Harbor loaded with munitions and other goods for England, France, and Russia, over German protests against the violation of America's declared neutrality. Most Americans sympathized with the Allies—but not with former president Teddy Roosevelt's call for a declaration of war against Germany. A presidential campaign was under way, and the Republican candidate was a former New York governor, Charles Evan Hughes. But Woodrow Wilson's reelection theme, "He kept us out of war," struck a deep chord with New Yorkers, as it did with other Americans.

In the early hours of Sunday, July 30, the war came to New York. At 2:08 A.M., a huge explosion rocked the city. All over Manhattan and Brooklyn, windows fell from buildings. Leaping out of bed, or thrown out, people ran into the streets in panic. The Brooklyn Bridge swayed, to the horror of New Yorkers driving home from their night's amusements. The shock from the blast was felt as far south as Philadelphia. An even larger explosion followed half an hour later. Those with a view of the harbor could see spectacular fires burning on the New Jersey waterfront. Shells and shrapnel rained down on Ellis Island. The immigrants detained there had to be evacuated to the mainland. Hundreds of policemen, in fleets of commandeered taxicabs, were dispatched downtown, where they found burglar alarms ringing on every block and sidewalks filled with broken glass. But the expected looting did not take place: even the criminals were frightened. Four people, including an infant hurled out of bed in Jersey City, were killed or presumed dead.

The next day, screaming headlines reported that two million pounds of munitions waiting to be shipped to the Allies had blown up near the Statue of Liberty on what was known as Black Tom Island—so named because, from the air, it supposedly resembled a black cat, though landfill had turned it from an island into a mile-long promontory jutting out from the Jersey shore. (Today the area is known as Liberty Park.) The cause of the explosion was unclear, but many suspected the work of German agents. Irish revolutionaries tended to feel an affinity for the Germans, based on shared hatred of the British. Jim Larkin, who had been deeply involved in German sabotage plans, decided that a quick trip to Mexico would be good for his health. A young woman named Meena Edwards, known as the "Eastman Girl" because of her appearance in ads for the company's cameras, was vacationing on the Jersey shore, twenty-five miles south, when she heard the explosion. She, too, had had dealings with German agents, though of a more personal nature, and she had heard Black Tom discussed as a likely target for sabotage. At New York City police headquarters, where detectives were actively engaged in countering spies and saboteurs, there was no question about whether America should get into the war. Under the reform mayor, John Purroy Mitchel, and his police commissioner, Arthur Woods, the police had been in it since the beginning.

Two years earlier, on August 1, 1914, the day before Germany presented an ultimatum to Belgium, commissioner Woods had formed a thirty-four-man bomb squad under the command of acting captain Thomas Tunney. These "special service" squads were the department's standard organizational response to unusual problems. Tunney, a burly forty-year-old, was well prepared for the job. He had joined the force in Roosevelt's time, spending much of his career working with another special service squad on bombings by anarchists and Black Handers.

If an act of terrorism similar to Black Tom occurred today, the Federal Bureau of Investigation would have jurisdiction. But in 1916, the FBI was in its infancy. In fact, law enforcement at the federal level hardly existed, and the NYPD, which had the country's largest and most experienced detective branch, filled the void. As far back as the 1870s, the department had maintained a lively interest in foreigners who could be seen as security threats. Under Inspector Byrnes, Sergeant Charles Jacobs and other "Red" experts kept an eye on places like Justus Schwab's saloon, near Tompkins Square, where

Johann Most hung out. Most exemplified the bomb-throwing radical for many Americans, although he is not known to have ever actually hurled one. A German-born socialist, he had come to New York after running out of European countries to agitate in. He had already done prison time in Austria (for leading a demonstration outside Parliament), in Germany (for making a revolutionary speech), and in England (for publishing an article celebrating the assassination of Czar Alexander III). His behavior didn't change much when he reached America in 1882, nor did his treatment by the authorities. In his newspaper, *Freiheit,* Most denounced the trial of the eight anarchists charged in the Haymarket bombing in Illinois—and was promptly arrested by Byrnes's men. He got a year in jail. After his release, he became part of a ménage à trois with two other East Side radicals, Alexander Berkman and Emma Goldman. In 1892, at the Carnegie steel plant in Homestead, Pennsylvania, ten people were killed in a battle between striking steelworkers and Pinkerton detectives. Most's two friends went to Homestead, where Berkman shot and wounded Henry Clay Frick, the plant manager. For this, Berkman drew sixteen years in a Pennsylvania state prison. He was denounced, unexpectedly, by Most, who in turn was horsewhipped at a meeting by Goldman. She herself was picked up by Sergeant Jacobs, who audaciously attempted to convince her to become a police informant. She threw a glass of water in his face.

Johann Most was a hard drinker, and there were times when he couldn't crank out quite enough copy to fill his small paper. In these periods, he resorted to reprints. In September 1901, he published a fifty-year-old article by a German radical urging the assassination of government leaders. President McKinley was assassinated the next day. The press, moreover, took to saying that his killer, Leon Czolgosz, had been inspired by Goldman, now something of a celebrity. Most tried his best to recall the unsold copies of his paper, but his readers at the Detective Bureau chose not to return theirs; instead, Most was arrested and put on trial. Sentenced to a year in prison, he died shortly after his release.

The killing of McKinley, along with Joe Petrosino's claim that federal authorities had ignored his warning of threats against the president, heightened the pace of the police's investigations of anarchists. In 1914, Tunney was still dealing with the aftermath of the murder of the king of Italy by Gaetano

Brescia. According to Tunney, the plot had its origins in the spring of 1900 at a meeting of anarchists in a house on Elizabeth Street. Brescia denounced some of the participants as cowards, and the meeting became so contentious that it broke up for fear the noise would bring police. Those who had felt Brescia's wrath responded with the ultimate accusation: he was a police spy. In anger, Brescia went back to Italy, where he murdered the king and was executed, becoming a martyr to the cause. In his honor, a group formed under the name the Brescia Circle. By 1914 it included nearly six hundred people meeting regularly in the basement of a shabby house at 301 East 106th Street in East Harlem, where they were often addressed by such famous radicals as Goldman and Berkman. The Brescia Circle also became involved with the IWW, which had sprung out of the great labor revolts in the West. Tunney saw little difference between the two groups. "If you scratched an anarchist," he observed, "you found an IWW underneath."

On the Fourth of July 1914, one of the Brescia Circle was arrested near the estate of John D. Rockefeller in Tarrytown, New York, twelve miles from the city. On the same day, three other members were making a bomb in their room at 104th and Lexington when it exploded and killed them. The bomb, according to the police, had been intended for the Rockefeller family. Tunney responded by insinuating a detective into the Brescia Circle, but the undercover did not speak Italian and his behavior was so aggressive that he quickly fell under suspicion and was twice put on trial by the circle, charged with spying. Both times he was acquitted, but finally he had to withdraw from the group, leaving the bomb makers to their work. On the radical's enemy list the Catholic Church held a high position, and in October 1914 bombs were set off at St. Patrick's Cathedral, seat of the New York Archdiocese, and at the priest's house of St. Alphonsus Church on the East Side. Tunney now assigned a more fitting operative to the case, a young Italian-speaking detective, Amedeo Polignani. As a result of his work, the department was ready the next time the bombers struck at St. Patrick's. In March 1915, while Bishop Patrick Hayes was celebrating Mass, two young men dressed as laborers entered the cathedral smoking cigars, which they removed and concealed in their hands. During the service, one of the men took an object from his coat pocket, set it on the floor, touched it with his lighted cigar, and quickly began to walk toward the door. Before he could leave, he was seized by a scrubwoman who had been washing the marble floor. In the meantime, an elderly man with white hair and beard extinguished the fuse attached to the device, and a tall, burly man seized the second saboteur, who was still sitting in a pew. So quickly and quietly did all these events transpire that few of the several hundred people at the service knew what had happened. The scrubwoman was Detective Patrick Walsh; the white-bearded "old" man was Detective Sergeant George Barnitz, second in command of the bomb squad; and the tall man who seized the second suspect was Captain Tunney. Barnitz's disguise was so convincing that when the group arrived at headquarters, Chief Inspector Schmittberger sought to bar him from the interrogation room where the suspects were being held. Charged and convicted in the attempted bombing, the suspects were all given substantial prison terms. When Polignani's identity became known, he received a number of death threats, and his picture was circulated in the anarchist community.

The Brescia Circle was child's play compared with the challenge that Tunney faced at the war's outbreak. Neither the United States nor Germany was prepared for an extension of the combat zone to America. The German ambassador, Count Johann von Bernstorff, however, was quickly allotted substantial funds to carry on sabotage, espionage, and propaganda. The problem was that he had very few agents with which to do so. Germany had only one spy in the United States, a New Jersey chemist, Dr. Walter Scheele (a reserve artillery officer in the Kaiser's army), who since 1893 had been performing industrial espionage. This made it necessary to employ diplomats in the dirty work. Two military attachés, Captain Karl Boy-Ed, a naval captain, and Franz von Papen, an army captain (later chancellor of Germany and, briefly, vice chancellor under Hitler), were assigned to lead a campaign of espionage and sabotage, with the commercial attaché, Heinrich Albert, serving as paymaster. New York, as the country's financial capital, its most influential journalistic center, and the principal port from which supplies were shipped to Europe, was more important than Washington, so Boy-Ed established his headquarters at 11 Broadway, overlooking the harbor. Von Papen, meanwhile, set up an intelligence center, disguised as an advertising agency, at 60 Wall Street; and Albert operated out of the Hamburg-America Shipping Line building at 45 Broadway, from which he eventually dispensed $30 million. The German high command sent agents to the United States from Europe, Latin America, and the Far East.

The German campaign was divided into two sectors, land and marine, New York being the principal focus of the latter. (In the first act of sabotage, a fire was set at a manufacturing plant in Trenton, New Jersey, on New Year's Day, 1915.) The mastermind of marine sabotage was a wealthy naval reserve captain, Franz von Rintelin, who slipped into the United States in April 1915 on a fake Swiss passport. Well connected in New York City from his previous duties as a director of the Deutsche Bank, he belonged to the exclusive New York Yacht Club, where the only prewar German members had been the Kaiser and his brother, Prince Henry. Using an import-export business as a front, von Rintelin and the attachés were able to call on the crews of ninety German ships that had been trapped in New York Harbor when the war broke out and were now being blockaded by British cruisers. At their disposal, too, were several thousand German army reservists who were unable to book passage out of the United States because the attachés could not secure enough fake passports for them.

Germany also drew recruits from the Irish-American community, whose hostility toward Britain was an old story in the United States, particularly in New York City, which provided the political and financial leadership of the revolutionary movement. A number of prominent Irish New Yorkers, including Judge Goff and the first police commissioner, Mike Murphy, had publicly urged violence against the British without being prosecuted for it. Larkin, though a Marxist and fugitive from Ireland, had many friends in the police force and was occasionally able to obtain information of value even to his non-Irish radical comrades.

Von Rintelin established a bomb factory in the middle of New York Harbor aboard an interned ship, the *Friedrich der Grosse*, eventually turning out fifty bomb containers a day. The devices were taken to Dr. Scheele's workshop in the predominantly German-American town of Hoboken, New Jersey, to be armed. Afterward, ship officers from the Hamburg-America and North German Lloyd lines distributed them to Irish-American stevedores, who planted them in the cargo holds of Allied ships, timing them to explode at sea. At least thirty-five vessels were sunk or damaged in this way.

The principal safe house for German agents in New York City was a four-story brownstone at 123 West Fifteenth Street, presided over by a dark-haired, buxom, middle-aged German opera singer, Baroness (via a forgotten marriage) Martha Held, alias Martha Gordon. Neighbors suspected the house of being a bordello, because of the strange men and unescorted ladies who entered through a basement door at all hours of the day and night. The neighbors were not exactly wrong. Using money supplied by the German government, Held had leased the house as a "recreational center" for German sea captains and other official visitors. Its existence meant that they would not have to patronize commercial vice joints, where their secrets might be exposed to the police. The attachés and von Rintelin used it to meet their agents. Held's dinner parties featured fine wine, rich cuisine, and beautiful "actresses" and "models," like the Eastman Girl, who often served as "escorts" for the guests. From time to time, hard-looking men in dockworker clothes also arrived with bombs, though according to some accounts, the most nerve-racking feature of a visit to Frau Held's establishment was having to listen to her hold forth with Wagnerian arias, since the evening's festivities never concluded until the fat lady sang.

The police would never have served the Union if Fernando Wood had been in charge of them in 1863. The Allies would not have had Tunney's bomb squad working for them, similarly, if John Mitchel had not been the mayor. At thirty-four, Mitchel was the youngest chief executive in the city's history. The "boy mayor," as the press dubbed him, was a Democrat and the grandson and namesake of an Irish-Catholic revolutionary leader. His maternal uncle was a New York City fire commissioner, and Mitchel's father had been a fire marshal noted for capturing arsonists. His family background might have made him acceptable to segments of the electorate to whom WASP reformers did not appeal. Mitchel, however, was enamored of high society. As mayor, he was photographed in Newport with the swells more often than with the regular Joes in Bushwick or Highbridge. He was temperamental and undiplomatic. His drive and independence had been assets when, as commissioner of accounts (or investigations) under McClellan, Mitchel had succeeded in obtaining the removal of the corrupt borough presidents of Manhattan and the Bronx. Later, his arrogance and insensitivity would make him many enemies. He was also unlucky. Reflecting eastern establishment opinion, he supported the Allies, and the war would drive a wedge between him and many of his Irish and German constituents. When he referred to the leader of the German-Americans, state (later U.S.) senator Robert Wagner, as "the gentleman from Prussia," even Republican legislators and Governor Whitman cried foul.

For police commissioner, Mitchel made a widely admired choice, albeit mostly by default. His first idea was to give the job to Raymond Fosdick, a young whiz kid who had written a book on European police administration. But Fosdick, who was only thirty years old, lacked gravitas as well as practical experience. With memories of Rhinelander Waldo still fresh in New Yorkers' memories, the boy mayor was not about to name a boy police commissioner; instead, he opted for a military man, Colonel George Washington Goethals, a West Point–educated army engineer who had supervised the building of the Panama Canal. Goethals was willing, but he insisted on the authority to dismiss and promote officers without being subject either to judicial review or civil-service procedures. Mitchel had a so-called Goethals bill introduced in the legislature to eliminate these inconveniences. The state government, however, was under the control of Tammany Boss Murphy at the time. To no one's surprise, Mitchel's proposal got nowhere in Albany, and Goethals was out of the picture.

The mayor now turned to his secretary, Arthur Woods, a socialite who had been a deputy commissioner under General Bingham and, more recently, a cotton broker. At forty-four, Woods was no schoolboy, and his experience in the department had taught him things that Groton and Harvard had not. Woods was quickly able to reward the mayor's confidence in him. Riding in a car with the mayor and two other city officials just a few days after taking office, he helped overpower a deranged man who took a shot at Mitchel and wounded the city tax commissioner.

Mitchel and Woods were so unashamedly in favor of intervention that, in 1915, both men volunteered for officer training at a camp in Plattsburgh, New York, established by Teddy Roosevelt's "preparedness movement." Thus, despite official U.S. neutrality, the bomb squad (which, as a sop, had been officially renamed the neutrality squad) established contact with Allied intelligence officers. Under the direction of Special Deputy Commissioner Nicholas Biddle, of the Philadelphia banking family, Tunney's men began their work by combing the sprawling waterfront—which included not only the piers in Manhattan and Brooklyn and the maze of streets and alleys that abutted them but large parts of New Jersey—searching for clues to the ships' bombings. The dockworkers were a clannish group. Many rackets flourished on the waterfront, and cops were definitely not welcome.

At first the detectives were not even sure what the bombs looked like, since the unexploded ones had been dumped overboard by the ships' crews. In May 1915, there was a break in the investigation: a ship from New York docked in Marseilles, and bombs were found in four sugar bags, which French military intelligence ordered returned to the city. The bombs turned out to consist of lead pipes divided by a copper disk into two compartments, one of them containing potassium chlorate and the other sulfuric acid. The action of the acid on the copper took place at a uniform rate and determined the amount of time that would pass before the two chemicals united to produce an explosion. The copper disk, in this case, had been too thick. Tunney's men checked sugar shipments from factory to vessel and purchases of potassium chlorate and sulfuric acid, but their investigation produced no leads. Then the French military attaché in New York City notified Tunney that an informant had been asked by a German to purchase TNT and deliver it to an address in Weehawken, New Jersey. The New York police had no jurisdiction across the river, but Tunney was undeterred. He assigned his deputy, the German-speaking George Barnitz, now an acting lieutenant, to set up a sting operation. Accompanied by Barnitz, the informant delivered the TNT, and the house where it was stored was kept under surveillance by detectives. When the occupant, a man named Faye, asked the informant to help him test the explosives in the nearby woods, Tunney called in the U.S. Secret Service, which did have authority in New Jersey, and detectives and agents surrounded the area. Faye and an accomplice were seized and a search of their house turned up dynamite, potassium chlorate, detonating caps, bomb cylinders, and four fully assembled bombs. There was also a chart of New York Harbor, and Faye was found to own a motorboat moored in the river. Even more interesting was Faye's identity. He turned out to be a German lieutenant who had been pulled out of combat on the western front and sent to New York to assist von Papen—that is, a member of the German armed forces had been assigned to bomb a neutral country. As a result of the arrest, Faye and three confederates

The Draft Riots (1863) were the largest urban insurrection in American history. Police repulsing a mob attack near the offices of Horace Greeley's *New York Tribune*. (© Museum of the City of New York)

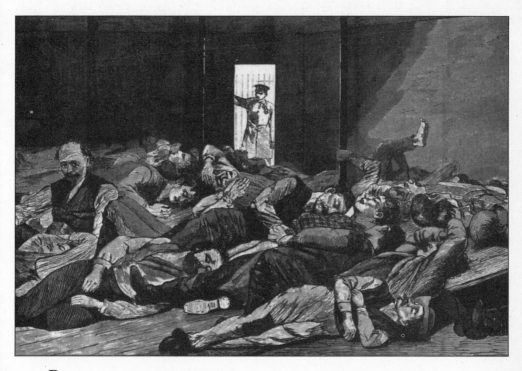

Police stations were the homeless shelters of the late nineteenth century. The practice was ended by Commissioner Roosevelt in 1896. (*Harper's Weekly*, February 7, 1874, Winslow Homer)

Tall and handsome—those were the requirements for membership in the
Broadway Squad (1880s); here a cop performs the unit's most common task: helping women and children across the street. (© Museum of the City of New York)

When trolley workers went out on strike, the transit companies would hire scabs; the entire police force was often mobilized to deal with the ensuing violence. (*Harper's Weekly*, February 9, 1889)

Superintendent William Murray *(seated in center)*, Detective Chief Inspector Thomas Byrnes *(standing behind Murray)*, and Inspector Alexander "Clubber" Williams *(standing far right)*, circa 1890 (© Museum of the City of New York)

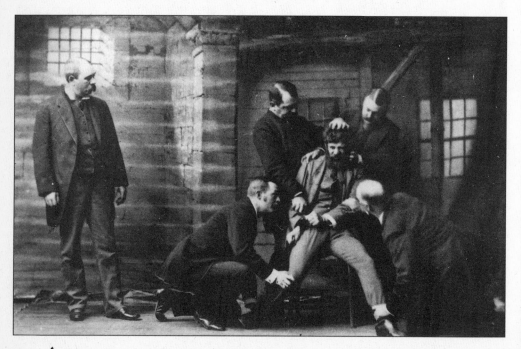

An 1886 photo staged by Inspector Byrnes *(standing at left)* for use in his book, *Professional Criminals of America* (© Bettmann/Corbis)

In a contemporary artist's rendering of the 1894 Lexow investigation, Captain Max Schmittberger sits in the witness chair, with committee counsel John Goff standing, and Reverend Charles Parkhurst seated at far left. (© Bettmann/Corbis)

The man on horseback during the 1898 police parade is newly appointed Chief William Devery, who, as a captain, had been fired for corruption. (© Museum of the City of New York)

Members of the unit formed to fight the Mafiosi and Black Handers, 1908. Its commander, Lieutenant Joseph Petrosino, is standing at the left. (© Daily News Photos)

Commanding officer of a squad working out of the police commissioner's office, Charles Becker, was electrocuted in 1915, after being convicted of ordering the murder of a gambler who squealed to the DA about police payoffs. (© Daily News Photos)

A police model from 1919, when the department owned only thirty-three cars. Six years later, it had more than six hundred. (© Daily News Photos)

In 1918, Lieutenant Richard Enright became the first career officer to be named police commissioner. Enright *(second from left)* had a penchant for photo ops, such as this mock holdup by a gun-toting society lady. (© Paul Thompson)

Detectives stand over the body of an off-duty police officer shot dead on a midtown street in 1941 when he attempted to question three robbery suspects. (© Daily News Photos)

For seven months in 1962 detectives trailed three professional thieves. After suspects held up a money courier, police moved in. More than thirty shots were fired; a detective and two bandits were wounded and the third killed. (© Daily News Photos)

Mounted police at at a demonstration in downtown Manhattan, ca. 1930 (© Daily News Photos)

Commissioner Lewis J. Valentine, seen destroying seized gambling equipment in Brooklyn (1935), was the department's leading corruption fighter. (© Daily News Photos)

Detective Mary Shanley *(at left)* escorts a female prisoner back to the United States from England, 1939. The woman on the right is a British detective. (© Bettmann/Corbis)

In 1911, Samuel J. Battle became the first African-American appointed to the New York Police Department. Despite a distinguished career, he was not promoted beyond the rank of lieutenant. (© Daily News Photos)

A looter arrested in the 1943 Harlem riot; the riot started with a police officer shooting a black soldier. (© Bettmann/Corbis)

Legendary detective Johnny Cordes *(far right)* comes out of retirement in 1956 to offer support to his protégé, former deputy chief inspector Frank Phillips *(far left)*. (© Daily News Photos)

Undercover detective Kitty Barry never allowed her photo to be taken during her years of work on drug cases and as a decoy in rape investigations (1959). (© Daily News Photos)

In the late 1950s Commissioner Steve Kennedy began to crack down on youth gangs. These four boys, wearing aluminum provective vests, were seized as they were about to engage in a rumble with another gang. (© Daily News Photos)

Captain Lloyd Sealy stands outside the Twenty-eighth Precinct. Harlem's first black commander, he was appointed after the 1964 riot. (© Lloyd George Sealy Library, John Jay College of Criminal Justice, CUNY)

Undercover transit cop Jack Maple in 1983.
Later, as a NYPD deputy commissioner, he played a key role in fashioning the strategies credited with cutting crime in the 1990s. (© Bruce Davidson, Magnum Photos Inc.)

A Hasidic Jew watches a car burning during the third night of the 1991 Crown Heights riot. The failure of the NYPD to bring the riot under control severely damaged the credibility of Mayor David Dinkins and Police Commissioner Lee Brown. (© Daily News Photos)

Left to right: Commissioner William Bratton, Mayor Rudolph Giuliani, and First Deputy Commissioner John Timoney in 1995. The following year, the mayor declined to reappoint Bratton or choose Timoney as his successor. (© Daily News Photos)

Cop on trial for murder, 2000. In 1999, four members of the citywide Street Crime Unit fired forty-one shots at an unarmed twenty-two-year-old West African immigrant named Amadou Diallo, striking him nineteen times. The cops were charged with murder and acquitted; Officer Sean Carroll weeps as he recalls on the witness stand the discovery of a wallet, not a gun, in the victim's hand. (© Associated Press Pool/*Albany Times Union*)

A Diallo case protester, 2000, stands by a silhouette with nineteen bullet holes. (© Daily News Photos)

were sentenced to the Atlanta federal penitentiary and two other collaborators interned.

An even bigger break came, it seemed, when Allied intelligence received word that a man named von Rintelin was directing the German sabotage campaign. Tunney was notified, and New York City detectives began trailing him. But the man they were following turned out to be a ne'er-do-well waterfront character with the same name as the millionaire sportsman. At this early stage of the war, the people von Papen referred to as "the idiotic Yankees" had a lot to learn about the spy business. In fact, von Rintelin's downfall would be a result of the attachés' jealousy. Von Papen and Boy-Ed even questioned his right to use the aristocratic *Von* and referred to him contemptuously as "Rintelin." In August 1915, they succeeded in having him recalled. His outbound journey was not as smooth as his entry. He sailed on a neutral ship, using his false Swiss passport, but the ship was intercepted by the Royal Navy on the basis of decoded German radio messages, and a boarding party removed von Rintelin. He was held in custody in Britain until the United States entered the war; then he was extradited, tried, and sentenced to prison, where he remained until 1920.

Tunney assigned his German-speaking detectives to infiltrate the bars, beer gardens, and restaurants of the Hoboken waterfront. One, Henry Barth, pretended to be a German secret agent himself, a ruse that led him to a seventy-year-old retired German sea captain, Karl von Kleist, whose job it was to deliver empty containers to Dr. Scheele and take the live bombs back to German captains on the waterfront. In the course of his work, von Kleist ran up $134 in expenses that Scheele failed to pay. So the captain wrote to 60 Wall Street to complain. The letter was intercepted by the police department, and Detective Barth, in his guise as a German intelligence officer, phoned von Kleist and arranged a meeting. The captain told his story to the detective and even took him home to show him an empty bomb cylinder. Barth arranged for him to relate his grievances to an aide of the German military attaché over a good shore dinner at a Coney Island restaurant. The solicitous aide, Lieutenant Barnitz, carefully wrote down the facts, had von Kleist sign the statement, and agreed to take him to the attaché's office to get paid. Instead they proceeded to 240 Centre Street. When von Kleist realized he was at police headquarters, he declared that he now understood why the gentlemen had been so polite to him. Von Kleist was interrogated by Tunney himself. During the questioning, a light fixture failed and an electrician was summoned to repair it. Then Tunney was called from the room. The electrician, a German-American, took advantage of the inspector's absence to strike up a conversation with von Kleist in his native tongue. The captain asked him if he was German. The workman said he was.

Von Kleist was a gentleman of the old school. He had been born into an aristocratic family, although as a boy he had run off to sea. His background did not prepare him for the Detective Bureau, where the spirit of Inspector Byrnes still prevailed. He asked if the electrician (actually Detective Henry Senf) could do him a favor and take some warning messages to his confederates. Von Kleist wrote out the notes and they were duly delivered—by detectives brandishing handcuffs.

A more wily target of the bomb squad was Paul Koenig, a detective for the Hamburg-America line who before the war had worked with the department in the investigation of thefts on the waterfront. When the war started, he was engaged to furnish bodyguards for the ambassador and attachés, and as early as September 1914 he sent two spies to Canada to sketch military installations. Koenig kept meticulous files, with each agent assigned a number. One of them, operative No. 4, was a New York City patrolman—and he wasn't working undercover. But he was a rare case. Almost always, the policeman's oath proved stronger for Irish and German cops than any ties of ethnicity.

To avoid tails, Koenig forbade his agents to enter 45 Broadway, preferring to meet them in the field. Attempts by Tunney's detectives to follow him to these rendezvous were unsuccessful. A good shadow was born, not made, Tunney believed, and many excellent detectives didn't have the knack. Some were too large and conspicuous, some were overzealous, some excited suspicion by being overcautious. Tunney compared a good shadower to a fisherman who knows just how much line to run out. And Koenig, according to Tunney, was "a slippery fish" who would slip around a corner with his shadower close behind him, only to "pop out of a doorway with a laugh for his pursuer."

The department turned to its wiretappers. But Koenig was prepared for them, too. To combat eavesdropping, he used a safety block system and code words. A street number in Manhattan named over the telephone meant that the meeting would take place five blocks farther uptown than the street mentioned. The Pennsylvania Railroad Station was really Grand Central; the Hotel Belmont was the bar at the Pabst, a German restaurant in Columbus Circle. Periodically, he changed the designations, so that instead of meeting five blocks up, the conspirators would meet five blocks down, and Borough Hall, Brooklyn, became the Pabst Bar. As often happens, the wiretappers struck pay dirt by sheer luck. A disgruntled spy whom Koenig had done out of $2.57 was overheard calling him a "bullheaded Westphalian." The police contacted him, and when he talked they had enough information to raid 45 Broadway, where they seized much valuable information. Because the United States was not at war, they were unable to charge Koenig. Later, when the United States did enter the conflict, the most that could be done was to intern him for the duration.

In July 1915, two months after the torpedoing of the *Lusitania* had mobilized American public opinion against Germany, the intelligence officers received a windfall. U.S. Secret Service agents Frank Burke and W. H. Houghton trailed Heinrich Albert and a German-American newspaper editor from the Hamburg-America building onto a Sixth Avenue uptown elevated train. The editor got off at Thirty-third Street, and Houghton followed him. Burke, who was one of the agents detailed by Chief William Flynn to assist Tunney in the New Jersey bomb-testing case, continued to follow Albert. It was a hot day, and the diplomat dozed off. When the train pulled in at Fiftieth Street, the startled Albert jumped up, leaving his briefcase behind. Burke snatched it. Realizing his loss, Albert looked back and saw Burke fleeing. The portly middle-aged attaché gave chase, but the young Secret Service man jumped onto a streetcar and escaped. Albert assumed that the thief was a British agent, but on the chance that it was an American criminal, he placed an ad in the newspaper offering a reward. By doing so, he denied himself the alibi that the material in the briefcase was not his in the event that it turned up in unfriendly hands. The papers it contained provided evidence of Germany's espionage and sabotage campaign and were rushed to Washington, where Secretary of the Treasury William Gibbs McAdoo personally examined them. Because a criminal case would be difficult to sustain under American law—indeed the lawbreaker was Agent Burke, a fact the U.S. was reluctant to admit—the Treasury leaked the information to the *New York World*, and the resulting story severely damaged the credibility of the German government. President Wilson ordered von

Papen and Boy-Ed expelled from the United States, but they left their network behind. Henceforth, Albert was referred to by his colleagues as "the minister without portfolio."

The success of Allied agents and American police in New York did not prevent the largest act of sabotage ever committed on U.S. soil, the Black Tom explosion. Although it was the most important ammunition transfer point in the United States, its security arrangements left much to be desired. On Saturday, July 29, the workmen quit at 5:00 P.M., leaving a number of freight cars sitting on railroad tracks and barges tied up to the docks, all loaded with ammunition. Responsibility for security was divided. The railroad property was guarded by half a dozen watchmen from the Lehigh Valley Railroad, while four private detectives protected the barges. Two of them were bribed by Paul Koenig, and that Saturday night two German officers rowed out to the island, where they were met by one of the workers, a man of Austrian birth. The three set off the explosion, causing $14 million worth of damage. Among those killed was the chief of security for the Lehigh Valley Railroad. Despite intensive investigation and many years of postwar litigation before a German-American joint claims commission, the saboteurs were never definitively identified. But the two German officers are generally believed to have been Kurt Jahnke and Lothar Witzke, and the Austrian accomplice is thought to have been Michael Kristoff. The case was finally settled in 1936, but the Nazi government blocked payment of claims. It was reopened after World War II, and the last payment was made in 1979. In 1918 Witzke was captured sneaking into the United States from Mexico and condemned to death. The sentence was not carried out, though, and after the war he went home to receive an Iron Cross. Jahnke's spying career for Germany extended into World War II.

In April 1917, the United States declared war on Germany. In the Civil War, the government had not dared to institute a draft until two years into the struggle, when it was desperate for manpower. The Wilson administration took a different course, enacting a draft law at the outset. The question was whether the law could be enforced, particularly in the immigrant capital of America, New York City. Half a century earlier, the streets had run with blood. In 1917, the immigrant population overwhelmingly rallied to the flag. The Irish Fighting Sixty-ninth Regiment went to war as part of the Rainbow Division (whose commanding general was young Douglas MacArthur). The colonel of the Sixty-ninth, "Wild Bill" Donovan, earned the congressional Medal of Honor and went on to become one of America's great corporate lawyers. An overaged East Sider who volunteered under the name William Delaney was so scarred that the examining physician asked him what wars he had been in. "A lot of little wars around New York," he replied. It was Monk Eastman. Accepted into the New York National Guard's Twenty-seventh Division, he fought so well in France that he returned loaded with decorations, and one of his frontline comrades, the son of Governor Alfred Smith, persuaded his father to pardon him. The draftee Seventy-seventh "Statue of Liberty" Division was composed of Jews and Italians from downtown—"hardy backwoodsmen from Hester Street," their general called them—and their "lost battalion" won immortal glory in the Argonne Forest. Harlem sent the famous "Hell Fighter" Regiment overseas. Somehow, there was no place for them with the American forces, though, so they served with the French and established an outstanding record.

Once America was in the war, cooperation between the police and military intelligence became so close that it was often difficult to determine where one agency left off and the other began. Deputy Commissioner Biddle became a colonel in charge of the New York intelligence office, the largest outside of Washington. His staff was composed of Ivy League graduates of impeccable social credentials. While Biddle's office was at 302 Broadway, he also supervised a contingent of "intelligence police"—New York City cops who were given the military rank of sergeant and the title of inspector and operated out of police headquarters on Centre Street. The department also cooperated with U.S. naval intelligence, headed by Lieutenant Commander Spencer Eddy, a Harvard graduate and New York socialite, whose office was located on Wall Street. The presence of gentlemen commissioners and deputy commissioners in the department during the early decades of the century and the influx of members of the social elite into the police intelligence network during World War I produced a cadre of well-connected New Yorkers to whom the police could turn for assistance and support.

Among the first targets of the military-police network were the Wobblies.

The neutrality squad kept a watch on the IWW office at 74 St. Marks Place and forwarded reports to Biddle. These were useful when Wobblies from all over the country were arrested and shipped to Chicago to be tried for obstructing the war effort by federal judge Kenesaw Mountain Landis (later the first commissioner of baseball), who eventually sent them to Leavenworth Prison. In New York, antidraft activity was quickly quashed. On June 4, 1917, the night before the law was to go into effect, a rally was addressed by Emma Goldman and Alexander Berkman. A group of soldiers in uniform armed with electric light bulbs, bricks, lemons, and stink bombs repeatedly interrupted the speakers. One young draft resister, Joseph Cain Jr., shouted, "Give me liberty or give me death," provocation enough for the soldiers to commence a free-for-all, apparently seeking, as one of the newspapers noted, "to satisfy Cain's second choice." The fighting continued in the streets, and a number of anarchists were beaten and arrested by police and soldiers. Berkman and Goldman were prosecuted and convicted for their part.

Even nonviolent, respectable antiwar opponents were crushed by the military-police apparatus. Roger Baldwin, an Ivy League–educated socialite and the head of the National Civil Liberties Bureau (NCLB), naively expected to establish a working arrangement with the authorities. Biddle himself would lead a burglary of the NCLB offices, confiscating documents. To his embarrassment, ten days later, in an official interview, Baldwin offered the intelligence chief copies of the very documents that had been stolen; nevertheless, Baldwin ended up in prison as a war resister.

Like his reform predecessors, John Mitchel was fated to be a one-term mayor. Though his campaign billboards portrayed him in uniform with rifle and bayonet fending off a Tammany tiger (which from the campaign rhetoric could have been construed as first cousin to the imperial German black eagle), he was overwhelmingly defeated in November 1917 by a Brooklyn judge named John F. Hylan, who had the strong support of William Randolph Hearst. Mitchel joined the army, and a few months later he was killed, falling from a plane during pilot's training. He had left his seat belt unfastened because it aggravated the chronic headaches that had plagued him since a bout of fever in South America years earlier. Arthur Woods also resigned and went off to the army, where he rose to lieutenant colonel. And the bomb squad lost another powerful patron with the death of Chief Inspector Schmittberger in October 1917, while on sick leave for nervous exhaustion. Tunney, now an inspector, moved en masse with twenty of his bomb-squad detectives into the U.S. Army, which made him a captain and sent him around the country to organize similar units in other police departments.

Although the Hearst papers had vigorously opposed America's entry into the war, Mayor Hylan did not dare cut back police cooperation with military intelligence. If the New York City government had tried to obstruct the war effort, Hylan would have had to face not only Wilson but Governor Whitman in Albany and Teddy Roosevelt of Oyster Bay. Hylan and his police commissioner, Richard Enright, wisely let Colonel Biddle run the department's counterintelligence operations for the duration of the war. Tunney even returned briefly, between stints in the army, to head the bomb squad. Indeed, the New York City police would be in the forefront of the drive to crush dissent—even to dragoon American citizens into the service.

People will "forget there ever was such a thing as tolerance," President Wilson had presciently observed before the war. "To fight you must be ruthless and brutal, and ruthless brutality will enter into every fiber of our national life, infecting Congress, the Courts, the policeman on the beat, the man in the street." Before 1917, law-enforcement efforts against spies and saboteurs had been relatively restrained, considering that bombs were exploding. As soon as war had been declared, military intelligence and police agents expanded their operations to go after war resisters. Congress passed the Espionage Act, making it a crime to convey false statements that might interfere with the war effort, and the Sedition Act, which made it a crime to utter "disloyal" statements. In a case brought under the Espionage Act, the Supreme Court laid down the test that the words spoken must constitute a "clear and present danger." In the wartime atmosphere, clear and present danger would become a very loose concept.

In 1918, a group of radicals printed leaflets attacking American intervention in the Russian Revolution. On an August morning of that year, one of the group was throwing them from the fourth floor of a hat factory at the corner of Houston and Crosby Streets on the Lower East Side. Passersby brought copies to the local police station, where a military intelligence officer reviewed them and sent NYPD intelligence agents to the factory. They captured the leaflet thrower, who led them to his accomplices—six Russian-born radicals, who were all arrested. Twenty-nine-year-old Jacob Abrams, who stood first alphabetically, gave his name to the legal case that followed. The defendants were tried under the Sedition Act, receiving sentences that ranged from three to twenty years. The case was eventually appealed to the Supreme Court, which upheld the conviction.

Even loyal Americans felt the power of the military-intelligence police apparatus. Many draft-aged men had been deferred; others had failed to register. The sight of able-bodied men who were neither working in the war industry nor fighting was a source of outrage to those who were, and to their families. In the summer of 1918, the army provost marshal issued a "work or fight order." To find the so-called slackers, police roamed through public places, accosting men more or less at random and demanding that they produce their draft-registration documents. Those who could not were taken into custody. Though official policy specified that only the police could make arrests, even departments as large as New York's had insufficient manpower for massive roundups. In practice, the police were "assisted" by soldiers, sailors, and members of the American Protective League (APL), an organization of citizen volunteers who had been given military intelligence credentials. In July in Chicago, 10,000 APL agents questioned 150,000 men and arrested 16,000 for failure to produce their draft cards. The largest drives, however, came in September 1918 in the New York area: 50,000 men were seized and detained that month by police, servicemen, and APL operatives. U.S. Senator William Calder of New York complained of men being "taken out of their places of business and crowded into vans, perhaps 50 or 60 packed in like sardines, and sent to the police station houses." One prominent New Yorker was having dinner with a young woman in a Brooklyn restaurant when the military police appeared and demanded to see his draft card. Because the draft board had never sent him one, he was arrested and hauled to a Brooklyn stationhouse, where he stood for five hours in a lockup without food or water. From the precinct, he was taken to a National Guard armory for further interrogation. Finally, a business partner found him and arranged his release.

The Armistice did not lead to the abolition of the police-military intelligence network. The Russian Revolution set off a "Red scare" and a crackdown even more severe than the wartime one. In February 1919, a general strike in Seattle was crushed by troops. In April, bombs were mailed to a group of prominent people that included J. P. Morgan and John D. Rockefeller. Riding the subway home, a New York postal clerk read a newspaper account describing the way the bombs had been wrapped. He recalled seeing sixteen identical packages in brown paper bearing the return address of Gimbel's department store; he had put them aside a few hours earlier for want of proper postage. He returned to the post office, the bomb squad was summoned, and the packages proved to contain powerful explosives. On May Day, there were riots in several cities, including New York. In June, a bomb detonated in front of the home of U.S. Attorney General A. Mitchell Palmer, leader of the government's anti-Red campaign. His neighbor, Assistant Secretary of the Navy Franklin D. Roosevelt, was alighting from a cab just as the bomb exploded, killing the bomber and two passersby. September brought a police strike in Boston, and at the end of the year, Emma Goldman and Alexander Berkman were deported to Russia. The federal investigative official responsible for their case, one J. Edgar Hoover, journeyed to New York Harbor to see them off. He was rewarded by the sight of Goldman and Berkman shaking their fists at him as their ship sailed away. On January 2, 1920, Attorney General Palmer ordered a series of raids all over the country. Federal agents, police, and military personnel seized four thousand persons for possible deportation.

In New York, the final act of the Red scare occurred on September 16, 1920. Just before noon, a rickety wagon drawn by a weary-looking old horse pulled up a few yards east of the intersection of Wall and Broad Streets— alongside the headquarters of J. P. Morgan and across from the U.S. Assay Office, with its statue of George Washington on the front steps, marking the site where he had taken the oath of office as the first president. Precisely at noon, a dynamite bomb exploded in the wagon, throwing more than five hundred pounds of shrapnel in every direction. Thirty-nine people were killed or died of wounds; ten times that many were injured. Windows fell in at the Stock Exchange, and the president walked quickly across the exchange floor (running was not allowed) to ring the bell, ending trading for the day. Police strength in the Wall Street District was at low ebb. Most of the reserves from the downtown precincts were on duty at a transit strike in Brooklyn; the few remaining were assigned to an Odd Fellows parade. One of those called away was the officer who normally stood in front of the Assay Office. At the scene, there was mass confusion. Wall Street had not seen anything like it since the Russell Sage bombing in 1891.

Before the explosion, a crew of government porters had been carrying hundreds of wooden boxes filled with gold ingots from the vault in the nearby subtreasury basement to the Assay Office, but they had quit for lunch and closed the doors of the subtreasury. With a fortune in the two government buildings, and the confusion of the bombing, looting was feared. A police sergeant stationed half a dozen cops with drawn guns in front of the federal buildings. Eventually, seventeen hundred policemen in commandeered cars and trucks arrived from all over the city; Mayor Hylan and Commissioner Enright took personal charge at the scene. This was not enough for the assistant U.S. treasurer, and in a throwback to 1877, he phoned the chief of staff of the army garrison on Governor's Island, demanding federal troops. Regulars of the Twenty-second Infantry were assembled, armed, loaded onto ships, and ferried across the water, double-timing into the Wall Street area with rifles loaded and bayonets fixed, just forty minutes after the call was made.

The general reaction was that it had to be Reds. The Morgan headquarters, temple of American capitalism, appeared an obvious target. The explosion had killed the firm's chief clerk, and a severed woman's head, still wearing a hat, had stuck to the outside wall of the building (the dents from the shrapnel can be seen there today, having purposely been left unrepaired). The statue of Washington was still standing—a reassuring fact noted in stories and editorials throughout the country, and the next morning the Stock Exchange opened its doors for business.

The nascent FBI, the U.S. Secret Service, and the NYPD all conducted investigations. Inspector Tunney was no longer around to lead the police efforts. After his return from army service in 1919, Enright had dropped him back to a captain's rank and put him in charge of the pickpocket squad—the man who for four years had fought the top agents of the German empire was now going to spend his time chasing dips. Lieutenant Barnitz, who had been a naval officer, was demoted to sergeant and sent out, in uniform, to patrol a precinct. It was the familiar story of a police commander being punished by a new administration for being a favorite of the old one. (Indeed, Tunney had been promoted to captain in the same department order in which Commissioner Woods had passed Enright over.) Tunney knew he had no future with the organization. Only forty-five, he retired to open a private detective agency. (In 1926, his cousin Gene Tunney won the heavyweight boxing championship of the world.)

The department's investigation of the Wall Street bombing was led by Captain John Coughlin, a highly regarded veteran detective in command of the headquarter's squads. His first important lead was a report of someone depositing papers in a mailbox at Cedar Street and Broadway, a two-minute walk from the site of the bombing, sometime between the 11:30 and 11:58 A.M. collections. Each had a slightly different message, a typical one being:

> Remember we will not tolerate any longer.
> Free the political prisoners.
> Or it will be sure death for all of you.
> American Anarchist Fighters.

In the debris, investigators found the steel knob of a safe that had apparently held the explosives in the wagon. There were no records of its purchaser. Horseshoes from the animal drawing the wagon were checked against those at four thousand stables. Investigators looked into the possibility that the explosion was meant to cover a robbery of the porters transporting the gold. Among the "odd fish" who always turn up in major investigations was, in this one, Edwin P. Fischer, a lawyer and former tennis champion, who had told friends weeks before the blast to stay away from Wall Street until after September 16 because sixty thousand pounds of explosives were going to blow up. Fischer, a former mental patient, was taken into custody in Toronto and returned to New York. He arrived at Grand Central Station wearing two complete business suits, one on top of the other, with a white tennis costume underneath; he told reporters that he always wanted to be prepared for a game. He could offer only one explanation for his prescient remarks: his psychic powers. Despite years of investigation and thousands of tips, the case was never solved.

The neutrality squad continued on under other names. In 1923 it became the radical squad, in 1931 the alien squad, and in 1946 the Bureau of Special Service Investigations (BOSSI). None of these units would achieve the same prominence. By the time World War II came along, the FBI was firmly established as the nation's domestic-security agency and the NYPD was cast in a decidedly secondary role. Security work had become a messier business, in any case. World War I was an old-fashioned struggle between nations. World War II and the Cold War that followed were ideological conflicts.

In the 1930s, the German-American Bund paraded openly in brown shirts with swastika armbands giving the Nazi salute. Other New Yorkers joined the Christian Front, whose action arm, the Christian Mobilizers, took over street corners and insulted or beat up Jewish passersby. A startling number of New York City police officers belonged to the front, and the department was often accused of being soft on them. Responding to an official questionnaire in the late '30s, four hundred cops identified themselves as front members. In 1940, a suspicious package was discovered at the British pavilion in the New York World's Fair. The bomb squad responded, and two detectives were killed while attempting to move the package. Their deaths opened the eyes of some cops who had been inclined to view the front with sympathy.

10

Shoofly

The ranks of the NYPD have always included a few highly trusted officers on whom the department could rely when it needed to get to the
bottom of an allegation against one of its own. George Walling, who
filled this role in the 1860s, told the story of a pickpocket who boldly walked
into headquarters one day to accuse two veteran detectives of shaking him
down. Walling and his boss, Superintendent John Kennedy, were reluctant to
believe the charge. But the pickpocket offered to overcome their skepticism;
so Walling accompanied him to Thirteenth Street, where he had supposedly arranged to meet the detectives in order to satisfy their latest financial
demand. With Walling sitting on a nearby cart, his face concealed under a battered hat, the rendezvous took place and the detectives headed off to a saloon
on Fourteenth Street. Walling found them at the bar.

"What'll you take?" one detective asked the other.

"I'll take the money that thief has just given you," Walling interjected.
Reaching into the detective's pockets, he removed a wad of bills that proved to
include one he had taken care to sign beforehand. When he laid out the facts
to the superintendent, Kennedy ordered the two men to hand in their resigna-
tions. (Like many of his successors, he preferred to dispose of these cases quietly and informally.)

The superintendents, chiefs, and commissioners who followed took to
forming their own confidential squads for sensitive matters such as the
enforcement of laws against gambling and the closely entwined problem of

police graft: sometimes the squads exposed it, sometimes they collected it, sometimes they did a little of each. As a deputy commissioner, Rhinelander Waldo created a headquarters unit composed of a sergeant, three roundsmen, and fifteen patrolmen for pretty much the sole purpose of nailing Max Schmittberger. But it was not until 1914, with the ascent of the "boy mayor" John Purroy Mitchel and his Ivy League–educated police commissioner, Arthur Woods, that the department at last had a confidential squad that was fully committed to the job.

The mayoralty aside, political control of the city in the first decades of the twentieth century rested largely with Tammany Hall, led by its boss, George Murphy, and his lieutenant for organized crime, Tom Foley (successor to Big Tim Sullivan). Foley had a friendly network of captains, inspectors, and plainclothesmen. His saloon at Centre and Frankfort Streets near the Criminal Court Building was the place to go for politicians, bail bondsmen, or gangsters looking to make "contracts," as such deals are still called in New York City. Commissioner Woods was an orator, and his descriptions of the rank and file—"brave as lions, true to each other, and true to the highest standards of honor"—betrayed a romantic cast of mind. Graft, he argued, went against men's nature. But in the prevailing political climate, he recognized the troops' need for some artificial stimulus to their powers of resistance to "these perversions of the spirit." So he created a commissioner's confidential squad, placing it under the command of "Honest Dan" Costigan, the former scourge of Chinatown's gamblers, whom he promoted to inspector.

It wasn't easy to find suitable men for such a unit or, having found them, to persuade them to accept. One who accepted and proved to have a gift for the work was Sergeant Lewis J. Valentine. The son of a fruit-store owner who had emigrated from Alsace, Valentine had a ruddy complexion, large ears, and a bulbous nose. Although he was handy with his fists, nothing about his early career pointed to a brilliant future or indicated any particular interest in catching grafters. Appointed to the force in 1903, he bounced around Brooklyn and Manhattan, taking ten years to win his first promotion. In the aftermath of the Becker case, he was one of a cadre of new sergeants transferred into the Tenderloin en masse. Instead of raiding joints with a vengeance, however, Valentine requested a transfer to a less demanding assignment, where, as he explained, he would have more time to study for lieutenant. Through a political connection in his neighborhood, he got his wish. To all appearances, he was just another plodding cop—one who might not have any appetite for graft himself but wasn't looking to buck the system. Then he hooked up with Costigan, who had an infectious enthusiasm for the work of nailing crooked cops and for making the officers around him learn, as he had, to consider the appellation of "rat" a badge of honor.

In one of Valentine's early triumphs as a shoofly, he got the goods on a patrolman named Sharkey, who had volunteered, for $300, to fix a murder case arising out of a brawl. Valentine and his partner disguised themselves as sailor buddies of the defendant's, who was a sailor himself, and made the pay-off in marked bills. Sharkey turned out to know Valentine's brother, and the patrolman's friends briefly entertained the idea of capitalizing on the connection. But Valentine was resolute. Convicted of extortion, Sharkey wound up in Sing Sing, while Valentine won a promotion to lieutenant, partly on the strength of the incentive points that came with the citation he received for his work on the case.

Internal affairs work, as it would come to be known with the creation of the first permanent unit two generations later, was not only personally offensive to many cops but also professionally hazardous, since, as anyone passingly acquainted with the city's history understood, reform administrations rarely lasted long. Many cops decided that it was better, from a long-term career perspective, to specialize in some other line of police work. Even among those who let themselves be wooed into units like Costigan's, there were officers who found ways of letting their colleagues know that they were less than 100 percent committed to the mission. Valentine and his partner, Sergeant Floyd Horton, took no such precautions. In the spirit of their mentor and commander, Costigan, they did not temporize. Sent to Bridgeport, Connecticut, to bring back a reluctant witness in a corruption case, they went about the job with such gusto that a local grand jury indicted them both for attempted kidnapping. In another case, Valentine resorted to the use of an emetic in an unsuccessful attempt to extract graft money from a policeman's stomach.

The professional hazards of so zealously serving a reform administration became clearer after the election of 1917. The new mayor's nickname, "Red Mike" Hylan, referred to the color of his hair and mustache; it also fit his temper, which was hot. Politics, a second career for Hylan, gave him an opportunity to vent some powerful emotions, which had fermented during his earlier period of employment as an elevated-train motorman. He had been fired from that post after his train very nearly ran over a superior with whom he had quarreled. The public generally loathed the private companies that operated the city's mass-transit lines; attacks on their venality and vows to maintain the five-cent fare were a staple of the political oratory of the day. But the personal intensity of Hylan's feelings against the transit barons gave him an extra edge, which, along with the backing of the press lord William Randolph Hearst and the Brooklyn Democratic organization, helped him land in the mayor's office. Once elected, he made the police band available to serenade Mr. and Mrs. Hearst at a succession of public events, including the opening nights of movies starring Hearst's mistress, Marion Davies, whose father, through Hylan's good offices, became a magistrate.

In his quest for a police commissioner, Hylan turned to one of Woods's civilian deputies, Frederick Bugher. He chose Bugher offhandedly, after a political ally had urged the name upon him, and he regretted the decision almost immediately. These feelings may or may not have had something to do with the pique of Hylan's brother-in-law, Detective Sergeant Irving O'Hara, who had offered the new commissioner some unsolicited advice. Bugher, a Prussian type, evidently treated Sergeant O'Hara brusquely; at any rate, he did not give his ideas the high value that the sergeant himself, and perhaps his brother-in-law the mayor, thought they merited. Twenty-three days into the new administration, Hylan had a dream that, as he explained later, strongly indicated the need for a different police commissioner.

Summoned to the mayor's office, Bugher entered, clicked his heels, and saluted, as usual.

Hylan gave him the news without a great deal of delicacy. "You're fired" were the precise words, imparted in a loud voice.

Dumbfounded, Bugher clicked his heels, saluted, and wordlessly withdrew.

At various times down through the years, mayors of New York City have, as the saying goes, "skipped over" certain high-ranking police officials in the process of selecting a new commissioner. No mayor has ever reached as far down in the ranks as Hylan did, bypassing 122 higher-ranking officers en route to his choice of Lieutenant Richard Enright as Bugher's improbable successor. One of the many people surprised by the choice was Enright himself. Soon after being ushered into the commissioner's office to assume his duties, the telephone rang and he leapt to answer it. "Lieutenant Enright speaking," he said.

Nowhere did the appointment cause greater astonishment, however, than in the ranks of the commissioner's confidential squad. Enright's main distinction, up until then, had been his leadership of the Police Lieutenants' Benevolent Association. In that capacity, he had made a number of vitriolic attacks on Commissioner Arthur Woods. At a lieutenants' association banquet attended by Enright's friend former president William Howard Taft, the lieutenant held forth on the problems of the New York City police: "During the last thirteen years, nine commissioners have come and gone, with an average service of a little more than one year," he observed. "With them have come and gone some thirty-three deputy commissioners. . . . Some have been lawyers, some have been judges, some have been railway men, some have been schoolmasters, some have been bookkeepers, some have been bartenders, some have been plumbers, some have been milliners, and some have had no visible means of support."

Commissioner (and former Deputy Commissioner) Woods was not amused. He passed over Enright three times, which in accordance with civil-service law sent him to the bottom of the captain's list. The Patrolmen's Benevolent Association, founded in the 1890s, was much larger than the lieutenants' organization, but there was still a reluctance on the part of many patrolmen to openly oppose so exalted a personage as the police commissioner. Enright, being a boss himself and no shrinking violet, had emerged as the department's first outspoken leader of rank-and-file opinion, inaugurating a long, intermittent tradition of acrimony between the various benevolent associations, on the one hand, and the various mayors and commissioners, on the other.

Officially, the associations existed for such purposes as the provision of widows' pensions above and beyond the benefits conferred by the city. Unofficially, they were political pressure groups. Early in the century, the PBA had raised a slush fund to successfully persuade the Albany legislature to enact a law requiring three platoons rather than two in the NYPD, thereby significantly reducing a cop's duty hours. To Dan Costigan, who loathed all politicians, Enright and his type were parasites eating away at the integrity of the organization. At Costigan's behest, Valentine and Horton initiated an investigation of the finances of the lieutenants' association. For once, they failed to come up with any evidence of wrongdoing. But Enright, of course, did not forget the episode.

Commissioner Enright showed no great eagerness to dispel the suspicions associated with Lieutenant Enright. He enjoyed the ceremonial side of the job. Under his aegis, the department invited a number of European police officials to a series of conferences that helped establish the city's, and Enright's, importance in the international law-enforcement community. He was on cozy terms with a number of celebrities and cultivated a group of rich friends whom the press dubbed "Enright's millionaires." These privileged citizens received gold badges, which some, at their own expense, had studded with diamonds. With the badges came so-called courtesy cards entitling the bearers to unspecified special treatment.

In picking Enright for the job of commissioner, Mayor Hylan may have been acting on a certain cumulative dissatisfaction with the series of top-hatted outsiders who, since the turn of the century, had been brought in to run (or, as it often turned out, to neglect) the department. Enright, if he was anything, was an insider, and he knew how to make his adversaries' lives miserable. Reporting for work one day to find that he no longer had a locker, Costigan hung his coat on a hook. When word of the incident leaked to the press, the commissioner issued a regulation prohibiting policemen from communicating with reporters. Costigan managed to contain himself briefly. His self-control ran out, however, when, at a meeting of the headquarters brass shortly after Enright announced his engagement to be married, the chief inspector, "Honest John" Daly, congratulated him and urged all the commanders present to pony up money for a wedding present. Costigan declared that he would not contribute a penny to such a cause.

His words seemed to awaken pangs of conscience in the commissioner: As much as he appreciated the spirit behind the gesture, he told his subordinates, he could not accept such a gift. Following the meeting, however, he disbanded the confidential squad, demoted Costigan to captain, and sent him to a precinct in the far northern end of the Bronx; for good measure, Costigan found that a detective had been assigned to tail him virtually around the clock, in quest of some transgression that would justify yet further humiliation.

Valentine wound up as a relief desk lieutenant in Brooklyn. He never knew where he would be assigned to work on a particular day; over time, he made the rounds of virtually every precinct in the borough. Although he thought about quitting, he was past thirty-five—only a few years away from pension eligibility—and had a wife and five children. Standing first on the captain's list, he was banking on his promotion and the $2,000-a-year captain's pension

($350 more than the pension coming to him as a lieutenant) to provide the money that he would need to buy a small home.

But Enright's vindictiveness knew no bounds. He passed over Valentine three times, sending him to the bottom of the civil-service list. In this, the commissioner could argue that he was simply doing what the reformers had done to him. He could not make the same case for his treatment of Lieutenant Horton. In December 1920, Horton was fatally wounded in a gunfight with some burglars he had encountered on his way home from his precinct. In the waning moments of his life, Horton managed to write down the license number of their car—a last act that led to their capture. The circumstances of his death brought him the department's top award, the medal of honor, which should have entitled him to posthumous membership in an organization of decorated cops known as the Honor Legion. The vengeful Enright pulled the strings necessary to have Horton excluded.

Valentine, frustrated by a series of senseless transfers and embittered by the treatment of his beloved partner, threw himself into yet another round of study for the promotional exam, hoping that the voters would give Hylan the heave in the elections of 1921. He was not a scholar. He had left school early, and like many bright blue-collar boys, he learned by watching and listening. To grasp the contents of a book, he had to read it aloud. Fixing up a corner of his basement next to the coal bin as a study, he used an egg crate for a desk and did his reading on a discarded kitchen chair without a back, lest he lose focus or be tempted to relax. Night after night, he sat by the coal bin reciting police texts. The transfers actually worked to his advantage, giving him an opportunity to see a variety of police units and perspectives and to observe different commanders at work. The knowledge that the administration was looking for an excuse to fire him gave him an extra reason to be careful.

Hylan's reelection was too much for Costigan, who quit to open a private detective agency. Valentine stuck with his routine. When it didn't appear that things could get much worse, he was on desk duty at the West Sixty-eighth Street station in Manhattan one day on the 8:00 A.M. to 4:00 P.M. shift. At two o'clock, he received a phone call from his wife. Their only son, Eddie, who was seventeen, had not awakened that morning. He had been rushed to the hospital, where doctors had determined that he had spinal meningitis. They gave him only a few hours to live. Under departmental rules, Valentine could not sign out until his designated relief—the lieutenant working the

4:00 P.M. to 12:00 A.M. shift—showed up. To walk out sooner would mean almost certain dismissal. He sat at the desk, toying with his gold shield and ink-well cover, gazing out the window, and praying. The relief lieutenant appeared unexpectedly early; he had been feeling bored at home, he explained, and had decided to come in to break the monotony. Valentine, who managed to see his son just before he died, attributed this act of grace to the power of prayer. (It is also possible, of course, that one of his colleagues called the night lieutenant to apprise him of the situation.)

Valentine's precinct, housed on Sixty-eighth Street near Broadway, covered the upper part of New York's night-life district—now called Broadway rather than the Tenderloin. Before the world war, Americans had known the Tenderloin as a sinful but distant place. In the 1920s, Broadway had a glamorous aura, and it replaced Main Street as the nexus of national culture. Everybody knew the city and its night life, at least from the movie screen. Americans were enthralled and appalled.

Even before the onset of official Prohibition in January 1920, the U.S. government enforced "wartime" prohibition. In August 1919, federal agents in army trucks raided dozens of bars and hotels. In October, thousands of places were closed, some of them none too gently. In one instance, agents invaded a Times Square saloon and opened fire, wounding a bartender and a customer. Prohibition killed such famous establishments as Louis Sherry's, Delmonico's, Rector's, and the Manhattan Hotel, where the cocktail of that name was invented. It replaced them with hotsy-totsy nightclubs and shadowy speakeasies. From the West Forties up into the Seventies could be found the hangouts of the not-quite-so-cute-and-colorful real-life approximations of Damon Runyon's guys and dolls. Lindy's at Fiftieth Street and Broadway was a major gathering place, and West Fifty-second Street was lined with speakeasies that included the 21 Club and Leon and Eddie's. The well-heeled guys dated the good-looking dolls from the Ziegfeld *Follies*, Earl Carroll's *Vanities*, and George White's *Scandals*, or visited the girls who held forth in the assorted townhouses of Polly Adler, a top madam of the day. Texas Guinan stood up in her clip joint and yelled to the customers, "Hello, suckers," while her girls worked the room picking up hundred-dollar tips. The suckers loved it. Some joints "dressed up" their tables with faux hoodlums and pointed them out to customers as "Tough Jake" or "Irish Paddy." They used ink eradicator to raise $30 checks to $3,000 and installed special buzzers to signal the arrival of the police.

The biggest man on Broadway, Arnold Rothstein, variously known as "A.R.," "the Brain," and "the Big Bankroll," was a racketeer apart. His father had been a respectable dealer in wholesale cotton goods. After starting out as a salesman—a job that bored him—Rothstein turned to gambling, initially as a diversion and then as a career. Early in the century, he was just another Lower East Side small-timer enjoying the protection of Tim Sullivan and the services of Monk Eastman as his debt collector. He also worked as a bail bondsman, which brought him into close association with a network of cops, lawyers, and judges. In 1909, Rothstein was one of the East Siders who moved up to the Tenderloin. He married a Broadway showgirl, and the best man at the wedding was Herbert Bayard Swope, the *World* reporter who later broke the Becker case. The political fallout from that episode, followed by the death of Tim Sullivan, paved the way for Rothstein's rise.

Politicians like Tom Foley no longer wanted a direct hand in the rackets. They needed an intermediary, and Rothstein got the job. As he grew more powerful, he became a banker for a drug syndicate, labor racketeers, and peddlers of stolen goods. If there was a buck in it, he was there. His lawyer, Bill Fallon, who wound up in the slammer himself, characterized Rothstein as "a man who dwells in doorways, a gray rat waiting for his cheese." By the First World War, his name was magic. The cognoscenti dismissed the rumors surrounding the Black Sox scandal and the fixing of the 1919 World Series— until Rothstein's involvement surfaced. Rothstein and his good friend Nicky Arnstein, who was married to Fanny Brice, participated in a number of Wall Street frauds, including the theft of $5 million in bonds. (One detail left out of the movie *Funny Girl*, the Fanny Brice biopic starring Barbra Streisand, was the murder of young bank and brokerage messengers. The face of one victim was mutilated with knife cuts to prevent identification.) When the fugitive Arnstein finally had to take the fall, he arranged to surrender at the Criminal Court, and he and Brice drove downtown in their open Cadillac. For part of the trip, they traveled behind the police department's annual parade, and Enright's cops did not molest them. While Brice and some friends waited in Tom Foley's saloon for Arnstein to post bond, their car was stolen. After one quick phone call invoking the name of Rothstein, the car was returned by an apologetic Monk Eastman. (Seven months later, Eastman was dead, shot by a U.S. Treasury agent with whom he may have had business dealings.)

Rothstein once mistook some raiding cops for holdup men and shot two of them. He was not arrested until after the Hearst press learned about it and accused Swope of the rival *World* of paying a bribe to square the rap for his pal. When the dust settled, the only one to go to jail was the police inspector in charge of the Broadway District, officially for perjury but actually for being unlucky enough to get caught up in Rothstein's affairs. (An appeals court later overturned the inspector's conviction.) Tales of cops made scapegoats for politicians and gangsters were part of the department's folklore. Billy Files, of Becker case notoriety, became a sergeant instructor at the Police Academy, where every rookie learned how Files had been crucified merely for being in the same hotel dining room as Herman Rosenthal on the night of his murder.

In the 1920s, many organized-crime figures owed their position to Rothstein. Waxey Gordon (Irving Wexler) switched from labor slugging on the East Side to bootlegging under A.R.'s patronage. By the Roaring Twenties, Waxey was a multimillionaire who owned breweries and distilleries, lived in luxurious homes, and maintained a fleet of expensive automobiles. Rothstein's Italian protégés included Frank Costello (Francisco Castiglia) and Charles "Lucky" Luciano (Salvatore Lucania). In 1914, the year after Mayor Gaynor's demise, the police had finally managed to nail Owney "the Killer" Madden on a murder rap and send him up. Released in 1923, he formed a partnership with "Big Bill" Dwyer and, backed by Jimmy Hines, the boss of Harlem, rose quickly to become one of the biggest figures in gangdom. In addition to bootlegging, he owned breweries, nightclubs, taxis, laundries, and, with Rothstein, a piece of the Cotton Club.

It was an atmosphere rife with financial opportunity for cops inclined that way. In the pre-Prohibition era, only saloons that wished to run outside of licensed hours had been required to pay off. Now any place that served liquor had to fork over. Inspectors, captains, and vice cops were raking in money; even an ordinary patrolman who stopped a beer truck could turn a nice dollar. The tough waterfront precincts, once seen in part as punishment assignments, were highly desirable because smuggled booze was landed in them. Luciano, a top bootlegger, claimed to have sent $10,000 to $20,000 a week to headquarters. Lucky was, of course, not totally reliable, but few people have disputed his assertion that headquarters was for sale. In some ways, there was less opprobrium attached to police graft now, since much of the public rejected Prohibition; even the governor, Al Smith, was an avowed "wet." Neither city cops nor federal agents, for the most part, made a serious effort to enforce the ban on alcohol. Yet two middle-aged, overweight former postal clerks, Izzy Einstein and Moe Smith, who in 1920 became federal agents in the New York City office, managed to make nearly a thousand arrests a year and became famous lawmen—too famous for the U.S. Treasury, which dispensed with their services in 1925. Now totally forgotten, Izzy and Moe illustrated an old-time Chicago mob fighter's dictum: "A one-armed cop on a bicycle can clean up a town—if he's honest."

Like the nation, the NYPD was being motorized. In 1919, it owned just thirty-three cars. Six years later, there were more than six hundred, and every precinct had two or three light runabout patrol vehicles, while three- and four-man detective squads roamed the city in heavy touring cars. Police cars were not equipped with radios, though, until 1932, so their crews, like foot cops, had to call in on the signal box every hour to receive assignments. Still, as the term "auto bandits" began to appear in crime stories, the department could claim that it was keeping up technologically. At the beginning of the '20s, cops still spent sixteen hours a week on reserve, but the use of cars lessened the need for them to do so; in 1926, the reserve requirement was reduced to eight hours, and in 1930 it was abolished. With the end of station reserve, cops had more free time, and department lore was increasingly passed along in cop bars rather than section rooms.

By the middle of the decade, however, the brazenness of the gangsters and the intimacy of their dealings with the police and other city officials had reached levels that worried some Tammany Hall regulars. When Tammany's candidate, state senator Jimmy Walker, captured the mayoralty in 1925, Governor Al Smith took him aside on the eve of his inauguration and treated him to a little talk about the facts of political life. Smith asked Walker for two pledges: one was to get rid of his mistresses and spend more time with his wife; the other was to clean up the police department. In fulfilling the first pledge, Mayor Walker was on his own. To help him out with the second, Smith proposed a candidate for the job of police commissioner: his superintendent of banking, George V. McLaughlin, a burly, red-faced, tough administrator sometimes sarcastically referred to as "George the Fifth" by fellow Irishmen.

Lewis Valentine, now in the eighth year of exile, was on desk duty at a precinct in the Greenpoint section of Brooklyn when the summons came for him to report to headquarters. Borrowing a pair of suitable shoes, he rushed to a meeting with McLaughlin, who gave him his new assignment. He was to take command of the Clinton Street precinct in downtown Manhattan—long a Tammany stronghold—and run it, McLaughlin said, for the department rather than for the politicians. The new police commissioner restored Valentine's captain's-list eligibility and soon gave him his long-awaited promotion. A few months later, Captain Valentine returned to headquarters as deputy inspector in command of a reconstituted, Costigan-style confidential squad.

With the commissioner's backing, the squad went after the high-level gambling games carried on by the Broadway crowd behind "Do Not Disturb" signs hanging on hotel-suite doors. A district inspector who honored the request could pick up ten years' salary. Valentine began hitting Rothstein's places and those of such big shots as "Nick the Greek." The gamblers retreated into what they had every reason to think were safer sanctuaries—Tammany clubhouses. Valentine infiltrated the games with undercovers, using unrecognizable rookies who had been plucked out of the academy and sent to New Jersey and Long Island to build up credible false identities before they commenced their work.

This kind of law enforcement was unheard of. The clubhouses had always been off-limits. Behind their doors, anything went, even murder. One night, a cab delivered two dying men to Bellevue Hospital. Valentine's detectives ascertained that they had been picked up outside the club of Harry Parry, the municipal court clerk, a district leader, and a Sullivan by marriage. There the cops found bloodstains and a couple of guns on the floor. The dead men turned out to have come to the clubhouse with $12,000 that they had just obtained in a holdup; after losing the money in a crap game, they had pulled their guns. Valentine's bold tactics undermined many of Mayor Walker's more influential supporters. As one Italian gangster observed about Harry Parry, "He mustn't have much power if he can't keep the cops out of his own club." When the bosses complained to McLaughlin about his overzealous shoofly, he made Valentine a full inspector.

To protect themselves, the gamblers relied on a network of police informants to alert them to raids. One of the biggest games was operated behind heavy steel doors and barred windows in Sheriff Tom Farley's clubhouse on East Sixty-second Street. Valentine's men smashed their way in only to find the guests, in a room thick with cigar smoke, busily engaged in packing baseball bats, rubber balls, maypoles, and other playthings for an upcoming club picnic. It was two in the morning. The police made twenty-six arrests, but Farley furnished bail, and the suspects were all released for lack of evidence the next morning. Commissioner McLaughlin, infuriated with the mayor over his obvious failure to support the police in their new zealousness, resigned after fifteen months to take a corporate job at $75,000 a year. (Later, as president of the Brooklyn Trust Bank, he had a controlling interest in the Brooklyn Dodgers.)

Walker had not exerted himself a great deal in office. But he didn't have to. Broadway and the smart set alike loved him for his wit and charm—a marked contrast to the burly saloonkeepers Murphy and Foley (both now deceased), who had run the political machine in the past. Walker was slim, handsome, and dapper. He was also a songwriter who could be depended on to perform his one big hit, "Will You Love Me in December as You Do in May?," at civic events. As mayor, he seldom rose before noon, and (against the advice of Governor Smith) he continued to spend his evenings with his mistress, Betty Compton, a fiery singer and dancer whose show-business career blossomed as "first lady of the night mayor." In an effort to get rid of her, the bosses had detectives bug her torrid phone conversations with a producer and delivered the recordings to the mayor. It didn't work. He was in love.

The 1920s was the era when Walker's people, the Irish Catholics of New York, finally arrived. Politically powerful since the middle of the previous century, they had continued for decades to eat at the second table and hide their lights behind more widely acceptable, Protestant front men like Mayors Van Wyck and McClellan and Police Commissioners McAdoo, Bingham, and Waldo. Now, at last, there were mayors and commissioners with names like Hylan, Walker, Enright, and McLaughlin; and the governor was Al Smith, another Irish-American. Joe Kennedy, who lived in Bronxville, and Tom Coleman of New York City were big players on Wall Street. Colonel Wild Bill Donovan's law firm represented major corporations. (But anti-Catholic sentiment cut down the normal Democratic vote when Al Smith ran for president in 1928, and it prevented President Hoover from appointing Donovan attorney general in 1929.) The Catholic archdiocese that covered Manhattan and the Bronx sent more money to the Vatican than did the archdioceses of all the countries in Europe combined. On St. Patrick's Day, March 17, the whole town became Irish for a day. And, as the city government's leading Irish institution, the police department occupied a central place in the Irish ascendance.

With the inconvenient McLaughlin out of the way, Walker scoured the horizon for a more pliable police commissioner. He soon alighted on his former law partner, Joe Warren, who accepted the job after a discussion in which Walker laid out in clear terms his desire to rid the city of Valentine and his noxious confidential squad. Summoned to a meeting with the new commissioner, Valentine anticipated another demotion and a protracted stay in Siberia. Instead, in a display of backbone that came as a shock to the mayor as well as to Valentine, Warren promoted him to deputy chief inspector. "Your duties are unchanged—I like your work," he explained. Valentine was now seen as the second most important man in the department, and the newspapers took to calling him "the Crown Prince."

He had an unusually sharp nose for the dodges and scams of police officers on the make. Few of his peers would have thought, for example, to question a piece of police heroism that filled the newspapers one winter day. A young patrolman had rescued a drowning man off the Brooklyn docks. While the rest of the department joined in celebrating the patrolman's derring-do, Valentine felt compelled to subject it to closer analysis. The amount of time spent in the frigid waters, the distance covered, the weight of the helpless victim—it added up to more of a feat than Valentine considered humanly possible. Rather than keep his suspicions to himself, he arranged to meet the young hero at an indoor swimming pool. After they had chatted for a while about swimming and rescue work, Valentine directed him to strip and dive in. The patrolman indicated a preference for remaining in the steam room, where they had begun their conversation. But in the face of Valentine's insistence, he did as ordered—and nearly drowned. It turned out that he couldn't swim. Valentine, without removing his clothes, plunged into the pool and rescued him.

Like many of his contemporaries, Mayor Walker seemed to expect the good times on Wall Street and Broadway to last forever. Politically, conditions started to deteriorate one night in November 1928, when Arnold Rothstein, seated at his usual table in Lindy's, was called to the phone. Following a brief conversation, he departed for the Park Central Hotel, the site of many of the era's grander card games. Shortly afterward, Rothstein was found staggering near one of the hotel entrances, shot in the abdomen. Cops heard that he had been up in Room 349. When detectives entered, according to Valentine's subsequent account, they found an overcoat bearing a label with the name of George McManus. According to the prevailing line of gossip, Rothstein had welshed on a gambling debt to McManus. The murder shook the underworld and the world of politics alike. Mayor Walker was at a roadhouse with Betty Compton when he got the news. The bandleader, Vincent Lopez, saw the mayor turn pale and asked him if everything was all right. Walker told him about the shooting and added that it meant "trouble from here on in." (Although McManus was indicted for murder, the charges were dismissed after the D.A. submitted a memo to the court that was virtually a brief for the defense.)

Rothstein lingered for two days, while investigators ransacked his files, finding, among other documents, evidence of the fixing of the 1919 World Series and links to Jimmy Hines, Waxey Gordon, Frank Costello, and Lucky Luciano. Walker was shaken and discouraged. But he awoke from his funk long enough to perceive the advantages of finding an underling who could be plausibly blamed for some of the violence and sleaze in which his administration now seemed to be entangled.

He and his police commissioner had a talk. It was Walker's opinion that Warren should resign immediately, citing ill health. Warren thought he should have a chance to solve the Rothstein case. His old friend the mayor gave him four days, and Warren labored strenuously but unsuccessfully. For a brief moment, he toyed with the idea of using his letter of resignation as an opportunity to blast the mayor and his regime. Then, as Walker had counseled him, he submitted a more conventional letter praising his boss and attributing his own decision to a desire to go back into private law practice. Soon after being relieved of his duties as police commissioner, however, Warren checked into a sanatorium. He died eight months later of a paralytic stroke.

Mayor Walker now turned to Grover Whalen, the city's official greeter. Whalen was a renowned poser, tall and handsome and impeccably groomed, with a magnificent mustache. In his silk hat and morning coat, with a boutonniere and a French Legion of Honor ribbon pinned to his lapel, he made a memorable impression. Equipped with a fine sense of public relations, he had perfected the ticker-tape parade, an institution that played a conspicuous part in New York life in the 1920s. Old newsreels show the mayor and his greeter, in top hat and tails, riding along with the likes of Charles Lindbergh, Commander Byrd, and Gertrude Ederle. These municipal celebrations, along with the St. Patrick's and police parades, raised public spirits, heightened civic unity in a polyglot city, served as homage to New York's Tammany masters, and gave the notoriously work-shy mayor an agreeable task to perform. Of course, some heroes—the Olympic archery champion or the president of Slobovia, for example—generated less excitement than others. But Whalen had that problem figured out. It didn't matter how obscure the celebrity was, he discovered; if you brought him up Broadway at noontime, there would be a ready-made crowd of hundreds of thousands of citizens gathered to celebrate lunch.

Before accepting the commissionership, Whalen went through a Hamlet-like agony of indecision, bowing to the call of duty, in the end, only after being assured by his regular employer, the John Wanamaker department store, that he would continue to receive his $100,000-a-year salary even as he served the city. This time, Valentine's dealings with the new commissioner were not marked by an unexpected burst of integrity. Whalen broke him back to captain, shaved $1,300 off his annual salary, and sent his squad of fifty officers scattering to the winds. "Gumshoeing and wiretapping are at an end," Whalen proclaimed with a righteous air. In explaining his treatment of Valentine, he drew an analogy with Charles Becker: here was another shoofly who had gotten out of hand.

"You're a fine lot of men," Valentine told the members of his disbanded squad, "and I'm proud to have known you. I know you'll be a credit to your commanding officers wherever you are. You were to me." Tears trickled down the cheeks of some of his former subordinates as they left the room. Valentine, for his own part, was sent to a backwater precinct in Queens. After checking out the new command, he telephoned his wife to say it was "a fine precinct" and stayed up all night in order to personally turn out three platoons and read the list of routine neighborhood complaints: one from a housewife about a Peeping Tom, another from a druggist contending against sneak thieves, a third about a noisy speakeasy. "Some people have been spreading rumors that I'm going to quit," Valentine said. "Get that out of your heads. I'm here to do a job and I'm going to do it. A good cop goes where he's told. I expect you to do that for me." Retirement was in his thoughts, though, if not in his words. He had already served long enough to claim his captain's pension, and he began looking forward to the day when he would have the time and the financial means to travel across America with his wife.

Whalen's eighteen-month tenure was a blaze of publicity stunts. A squad known as "Whalen's whackers" mounted splashy raids. Headquarters was sandblasted and its gold dome regilded and illuminated at night by multihued spotlights. The politicians were delighted; the gamblers and gangsters were equally pleased. The new commissioner also spent a lot of time denouncing the Red menace, and he had fifty rookie cops assigned to work undercover in the Communist Party. At the funeral of one party activist killed by the police, four of the sixteen-man guard of honor were undercover detectives. On May Day 1930, the Communists held a rally in Union Square and attempted to march on City Hall. The cops broke up their procession with nightsticks, Tompkins Square–style. Whalen's identification with Wanamaker's was well known, so the fleeing marchers got a measure of revenge by breaking the windows of the department store.

Whalen's administration was the last act of the Roaring Twenties NYPD. In October 1929, the stock market collapsed. A few months earlier, Whalen had organized a "spontaneous" rally of prominent citizens who demanded that Walker run for reelection. The Republican candidate, Congressman Fiorello La Guardia, ran a hard-hitting campaign. The police, he charged, knew who had murdered Rothstein but didn't dare bring the killers to trial for fear of what they might say about the administration. Reform's moment had not quite arrived, however, and Walker was reelected by a wide margin. Then, as the country slipped into the Depression, the mood of the electorate changed. Conditions became ripe for another of the great scandal-and-reform dramas that seemed to come at twenty-year intervals. A few weeks after the election, the Tepecano Democratic Club of the Bronx was holding a banquet in a restaurant to honor a magistrate named Albert Vitale. The crowd was made up of the usual assortment of politicians, mobsters, and city job holders, with a few cops sprinkled among them.

Seven masked gunmen burst in and robbed the guests of money, jewelry, and, in the case of a veteran detective, his revolver. When they left, the magistrate told the cop to keep quiet and all would be well. Three hours later, the officer's gun was returned to him. When word of this incident leaked out, the cop told investigators that he had surrendered his weapon on orders from the magistrate. Vitale was found to have banked an unusual amount of money in recent months, and one of his markers had turned up among the dead Arnold Rothstein's effects. Samuel Seabury, a prominent lawyer who had been the judge at Becker's second trial, was appointed by Governor Franklin Roosevelt to conduct an investigation of judicial corruption. His probe led to Vitale's removal from office.

Still, it was low-level stuff. Magistrates were small-time lawyers who couldn't make a living practicing and didn't have the connections or money to be made regular judges; their virtue was always suspect. Then, in August

1930, Joseph Force Crater, a Tammany man recently elevated to the state supreme court, interrupted a Maine vacation with his wife to return alone to New York City. He visited his chambers, filled several portfolios with private papers, and drew $5,150 in cash from the bank. After purchasing a ticket for a Broadway musical, he stopped at a popular restaurant, ran into a lawyer friend out with a showgirl, and joined them. Lingering long after curtain time, he left, hailed a cab, and was never seen again.

About six weeks after Crater's appointment to the bench, an investigation revealed, he had raised from his bank account and the sale of securities a little over $23,000—slightly more than a supreme court justice's annual salary of $22,500. It was commonly understood that a year's pay was the accepted price for a judicial robe. With Seabury beginning to consider the issue of the buying of judgeships, Crater might have been worried. As a lawyer, he had been the administrator of a bankrupt hotel, which was sold to a buyer for $75,000. Shortly afterward, the buyer turned around and sold it to the city for $2.85 million. Among the judge's effects was a note to his wife telling her that he expected to receive a large sum from the sale. That transaction, too, was beginning to arouse interest. Despite a mammoth investigation, the police could not find Crater. His girlfriends from the chorus lines had no idea where he was, nor did a former mistress who was suing him for breach of promise.

In a subplot of Judge Seabury's examination of the magistrates, it emerged that some of the city's vice cops had six-figure bank accounts on salaries of, typically, $3,000 a year. The lieutenant in charge of plainclothesmen in the Broadway area and his mother had jointly banked nearly a quarter of a million dollars. Under interrogation, the lieutenant's mother claimed that she had saved up the money over a lifetime, always putting away nine dollars out of every ten. It was pointed out, though, that the account had contained only $5,000 six years earlier. The fact that vice cops were paid off was not exactly hot news to most New Yorkers. Ears perked up, however, when the probe uncovered a lowlife named "Chile" Acuna, who admitted that he and others like him worked regularly with plainclothesmen to set up women on prostitution charges—in order to shake them down. The press referred to Acuna as the "human spittoona." In the midst of these stimulating revelations, Seabury was handed what appeared to be another Becker case.

In February 1931, a woman named Vivian Gordon visited his office to make an accusation against a Manhattan vice cop named Andy McLaughlin.

Eight years earlier, she claimed, he had framed her on a prostitution charge, enabling her estranged husband to obtain a divorce. Seabury's investigators told her to produce papers and come back. Before she could comply, she was found dead in Van Cortlandt Park up in the Bronx, strangled with a rope. A preliminary investigation disclosed that her husband had been granted his divorce on the very day of her conviction in 1923. Where was Detective McLaughlin? He was still a Manhattan vice cop—one who, a few days after Gordon's story got out, had departed for Bermuda, where he had still been at the time of her murder. His alibi was suspiciously good, skeptics declared. As a vice cop, McLaughlin would be acquainted with the kind of organized-crime figures who would willingly arrange a hit for him, especially if their own interests were served at the same time. That's how the leaders of New York's institutionalized reform movement figured it, anyway. Meanwhile, the press discovered that Gordon, as a result of her divorce, had lost custody of her daughter, now sixteen and living quietly in New Jersey. Ten days after her mother's death, the daughter committed suicide. The affair looked like a rerun of Becker-Rosenthal nineteen years earlier.

Seabury, who had sentenced Becker to the electric chair, was not unaware of the political possibilities. He had ostentatiously bowed out of the political arena in 1916, after a gubernatorial campaign stymied by a double-cross from Teddy Roosevelt and sabotage by Tammany Hall. Tall, white-haired, and physically imposing, Seabury had the right social credentials, being a direct descendant of John and Priscilla Alden.

Detective McLaughlin was beginning to look like a candidate for the electric chair. Luckily for him, however, Grover Whalen was no longer the police commissioner. As the Seabury investigation heated up, Whalen decided that he was needed back at Wanamaker's. Mayor Walker replaced him with the chief of detectives, Ed Mulrooney. The second career cop to be named commissioner, Mulrooney was one of those solid commanders who held the force together in good times or bad. A quiet man, he dreaded public speaking; his mouth, when he opened it, poured out such stereotypical bits of New Yorkese as "thoid" (for *third*) and "berled" (for *boiled*). He had started as a pilot on Hudson River barges and, after joining Teddy Roosevelt's department at twenty-one, had spent a number of years in the Harbor Unit chasing river crooks and making rescues. (It was Mulrooney who had taken twenty-nine bodies out of the hold of the *General Slocum*.) Under Mulrooney's scrutiny, a number of things about the Gordon case and the allegations against McLaughlin did not fit. Gordon had twice served time in the New York State women's prison at Bedford Hills after pleading guilty to prostitution. She was known for sending letters to johns and threatening to expose them if they refused to pay off. In a search of her apartment in the swank Murray Hill section of the East Side, detectives found the names of forty girls and more than five hundred johns. Gordon liked to sashay around in a fur coat and jewelry, and had been wearing such an outfit on the night of her death—but not when her body was found. Her husband demonstrated that he had filed his divorce action before his estranged wife's arrest; the granting of the decree on the date of her conviction was coincidental. The police eventually charged three Broadway thugs with Gordon's robbery and murder, and one of them turned state's evidence against the others. Because an accomplice's testimony was insufficient for conviction, the defendants went free, but they were later convicted on other charges. Andy McLaughlin did not become another Becker, but he was fired for collecting graft as a vice cop.

The Seabury investigation moved on to the operations of New York City government in general. Laughter tinged with anger greeted Sheriff Farley's explanation of his large bank deposits: they had come from a "marvelous tin box" he kept at home. Captain Costigan, now in retirement, gave timely advice to Seabury; and the exiled Captain Valentine testified about the raids that he had made on gambling houses and the price paid for them. The stockmarket crash had put a serious damper on the Broadway scene, and crime seemed to be out of control. By 1931, the signs of economic distress were everywhere. Sixteen cops were killed that year, mainly in run-ins with gangsters. In one spectacular escapade, three holdup men ambushed the manager of a Bronx fur plant as he was taking a $4,600 payroll to his office. When a police officer guarding him reached for his gun, he was shot in the heart. As the robbers sped from the scene, they fatally wounded a motorcycle policeman who threatened to obstruct their escape. An off-duty fireman grabbed the officer's gun and began blazing away, until he, too, was shot, though not fatally. The gunmen sped toward Manhattan, shooting at everybody in their path. Traveling in a passing car, a couple and their four-year-old daughter were wounded by gunfire, the child mortally. Then a detective and patrolman joined the chase in a commandeered taxicab, the detective blazing away from the running board. After crossing a bridge into Manhattan, the getaway car hit a truck and finally came to a stop. Police poured a hundred shots into the vehicle, hitting each of the three bandits at least a dozen times and killing the lot of them. Around the same time, a four-year-old boy was killed in an exchange of gunfire between Dutch Schultz's gang and "Mad Dog" Coll's.

The public didn't mind gangsters bumping each other off, but this was too much. In 1931, a baby-faced cop killer named "Two Gun" Crowley and a companion held 250 officers at bay until Crowley surrendered. The siege seemed to dramatize a world gone mad. In May, Mayor Walker, fearing a hostile reaction, decided to skip the annual police parade. At the last minute, he told Commissioner Mulrooney that he would walk along for a few blocks. Marching at the head of six thousand cops up Broadway and then Fifth Avenue, Walker attracted a smattering of boos; then he heard cheers that inspired him to go the whole route. But in 1932, with his troubles coming to a head, he canceled the parade altogether; after seventy-five glorious years, it was never held again.

At the Seabury hearings that year, Walker was unable to explain some "loans" he had received from people doing business with the city. Seabury leaned on Governor Roosevelt—by now the likely Democratic presidential candidate that fall—to have Walker removed from office. The mayor submitted his resignation and, in the tradition of Oakey Hall and Richard Croker, sailed for Europe with Miss Compton on his arm. After some dickering, the bosses replaced him with surrogate judge John P. O'Brien, who enhanced his reputation as machine puppet by remarking, when asked about the identity of his police commissioner, "I haven't gotten the word yet."

As the reformers were casting about for a mayoral candidate in the 1933 elections, Judge Seabury expressed a preference for Fiorello La Guardia. The Italian Jewish "Little Flower" was considered uncouth by many goo-goos: he wore a ten-gallon hat—an affectation picked up during his boyhood on a western army post, where his father had been a regimental bandmaster—and he was constantly berating somebody or something at the top of his lungs. After the war, he had become president of the Board of Aldermen and had been elected to Congress from East Harlem, at that time the uptown Little Italy. In the House of Representatives, La Guardia was closer to the La Follette Progressive wing of Republicanism than the New York State conservative kind. In 1932, he lost his congressional seat in the Democratic landslide. But the fusionists needed Seabury, and eventually a deal was cut that, in a three-way race, produced victory for La Guardia. His principal reform rival, General

John F. O'Ryan, had stepped aside in the interests of unity; O'Ryan thus became the obvious choice for police commissioner, but it was equally necessary for Valentine to occupy a prominent place in the new scheme of things at headquarters. At La Guardia's direction, the old shoofly returned as chief inspector, quickly settling back into his routine. Some of his longtime adversaries were in a mood to kiss and make up. A delegation from the Honor Legion arrived at his office to present him with an honorary membership. Valentine refused, recalling their treatment of his partner Floyd Horton fourteen years earlier.

General O'Ryan did not hit it off with La Guardia. Valentine did, so the mayor quickly fell into the habit of bypassing the commissioner and going directly to the chief inspector on sensitive matters. Soon there was a more decisive break. By 1934, the city swarmed with strikers and protesters demanding economic assistance. Some of them blocked the entrances to office buildings; a taxicab strike led to violence. The general felt that nightsticks were the answer. La Guardia, a former labor lawyer, disagreed. In September, O'Ryan resigned, and La Guardia wasted no time in announcing that Valentine would take command of the department. For the first time in its history, a shoofly had become police commissioner.

When Valentine moved into the commissioner's office in Room 200 of the headquarters building on Centre Street, he put pictures of La Guardia and Seabury on the wall of that dark, dour, wood-paneled chamber; and though he didn't do the same with his old friends Floyd Horton and Dan Costigan, their spirits also occupied the office. Having reestablished the commissioner's confidential squad, he took a strong personal interest in disciplinary proceedings. Facing dismissal, accused cops would plead tearfully for mercy. "You're fired. Take this bum outta here," was Valentine's customary response. In his first five years as commissioner, eighty-three officers, including several high-ranking ones, committed suicide. But while not widely loved by the rank and file, Valentine had a tender side. Any patrolman who felt mistreated by his superiors was invited to tell the commissioner about it face-to-face. He also let it be known that he would personally extend a loan to any cop who needed money to tide him over a difficult period. Several times a week, on average, subordinates took him up on the offer.

11

The Celebrity Cops

Johnny Cordes, the only New York City police officer ever to win the departmental medal of honor twice, was not one of those kids who always wanted to be a cop. At the age of twelve or so, he had a nice little racket going as a door-to-door seller of clothesline. The night before he visited a building, he would be up on the roof removing the line that the tenants had already strung there. Many of his boyhood companions wound up with police records. A few died in the electric chair. Later in life, Johnny's intense dislike for crooks was tempered by an awareness that, as he put it, "The border-line between me and them was very thin." In his combat skills and powers of improvisation, he conceded nothing to such contemporaries as Mad Dog Coll, Lucky Luciano, Dutch Schultz, and Legs Diamond. Had he chosen a life of crime, he might be as well-remembered as they are.

Cordes, who had wide blue eyes, thick eyebrows, and straw-colored hair, grew up in Greenwich Village before it was bohemian and Harlem before it became mostly black. His father was Alsatian. (The name was COR-deez, with the accent on the first syllable.) After health problems knocked him out of the workforce, Johnny's mother, who had come over from Germany, moved the family uptown and became the janitor of their tenement building. Johnny, the eldest of five children, helped out by selling newspapers, setting up pins in a bowling alley, and doing errands for a brewery, in addition to his clothesline enterprise. At thirteen, he dropped out of school and went to work as a runner and order clerk on Wall Street. Later, weary of the financial world, he earned a

213

living as a six-day bicycle racer at the Velodrome in Newark and, between races, as a five-dollars-a-head recruiter for the O'Brien Civil Service Institute. His strategy was to prowl the places where big men did backbreaking work—the docks, the stables, the packinghouses—and evangelize about the easy life that awaited those who, with the O'Brien institute's help, passed the police test. A free spirit, Cordes gave no thought to a police career for himself until one evening when, on a visit to the institute gymnasium, he was moved to offer some unsolicited weight-lifting advice to a huge man who was training for the exam.

His pupil—a beef lugger by day—was ungrateful. "I suppose you think *you* could get on the cops," he sneered.

"Certainly I could," Cordes replied.

They bet on it. Cordes, who had the slim physique of a bicyclist, passed. The beef lugger failed.

After joining the department in August 1915, he was plucked out of the Police Academy by Inspector Dan Costigan. With his slight build, fresh complexion, and ready smile, Cordes didn't look like a cop, and, vindicating Costigan's judgment, he proved to be a gifted undercover. On the confidential squad, Cordes was called on to portray, among other roles, a sailor, a streetcar conductor, a longshoreman, a young playboy, and, in the words of his Boswell, the journalist Joel Sayre, "a whole stock company of bums."

Although Cordes had no use for what he called "take guys," his specialty under Costigan was not police corruption but gambling, and he was far from a zealot on the subject. One duty of his boyhood job with the brewery had been to deliver ailing horses to a blacksmith named Jimmy Hines—now a significant force in Tammany Hall and the protector of many an eminent figure in the bookmaking and numbers rackets. Cordes had remained on good terms with Hines, and the connection served him well after the pendulum swung Tammany's way in 1917. Like everyone who bore the taint of association with Honest Dan, Cordes paid a price for it when Richard Enright became police commissioner. But Cordes's punishment—a brief stint in uniform—was nothing like that endured by Lewis Valentine, Floyd Horton, or Costigan himself. After six months, Cordes caught a gang of robbers and became a detective again, this time with a squad working out of the East Sixty-seventh Street precinct in Manhattan.

Heading to work on the evening of March 29, 1923, Cordes stopped at a cigar store on Lexington between Sixty-ninth and Seventieth Streets. His brother Freddy, who had given him a lift, was parked outside in his Studebaker. Johnny, whose tour of duty was scheduled to start in ten minutes, didn't pay much attention to the two men behind the counter, and he was on the brink of placing his order for Optimo Blunts when he noticed that they were dressed funny for salesclerks. They had caps on, for starters. In addition, the taller of them was wearing an overcoat and had his hand concealed in it in a way that suddenly made Cordes uneasy. He glanced quickly at the shorter man, who, indeed, was very short, only about four foot ten. He was pointing a .38-caliber revolver at something or somebody on the floor. Cordes had walked into a stickup.

The stickup men—Patrick Ahearn, twenty-three, and John Whitton, eighteen—were drug addicts and members of the Hudson Dusters, a gang native to the West Village streets on which Cordes had played and scrapped as a boy. Whitton, known to his friends as the Mutt, had escaped from the East View Penitentiary in Westchester County the previous weekend. He was the brains of the partnership. Ahearn was the brawn. They had entered the store a few minutes earlier and with guns pointed at the manager—the shadowy figure now cowering below the muzzle of Whitton's revolver—had removed $16.98 from the cash register. On their instructions, the manager had opened up a safe and turned over an additional $80 in bills and coins.

Cordes was wearing a green cap and a red-and-brown-checked camel's-hair overcoat. He was not armed. "I don't see the particular type of cigar I smoke," he said in a casual tone of voice, as though he had noticed nothing out of the ordinary. "Guess you're out of them. Well, I'll be in again." He turned to leave.

"Just a minute, mister," Ahearn called. "You'll get your smokes."

Nearly out the door by now, Cordes looked back. What he saw made the pretense of ignorance hard to maintain. The store manager was standing next to Whitton, obviously petrified with fear. He stared at Cordes in a silent cry for help.

The barrel of Whitton's gun shifted toward Cordes, who instinctively placed his right hand over his heart. Whitton fired. The bullet passed through Cordes's hand, nearly tearing his thumb off. It continued through his coat and into his chest, knocking him to the ground.

"Give it to the son of a bitch!" Whitton shouted, spotting signs of life. Ahearn was nearer the gate that divided the counter area from the rest of the store, and in a better position to follow up. Pulling the revolver out of his coat, he ran out to the fallen detective and bent down, preparing to administer the shot that would finish him.

From his prone position, Cordes snatched away Ahearn's gun and shot him in the stomach. Ahearn went down. Cordes traded gunfire with Whitton, his shots going wild because he was using his uninjured hand—his left. Whitton, shielded behind the cash register, fared better, striking Cordes in the right shoulder and the left thigh. When it became clear that Cordes was out of ammunition, Whitton burst out through the gate, intending to complete the job his partner had bungled. But Cordes managed to seize his gun too and, with another blast of left-handed gunfire, sent Whitton running for his life into a stockroom.

Dragging himself to his feet, Cordes went to inspect the manager. Unhurt, he gave Cordes some happy news: the stockroom had only one door. Now Cordes stumbled out onto Lexington Avenue and into the path of his brother Freddy, who had heard the shots and was coming to investigate. He had just entreated his brother to go for help when a shot rang out, and Cordes was hit by another bullet—number four of the night. This one, it turned out, had been fired by a fellow police officer, an off-duty sergeant. Partying with a lady friend nearby, he had heard gunfire. Although heavily intoxicated, he responded to the call of duty by staggering across Lexington Avenue in the direction of somebody he mistook for a robber: Cordes. His shot hit Cordes in the back of his right shoulder, knocking him flat and sending his gun— the one he had seized from Whitton—skidding across the pavement. The approaching sergeant got off two more shots. One went crashing through the cigar store's plateglass window. The other shattered the window of a neighboring business.

Cordes pulled himself to his feet and held out his detective's shield. "Please don't kill me, mister," he begged. "I'm a policeman."

The sergeant moved closer. With his gun muzzle against Cordes's left cheek, he pulled the trigger once more. The bullet narrowly missed the jugular vein, winding up behind Cordes's left ear. The shot spun Cordes around, but miraculously he found his balance and, anesthetized by rage, gave the sergeant a stiff kick in the groin. The gun went off again, striking Freddy Cordes in the elbow. Johnny picked up Whitton's gun and, using his right forefinger to stanch the flow of blood from his cheek, reentered the cigar store. Stepping over the unconscious Ahearn, he proceeded to the stockroom and ordered Whitton out at gunpoint.

By the time Cordes and his prisoner reached the street, a passerby was administering first aid to the detective's brother, and the sergeant had absconded. There were no other police in sight.

Sensing that he might not have much consciousness left in him, Cordes marched Whitton toward Presbyterian Hospital, at Seventieth Street and Park Avenue.

"You're gonna die, mister," Whitton said en route. "Lemme go and I'll say a prayer for you."

Cordes told him to save his prayers. "Anyway," he added, "if I thought I was gonna die, I'd kill you first."

Taking inventory of the damage later in the evening, the surgeons tallied three fractures of Cordes's right jawbone and two shoulder wounds, plus bullet holes in his right hand, left leg, and chest. He was a bloody wreck. Just the same, the clerk at the main entrance of the hospital refused to admit him and his prisoner (this was Park Avenue, after all), firmly directing them to the emergency-room entrance on Seventy-first Street. There Cordes was finally able to phone the precinct and get medical attention after several of his fellow detectives took custody of Whitton (and caught him in the act of trying to ditch the stolen cash).

The incident, with the facts sanitized in the sergeant's favor, made the front page of the *New York Times*:

POLICEMAN IN ERROR SHOOTS A DETECTIVE WHO FIGHTS ROBBERS

Officer Surprises Thieves Robbing United Cigar Store and Uses Pistol.

SERGEANT ENTERS AND FIRES

Officers Mistake Each Other for Bandits and Three-Cornered Battle Follows

ONE IS WOUNDED 4 TIMES

Two Robbers Captured, One Mortally Hurt—Detective Cordes Also Dying and His Brother Injured

Like Whitton, the doctors who operated on Cordes didn't think much of his chances. A mere six days later, however, he snuck out of the hospital by a back staircase in a suit of clothes that his wife had smuggled in. Less than a week after that, at home with his hand and shoulder bandaged and his fractured jaw wired up like a suspension bridge, he received an unexpected visit from a man he had arrested for forgery the previous year; the man attacked him, proclaiming that it was God's will that Cordes die. Though not at his physical best, Johnny managed to level his assailant with a dining-room chair. But the incident made an unfavorable impression on Mrs. Cordes. Sensing that her husband might not be altogether safe under his own care, she spoke to his doctors, who spoke to his superiors. The department had him shipped upstate to a police vacation and convalescence camp in Tannersville, in the Catskills, where the superintendent was Syd Enright, the commissioner's nephew. When Uncle Richard visited the camp, Cordes, in his new status as hero, was emboldened to ask the commissioner for a promotion to first-grade detective. Enright, remembering the former shoofly, harrumphed and moved on.

Cordes suffered from chronic headaches the rest of his life, and his left ear was mostly decorative. He could almost surely have qualified for a disability pension, but, as he told Mayor Jimmy Walker a few years later, he wouldn't have known what to do with himself. "I don't drink, I don't smoke, I don't play the races, and movies bore the hell out of me," he said. "My only fun is putting these hoods in the box."

Not surprisingly, Cordes's near-death experience affected his view of the world. For years afterward, he clung to the green cap he had worn that night, and to the practice of leaving his gun in his locker at the precinct. The NYPD required its men to be armed at all times, but Cordes, who often worked undercover, was famously reluctant to do so, lest he be mistaken for a criminal again and get into a shootout with another fellow cop. His superiors tended to turn a blind eye to such transgressions when Cordes was the one committing them.

When the NYPD bestows medals of honor, it tends to look for officers who have been shot at or, better still, have actually been shot. Johnny Cordes won his first for the cigar-store escapade. His second, in 1927, came after another incident in which he went up against a couple of gunmen—ones who, in this case, had kidnapped a prominent bootlegger. Cordes, unarmed again, enlisted the help of a passing motorcycle cop before his final confrontation with the suspects, at the corner of Sixty-sixth Street and Central Park West. He disarmed one of the thugs before he could fire. The motorcycle cop shot the other one as he was preparing to get off a second shot at Cordes from close range.

But while it was daredevil feats like these that brought Johnny to the notice of the gossip columnists Walter Winchell and Ed Sullivan and their readers, it was his sheer doggedness more than his invincibility that caused other detectives to shake their heads in wonder. Not long after his second wounding, Cordes left Tannersville to hunt down a member of a West Side gang responsible for a series of stickups. Cordes maintained his stakeout, unassisted, for nine days, grabbing only the few hours of sleep he needed each night and using the men's room of a nearby Elevated station when necessary. He was climbing the stairs to the El at 4:00 A.M. when he noticed a commotion in the street. A crowd had formed around an ailing horse harnessed to a Borden Milk Company wagon. On the edge of the crowd, Cordes spotted his suspect, Eddie Purtell. Cordes hurried back through the turnstile and down the stairs.

"Why hello, Johnny," Purtell greeted him. "I thought you was hurt real bad."

"Superficial flesh wound," Cordes said nonchalantly.

"What brings you out this early?" Purtell asked.

"You," Cordes said. In a quick bit of improvisation, he added, "Coughlin told me to bring you in."

Assistant Chief Inspector John J. Coughlin, the commander of the Detective Bureau, was a tall, muscular, and striking-looking man who dressed like a banker and wore a pince-nez. As a detective captain, he had led the investigation of the Wall Street bombing in 1920. Once, as a sergeant in Chinatown during the tong wars, he had sat on a stage to protect a comedian threatened with assassination. The performance came off without a hitch; later that night, however, a tong hit man slid down a rope and shot into the comedian's flat, killing him. Coughlin was a bachelor who lived with his sister in the Bronx. The police force was his life, and his knowledge was encyclopedic. With Coughlin, the mention of almost any block in the city seemed to bring forth the story of a murder, robbery, or burglary that had occurred there.

"You're supposed to be in Tannersville," Coughlin noted coolly when Cordes and his prisoner appeared.

"Sure," said Cordes. "But don't you remember you phoned me there last night and told me to bring Purtell in? Well, here he is."

"I did no such goddamn thing," said Coughlin.

"I guess you must have been drunk when you called me," said Cordes, who had an easy manner with persons of all ranks and social stations. "Well, anyway, now we got Purtell here, it's a shame to waste him. Let's take him over to Long Island City and have a guy there in the hospital look at him."

The guy in the hospital—a wounded cashier—identified Purtell as his assailant, and with the testimony of three more witnesses, he was booked for robbery (and sentenced, eventually, to thirty years in Sing Sing). "Now are you satisfied that you told me to come down and collar that guy?" Cordes asked Coughlin.

"Yes, I am, you fresh little bastard," Coughlin replied.

The Detective Bureau was no longer the tiny fiefdom it had been in Thomas Byrnes's day, though his spirit still ruled it and for a long time his old boys ran it. Steve O'Brien and "Chesty" George McClusky played musical chairs as chief of detectives. McClusky replaced O'Brien when Roosevelt's reform administration fell and, after falling out with Devery and coming back under McAdoo, was himself replaced by O'Brien. Organizationally, though, the twentieth-century Detective Bureau was created by Arthur Woods. After he returned from a scholarly inspection tour of Europe's police forces, Woods kept another Byrnes man, Jim McCafferty, as chief of detectives as he modeled the bureau along Continental lines, creating the homicide, robbery, pickpocket, and safe-and-loft squads, among other specialized units. Woods also promoted the use of scientific methods of investigation. In 1904, Detective Sergeant Joseph Faurot had been sent by Commissioner McAdoo to London to study the fingerprint system of Scotland Yard. By the time he returned, McAdoo was out as commissioner and his successor, General Theodore Bingham, was not interested. But with Woods's support, Faurot was allowed to fingerprint the suspects in a burglary at the Waldorf-Astoria, and the prints were sent to Scotland Yard, where one was identified as belonging to an international hotel jewel thief. In 1908, Faurot used fingerprinting to solve the murder of a nurse. In 1911, now a captain working on a case involving a loft burglar named Caesar Zolla (a.k.a. Charles Christi), he was able to demonstrate the reliability of the new approach in court by having fifteen men press their fingers on an ink pad. Then, with Faurot out of the room, one of them touched a glass, and the detective, invited back into the chamber, correctly identified him. From then on, New York courts accepted fingerprint evidence as scientific.

Woods knew American detectives were decades behind their European counterparts. There, criminal investigators were university men, and the police maintained a close working relationship with academics. The police chief of Vienna, Johann Schober—later the chancellor of Austria—remarked that "scientific study is as much a part of our police training as is the schooling of our men in matters of self-defense." The intellectual leader of European criminal investigation was Hans Gross, a real-life Sherlock Holmes, who learned how to question suspects and analyze evidence as an Austrian magistrate before he was called to a law professorship. As police commissioner, Woods created a homicide clinic and sex offenders laboratory in 1914.

Commissioner Enright, who succeeded Woods, had little use for clinics and labs and discontinued them. When Enright hosted international police conventions in New York City, acting captain Cornelius Willemse, commander of the First Detective District, was assigned as a liaison because of his fluency in several languages. Willemse mingled with European policemen who argued theories of criminal anthropology, sociology, psychiatry, and jurisprudence, and discussed the greats of criminology and psychology, Lombroso, Ferri, and Krafft-Ebing. Some of these officers had attended lectures by Hans Gross, and all regarded his writings as their bible. Willemse could only offer the visitors a "frisking tour," a gun-hunting raid with plenty of "blackjack action," and the ritual trip to Chinatown. The Europeans could barely conceal their boredom. The only thing that impressed them, it was said, were the beautiful girls on Fifth Avenue and the massive skyscrapers.

Willemse, who began his own detective career in the first generation after Byrnes, was a notably unscientific policeman. As a young detective, though, he was assigned to the Manhattan district attorney's homicide squad, where he worked under the direction of the rigorous Frank Moss. In his murder investigations, Willemse became friendly with the chief medical examiner, Dr. Charles Norris. Before the establishment of the M.E.'s office in 1918, homicide investigations were conducted by coroners—political appointees with no medical training. The tall, bearded, aristocratic, and wealthy Dr. Norris had no time for politics and used his own funds to supplement the office budget.

In the 1920s, when Cordes was a rising star in the bureau, Homicide was still commanded by Deputy Inspector Arthur Carey, another Byrnes veteran who had been Arthur Woods's favorite commander. Homicide handled the big murder cases—the ones splashed across the front pages of the city's racy new tabloids, the *Daily News* and the *Daily Mirror*, which illustrated these tales, whenever possible, with gruesome photos of the deceased. (The old hell-raising *Herald* and *Tribune* had merged into the upmarket *Herald Tribune,* which disdained sensationalism, as did the *Times.* The *World* could go all out on a politically charged affair like the Becker case, but it was not so readily aroused over dead blonds in a love nest.) At the end of 1928, Commissioner Grover Whalen would sack Carey for failing to solve the Rothstein case (even though he produced compelling evidence linking McManus to the crime), thus ending the career of one of the most capable and thorough investigators the NYPD had produced.

The safe-and-loft squad investigated big-time burglaries and hijackings. The yegg trade still flourished, and a good safe-and-loft man, analyzing the modus operandi of a a particular job, or sometimes just the tool marks, could tell which crew was responsible. Safe-and-loft men also encountered a substantial number of supposedly honest merchants who, seeking an insurance windfall, would report bogus burglaries or even have their premises torched when business was slow.

The Detective Bureau was the one place in the NYPD where female officers could make their mark. Uniformed patrol and promotional exams were for men only. But a woman in plainclothes could often go unnoticed by criminal suspects. (European intelligence bureaus and American private detective agencies used female agents long before U.S. police departments did). The Irish-born Mary Shanley was a star of the pickpocket squad, with more than a thousand arrests of shoplifters, confidence men, and pickpockets to her credit. Assigned to the bureau in 1935, she rose quickly to first-grade detective. Mary, as she was known throughout the department, was a tough street cop, five feet eight inches tall and weighing 160 pounds. Pickpockets were skilled professionals who used the same tactics generation after generation. Dips, by this time more commonly called "cannons," still worked in teams. If the victim was female, two "moll buzzers" would walk in front of her while their accomplice, the "hook," passed behind her. The moll buzzers would stop abruptly, engineering a collision with the victim, and apologize profusely to her, giving her a good jostling in the process. Meanwhile, the hook would open her bag and steal the valuables. One of Mary's first collars was a notorious hook, "Chinatown Charlie," who preyed on the shoppers along Fifth Avenue.

Another of Mary's targets were the "seat tippers" who worked the theaters around Times Square. They would sit behind women who had come to the movies alone. When the viewer was wrapped up in the story (tearjerkers were best for this purpose), the thief would use his feet to tip up the seat where the victim had placed her purse, which would fall through the gap into the seat tipper's hand—and Mary Shanley would collar him. If the thief was a woman, Mary would grab her by the shoulder, whispering, "This is a pinch, honey." If it was a man and he tried any funny business, Mary was not adverse to letting off a few shots. "You have the gun to use, and you may just as well use it" was her philosophy, which earned her the nickname of Annie Oakley. Once, while arresting a female seat tipper she had followed out of St. Patrick's Cathedral, Shanley fired two shots in the air to halt a male accomplice. In 1941, she was temporarily demoted from first grade after firing her revolver, while off duty, in a tavern in Jackson Heights, Queens. She was always on the lookout for women she thought might need protection. Near the end of her career, while patrolling Fifth Avenue, she saw a beautiful blond shopper being followed by a crowd. Mary moved in and attached herself to the woman, and for the next two hours Grace Kelly shopped in safety.

While Mary might blend into a crowd, in a one-on-one situation her Irish brogue and big, tough appearance would mark her as a cop. More petite women were required for undercover work. In 1949–50, when the Brooklyn district attorney was investigating a top gambler named Harry Gross, a slim young policewoman named Theresa Scagnelli was assigned to work as a maid in the hotel where Gross lived. Unbeknownst to him, every day, after Gross departed, Scagnelli took papers from his desk to the district attorney's office. Later, under her married name of Melchionne, she would head the Police-women's Bureau and rise to deputy commissioner in charge of community affairs and the Youth Bureau.

One of the city's top narcotics investigators in the same period was 110-pound first-grade detective Kitty Barry. A sergeant's daughter, she was not afraid to go alone on a drug-buying mission into an apartment with a dozen junkies, or to stroll across a public park after midnight, making herself the target for a serial rapist. Although Barry made many outstanding collars, her picture never appeared in the newspapers, lest her identity be compromised.

Every precinct had its own team of detectives—generalists who ran the gamut of crime categories. Although they shared a stationhouse with the patrol force, their upstairs offices were off-limits to uniformed cops, and the cops sometimes got the impression that detectives, with their gold shields and higher salaries, were above them in more ways than location. A precinct detective squad was generally divided into two rotating teams. One stayed in the office "catching squeals"—that is, arrests brought in by the patrol force or citizen complaints. The other group of detectives would be out investigating, or "pitching," cases. The night-shift catchers would be on duty from 4:00 P.M. to 8:00 A.M., occasionally napping on cots provided by the department. The prestige of precinct detectives, like that of patrolmen, varied with the price of the local real estate. Manhattan had more status than the outer boroughs; midtown was preferable to uptown. In any part of city, the precinct detectives were the ones who did the bulk of the work, and some exceptional men served their entire careers in that capacity.

William Quaine, born in Ireland, attended Dublin University with the idea of becoming a priest. He wound up taking a degree in law and emigrating to the United States at the age of twenty-three. In 1907, he joined the NYPD as a newly minted U.S. citizen. Quaine had a ready smile and a thick brogue, but there was steel in him. Assigned to the East Harlem precinct, he was walking a post one day under the Third Avenue Elevated when he saw a runaway horse pulling an express wagon toward a crowd of children on the sidewalk. Quaine seized the horse's bridle and managed, after a struggle, to steer it aside. Battered and bruised, he sat down to catch his breath only, to hear a cry of "Help, police, thief!" from a window. The exhausted Quaine raced three flights up, met the thief coming down, grappled with him, and knocked him cold. A few months later, he trapped a robbery suspect on a crowded Elevated platform. The suspect fired at Quaine and missed. Quaine kept on coming and knocked him out with a right to the jaw. He hadn't shot back, he explained later, for fear of hitting a bystander.

In 1912, still a patrolman, Quaine chased a holdup man from the scene of his crime, on East Ninety-seventh Street, to a tenement at 101st and Second Avenue. Quaine recognized the suspect as a member of the Car Barn Gang—toughs from the East Side docks, who had earned their name by boldly posting a "Cops Keep Out" sign at the boundary of their turf near a streetcar barn at Ninety-seventh Street and Second Avenue. When the holdup man resisted arrest, Quaine beat him unconscious and took him to the station. The suspect turned out to be wanted for the murder of a Bronx saloonkeeper. The police commissioner at the time was Rhinelander Waldo, and Quaine was tapped for duty with one of his antigangster squads. His squad got the mission of breaking up the Car Barn Gang, which soon ceased to exist. Quaine then moved back to the precinct detective squad in East Harlem.

The hoods of the uptown Little Italy found Quaine annoying. One night, he got a call from a man offering to meet him at 116th Street and Third Avenue with valuable information. Quaine suspected a trap. He went anyway. As he arrived, he noticed movement, and the glint of a revolver, behind one of the Third Avenue Elevated pillars. Whipping out his gun, he fired, striking the gunman. Half a dozen other hoods were lying in wait. Quaine shot three of them, and the rest fled. The Galucci Gang, which had put a price of $10,000 on his head, quickly thought better of the idea.

Quaine knew every inch of the precinct. One day, a young woman employed by one of the big department stores vanished on her way home. Looking at her picture, Quaine gasped. He had seen her walking alone a couple of hours earlier, and he had a good idea about what had become of her. Accompanied by two fellow detectives, he went to a tenement on East 104th Street, where a woman known as "the Little White Sister," suspected of involvement with a narcotics gang, made her headquarters. The detectives kept her apartment under surveillance until she emerged and made her way to an adjoining building. They followed her, broke into a shabby flat, and found the missing girl on the floor, gagged and bound. The gang's intention, apparently, was to turn her into a prostitute. Quaine's stoolies were among the best, and he could often provide information of value to his colleagues at headquarters. Because he worked out of the Broadway limelight and had no connections—and because he treated gamblers and fixers with conspicuous disrespect—Quaine remained a precinct detective until shortly before his retirement, when he was transferred to the district attorney's office. After leaving the force, he returned to Ireland.

Francis D. J. Phillips, known to his friends as Frankie, joined the NYPD in June 1926. He was small, wiry, and ambitious. Transferred to a station on the Lower East Side, the traditional spawning ground of the city's criminals, Phillips carved out a name for himself by making collars: a street robber here, a store burglar there. One day, Phillips and one of the precinct veterans, Patrolman Eddie Flood, caught a couple of opium peddlers after a frenzied chase along Grand Street. Like Quaine, Phillips won praise for not firing into a crowd. Before long, he was working as a precinct detective in Sheepshead Bay, at the far end of Brooklyn.

In July 1928, Phillips was summoned downtown, to Coughlin's office. He had performed well in his Brooklyn tryout, and he was hoping for a chance to test himself in a livelier and more central area of the city. To Phillips's surprise, Coughlin informed him that he would be working at headquarters—and not just at headquarters, but on the most prestigious of the headquarters detective units, the main office squad, which got the toughest cases. For a twenty-four-year-old cop with two years on the job, this was a great opportunity. Then Coughlin threw in a piece of news that left Phillips in a state of blissful amazement: he would be working with Johnny Cordes.

Cordes was a near-mythical figure in the department by now. He was also a favorite of the main office squad's commanding officer, Inspector John J. Lyons, who had taken Cordes with him through three successive assignments. With the appointment of George McLaughlin as commissioner in 1926, Lyons's squad, along with Valentine's raiders, became the crack troops of the city's war on organized crime. Phillips would be joining the team as it took on a new mission: Legs Diamond.

Jack Diamond—his proper name—was a gunman who had worked for Arnold Rothstein, among other gangsters, before setting up a bootleg distillery in the Catskills. Although he sometimes described himself as a "bodyguard," Diamond had a proactive understanding of the role. Whenever possible, he liked to make sure that his clients' enemies were foiled not just in their attacks but in their hopes of remaining on the planet. People who succeeded in winning large sums of money at Rothstein's gaming tables sometimes failed to reach home with their winnings intact. "That's the kind of bodyguard Legs was," Cordes told Phillips.

Cordes's squad had established a wiretap on Diamond's suite at the Harding Hotel on West Fifty-fourth Street. The law on intercepted communications was murky, and a lot of people were put off by the idea of wiretapping, so the department avoided the term; detectives spoke instead of "supervising" someone's phone. The fierce prosecutor Frank Moss, acting as counsel to a state investigating commission, had once jumped on Commissioner Woods about the practice. Woods had lashed back, telling him: "You know that you cannot do detective work in a high hat and kid gloves." He added, "There is too much snappy talk about the rights of the crook. He is an outlaw and defies the authorities. Where do his rights come in? If people spent less time talking about the dear criminals and more time helping the police to run them down we would have fewer criminals."

Cordes and Phillips spent many long hours in a dank basement down the block, listening to phone calls. Occasionally, they would hear arrangements being made for a rendezvous, and Phillips would get the job of following Diamond or his henchmen, to see where they went and whom they met. Cordes, the master tailer, was too familiar a face for such duty now. "Nobody uptown knows your kisser," he told Phillips, "and that's good." Phillips was in his mid-twenties, but he could pass for a teenager. In a T-shirt, standing by a newsstand with a racing form in his hand, he cut a very low profile.

Cordes liked to talk. Phillips liked to listen, and he milked their time together for its full educational value. "Now lemme tell you something about when you're tailing some punk," Cordes would say. "You always gotta be casual-like. Never make no quick moves, even if the guy should turn around and look right at you. Never get too close to your man. If you think they've made you, drop 'em. Yeah, as soon as they get suspicious, lose 'em. It may throw them off the track. If you're sure they've made you, get on the phone to the boss or me, and we'll send someone else out."

Phillips and Cordes's more routine days usually began at the 9:00 A.M.

lineup, where known criminals and suspects were paraded. The lineups were a way for detectives to keep current on who was who in the criminal world; they also reinforced the department's basic values. First-time offenders who had not hurt anybody were treated gently, the theme being "Look, son, you made a mistake, but you can straighten out." Old-timers caught in the act, and on their way up the river for life as three-time losers, did not usually deny their guilt and tended to be philosophical about what lay ahead. Cops treated them as professional soldiers would treat a defeated brother in arms. Smart punks and vicious thugs could expect a going-over. When one of them came to be questioned by the officer conducting the lineup, usually someone of high rank like Inspector Lyons, he would be asked about his past crimes and present activity. If he played dumb, the inspector, glancing at the yellow criminal-record sheet in front of him, might say, "You had a problem in the Bronx a few years ago, didn't you?" After a lot of stalling, the suspect might admit that he had been sent up for a jewelry-store holdup in that borough. More prodding by the inspector might elicit an admission of additional holdup raps. When asked to explain his present predicament, the suspect might say he had been socializing with a few friends in a Broadway nightspot when detectives burst in and grabbed them, omitting the fact that one of his pals had a gun on him and that all had serious criminal records. With this, every detective in the room made a mental note to look up the suspect and his friends the next time a store was heisted. Sometimes a high official, even the police commissioner, would attend and deliver a pep talk. Some of the prisoners on stage had been arrested by uniformed cops who were present in the audience. In such cases the big boss conducting the lineup would be sure to single them out for praise, while they sat beaming like students who had aced their exams. If the collar was a really good one, the chief of detectives or police commissioner might ask the cops involved to "report to my office after this is over." Soon they would be wearing detective shields. When a police officer had been killed the night before, the ranking officer would note the facts of the case, exhort the men to greater vigilance, call attention, and order a salute while he proclaimed the department's motto, "Faithful unto Death."

Working with Cordes, Phillips learned the ins and outs of the Bureau of Criminal Investigation. Most cops, Cordes said, knew only one way to use the BCI: they would walk in and say, "I want a yellow sheet on Joe Jerk." In addition to its files of arrest records, the BCI maintained an elaborate index of suspects by modus operandi, with types of crime listed in alphabetical order: arsonists, auto thieves, baggage thieves, bank robbers, bogus representatives, bomb throwers . . . all the way to white slavers and worthless check passers. Under the robbery heading, for example, were such subcategories as inside, outside, from women, snatchers (payroll), and snatchers (pocketbooks). In a separate file called "the gallery," suspects were organized by race, height, and distinguishing facial features.

Captain Fred Zwirz of the BCI was proud of his domain. While he was showing Phillips around one day, a detective came in with word of a new brand of thief—a woman who worked the ladies' room at Bonwit Teller. Waiting until she heard a toilet flush, she would reach over the stall door, grab the bag that the occupant had left hanging from a hook on the inside, and run. "Look under the Ts," Zwirz replied, wearily. "There it is. Toilet workers." They found several women under that heading, including one who matched the description that the detective had gotten from a victim. "Go pick her up," said Zwirz, handing the detective a photo. "There's nothing new in crime," he added. "I've been here fifteen years, and none of you boys ever bring in anything new."

Still, Cordes was a traditionalist, arguing that "the most important pinches I've made came because some stool I knew phoned me and said, 'You'll find the hood that pulled the West Side killing up in Room 514 at the Bedford Hotel.' " Stool pigeons could only do so much, though. Cordes's team knew all about Legs Diamond, but witnesses who were prepared to testify against him had a habit of disappearing. Diamond co-owned an uptown establishment known as the Hotsy Totsy Club. One night, three hoods walked in, ordered drinks, and picked a quarrel with Diamond and an associate named Charles Entratta. Hymie Cohen, Diamond's partner in the Hotsy Totsy, told the orchestra to play louder. With the music drowning out the noise, Diamond shot one of the hoods, Red Cassidy, three times, twice in the head. Entratta shot the other two.

There were twenty-five customers in the club at the time, plus a number of waiters. But the police didn't have a single cooperative witness by the time Diamond finally presented himself, voluntarily, for arrest. Diamond, for his own part, had come up with a couple of witnesses who were ready to testify to his innocence. "You know, Jack, we got everything but a picture of you bending over Cassidy and putting three bullets in his head," Cordes told him.

"I guess you'll need to have a picture if you're ever going to get me," Diamond replied.

"I guess you're right," said Cordes.

Diamond was considerably less cautious with fellow criminals than with the law. In the end, it was underworld rivals who got Diamond, assassinating him in Albany as he was on his way to a liaison with a girlfriend. "The son of a bitch crossed us," Cordes commented.

They had better success against other targets. In December 1930, Cordes's team went after three men who had been hitting Brooklynites over the head with gun butts and lead pipes and stealing their wallets, purses, and jewelry as they emerged from the subway on their way home. "The sluggers," they were dubbed. (The term *muggers* had not yet achieved currency.) A snitch led the detectives to one Julius Levy; while he denied his involvement, his arrest had an interesting effect on the robberies: now they were being committed by two perpetrators (or "perps") instead of three.

In an effort to find Levy's associates, Cordes and Phillips paid a visit to a Lower East Side saloon that he had frequented. The bartender, speaking in front of an audience of customers, praised Levy as a quiet drinker and generous tipper. Looking squarely at Phillips, he added, "I get off at two, and lots of times Julius would drive me home." At 2:00 A.M., the detectives were waiting outside. "We'll give you a lift home tonight," Phillips said. The bartender nodded, got in, and quickly changed his tune, describing Levy as a "strong-armed bum" and volunteering the names of his two accomplices, Sam and Jake Cohen. He added that they usually came by his saloon around 8:00 P.M. for a shot or two.

"Sam and Jake Cohen," said Cordes. "I know them rats well."

The following night, Cordes, Phillips, and another well-known headquarters detective, Johnny Broderick, were parked across the street when a large car pulled up outside the saloon. Cordes, who had a remarkable memory for faces as well as voices, recognized the Cohen brothers instantly. "They're our babies," he proclaimed.

There were five men in the car, and they came out swinging. After what the *World* described as a "short but desperate fight," the three detectives—"noted for their fistic ability"—emerged victorious, and their five prisoners were delivered to the nearest precinct.

In 1934 the main office squad blew a golden opportunity to apply the techniques of forensic psychology to the chief suspect in the crime of the century. For two years after the kidnapping and murder of the Lindbergh baby, bills from the ransom money appeared in New York City. Acting Lieutenant James Finn, in charge of a squad of twenty-three NYPD detectives assigned to the case, believed that it was only a matter of time until there would be a capture, probably in New York City. Then would come the interrogation. To prepare for it, Finn, on his own initiative, consulted a prominent New York psychiatrist, telling him about the ransom note and other details of the case. The psychiatrist constructed a profile of the kidnapper as someone out to demonstrate his superiority to a national hero. When the suspect was captured, he advised Finn, he would never talk if he were hauled to a police station and subjected to the usual grilling. The way to get the story out of him, the psychiatrist continued, was to take him to a private setting (something like a psychiatrist's office) and question him in a soothing manner. In 1934, a gas station attendant jotted down an automobile license as the driver passed a gold certificate, and a task force of FBI agents, New Jersey troopers, and New York policemen arrested Bruno Richard Hauptman in his car near his home in the Bronx. With preliminary jurisdiction in the case, New York City detectives conducted the initial interrogation. Instead of taking him to a simulated clinical setting, however, they brought him to an out-of-the-way precinct on Greenwich Street in Lower Manhattan, where he was put through a standard police interrogation by detectives under the direction of Inspector Lyons. Hans Gross would not have approved, and in the end, Hauptman did not confess, although he was executed for the crime anyway.

The other star of the bureau was Johnny "the Boff" Broderick, who had been a Gashouse District tough guy, a former labor slugger, and, briefly, a city fireman before joining the force in 1923. He often worked with Cordes, and the two Johnnys were both favorites of the gossip columnists and police reporters. Broderick had started out on the gangster squad. His commander, an ex-boxer, explained their mission in terms that Broderick, a formidable boxer in his own right, could appreciate: "Now lemme tell ya what we're gonna do. We're going after the shakedown mugs, the tough guys, the muscle guys. But we're not . . . gonna arrest them. . . . We're gonna beat them up. This ain't according to the book. When we get through with them, they're either going to be too scared to shake down the storekeepers, or they're gonna be in the hospital."

Broderick had a left hook that he patterned on Jack Dempsey's. (He was a good deal taller and heftier than Edward G. Robinson, who played a cop modeled on him in the 1936 movie *Bullets or Ballots*.) He demanded that gangsters tip their hats to him. Once, after a few words, he left Legs Diamond upside down in a garbage can. On another occasion, he went to the funeral of a Hudson Duster and spat in the dead man's eye. But he was capable of a certain subtlety. Sometimes he would stroll down his beloved Broadway with a lead pipe wrapped in a newspaper. Encountering a hoodlum of his acquaintance, Broderick would walk right up to him and start hitting him with the newspaper; to an onlooker, it looked as if he were giving an old friend a playful tap.

Broderick was skeptical of the niceties of due process. He encouraged the victims of crime—young women especially—to think of him as an informal protection service. A chorus girl, for example, might be under pressure from some creep looking to turn her into a prostitute. She could go to court, secure an order of protection, and beg the police to honor it, living in terror all the while. Or she could contact Broderick, and the upshot would be simpler. After an encounter with his rolled-up paper and a headfirst landing in a trash barrel, the aspiring pimp would not bother her again.

The bureau in its heyday bred colorful cops. Barnett "Barney" Ruditsky, a Jewish detective who had lived in London and South Africa as a boy, was not a formidable specimen to look at, but he was as rough and fearless as the Boff, with whom he frequently teamed up. Returning home after celebrating a wedding anniversary one night, Ruditsky and his wife spotted two men holding up a candy store. Ruditsky seized one of the perps and grabbed his revolver. Turning the weapon over to his wife, he told her to hold the prisoner while he pursued (and captured) his accomplice. In time, departmental opinion would turn against the celebrity detectives who hung out at nightclubs and palled around with gossip columnists and gamblers. The eternal question hung over the bureau: Were detectives and their informants too close?

In 1941, Barney Ruditsky retired and moved to Hollywood, where he served as technical adviser on a series of crime movies. His reputation with the Los Angeles Police Department was not good. Ruditsky was accused of collecting bad debts for Bugsy Siegel and operating a Sunset Strip nightclub frequented by gangsters. The well-known mobster Mickey Cohen was once shot leaving the place. In 1947, Broderick was compelled to leave the force after a district attorney's wiretap caught him in some highly compromising conversations with underworld figures.

Some of the men who would run the NYPD in later years were not enamored of the Detective Bureau. "Only on a neat organizational chart was the Detective Bureau a province of the larger jungle that was the NYPD," Patrick V. Murphy, the commissioner brought in after the Knapp commission scandal of 1970, commented. Murphy described the bureau as a "breakaway entity, with its own laws, customs, and marching orders." Detectives spent much of their time in bars, according to Murphy, "either shaking down the owner or planted on a bar stool listening for 'information.' "

In the 1930s, though, the bureau rode high. Commissioner Valentine's ideas about the proper treatment of hoodlums were nicely in tune with Broderick's. Viewing a lineup one day, Valentine was appalled to see a young gunman, freshly arrested for murder, wearing a pearl-gray fedora and a velvet-collared overcoat. Valentine was in a bad mood: a number of merchants had been shot by robbers recently, and only the night before, he had visited a dying policeman who had interrupted a holdup. The sight of the smug young killer in his snappy attire was the clincher. "He's the best-dressed man in this room," Valentine observed with disgust, "yet he's never worked a day in his life. When you meet men like this, don't be afraid to muss 'em up. Men like him should be mussed up. Blood should be smeared all over that velvet collar. Instead, he looks as though he just came out of a barber shop."

Valentine held out the promise of promotions for cops who "kick the gorillas around." Once, when a stickup man died after being brought in covered with bruises, Valentine dismissed the affair as "just another dead criminal, a small loss." Gangsters, in his view, should be taught to "tip their hats" to the police—a policy that Johnny Broderick took literally. The "muss 'em up" speech elicited a storm of protest from editorialists and civil libertarians, and some of the critics appealed to the mayor to set his police commissioner straight. They got no satisfaction from La Guardia. He was a committed liberal when it came to the rights of labor unions and political dissenters, including Sacco and Vanzetti. But La Guardia, like Valentine, had a visceral hatred for hoodlums. On the day he took office, he announced that Byrnes's old boundary line for criminals was now the city limits. In the same tradition, he encouraged the police to knock transgressors around. When a group of arrested jewel thieves showed up in court with their faces battered out of shape, La Guardia's comment was, "Just too bad."

The press, for the most part, thought the same way. One night, at the fights in Madison Square Garden, Broderick took a couple of tough-looking characters to task for failing to tip their hats in the manner that he required. They turned out to be respectable out-of-town businessmen not familiar with New York etiquette, and when they landed in the hospital, Broderick was in trouble for a while, until his journalist friends came to his rescue.

Johnny Cordes landed in hot water for being too accommodating to an accused killer. When George McManus called the police to arrange his surrender in the Rothstein murder, Cordes got the assignment of bringing him in. McManus had a brother in the church and another who had been a first-grade detective, and he was generally considered a good guy by the theater and sporting set. He also enjoyed the protection of Jimmy Hines. So when he met Johnny at a barbershop and asked for time to be made presentable—his picture would be on the front page of the newspapers, after all—Cordes consented. After reporters got wind of the police-supervised haircut, Cordes endured a torrent of criticism, and Commissioner Grover Whalen briefly busted him back to uniform. But the press soon lamented the fall of its favorite, and he was restored to the bureau.

At times, the bureau men could act with surprising restraint. In 1931, when "Two Gun" Crowley and his buddy "Fats" Duringer were holed up in a building on Ninety-first Street near West End Avenue, Cordes, Phillips, and Broderick rushed uptown and, with the local commander's approval, climbed the stairs to the landing outside the apartment in which Crowley and Duringer were making their stand. "Crowley, you'll be dead in a few minutes," Broderick shouted. "Give up now and I promise no one will lay a hand on you." Broderick wound up capturing both men without firing a shot. They were convicted of first-degree murder and sent to the electric chair.

Cordes's hesitancy to carry a gun was not the only attitude that made him unusual among his peers. He was strongly opposed to capital punishment and disdained the third-degree methods commonly used with suspects at the time. When it came to the young punks who accounted for much of his workload over the years, Cordes believed in rehabilitation and, indeed, sometimes helped bring it about. One day in the late 1920s, he received a letter from "the fellow that was playing tag with you that night in the cigar store when you tagged me out." His correspondent, who signed his name "Paddy," was Patrick Ahearn, the man he had shot in the stomach. After a recovery nearly as miraculous as Cordes's, followed by eighteen months in prison, Ahearn had become a longshoreman. Now, several years later, he was out of a job. "I seen your name in the paper this morning saying you were one of the best men in the department," he wrote. "That was what made me think of you."

Cordes found him another spot and watched over him long enough to be satisfied that Ahearn had gone straight. Ahearn's buddy John Whitton, after fifteen years in prison, also landed a job on the docks—until a superior learned about his record. "He's a murderer," Whitton's boss told Cordes, who had come in to make a plea on his behalf. "I don't want him around here."

"It wasn't you he tried to murder," Cordes countered. "It was me. And if I don't hold it against him, why should you?" By the late 1930s, worn out from long hours and his wounds, Cordes had transferred to the waterfront squad, where he had been made an acting lieutenant. This gave him a connection to the shippers, so he was able to find a place for Whitton on another pier. A few weeks later, after a shipment of disassembled machine guns disappeared en route to the British Army, the waterfront squad received an anonymous tip from a caller who asked for "Johnny."

"The lieutenant's not here right now," the detective on duty replied. "Can I take the message?"

The caller gave the name of a haberdasher's on Fifteenth Street, where, as he'd promised, the police found the machine guns—assembled and wrapped in burlap bags. The next day, they fished Whitton out of the Hudson, with three bullet holes in him.

Cordes's protégé, Phillips, had a distinguished career in the bureau, rising to the rank of deputy chief in charge of all the central-office squads, with, it seemed, a good shot at moving up to chief of detectives in the next big command shuffle. Phillips, like Cordes, preferred professional criminals to amateurs. His idea of a worthy adversary was the great bank robber Bill Sutton, whom the tabloids dubbed "Willie" and, because of his penchant for disguise, "the Actor." It was a matter of pride with Sutton that, in the commission of some sixty major robberies and burglaries, he had never physically injured anyone, though he had originally come to serious police attention as a murder suspect.

A small, frail-looking man with high cheekbones, Sutton grew up on the Brooklyn waterfront. When he was just twenty years old, one of his neighborhood gang buddies was murdered, and stool pigeons named Willie as the killer. Sutton went into hiding, and it took the cops two years to find him. When they did, according to his account, they gave him a bad beating, though he was acquitted on the murder charge. Forever after, Willie eschewed violence and was polite with cops. Questioned by Phillips after being busted for a bank job in 1930, Sutton recalled his boyhood jaunts in Prospect Park and grew dewy-eyed when he spoke of the flowers and shrubs of the Brooklyn Botanic Gardens and his early dream of becoming a gardener. Phillips eventually brought up a jewelry-store job on Fulton Street. "Look, Frankie," said Sutton, "I never went in for penny-ante jobs. I read about that stickup, and I remember thinking what jerks the men were who pulled it."

Phillips thanked Sutton for what he took to be a truthful answer, since the police already had three suspects.

"So long, Frank, I'll be seeing you again," Sutton said at the end of their talk.

"I doubt it, Bill," Phillips replied.

Sutton was sent to Sing Sing with a thirty-year sentence for the bank job. But in December 1932, he and a buddy escaped, climbing over a thirty-five-foot wall into a waiting car. In fairly short order, the Corn Exchange Bank at Broadway and 110th Street was robbed by three men. One of them was wearing a police uniform. Nobody was hurt. Phillips and his colleagues discerned Sutton's handiwork.

After a second bank robbery, acting captain Patrick McVeigh summoned Phillips and four other top detectives and told them to drop everything else and focus on Sutton. "Bring him in," McVeigh said.

The detectives made the rounds until they found a midtown hotel clerk who recognized a photo of Sutton's associate Eddie Wilson. The previous summer, according to the clerk, Wilson had stayed at the hotel under a pseudonym. Examining his phone records, the detectives eventually located another member of Sutton's gang, Joseph Perlango, alias Joe Plank, who was living on Chrystie Street. Phillips put in a wiretap, and after getting a group of Corn Exchange Bank employees to describe the voices of the robbers, he settled down to monitoring Perlango's phone calls. On Saturday, February 3, 1933, he heard a voice that made him raise his hand.

"Is this you, Joseph?" asked the caller.

"Good to hear from you, Eddie," Perlango said. "How's everything?"

"Splendid, splendid. Bill sends you his best. He and Irene are fine."

"They can have that town," said Perlango.

Eddie Wilson—for it was certainly he—mentioned that he would be "driving down to New York" the following night to see friends. He would return home directly, he added, trying to assuage Perlango's concerns, since "I'm only about five blocks from the city line."

The detectives guessed that Wilson was in Yonkers. And since Wilson also spoke of having just picked up his 1934 license plates, they decided that he had probably obtained them at the office on 181st Street, in Washington Heights. With a call to the appropriate authorities, they learned that the motor-vehicle bureau had issued a license to Kenneth Morley, a pseudonym that Wilson had used in the past. The car was a Chrysler sedan with the license plate 3-Y-2663.

At ten-thirty the next night, they saw the Chrysler heading south on Broadway, followed it, and nudged it over to the curb. Phillips flew out of the detectives' car, ordering Wilson to put up his hands. Wilson drew a gun from his waistband. Phillips fired, striking him between the eyes, and hopped onto the running board. Wilson's companion, a young woman, screamed as the car continued on, driverless. Phillips managed to reach inside and knock the gun from Wilson's hand, but the car didn't come to a stop until another detective grabbed the steering wheel.

Sutton's robberies were so impeccably planned and executed that there was no way he and his associates could be caught (or so he believed), as long as they resisted the temptation to rat on one another. Sutton himself set a high standard of noncooperation. Wilson—one of the few associates who could match his fortitude—did not talk. But the police used his arrest to extract a statement from Perlango. "Smarten up, Joe," Captain McVeigh told him. "Wilson is dying. You know he'll come clean before he goes. If you beat him to it and tell us where Sutton is, that won't hurt you any when your trial comes up."

Perlango led them first to Trenton and then to Philadelphia, where the detectives enlisted the aid of that city's chief of detectives, Jim Malone. They broke in through Sutton's door and seized a .45 automatic from his waistband.

"Captain Malone and Captain McVeigh and Frankie Phillips from New

York," said Sutton by way of greeting. "They sent the first team, didn't they? I told you I'd see you again, Frank, remember? How did you guys ever make me?"

"We got Eddie Wilson and Perlango yesterday," McVeigh said.

"Wilson never talked, Captain, not Wilson," said Sutton.

"Phillips had to shoot him," McVeigh reported. "He's in bad shape. If he lives, he'll lose his eye—maybe both eyes."

"That's tough, real tough," Sutton said. "Wilson was a great guy to have along."

They found three machine guns in addition to a stash of revolvers, tear gas bombs, handcuffs, and police and post office uniforms, as well as $51,000 in stolen bills.

After confessing to the bank jobs, Sutton congratulated Phillips on a piece of police work deserving of a promotion. "I'll be seeing you again," he added. True to his word, Sutton escaped for the third and last time in 1947. He remained at large until 1952, when a twenty-three-year-old clothing salesman named Arnold Schuster spotted a man who resembled Sutton on a subway train. When the suspect got off at a Brooklyn stop, Schuster followed him to a filling station, where the man bought a battery for his dead car, which was parked around the corner. Schuster spotted some cops parked in a patrol car and apprised them of his suspicions. Their method of checking out the suspect was to ask him if he was, in fact, Willie Sutton. "No, my name is Gordon," he replied. Satisfied, the cops departed. When they went into the precinct and told their story to a detective, he insisted on accompanying them back to the scene. The suspect was still tending to his car, but he admitted his true identity when grilled by the detective. All three cops were promoted to first-grade detective immediately. The salesman's role in the case was not revealed. When the newspapers lamented the police officers' ineligibility for $200,000 in reward money, Schuster went public in hopes of claiming the money for himself. Two weeks later, he was shot dead. Sutton had nothing to do with the assassination: it turned out that the gang lord Albert Anastasia had been enraged by the sight of the salesman on television. "I can't stand squealers," Anastasia had exclaimed as he ordered the hit on Schuster. In fact, there had been no rewards offered for Sutton's capture; it was all talk. There were, however, rewards offered for Schuster's killer. Sutton himself, genuinely shocked by the crime, tried to put up $10,000.

On another occasion, an informant warned the police that Sutton, having heard about what Phillips had done to Wilson, was gunning for him. Phillips assured his wife that Sutton was too much of a professional to be carried away by personal animus. Sutton confirmed this later. "Shooting a cop is for these trigger-happy young punks who are loaded with junk," he told Phillips. "I'm a bank robber, not a killer, Frank." But there had been days, he added, when he had felt ill will toward Phillips. Sutton was a Dodgers fan. Phillips was just about the only Giants fan in the borough of Brooklyn. Sutton had read that Phillips never missed a Dodgers-Giants game. As a precaution, therefore, Sutton had stayed away from those games. That, he said, was his only grievance against Phillips.

The NYPD was not as forgiving. In 1956, Phillips was called in front of a grand jury in Suffolk County, on the east end of Long Island. The grand jury was probing a gambling casino that Phillips had visited while off duty. At first, he denied an acquaintance with the owner; then he went back to the jury and admitted knowing the man under a different name. It seemed to be a fine point, but Phillips was indicted, and the new regime at police headquarters, under a bookish commissioner named Steve Kennedy, cut him no slack. Phillips was compelled to retire. The era of the celebrity detectives—the cops with nine lives and the same kind of flash as the criminals they chased—had come definitively to an end.

12

Battle in the Lead

A s the Jackie Robinson of the NYPD, Sam Battle displayed some of the same qualities as the great second baseman who signed with the Brooklyn Dodgers in 1946. After joining the force in 1911, Battle spent his first few years enduring the methodical silence of his colleagues and the stares and taunts of white citizens. On reserve duty at the West Sixties precinct, he had a sleeping perch of his own up in the flag loft, where he occasionally mused on the incongruity of the Stars and Stripes over his head and the segregation below. Not until he was joined by a white sergeant seeking a quiet place to study for promotion did Battle have any company.

By the teens, San Juan Hill was losing its status as the city's principal black neighborhood. Spurred by the 1900 riot, black churches and their congregations began to settle in Harlem. In 1913, the NYPD recognized the shift in population by transferring Battle to the West 135th Street station. There, too, he was something of a curiosity, and his fellow cops were standoffish. Reporters would occasionally come around and try to prod Battle into saying something disparaging about his coworkers. But he could not be provoked.

In Harlem, Battle was no longer a lone pioneer: Robert Holmes, the second black officer appointed to the NYPD, was assigned to the same precinct. Like Battle, he was an active street cop and one who apparently had friends in the community—many of them. In 1917, Holmes was shot to death by a burglar he had been pursuing. Twenty thousand Harlem residents turned out for Holmes's funeral. Harlem's black population was largely composed of people like Holmes's mourners: hardworking, churchgoing, innately conservative men and women. If enlightened political leadership had reached out to them, giving them the same chance at jobs, housing, and education as other groups and bringing them into public agencies such as the police department in significant numbers, a large, stable, urban black middle class might have developed. Instead, blacks made slow progress.

In 1916, there were just fifteen blacks on the force, including Battle and the two from Brooklyn who had been merged into the NYPD in 1898—Battle's brother-in-law Moses Cobb and John Lee. All were patrolmen. In Chicago, by contrast, where blacks constituted a significant part of the then-dominant Republican Party's political base, far more of them won jobs on the police force. The Chicago department, though less than half the size of New York's, had 131 blacks, including a lieutenant and ten sergeants.

World War I spurred the migration of blacks from the rural South to the urban North. Between 1910 and 1920, the number of blacks in Manhattan (mostly in Harlem) nearly doubled, from 60,000 to 109,000—almost 5 percent of the island's population. The experience of making the world safe for democracy put some black soldiers in less of a tolerant mood when it came to second-class citizenship at home. In 1919, race riots broke out in many cities; thirty-eight people were killed in Chicago and six in Washington, D.C. In Harlem, which still had a substantial white population, a racial argument between two men ended in gunfire, with the black man shooting at the white man and hitting two innocent bystanders. Police who responded were also fired on.

Battle decided to study for the sergeant's exam that year and, like many of his white brethren, applied to Delahanty's, a cram school where police officers prepped for promotion. Word came back that his request would be put up to a vote of the other students. A few days later, in the early morning hours of September 16, a group of blacks congregating near the corner of 135th Street and Lenox Avenue began taunting people who were wearing straw hats, which had been out of season since Labor Day. Some of the taunters snatched or crushed the offending headgear. Not everyone took it as a joke.

One who didn't was Amanda Hayes, a white police officer from the 135th Street precinct, out of uniform and on his way home. As he started down the subway steps, a black man leaned over and grabbed his hat away. The officer gave chase, caught the man, and struck him. The mood on the street turned from lighthearted to serious. A crowd of blacks jumped Hayes, knocked him down, and broke his jaw. He pulled his revolver and fired two shots, killing a black man in the crowd. White passersby intervened on Hayes's behalf. Word quickly reached the station, and the reserves came charging to the scene, with Sam Battle leading the way, as usual. "That's a police officer you're fighting," he shouted, breaking through the crowd to rescue Hayes. A few days later, Battle was admitted to the Delahanty course by unanimous vote.

Acceptance by his peers was grudging; by the department, it was even slower. Although Battle scored high on the exam, Tammany was in power, and Commissioner Richard Enright refused to promote him. Battle set his sights on joining the Detective Bureau instead. He was forced to earn his appointment the hard way, by volunteering to share a cell in the Tombs with a black murder suspect. The plan, devised by the reckless captain Cornelius Willemse, was for Battle to pass himself off as a fellow criminal in an effort to get the suspect to talk. As Willemse might have anticipated, Battle was recognized, touching off a riot in the cellblock before guards could extricate him. Battle, who could easily have been killed, was duly made a vice-squad detective as a reward for his efforts.

He started out well in this new phase of his police career. On orders from Mayor John "Red Mike" Hylan, Battle and a group of his fellow vice cops raided a Republican club in Brooklyn that was renting its premises to sex-show promoters. Afterward, bringing the prisoners back to be booked, Battle had the presence of mind to tell the patrol-wagon driver to go past Hylan's house with the bell clanging, so the mayor would know the outcome. Before long, though, Battle got carried away, raiding a protected joint, and Enright shifted him to Canarsie, the last subway stop in Brooklyn. The Eightieth Precinct (as it was numbered then) had a reputation as the department's most forbidding Siberia. It was where the sewer pipes emptied out the waste of New York City toilets into the bay and the precinct was known in the NYPD, accordingly, as "the Shit House." When Battle reported to his new command, a sergeant told him to look up at the station door and tell him what he saw written. "Eightieth Precinct," Battle replied, puzzled. Wrong, said the sergeant: if Battle looked a little harder, he could see the unofficial station motto, "All Those Who Enter Here Leave Hope Behind."

With the arrival of Mayor Jimmy Walker in 1926, Battle managed to escape exile. Like Lewis Valentine, he was called in by the new police commissioner, George McLaughlin, who promoted him to sergeant and assigned him to detective duty in Harlem. By then, there were forty-nine blacks on the force. In January 1934, the first month of the La Guardia administration, Battle was made an acting lieutenant; a year later, he was promoted to a full one. But he advanced no further in the NYPD.

By the late 1920s, the postwar tensions had faded, and Harlem was widely regarded as a fun place where chic whites went (as the song said) "in ermine and pearls" to hear the music of Louis Armstrong and Duke Ellington. The fabled Cotton Club, owned by Arnold Rothstein and Owney Madden, would not even admit black customers. After the Depression hit, though, the atmosphere in Harlem turned grim. The unemployment rate among blacks reached 40 percent in 1935. (It was 15 percent for the rest of the city's population.) The situation was made more galling for many Harlemites by the employment practices of white-owned stores on 125th Street, the principal commercial thoroughfare of the area. There, out of a workforce numbering roughly five thousand in all, only about a hundred employees were black, and they worked mostly as porters or maids.

In the mid-1930s, virtually all of the city's 125 black officers, including two sergeants and Lieutenant Battle, were stationed in the black areas of Harlem or Brooklyn. Even in these neighborhoods most cops were white, and some had been sent there for punishment. In the 1930s, blacks made charges echoed in later generations: the police were an army of occupation; they did not provide sufficient protection; they were corrupt; they stopped and searched people with abandon. Among cops, Harlem was considered a dangerous assignment. The worst beat was known as "Beale Street" (actually 133rd Street between Fifth and Seventh Avenues), where, as one black writer noted, "a knife blade is the quick arbiter of all quarrels." Eleanor Roosevelt wrote La Guardia, urging the city to hire more black policemen. Such an effort might not be warmly received in Harlem, he pointed out in his reply, because some of the black cops who already worked there were perceived as "too rough."

Riots aren't supposed to happen outside the warm months or under a liberal mayor. But Fiorello La Guardia experienced two major riots in Harlem, and the first began on a chilly day in March 1935 when a sixteen-year-old boy named Lino Rivera stole a pocketknife from the counter of the S. H. Kress department store on West 125th Street. While about five hundred mostly black customers looked on, the manager and a couple of employees chased Rivera through the store and caught him. Struggling to escape, he bit at least one of his captors. The manager, fearing trouble, decided to take the boy into a rear office and let him go home after things had calmed down. But word quickly spread through the crowd that Rivera had been removed in order to be beaten. The arrival of an ambulance seemed to confirm the rumor, though, in fact, it had been called for an injured employee.

The store erupted, with customers overturning counters and throwing merchandise on the floor. Patrolman Tim Shannon of the West 123rd Street Station was walking a nearby beat, heard the commotion, ran inside, and called for assistance. Police reinforcements managed to disperse the crowds in and around the store. By 5:30, most of the cops had withdrawn from the area. But the most serious trouble lay ahead, fueled by a mistake that police officers would often make in situations of this sort. The subject of the protest, Lino Rivera, had been quietly released through the back door during the earlier disturbance; unfortunately, no one thought to inform the crowd of this. When people asked the bluecoats what was happening, they were given the usual: "Move along" and "Mind your own business."

At 6:00 P.M., just before closing time, a group of black and white pickets from the Young Liberators League paraded in front of the store. Daniel Miller, an unemployed young man from the South Bronx, mounted a hastily made platform and began to speak. Within minutes, he had attracted a crowd of about a thousand. According to the tale now passing from one onlooker to another, a ten-year-old boy, arrested for stealing a candy bar, had been beaten to death by police. Protesters threw bottles through two large plateglass storefront windows. Police reinforcements were ordered back to the scene, while the crowd grew to about three thousand. The police got some of the people in front of the store to leave, but others gathered in the back, where they began collecting bricks. Coincidentally, a hearse drove by: "There's the hearse come to pick up the boy's body out of the store," a woman cried. Belatedly, some cops made an effort to reassure people that the boy had not been killed, or even arrested. It was no use. Once again a mob stormed Kress's while rioters surged up and down 125th Street, breaking windows and looting other stores. By 9:00 P.M., there were seven hundred police officers in the area.

Near the corner of 127th Street and Eighth Avenue, a police officer fired a shot in the air after seeing a white man jumped by several blacks. As the attackers fled, the officer fired at one of them, hitting him in the back; the cop claimed later that the man had ignored an order to halt. Over the course of the night, several more black men were shot by police, and the brass finally decided to demonstrate that Rivera was alive and well. The teenager was accordingly fetched from home and, at 2:00 A.M., put on exhibit in front of Kress's.

By now the riot had spread many blocks from the original flash point. It took the police all night to restore order. More than a hundred people were injured and 250 store windows smashed. Three men were killed or died of bullet wounds inflicted by the police. Only when a community paper printed a picture of the youngster with the popular Lieutenant Battle did the truth become generally accepted. An investigating commission appointed by Mayor Fiorello La Guardia concluded that the riot had been largely a result of social conditions in the area. Its report was particularly critical of Commissioner Valentine and the NYPD, demanding that a citizens' committee be formed to investigate the department. La Guardia suppressed the report, but portions of it leaked out.

Valentine was an easy target for criticism sometimes, because he had a reflexive tendency to defend his men when they were enforcing the law. Just the previous year, though, he had called a sergeant on the carpet for using tear gas to disperse a crowd in Harlem. The sergeant took the position that he had been forced to use the gas in order to keep people from getting hurt; Valentine countered that there had been no disorder until the police arrived. It was Mayor La Guardia's policy, he said, "to give such meetings the fullest latitude."

The sergeant was uncomprehending. The demonstration leader wouldn't cooperate, he protested.

Valentine laughed. "Get used to it," he said.

La Guardia was a master of ethnic politics. The once-mighty German vote, for example, was now minuscule compared to that of the Jews and Italians; so La Guardia criticized Hitler but had little to say about Mussolini. Blacks, too, were a small voting bloc, and La Guardia hardly gave them a thought when he decided to attend a rally for Italian war relief during Mussolini's invasion of Ethiopia. On other occasions, though, he managed to work magic in Harlem. During his 1941 reelection campaign, La Guardia arrived at a rally in a Harlem park to the sounds of Cab Calloway's orchestra, while twenty thousand black New Yorkers greeted him with cries of "That's our mayor!" After La Guardia spoke, he announced that "the mayor of New York now welcomes the mayor of Harlem" and summoned Bill "Bojangles" Robinson, the country's most popular black entertainer, to the microphone. That same election year, in another canny move, La Guardia appointed Sam Battle a city parole commissioner. But the office was a minor one, passing on parole applications from prisoners serving short sentences in city jails. Yankee baseball great Lou Gehrig, stricken with his fatal illness, had been appointed to the same board in 1939 to give him something to do. Battle, a vigorous fifty-eight-year-old, would have been better utilized as a deputy police commissioner. (Despite the "bad heart" diagnosis that almost kept him off the force, he lived to the age of eighty-three.)

In 1941, La Guardia's principal black critic was a thirty-three-year-old minister, Adam Clayton Powell Jr., whose father had founded Harlem's Abyssinian Baptist Church early in the century. Eventually it became the nation's largest black congregation. In 1937, the son had succeeded his father as pastor, and from his pulpit he targeted the police department. No love was lost between the minister and Commissioner Valentine. In 1942, when Powell scheduled a rally to protest the police killing of a black man, Valentine advised La Guardia to urge Powell to cancel the rally while a grand jury investigated the shooting. "This type of rabble-rousing is dangerous and might result in serious disorder," Valentine warned the mayor. Powell would not back down. New York had a "racist police force and a prima donna mayor," Powell said.

In June 1943, after a race riot that left thirty-four people dead in Detroit, the army had to be sent in to restore order. Powell called for an immediate meeting with the mayor. If there were a similar riot in New York City, he said, "the blood would rest on the hands of La Guardia and Valentine." Even before the Detroit riot had ended, La Guardia had dispatched two officers to study the situation; one of them, acting lieutenant Emmanuel Kline, was black. In Detroit, the disturbances had broken out on a Sunday night, at a time when few supervisors were on duty, leaving rank-and-file cops to use their own judgment. Many had used it badly. The Detroit police had been especially free in the use of firearms. Of the twenty-five blacks who died in the riots, twenty-three were gunned down by the police. The Detroit riot spurred a review of NYPD policies. La Guardia and Valentine decided to place the preservation of life over that of property—there would be no shooting to prevent looting—and they would have superior officers present in large numbers.

They did not have to wait long for their plans to be tested. On Sunday night, August 1, at the Braddock Hotel on West 126th Street, an argument broke out between employees and a black female guest. The Braddock had frequently been raided for prostitution and narcotics, and, following a customary police practice of the day, an officer had been posted to the "raided premise." Patrolman James Collins of the Twenty-eighth Precinct had drawn the assignment this particular night. Police antivice practices were a sore point with Harlem residents; some cops, it was said, took it on themselves to bar interracial couples from registering at the Braddock. Three months earlier, the police had shut down the famed Savoy ballroom, supposedly for encouraging prostitution; the real reason, in the opinion of some black critics, was the presence of a conspicuous number of interracial couples on the Savoy's dance floor. The police, critics charged, were not nearly so zealous in their enforcement efforts against equally licentious downtown dance halls, which a Harlem paper referred to as "meat markets." (Actually, Valentine was tough on vice across the board, and the puritanical La Guardia shut down mildly risqué bump-and-grind burlesque houses whose chief attractions were the likes of Abbott and Costello and Red Buttons.)

The desk clerk at the Braddock asked Officer Collins to intervene. Collins advised the woman to leave. She refused and began verbally abusing the officer, who arrested her on a charge of disorderly conduct. All this was witnessed by another guest, a black domestic from Connecticut who was visiting her son, a military policeman. She intervened on the first woman's behalf. Collins told her to mind her own business. Her son, Private Robert Bandy, joined in, and a struggle ensued in which the soldier grabbed Collins's nightstick, according to a police report. Bandy insisted that he was simply trying to defend his mother. When he refused to surrender the club, Collins shot him. Mother, son, and cop were swiftly taken to the hospital.

Bandy had merely been grazed, but, once again, rumor turned the incident into murder: a white cop had killed a black soldier who was protecting his mother. Several thousand people gathered at the Braddock and at the 123rd Street precinct. Police reinforcements were sent in from neighboring precincts.

Under the watchful eyes of the police, the protest started out as an orderly affair. But by ten-thirty, people were breaking windows on 125th Street, and cops were firing in the air to disperse them. Claude Brown, the author of *Manchild in the Promised Land*, was six years old at the time; he woke up to the sound of crashing glass and assumed that the Germans or Japanese were bombing New York. The novelist Ralph Ellison recalled "distant firetrucks, shooting, and, in the quiet intervals, the steady filtering of shattered glass."

Heading uptown without delay, Mayor La Guardia ordered the Braddock closed. By early morning, there were five thousand police officers in the area. (Parole Commissioner Battle was also on hand.) Before the rioting was over, six people had been killed, all of them black; four were shot by the police, one by a bartender, and one by a member of a private security patrol. Two of the shootings by police had been in self-defense, investigators found. Two, though, were "looters" shot dead by "Big Ben" Wallace, a much-decorated black cop with a particularly fearsome reputation. (Three years later Wallace was showing a rookie around his beat. Entering a tavern, he spotted a man he suspected of being armed and ordered him to stand still. The man whipped out a gun and shot Wallace dead.)

Detroit had given the department time to plan, and many black leaders praised the mayor and the police for their relatively restrained response. Although the riot started on Sunday night, high officials swung quickly into action: La Guardia made two radio broadcasts in the early hours of the morning and three more the next day, calling for calm. The NYPD's sheer size helped: the five thousand cops brought into the riot zone added up to a bigger force than the whole Detroit police department. Not feeling outnumbered, officers were less prone to use their guns. Thanks to the war and the attention to civilian defense, the city had a strong auxiliary police force, and many blacks had been encouraged to join. The department was thus able to mobilize some fifteen hundred black citizen volunteers, who were issued batons and helmets and put out on patrol. Military police also swept through the area, clearing Harlem of black soldiers.

Postwar New York was transformed by the great migrations of southern and Caribbean blacks, on the one hand, and Puerto Ricans, on the other. The number of blacks on the NYPD also rose, but not in proportion to their numbers in the population. By 1950, the city had 368 African-American cops.

This was less than 2 percent of the force, and the highest-ranking of them was Emmanuel Kline, an acting captain in command of the fifteen-officer Juvenile Aid Bureau in Harlem. Kline was never given command of a precinct. Not until 1953 did a black officer in Brooklyn, George Redding, become a civil service captain. (Chicago had appointed a black captain in 1940.)

In 1947, a builder named William Levitt opened a low-priced development of tract housing on Long Island. A two-bedroom house with one bath, a living room, and a kitchen built on a twenty-five- by thirty-foot concrete slab (no basement) could be had for $6,990, or $58 a month, no money down. Levitt had created an ethnic, blue-collar city dweller's dream—a house of one's own in suburbia—and the G.I. Bill made it affordable. Veterans' benefits, meanwhile, opened college doors for many upwardly mobile whites, who in time moved into well-paid careers that gave them entrée into middle-class suburbs. As they left, blacks and Hispanics moved into their old city neighborhoods. The total black and Puerto Rican population in New York City grew from 520,000 (7 percent of the total) in 1940 to 1 million (12 percent) in 1950 and 1.7 million (22 percent) by 1960. For most of these newcomers, there were no invitations to suburbia. The czar of New York's state and city public works, Robert Moses, built the overpasses on his suburban highways too low for buses, in order to keep the public parks of Long Island as free as possible of dark-skinned people from the inner city.

With the departure of Mayor La Guardia at the end of 1945, Tammany had managed to install former Brooklyn district attorney William O'Dwyer as mayor. In 1950, a massive police corruption scandal forced O'Dwyer to resign.

O'Dwyer's replacement as mayor, Vincent Impelletieri, was a minor city bureaucrat who had been put on the ticket to provide ethnic (Italian) and geographic (Manhattan) balance. His three and a half years in City Hall were not notable for any accomplishments, and the police department drifted. In 1949, the FBI refused to publish New York City crime figures in its annual reports, on the grounds that they were unreliable. For years, it seemed, New York's greatest crime fighter had been "Detective McCann." Even under La Guardia and Valentine, it was common police practice to file the records of many ordinary robberies and burglaries in the garbage can. (This could help explain why, in 1939, Detroit, with only a fourth of New York's population, reported about the same number of robberies and burglaries as New York but only about a fourth as many murders—murder being a far harder crime to ignore.) Sometimes, of course, the victim's stolen property was covered by an insurance policy. If an insurance investigator had difficulty locating a crime report and asked a desk officer for assistance, the latter would smilingly reply that the case had been assigned to Detective McCann. Nothing more needed to be said. The insurance company, which valued its good relations with the police, would pay the claimant. In 1950, the NYPD moved responsibility for crime records from the precincts to headquarters. The first year after the change, the incidence of robbery jumped by 400 percent, and burglaries shot up 1,300 percent. An army of criminals had not suddenly descended on the city; Detective McCann had simply been sidelined.

In 1953, Tammany boss Carmine DeSapio brought forth Robert Wagner, son and namesake of a famous U.S. senator, who unseated Impelletieri. At first it looked as if Tammany had just changed faces at City Hall, but, in fact, the middle class was taking charge of the city government and the police were beginning to break loose from political control. Wagner appointed a prominent lawyer, Frank Adams, as police commissioner. In 1955, when Adams left, Chief Inspector Steve Kennedy replaced him.

Like Valentine, Kennedy was a career-cop "reform" commissioner, not popular with the troops. Prior to joining the force in 1929, he had been a longshoreman and an amateur boxer. He had also learned stenography during a period of clerical work in the Manhattan office of U.S. Steel. The department accordingly used him to take statements in criminal cases and for various administrative duties; after his promotion to lieutenant, he was posted to La Guardia's City Hall as a police aide. There, watching the bright reformers come and go, Kennedy became aware of his educational shortcomings and was inspired to complete high school, college, and law school, all at night, while learning to speak in a voice more Shakespearean than Brooklynese. Colleagues found him pretentious, and in 1954 his rise to chief inspector over the heads of eighteen higher-ranking officers was singularly unpopular at 240 Centre Street. As commissioner, he blustered in public at the force's shortcomings, transferred erring members wholesale, and, in Lewis Valentine fashion, told cops to lock up criminals and take no guff from them.

Kennedy was one of the first police leaders to sense the youth rebellion that was emerging in America. He didn't like it. "Apply the law and apply it vigorously" was his stated philosophy. "It's not your job to become bemused with the vagaries of the why, oh why school," he told cops. "The policeman has a job to do and if he does it honestly and intelligently, he gains respect. That's a damned sight more important than being liked." Recalling his own youth, Kennedy noted that the cops on the beat had never asked him, "What are your needs? . . . Are you happy?" It was, " 'Look, bud, do this.' And if you didn't do it you got belted."

On an August night in 1959, a sensational crime appeared to demonstrate the need for Kennedy's approach. *West Side Story* had opened on Broadway two years earlier; now life imitated art. Shortly after midnight, a sixteen-year-old Puerto Rican, Sal Agron—dressed in a dark blue, red-lined, Dracula-style cape—stabbed two young men to death in a playground on Manhattan's West Side. Nicknamed "the Capeman," Agron and a companion, Tony "the Umbrella Man" Hernandez, were quickly arrested. According to the police report, six teenage boys and a girl, all of them Anglos, were in the park when Sal, Tony, and eight or ten other gang members entered. When the Anglo kids got up to leave, the new group blocked their path, and a melee ensued. "When organized gangs invade playgrounds and blindly, and wantonly, commit murder," Mayor Wagner declared, "the handling of the matter has passed from the social agencies to the police."

Kennedy was dealt a stronger hand than most police commissioners. In 1952, Bruce Smith of the New York City Institute of Public Administration conducted a management survey of the department. The IPA was a bastion of the professional-management school of government, which argued that administration, based on scientific principles, could be separated from politics and policy making. Naturally, Smith's report urged these ideas on the NYPD. By the standard of some of Smith's earlier studies, his proposal was modest. Twenty years before, he had recommended that the entire Chicago police force be fired.

Mayor Wagner was a pleasant Yale-educated man who had given Commissioner Adams carte blanche to run the department "without let or hindrance," as Adams later noted. "The department," according to Adams, was "a military organization that must be run by the commissioner alone." But no one had ever precisely delineated the line between policy (politics) and administration. Kennedy's vision, in any case, was not shared by most of his cops. A captain sporting a college ring might aspire to be recognized as a professional in the same way as a doctor or lawyer, but wages and working conditions were more important to a rank and file that, for the most part, had joined the department in quest of job security. "If it ain't in the paycheck, it doesn't count," cops often said. They were prone to the occupational disease of cynicism—toward life and toward the job itself. Many rank-and-file cops looked for leadership not to Commissioner Kennedy but to the head of the Patrolmen's Benevolent Association, John Cassese. In the 1950s, the PBA began to exhibit a new stridency. Cassese repeatedly clashed with Kennedy. In retaliation for one attack, Kennedy had Patrolman Cassese out directing traffic at an isolated post. The union president struck back by assembling his members to boo the commissioner when he appeared in public.

In his early days as commissioner, the public-relations-conscious Kennedy was hailed by the press. He even made the cover of *Time* magazine. It was a heady experience; sometimes Wagner would indicate that he did not entirely agree with his police commissioner on a certain issue—and Kennedy would fire back at his boss. When Kennedy canceled days off during a visit to the United Nations by Soviet Premier Nikita Khrushchev and Cuban leader Fidel Castro, Jewish cops complained about being compelled to work on their holidays. The commissioner summarily dismissed their protest: some men, he noted, were religious only a few days a year. When Jewish leaders protested to the mayor, Wagner ordered the commissioner to apologize. Kennedy ignored the mayor's directive (nor did he deign to rebut charges of anti-Semitism by mentioning that his wife was Jewish). Eventually, it became necessary for Wagner to note that he was "the mayor of New York, and everybody had better understand that." The "everybody" he meant seemed to be his police commissioner. In February 1961, the commissioner's term expired. Before he would agree to stay on, Kennedy said, cops would have to be given an immediate $600 annual pay raise. Kennedy knew that Wagner could not single out the police alone for a salary increase; his demand was probably a grandstand play. Wagner's response was to name a new police commissioner, Chief Inspector Mike Murphy.

In the 1950s, the new professionally minded NYPD did not place great emphasis on relations with minority groups. By 1963, though, with Martin Luther King Jr. marching through the South and the Kennedy administration promoting a civil-rights agenda, the NYPD was beginning to find a few black men it deemed capable of commanding precincts. Lloyd Sealy, the third captain of his race, was a janitor's son who had grown up in Brooklyn. As one of only a dozen blacks at Thomas Jefferson High School, he had been elected president of the student government. His career started out in a "black" precinct—the one covering the Bedford Stuyvesant area of Brooklyn. After seven years on patrol, Sealey was assigned to the Juvenile Aid Bureau. Meanwhile, he went to college and law school and began moving up in rank. Tall, handsome, calm, and courteous, the child of immigrants from Barbados, Sealy was well regarded at headquarters. In 1959, as a lieutenant, he was accepted for management training by J. Edgar Hoover's FBI academy. In 1964, his career got another boost after a white cop killed a black youngster in an unlikely spot for racial disorder—Manhattan's Upper East Side.

The trouble began on a hot Thursday in July. Some black summer-school students at a local high school were in the habit of sitting on an apartment-building stoop; sometimes they walked on the grass or littered the grounds, to the annoyance of the building's superintendent. That afternoon, the super sprayed the kids with a garden hose. They retaliated by throwing bottles and garbage-can lids, among other objects. When he retreated into the vestibule of a building, a fifteen-year-old named James Powell followed him. Nearby, in a TV-repair shop, was a thirty-seven-year-old off-duty police lieutenant, Thomas Gilligan. Hearing the commotion, he ran outside. According to Gilligan's subsequent testimony, Powell advanced on him, knife in hand, and refused to halt even after a warning shot had been fired. Gilligan fired two more shots, killing Powell. Other students gathered at the scene, some of them weeping. A crowd of three hundred began throwing rocks and bottles at police. Eventually, they were dispersed by seventy-five helmeted officers. Powell, who had lived in a housing project in the Bronx, had an arrest record for attempted robbery and vandalism. Gilligan, for his part, had nineteen citations for good police work. To the cops, the case seemed open and shut: an officer had defended his life and that of a citizen against an armed assailant. Many blacks saw things differently: a five-foot, six-inch kid who weighed 122 pounds was dead at the hands of a six-foot-two, 200-pound cop, over some juvenile hijinks, at worst. Interviewed by police officers and reporters, witnesses (or people who claimed to be witnesses) gave contradictory statements: Powell had a knife, or he did not (though his friends said that he had left home with two knives); he advanced on the cop, or he did not. The cop's own statement was kept secret for six weeks, until the district attorney completed a grand jury investigation. The day after the shooting, members of the Congress of Racial Equality (CORE) demonstrated while fifty officers stood by. "Save Us from Our Protectors," proclaimed a sign carried by one of the protesters.

On Saturday, demonstrators gathered in central Harlem outside the funeral home where Powell was being mourned. Then they marched to the local precinct, though the shooting had occurred well beyond its boundaries. On arrival, they were met by barricades and a cordon of cops. A delegation entered the station in order to demand Lieutenant Gilligan's suspension from the force. The inspector in charge replied that the D.A. was investigating the case. He gave the leaders a bullhorn to address the crowd and calm the tension. But as they spoke, bricks rained down from the roofs of nearby buildings. Some policemen rushed up to the rooftops while other cops struggled with demonstrators and made fourteen arrests. The inspector ordered his men to move the crowd back. Two blocks away, at 125th Street and Seventh Avenue, black nationalists were holding their usual Saturday night rally. The marchers and rally-goers merged; by 10:00 P.M., a thousand people were milling about, many shouting insults at police and whites in general. A compact car with a white couple in it was surrounded and damaged by demonstrators before the driver managed to zoom off.

"Go home!" a police commander shouted through a bullhorn. "We are home! You go home!" demonstrators shouted back. The retort would become standard in such confrontations, but in 1964 it seemed fresh and humorous. So far, only Philadelphia, among major cities, had experienced a riot in the postwar era.

From the 1930s through the '50s, the NYPD had looked to the Emergency Service Unit to spearhead its response to potential riot situations. Formed in 1930, after the abolition of precinct reserve duty, the ESU was composed of specially trained and handpicked officers. They were routinely used to deal with barricaded gunmen, deranged people threatening to jump off buildings or bridges, and riots. Because emergency-service officers rescued people as well as arrested them, the image of the unit was more that of firefighters than of heavy-handed enforcers.

In 1959, the department formed the Tactical Patrol Force (TPF). It had a different image. The TPF was composed of tall, physically fit officers trained in the martial arts. Its mission was partly to serve as a mobile anticrime unit and partly to handle civil disorder. While the day-to-day work of ESU officers involved helping the sick and injured, TPF men faced a regular diet of crime and disorder. ESU officers ranged from young to advanced middle age; TPF officers were all under thirty, and many were former marines or paratroopers who, as one member put it, wanted to "keep their jump boots." When trouble started outside the Harlem precinct, TPF units from elsewhere in the city were bused in. The borough commander ordered the area cleared. Advancing in ten- to twelve-man wedges, with a sergeant out front, the TPF men raised their clubs on cue and yelled, "Charge!"

Baton charges had a long history in the NYPD: Walling at the battle of the barricades, Murray at Tompkins Square, Devery in San Juan Hill, Whalen's men at Union Square. Some of them worked. This one didn't. As the police charged, a group of demonstrators ran south on Seventh Avenue pulling fire alarms, setting fire to rubbish baskets, and chasing and beating any whites they met. A larger group went north from 123rd Street, turned on Lenox Avenue, and continued to 135th Street, looting stores along the way. At 10:30 that night, a Molotov cocktail landed beside a police car and began to blaze in the street. One patrolman's leg was severely burned. Other cops drew their guns and fired into the air.

The press poured into the area. White reporters, who tended to consider themselves immune from harm when they covered Harlem, were beaten up. The night was filled with sounds of broken glass and gunshots. While whites who wandered into the area were badly beaten, the casualty list among blacks was longer. Some were shot, others clubbed. Harlem Hospital reported seventy-five injury cases; Sydenham, thirty.

Because Mayor Wagner was in Europe, Police Commissioner Mike Murphy directed the city's response. Arriving at the precinct at 4:30 in the morning, Murphy approved orders for his men to fire into the air. Not until 7:00 A.M., when many more policemen were on the scene and the rioters were tired, did the disturbance subside. On Sunday night, Powell's funeral services set off another round of disturbances, which continued until 1:30 in the morning. Unlike the riots of 1935 and 1943, the disorder was not confined to Harlem; this time, it spread to Bedford Stuyvesant in Brooklyn. Not until six days after the riot started did the two neighborhoods return to normal. In the aftermath, Captain Sealy was appointed commander of the Harlem precinct; twenty-nine years had passed since the need to put a black man in that position had been made evident by the riot of 1935.

After investigations by both the NYPD and the district attorney cleared

Lieutenant Gilligan, minority groups expressed their outrage and called for the creation of an independent civilian complaint review board, to hear charges against police officers. (Such proposals had surfaced in a number of cities by then. New York itself had, in 1955, created a review board within the department; it was supposed to hear civilian complaints against officers and make recommendations to the police commissioner.) The notion of civilians—outsiders—having input into police discipline ran counter to the doctrine of police professionalism; principle aside, a lot of cops found the idea threatening, and Commissioner Mike Murphy made it clear that he wouldn't allow such a thing. True to his credo of deferring to professional managers, Wagner sought a compromise. But Commissioner Murphy was adamant, and in June 1965 he quit.

It was in the last years of the Wagner administration that crime began to rise significantly. In 1961, the NYPD had reported 390 murders; by 1964 the figure was 637, up nearly two-thirds in three years. In 1964, a single homicide became symbolic of an ominous change taking place in big-city life. In March of that year, in a quiet Queens neighborhood known as Kew Gardens, Katherine "Kitty" Genovese was stabbed to death. Genovese managed a tavern and was in the habit of driving home late at night. It was after 3:00 A.M. when she got out of her car. Sensing that she was being followed, Genovese managed to run almost to her door before being caught and stabbed by a man with a knife. Thirty-eight neighbors heard her repeated screams, not one of them called the police. Instead, they watched the killer stab her and Genovese stagger down the street, stumble into her doorway, and collapse, while the assailant sauntered back and forth for ten minutes. The police quickly arrested a young black man who explained that, from time to time, he got an urge to go out and cut up a woman. The case, with its racial overtones and the massive apathy displayed by the witnesses, resonated deeply with New Yorkers.

In eerie parallel, the passivity of Kitty Genovese's neighbors and the fury of the Harlem rioters sent the same message: a worrisome number of New Yorkers were no longer prepared to take the responsibilities or follow the rules that bound the city together. A public-service announcement began to air on local radio and TV stations: "It's ten P.M. Do you know where your children are?"

In 1965, a Republican congressman from the silk-stocking district of the Upper East Side ran for mayor as a fusion candidate. In October, he held a rally near the site of Kitty Genovese's murder. "We must give the people of

New York faith," John Lindsay said. "It will require citizens to rally to the defense of their neighbors when crime strikes. Something has gone out of the heart and soul of New York City."

As a candidate, the tall, movie-star-handsome Lindsay had a good deal to say about the police. As mayor, he made it plain that he was going to be more heavily involved in police affairs than his predecessor. Considering the intensity of his interest, though, his method of choosing a police commissioner was strangely offhand. Lindsay had backed the idea of a civilian review board independent of the police department. He and his aides, accordingly, looked around for a big-city commissioner who could live with such a thing. There was only one obvious candidate. Philadelphia had a civilian review board—the only one already up and running in a big city. Philadelphia's police commissioner, Howard Leary, was an Irish-American career cop with a law degree. He professed to have no difficulty working with the board. He could hardly have said otherwise, of course, since his boss, the mayor of Philadelphia, was in favor of it. Pretty much on that basis alone, Leary got the nod as police commissioner of New York.

Lindsay moved swiftly to make good on his review-board promise—perhaps a little too swiftly. He established the Civilian Complaint Review Board, by executive order, in April 1966. Given some time to make a record for itself, the new entity might have overcome the resistance of the police rank and file. But the PBA made sure it wouldn't have much time. No sooner had Lindsay issued his order than the PBA lawyers were in court seeking a ruling: the imposition of civilian authority over police discipline, they argued, required an amendment to the City Charter, and that move, in turn, had to be approved in a public referendum. The issue was one of public safety, the public-relations man for the union argued. If a cop expected to be second-guessed by a civilian, he might hesitate to act in an emergency, thus placing New Yorkers' lives in jeopardy.

There was already some grumbling among cops around the country about a 1961 Supreme Court decision that applied the federal exclusionary rule to the states. No longer could an officer who conducted an illegal search use a weapon or stolen goods as evidence in a trial. To some cops, the civilian review board looked like yet another restraint on the police at a time when, as they saw it, criminals were running wild.

The referendum fight also had a strong racial subtext. The CCRB was high on the agenda of a number of civil-rights organizations. In 1962, the NYPD had dropped a requirement, dating back to 1937, that police live within the city limits; now they were free to move to any of six suburban counties, and many were exercising that newfound right. The PBA, in the person of its president, John Cassese, was increasingly prone to view the world through a racial lens. Cassese allowed that he was "sick and tired of giving in to minority groups." The minorities, he added, will "not be satisfied until you get all Negroes and Puerto Ricans on the board and every policeman who goes in front of it is found guilty."

The PBA launched an ad campaign against the proposal. In one provocative ad, a white girl was shown walking alone on a street filled with dark shadows. In the face of this onslaught, Commissioner Leary had nothing more to say than that he could live with the board; but, as he left no doubt, he could also live nicely without it. The proposal was beaten by a two-to-one margin. And though Lindsay sought to reassert himself with a new executive order, creating a mixed board of police officers and civilian employees of the department (named by the commissioner), the referendum had been a crushing defeat, and it had a profound influence on the Lindsay administration's subsequent dealings with the police. The mayor and his advisers had glimpsed the power of the PBA, and they would not readily do anything that might incur the wrath of the rank and file again. As for the substitute board that Lindsay had created, it lingered on for the next twenty-five years—a body that was neither civilian nor independent of the department but would add up to a time-consuming mechanism that further blurred the responsibility for police discipline.

In the postwar period, the city's Latin population began to grow, fueled by heavy immigration from Puerto Rico. Every day at a small airport in New Jersey, antiquated charter planes landed passengers who had paid as little as twenty dollars for the fourteen-hour standing-room-only flight from San Juan. By late 1947 there were an estimated quarter of a million Puerto Ricans in the city, and two thousand more arrived every month. The main area, or "barrio," where they settled was East Harlem between Ninety-seventh and 116th Streets. As it had with the Italians a half century earlier, the NYPD realized it had an urgent need for Spanish-speaking cops, but in 1953 there were only five on the force, and not all of them were from Puerto Rico.

Tony Bouza, born in Spain, had been raised in Brooklyn by his mother.

After two years of army service, he came home to a routine job, and like the John Travolta character in *Saturday Night Fever*, the six-foot, four-inch young man spent his time dancing and partying. His family worried about his future, and a sister who was married to a cop persuaded him to take the police test. Appointed to the force in January 1953, Bouza moved up rapidly. After a few months in a precinct, he was assigned to a youth gang squad in Manhattan, though he spent most of his time as an interpreter for the Detective Bureau. In 1955, a Columbia University professor named Galindez, known for his criticism of dictator Rafael Trujillo of the Dominican Republic, disappeared from a lower Manhattan street. The case became a cause célèbre, and the NYPD mounted a major investigation. Bouza was detailed to the Detective Bureau to work on it. The disappearance was not solved, but Bouza was introduced to the world of political intrigue as he dealt with the conflicts of pro- and anti-Trujillo factions. For his good work, he was given permanent appointment as a third-grade detective and assigned to a downtown precinct. Had he concentrated on Hispanic crime, he might have become a Latin Petrosino. But unlike the patient, plodding Italian immigrant, Tony Bouza found detective work boring. He was an intellectual who read Sartre and hoped to be a writer; in fact, he wrote a novel about the Galindez case, though he failed to find a publisher. Over the years, he picked up bachelor's and master's degrees and more promotions. In 1958 Bouza was made sergeant and assigned to the Bureau of Special Service Investigations. There he spent his first years monitoring the struggles between pro- and anti-Castro forces. The two groups battled over everything, even a statue of Cuban patriot Jose Martí that the city was preparing to erect in Central Park. Each claimed Martí as their hero and demanded pride of place at the ceremony. The city's parks department suddenly announced that it had "lost" the statue. Not until long after the trouble subsided did the department "find" the statue and erect it.

Despite their growing numbers, Puerto Ricans were ignored by the city government; they had never rioted. Instead, in the 1960s, Bouza, as a lieutenant, often found himself in Harlem, listening to speeches by Malcolm X, among other radicals. In 1967 the country was swept by riots. In New York, on a hot Saturday night in July, trouble broke out in the East Harlem barrio when an off-duty policeman tried to stop a street quarrel between two men. One of them ran away; the other came at the officer with a knife. A second off-duty policeman intervened, ordered the man to drop the knife, and when he kept coming, shot and killed him. Within an hour three hundred people were milling about, picking up bottles and throwing them at the police. Eventually a thousand officers were deployed in the area. For two nights, the police managed to contain the disorder; then it spread over a hundred-block area. Tony Bouza, now a captain, was in the forefront of the police ranks. Two residents, a sixteen-year-old boy and a forty-four-year-old woman, were killed by .38-calliber bullets, apparently from the gun of an officer firing warning shots. The situation was explosive, and police brass feared that the disorders would spread to other Hispanic areas in the Bronx and Brooklyn. Bouza, who was hit three times by flying bottles, remained at his post. At 4:00 A.M. a heavy rain came down. The downpour continued over the next two nights, ending the trouble. The Puerto Rican community began to get more attention from City Hall and police headquarters.

With more minority officers and commanders, the NYPD would have been in a better position to mobilize the support of inner-city residents. As things stood, the force had precious few blacks or Hispanics in the command ranks, and they were spread thin. Two months after Lindsay became mayor, Lloyd Sealy, now an inspector, was jumped up to assistant chief inspector and named borough commander of Brooklyn North, an assignment that put him in charge of eleven precincts. In his new role, Sealy often found himself at the center of civil disorder. His customary practice was to show up in full-dress uniform, marching out in front of his troops and bantering with the crowds. He wanted people to see that someone in charge understood their concerns. "Take off your black mask and show us your white face," a skeptical teenager would shout now and then. But Sealy was usually able to calm things down. Mayor Lindsay, too, walked the ghetto during tense times, and he liked to be accompanied by Sealy. But in 1969, Sealy retired, at the age of fifty-two. A few months earlier, the post of chief inspector had become vacant; no one, apparently, considered him for the job or made any effort to keep him in the department.

13

On the Pad

The police scandal of 1912 could be traced back to the Elks Club ball, where Lieutenant Charles Becker met Herman Rosenthal. The first two great postwar scandals also began with chance encounters. Jimmy Reardon, who joined the NYPD in 1942 at the age of twenty-four, was in the Becker mold, a six-foot-two, 215-pound tough guy on a vice squad working out of the chief inspector's office. One summer afternoon in 1947, while off duty and en route to Ebbets Field to see the Dodgers play, he stopped at a local bar, where he observed a short, stocky, wavy-haired young fellow taking bets. Reardon sized him up as an "outlaw"—the police term for a gambler not on the pad, or payoff list of those allowed to operate. Reardon put down a few bets before breaking the news that he was a cop. The gambler, Harry Gross, despite a disconcerting nervous tick in his right eye, was a personable young man fresh out of the army and just starting out. He begged off arrest, promising to make it right, and the two men agreed to meet at a bar after the game. When they did, they hit it off beautifully.

William O'Dwyer, New York's first postwar mayor, had entered office with heavy baggage. A burly, silver-haired, smiling Irishman from County Mayo, "Bill O" had been one of New York's Finest for seven years, including a couple spent as a vice cop. As a rookie in a Brooklyn waterfront precinct in 1917, O'Dwyer had killed a man. It was the kind of case that cops dreaded. He had been stopped on the street by a boy, who had told him that his father was assaulting his mother. When O'Dwyer entered the family flat, the father leveled a gun at him and the officer fired. In later years, O'Dwyer contributed to the boy's support. In 1924, after picking up a law degree and passing the bar, he left the force. He rose to become a judge and, eventually, Brooklyn district attorney, the job that left him with the baggage.

In 1941, a hoodlum named Abe "Kid Twist" Reles, hoping to save himself from a murder rap, began to give information about a killing-for-hire syndicate, which the press promptly dubbed "Murder Incorporated." Among its customers was Albert Anastasia, boss of the Brooklyn waterfront. Reles was placed in protective custody in rented quarters maintained by the D.A.'s office in the Half Moon Hotel on the Coney Island oceanfront. On November 12, 1941, at around 6:30 A.M., despite the protection of a six-man police guard detail from O'Dwyer's office squad, Kid Twist lowered himself out of a sixth-floor window, using a makeshift rope of bedsheets and wire, and "fell" to his death. Afterward, O'Dwyer's office dropped the case against Anastasia.

In World War II, O'Dwyer served in the army, rising to brigadier general and dealing with European refugee problems. During his war service, however, he found the time to visit the swank Central Park West apartment of Frank Costello, who was the de facto boss of Tammany Hall in addition to his more shadowy underworld position. When word of their wartime meeting came out during O'Dwyer's mayoralty, he claimed to have been there on military business, investigating fraud in army contracts. But he had never made an official report of the visit, whose true purpose, it seemed obvious, had been to seek Costello's backing for the mayoral nomination. With Tammany's help, O'Dwyer won the election in 1945.

La Guardia and Valentine had held the line against corruption. From 1935 on, the racket buster Tom Dewey was in office either as special prosecutor or as district attorney of New York County. After he quit in 1941, Dewey was succeeded by the able Frank Hogan. Now only Hogan was left, and his jurisdiction was limited to Manhattan. Valentine's successor as police commissioner, Arthur Wallander, had spent most of his career at the Police Academy or in special units such as Aviation, Emergency Services, and Civil Defense, all of them far removed from the vice squads and the hot-spot precincts. Wallander had been O'Dwyer's training sergeant in the Police Academy, and the outgoing mayor had cleared the appointment with the incoming one. But the new commissioner was no Valentine, and it was not difficult for City Hall or the police bureaucracy to work around him.

The O'Dwyer administration was to be a last hurrah for the old style of New York politicos. Like Jimmy Walker nearly twenty years earlier, O'Dwyer wound up in exile, propelled there by Jimmy Reardon and Harry Gross. By late 1949, they were partners, and some of Reardon's fellow cops had taken to calling him the "Connecticut Squire," thanks to the elegant digs he had found for himself in Westport, Connecticut. He was not a subtle operator. Indeed, word of his activities had apparently reached the mayor himself. Foreseeing a scandal, O'Dwyer was said to have urged the department to get rid of "the young plainclothesman out in Brooklyn with piles of money." Feeling the pressure, Reardon resigned from the force and became a full-time gambler.

At this point, Ed Reid, an enterprising reporter for a popular daily, the Brooklyn *Eagle*, published a series of articles about the alliance between "Mr. G and the Squire." The *Eagle* series said enough to catch the attention of the Brooklyn D.A., Miles MacDonald, who was a former subordinate of O'Dwyer's, but no fan of his. In January 1950, MacDonald convened a Kings County grand jury investigation. The judge overseeing the inquiry, the irascible and ambitious Sam Liebowitz, had been a top criminal defense lawyer—the defender of the "Scottsboro Boys," among other clients. (They were a group of young black men accused of raping two white girls in Scottsboro, Alabama. The case had been tried and retried in the '30s, attracting national attention. Eventually, some of the defendants were released, while others served prison time.) Liebowitz decided to take personal charge of the Gross case.

With MacDonald on the brink of indicting cops, O'Dwyer realized that the game was over. Within a matter of days, President Truman had conveniently named him ambassador to Mexico. "My country needs me," O'Dwyer tearfully told reporters, doing his best to imply that he was going on a secret mission to counter Communist subversion south of the border. Left to face the music was Police Commissioner William O'Brien, Wallander having retired. O'Brien's initial response was to blame his problems on a Communist conspiracy. Judge Liebowitz then summoned him to the Kings County Courthouse, where the commissioner was treated to a performance of the wiretapped recordings of Gross and his lieutenants as they openly discussed their payoffs to cops. O'Brien and Liebowitz got into a public row in the court-house hallway, oblivious to the reporters standing around them. "What are you going to do about it?" Liebowitz thundered. "It's the same all over the city . . . ice, ice, ice!" ("Ice" meant graft.) The commissioner argued back, but after a meeting in Liebowitz's chambers, emerged a chastened man. Congratu-lating the judge, the district attorney, and the grand jury for their excellent work, O'Brien promised that heads would roll. The first was his own.

Liebowitz held Gross and Reardon on high bail. Reardon adhered to the plainclothesman's code of silence. Gross, at first, refused to name names. How, he said, could he possibly turn against his good friends in the police depart-ment? After all, he had "been in their homes, been at their [children's] gradua-tions." Faced with jail, however, he caved. On the basis of his grand jury testimony, eighteen officers, including some of high rank, were indicted, and a number of others named as unindicted coconspirators. Many more quit, two shot themselves, and one jumped out of a courthouse window. O'Dwyer, by his own account, was tempted to do the same. "You would look out over the city from someplace high above it," he said later, "and you would say to your-self, 'Good Jesus, it's too much for me.' "

A guard detail of six cops hadn't been able to keep Kid Twist alive. Now, after Harry Gross was released from jail under police escort, the black comedy conti-nued. When one of the guards set his gun down on a shelf, the gambler's six-year-old son fired a bullet past his three-year-old sister's head. When another bodyguard went off to eat, Gross fled. Although the alarm went out immediately, no member of the NYPD could find him. He remained at large for two days, until a racetrack guard in Atlantic City recognized him from his picture. The star witness explained that he had been bored—he had needed some diversion.

The trial got under way in September 1951, with not-guilty pleas by the surviving police defendants. Gross, called to the stand, stunned the prosecution by refusing to testify. Even when Judge Liebowitz threatened to chain him to the witness chair and lock him up for a hundred years, it was no dice. Accord-ing to highly plausible underworld rumor, Gross had been slipped a payment of $75,000—and coached on what to do at the trial—during his brief trip to Atlantic City. In any event, the case evaporated, and double-jeopardy rules barred prosecutors from trying it again. Gross did testify later, at a number of departmental trials, and over fifty cops were dismissed from the force. (Seven years after that, Gross was released from prison. He moved to California, and

ended up in San Quentin for the killing of his father-in-law.) Reardon, after re-
fusing a final offer to cooperate, was sentenced to three and two-thirds years.
(In the 1960s, after his release, he was prosecuted by U.S. Attorney Robert
Morgenthau for running a gambling operation in Greenwich Village.)

By the time the next scandal rolled around, in 1970, the political landscape
had shifted dramatically. Tammany Hall was broken once and for all, and the
city had another fusion mayor, John Lindsay—the very antithesis, it seemed,
of the old-fashioned municipal politician. Lindsay, in turn, had brought in another putative reformer, Howard Leary, as police commissioner. Yet underneath all this newfangledness, conditions in the police department proved to
be depressingly familiar. What would come to be called the Knapp commission scandal, like the Gross scandal, involved plainclothesmen and gambling
pads in the Bronx as well as Brooklyn. But this time, the chance meeting that
set the process in motion was between two cops. And the scandal happened
because they were determined to make it happen.

David Durk had an odd pedigree for a New York City cop. The son of
an eye surgeon, the descendant of eastern European Jews on both sides of
his family, he had gone to Amherst and spent a year at Columbia University law school before joining the force, on a lark, in June 1963. He was a
troublemaker from the outset. One day, not long after reporting to his first
assignment—the Eighteenth Precinct, in midtown—Durk was given the
assignment of cleaning the borough chief's office. He unhesitatingly informed
his sergeant that the task was not in his job description.

Durk's coconspirator, Frank Serpico, was the son of a devout, hardworking
couple from a town outside Naples. His father had a shoe repair business in
Brooklyn. His parents taught him to regard gangsters as bad guys and cops as
good guys—a lesson reinforced by the radio show *Gang Busters*, which Serpico
never missed, and by more than one occasion when, as a slighter-than-average
kid with a shoeshine box, he was robbed by local toughs.

Like Durk, Serpico loved the job. Not the department, but the job. In their
feelings about the police, however, there was an essential difference. Although
both men were aware of the distance between themselves and other cops, this
was a gap that Durk hoped to bridge. He believed that his values and theirs
were, at heart, the same. Serpico's mental trajectory was carrying him away
from the police world. Durk and Serpico were about the same age (thirty
and twenty-nine, respectively), but while Durk was a product of the 1950s,

Serpico was molten material for the '60s. Around the time of his transfer to plainclothes, Serpico left Brooklyn and moved into a basement apartment on Perry Street, in Greenwich Village. There he came into contact with the anti-war movement, among other belief systems foreign to his upbringing. He responded warmly to them, becoming a sort of hippie cop. Taking advantage of the liberal dress code of plainclothesmen, Serpico grew long hair and a beard and began to wear leather jerkins, lederhosen, and other exotic items of attire. An intellectual rebel, Durk was never a cultural one. Tall, slim, good-looking, and married with children, he dressed neatly in a suit and tie and lived in a middle-class apartment building uptown.

They met in January 1966, as newly appointed plainclothesmen in a Police Academy training program devoted to prostitution, undercover work, and gambling in all its local varieties. What drew them together—and set them apart from their classmates—was the pleasure they took in the curriculum: the ins and the outs of such games of chance as bolita, and the dos and don'ts of undercover work. (A good way to blend into the scenery of a neighborhood bar, one instructor told them, was to wear bedroom slippers and bring along a poodle.) During class breaks, Durk and Serpico were taken aback to discover that what many of their fellow students wanted to talk about was the payoffs that would come their way as soon as school let out.

From the training program, Serpico was dispatched to a lowly division plainclothes unit in Brooklyn. His ambition was to be a detective, and he had gone into "clothes" because it was on the semiofficial career path to the Detective Bureau. The savvier and better-connected Durk, meanwhile, had snagged a place on an elite citywide antigambling unit, from which he soon moved on to the city's Department of Investigation, whose mandate was to combat waste and corruption in city government. The attorneys and investigators who worked there often talked about heavy-duty problems like the buying and selling of judgeships, but it seemed to Durk that most of the cases they actually pursued were small potatoes—a sign painter accused of taking home a few gallons of city-owned paint, for example. "We spent thousands of dollars trying to prove the theft of about five dollars' worth of paint," he recalled. Serpico, meanwhile, had become a regular guest at the Durks' apartment on West Seventieth Street. So it was only natural that when his fellow plainclothesmen began trying to entice him into their financial arrangements, he should seek Durk's advice.

Durk, as it happened, was full of advice, and after a certain amount of grumbling, Serpico followed most of it. At first, though, Serpico was hesitant. On his own, he had talked to a straitlaced captain, who had gotten him transferred to the Bronx, where, contrary to the captain's assurances, the pad was flourishing as much as in Brooklyn. Next, Serpico gave some information to the local D.A. that led to the indictment of ten Bronx plainclothesmen. This, however, was not the kind of all-out assault that the two young cops envisioned. So, over a period of more than two years, they went, separately and together, to a succession of what Durk was wont to call "people with flags in their offices," two of them prominent members of the Lindsay administration. When none of these worthies evinced much interest, Durk introduced Serpico to a budding muckraker on the metropolitan desk of *The New York Times*, David Burnham.

Burnham was as much of a firebrand as Durk, but his superiors at the *Times* were wary of resting such an important story on, as they saw it, two oddball cops and a bevy of anonymous sources. To overcome their resistance, Durk and Serpico persuaded a resolutely honest inspector, Paul Delise, to meet with Burnham's editors and share his impressions of corruption stretching back over the span of a three-decade-long police career.

"I've got six kids—you know what I mean?" was Delise's first reaction when Durk put the idea to him. A few days later, though, Delise chewed it over with Serpico, who had been transferred to a unit that Delise headed. Serpico said he knew about the *Times* meeting—he would be there. "Are you going down?" he asked. Delise repeated the concerns he had expressed to Durk but said that he would go if Durk and Serpico wanted him to. "You do what you have to do. I'll back you up a hundred percent," he said.

The fruit of all these labors was a page 1 story that appeared in the *Times* on April 25, 1970, under the headline

GRAFT PAID TO POLICE HERE
SAID TO RUN INTO MILLIONS

Survey Links Payoffs to Gambling
and Narcotics—Some on Force
Accuse Officials of Failure to Act

Now that police corruption had been officially discovered, reporters, prosecutors, legislators, and elected and appointed officeholders of every imaginable kind swarmed in, looking for a piece of the territory to call their own. In the history of New York City, there had been few choicer demonstrations of the capacity of a newspaper article to refocus the minds of those in power. Lindsay, after a couple of false starts, was compelled to appoint an investigating commission, headed by a prominent lawyer named Whitman Knapp.

Once again, as had happened at twenty-year intervals since 1894, there were hearings featuring rogue cops, ambitious lawyers, and white-haired eminences. Again the crusaders bonded with the press; and in Patrolman William Phillips, who wound up in Sing Sing serving a life sentence for the double murder of a prostitute and her pimp, the investigators found a rogue cop of an order of villainy to rival Charles Becker. (Phillips also protested his innocence.) Like the earlier scandals, too, this one spelled the undoing of the police commissioner, Howard Leary, whose appointment, it was now realized, had been a very large blunder, dictated by Lindsay's preoccupation with a single issue: his plan to establish the Civilian Complaint Review Board.

Had Lindsay's aides done their homework, they would have found that the Philadelphia police department, Leary's alma mater, was a long way from a model force, and its commissioner was generally judged to have done little to change it. As an outsider, Leary was even less effective in New York City. One headquarters old-timer likened his appointment to making the archbishop of Canterbury pope. With a police commissioner plugged into the department's inner life, the NYPD might have been able to head off the scandal. Commissioner Valentine had managed to avoid major problems by forcing out or demoting captains and inspectors who could not control their men. Leary's top command—his college of cardinals, as it were—were so polarized that when the first deputy commissioner wanted to get some information from the Detective Bureau, he was refused. He then went to one of his own faction, the head of the Internal Affairs Bureau, and got him to surreptitiously enter the bureau office at night to seize the files. The plot was leaked to the chief of detectives, who ambushed the top shoofly, whereupon the two bosses began swapping punches. In the end, the first deputy had to go hat in hand to the commissioner to get the files.

The civilian review board fiasco had given Lindsay's people a motive of their own for hesitating to challenge police corruption. The 1960s was a time of widespread urban riots, and City Hall feared that a vigorous probe of the department would upset morale and impair the force's ability to control civil disorder. In effect, the department's traditionally most important task, maintaining peace among the city's diverse population, was seen as requiring it to be less assertive in dealing with its traditionally largest source of grief, corruption. There were no secret meetings or confidential orders given to soft-pedal corruption, but like so many things in the culture of the NYPD, it was "understood." Lindsay, never popular with cops (particularly after the CCRB fight) tried to placate the police by giving them large pay raises and increasing the strength of the force to an all-time high of nearly thirty-two thousand.

After hanging on for several months, Commissioner Leary resigned in September 1970 and sailed to Europe for a holiday. Later he took a security job with a department store, then a second such position, and wound up teaching at a small New Jersey college. With Leary gone, the Lindsay people finally did their homework and appointed the police commissioner they probably should have named in the first place.

Patrick V. Murphy, who had grown up in the Flatbush section of Brooklyn, came from a police family. His father was a sergeant, his two brothers patrolmen. Five foot nine, slender, and serious, he was the son marked for the priesthood. During the war, though, he had been a navy pilot, and when he came home, married with a child (the first of eight), he needed a paycheck quickly and entered the family business. Rising steadily up through the ranks, he spent time as an instructor at the Police Academy and ultimately became a protégé of commissioner Mike Murphy (to whom he was not related). In the early 1960s, Pat Murphy left the city to run the police force of Syracuse, New York. When he came back, Mike Murphy appointed him a deputy chief. After retiring in 1965, he took a position at the Justice Department in Washington. The attorney general, Ramsey Clark, was so impressed with Murphy that he installed him to run the Washington, D.C., police department—long subject to direction by conservative southern congressmen. After the Democrats lost the 1968 presidential election, Murphy was appointed police commissioner of Detroit.

Unlike Leary, he knew how the NYPD worked. He named a straight arrow, veteran commander Mike Codd, as chief inspector and appointed a friend, former captain Bill Smith, as first deputy commissioner, thereby ensuring there would be no rival power centers in the department. Murphy also temporarily outmaneuvered the PBA. In the winter of 1971, patrolmen angered over a city lawsuit disputing the award of some pay increments staged a job action, refusing to leave their precincts except to answer emergency calls. The disappearance of cops from the streets would soon be noticed by the criminal element, and even ordinary citizens, without having to fear a bluecoat in the vicinity, might help themselves to the goods in shop windows. By canceling days off for detectives and superior officers and putting them on twelve-hour shifts, Murphy managed to staff enough radio cars to show the flag. Perhaps because the city was gripped by a deep freeze, crime stayed low, and after six days the PBA decided to return to work. In the aftermath, the detectives should have been Murphy's fair-haired boys. Instead, he determined to clip their wings. His experiences in the department had given him a low opinion of the bureau.

Murphy appointed a flamboyant detective commander named Al Seedman as chief of detectives. With his flashy jewelry, the tough-talking, cigarchomping Seedman was the kind of Broadway cop who had flourished in the days of Johnny Broderick. He had once been snapped by a press photographer jerking up the head of a cop killer to make him pose for a picture, as a result of which he temporarily lost a scheduled promotion. Under Seedman, the bureau would lose all of its eight hundred narcotics detectives to the new Organized Crime Control Bureau; detectives would no longer sit around waiting to catch "squeals" but be assigned a regular caseload; there would be much stricter supervision and no more promotions beyond third-grade (at least while Murphy was commissioner). The days of powerful detective chiefs running an autonomous operation and first-graders moving about like princes of the city were over.

Murphy's three-year commissionership was probably the most fertile moment in the saga of the NYPD's management from the mid-1940s until the early 1990s. Among other things, women came into their own in the department. In 1963, a lawsuit brought by policewoman Felicia Spritzer resulted in a court ruling that female officers could take promotional examinations. The following year, Spritzer and Gertrude Schimmel were made sergeants. By 1971, there were 327 women on the force, including three lieutenants and ten sergeants, and in that year Schimmel became the first female captain. (In 1978 she was the first to be made a deputy chief.) Murphy assigned women to regular patrol duty and in 1976, Captain Victoria Renzullo became the first female precinct commander.

Fighting corruption, though, was the theme of most of the new ideas introduced on Murphy's watch; his role, as he saw it, was to clean up the mess he had inherited and minimize the risk of ongoing scandal. In that spirit, Murphy expanded the old confidential squads into a full-fledged Internal Affairs Bureau and created a network of "field associates"—cops recruited to spy on other cops. He made commanders accountable for conditions in their units and, to drive the point home, resorted to an old routine of forwarding to a commanding officer a complaint about a gambling or after-hours joint that headquarters knew was operating on his turf and then sitting back to wait for the response. If the C.O. reported that his men found no violations, the place would be raided by a headquarters squad and the commander told to "put in his papers"—his retirement papers. Roughly 90 percent of the inspectors and chiefs on the scene when Murphy took over were gone within two years. Murphy took it on himself to downgrade the importance of gambling arrests, and the pictures of "K.G.s" (known gamblers)—a feature of stationhouse bulletin boards since time immemorial—were duly removed and replaced by photographs of muggers and stickup men. By 1972, the number of murders was close to 1,700, having quadrupled over the previous decade. In a city with crime at record levels, gambling, even big-money gambling, seemed petty. (The political establishment, meanwhile, had moved to set up a state lottery and a city-run network of offtrack betting parlors.) To head the new Organized Crime Control Bureau, Murphy recalled a famously honest and zealous commander, William McCarthy, from a golfing and teaching retirement in Florida.

Like most reform commissioners, Murphy was not popular with his troops, and, like Valentine, he seemed content with his unpopularity. Unlike Valentine, though, he was perceived as insufficiently supportive of his men. During his time, a number of police officers were assassinated by black militants. In 1971, two officers in a patrol car guarding the home of District Attorney Hogan in upper Manhattan were riddled with machine-gun bullets fired from an automobile, leaving both men permanently disabled. The district attorney was under guard because he had prosecuted (unsuccessfully) a group of Black Panthers for alleged acts of terrorism. A few days later, two cops, one white and one black, were shot to death while walking through a housing project on the site of the old Polo Grounds baseball field in upper Manhattan. Early in 1972, a foot patrol team of black and white officers in the East Village was shot and killed without warning by several men they passed on the street. The Polo Grounds assassins were eventually linked to attacks on police officers in San Francisco. The gun of one of the dead officers in the East Village was later found in the possession of a man who shot it out with police officers in St. Louis. Some detectives argued that there was a well-organized national conspiracy to assassinate police officers by a group known as the Black Liberation Army (BLA). Deputy Commissioner for Public Information Bob Daley, a former reporter (and future crime novelist), strongly urged the department to go public with the information. Others in headquarters were against it. They took the position that the evidence of an organized conspiracy was not firm. If the information was released, they said, cops would overreact and demand to be equipped with shotguns in their cars. Murphy delayed a decision and ultimately let some of the evidence out as part of a low-key interview with a *New York Times* reporter.

The incident that rankled most with cops occurred when two Twenty-eighth Precinct officers responded to a false 10-13 (officer needs assistance) call in a Harlem mosque. Both were beaten and one was fatally shot. To calm tensions, the Muslim suspects were released by superior officers on the scene, who accepted a community leader's pledge that they would voluntarily appear at the precinct; they did not. Headquarters hesitated in defending the officers who had gone into the mosque; in fact, the police had a standing agreement with the minister, one Louis Farrakhan, not to enter without the permission of a supervisor, who would seek the consent of mosque officials. Again, Deputy Commissioner Daley urged the police commissioner to speak out in support of his men. Murphy was cautious, and only after some delay did he go public. The commander of the Twenty-eighth Precinct blasted Murphy for failing to back the slain officer and resigned from the force.

The Knapp commission was in the mold of previous investigating bodies. It got some cops, like Phillips, to confess wrongdoing and others to claim they had seen the light. But while men like Costigan and Valentine had been invited to play a prominent role in past scandals, the Knapp probers tried to ignore Serpico and Durk, dismissing them as long on rhetoric and short on legally admissible evidence. Serpico, while working narcotics in Brooklyn, had been shot in the head during a raid. Some people thought he had been set up; others, including Commissioner Murphy, considered him just another casualty of the drug wars. The argument was moot in the squad rooms and cop bars where department lore was formulated. Serpico talked; Serpico got a bullet in the head. Whether the two events were related was irrelevant. The latter was not a good inducement for doing the former. After the shooting, Serpico was finally awarded a detective shield. He resigned from the department and went to live in Europe on the proceeds of the book and film about his career.

Durk, marginalized in both accounts, was bitter about their theme that the system always triumphed over those who sought to change it, and in the great tradition of reformers, the two men feuded and quit talking to one another. Durk's relations with the Knapp commission were also stormy. He expected the commission to zero in on the culpability of those in power. Far more than he liked, the Knapp people seemed interested in the crimes of the rank and file. In an initial round of hearings, all the witnesses were cops, and Durk demanded to know when the commission would shift its gaze upward.

In fact, Whitman Knapp and his chief counsel, Michael Armstrong, had decided to sidestep what Armstrong called the "muddy exercise" of publicly exploring the Lindsay administration's culpability, reasoning that such an inquiry would be seen as an attack on a Lindsay presidential candidacy, which was brewing at the time, and "would have detracted from our purpose, which was to focus on the police department."

The commission had therefore resolved not to call either Durk or Serpico, and even after it relented, under pressure from reporters and a Democratic city council leader, Durk and the commission staff continued to argue over the content of his testimony. Armstrong wanted Durk to describe the corruption he had seen among his fellow cops in the Eighteenth Precinct. Durk refused, explaining that if he talked about such things, he would be both slandering cops who had merely gone along, modestly, with the system and undermining his credibility inside the department.

"You're just like everybody else," Armstrong told Durk. "When it doesn't serve your agenda, you're not willing to testify—you're not willing to make the kind of sacrifice that you don't hesitate to ask of others. You expect guys to get out there and be heroes. You condemn everyone else because, according to you, they weren't willing to upset their good relations with the police, and here you are telling me that you won't upset your good relations with the police."

Durk stood firm and didn't testify about cops. He did testify about his efforts, along with Serpico, to find a public official bothered enough by corruption to do something about it. The average cop, he declared in his opening statement, longs to be honest but is convinced that "he lives and works in the middle of a corrupt society." The police department had become "a home for drug dealers and thieves" in which "men who could have been good officers, men of decent impulse . . . were told in a hundred ways every day, 'Go along, forget the law, don't make waves and shut up.' " Any anticorruption campaign that failed to fix responsibility outside the department as well as inside—and in high places as well as low—would be viewed by cops as a "swindle," he said. To most people, police corruption was a nasty but abstract problem; to Durk it was what stood between cops and their pride. At the end of his statement, fighting back tears, he stalked out of the room, leaving the audience to applaud the chair in which he had been sitting. Chairman Knapp, visibly nonplussed, called a brief recess so that people could collect themselves.

The scandal did take its toll on the city's highest officials. Lindsay, whose run for the 1972 Democratic presidential nomination collapsed early on, announced in 1973 that he would not seek another term as mayor. Though he didn't have to go into exile in Europe or Mexico, he was dead politically. In 1980, he entered the primary for the Democratic nomination for U.S. senator, and finished last in a four-way race. The fall of Lindsay also meant the end of the reform commissioner, Murphy. Like Teddy Roosevelt, he executed a glorious retreat to the Washington-based Police Foundation, a new Ford-funded think tank. Only fifty-three when he left New York, Murphy spent the next twelve years at the foundation. Though he was frequently touted as next in line to be FBI director or chief of another big-city force, nothing ever materialized. Perhaps the clearest winners were the makers of the hit movie *Serpico*, which affirmed two of the NYPD's most enduring maxims: "You can't change the job" and "Don't stick your neck out."

14

Twenty and Out

Michael J. Codd, a tall, broad-shouldered inspector with the upright bearing of the army major he had been in World War II, was the commanding officer of the Tactical Patrol Force in the early sixties. Robert Leuci, a short, chunky, boyish-looking patrolman with an ingratiating air of naïveté, was a highly productive member of the unit and a favorite of Codd's—enough of one, anyway, that he could directly approach the boss, known for his personal integrity, about his desire to get out of uniform. Leuci was also shrewd enough not to jump at the first opportunity.

"If you had a son working here," he asked Codd, "would you tell him to go into plainclothes?"

"Why do you ask that?" Codd replied.

Plainclothes, Leuci had heard, was a "really dangerous place" from a corruption standpoint.

"You're right—stay where you are," Codd counseled him.

A few months later, Leuci sought Codd's advice again—about a transfer to Narcotics.

This time he got the all clear. "There's not a cop in the world who would take drug money," Codd assured him.

Codd was invoking the historic distinction that even rogue cops made between "clean" money, which involved gambling or liquor-law violations, and "dirty" money, which had to do with crimes viewed as more harmful, such as robbery, murder, and drug dealing. But his information was out of date.

Narcotics might not be associated with the kind of systemic and routinized graft that had swiftly reestablished itself in gambling enforcement after the Gross scandal. In Narcotics, the money was more catch-as-catch-can, but there was far more of it out there. Gambling was the corruption of the past. Narcotics was the future.

In 1964, the year Leuci commenced his career as a narcotics cop, New York was waking up to an epidemic of heroin use—the second since the drug had come on the market in 1898. (It was promoted originally as a cough remedy and later, by some gushing enthusiasts, as a supposedly nonaddictive substitute for opium and morphine.) In the first big wave of heroin addiction, which struck in the teens and twenties, the victims came from the middle and lower classes, but many were gang members, gamblers, and prostitutes. Virtually all, in any case, were white. The second time around, in the 1950s and '60s, the heroin business benefited from the financial backing and administrative know-how of the Mafia, which shrewdly directed its marketing efforts at the ghettos. At the beginning of the sixties, there were perhaps fifty thousand heroin users in the country; by the end of the decade, there were an estimated half a million.

Cocaine, introduced in the mid-nineteenth century, was originally seen as a tonic for sinusitis and hay fever, and later used as a local anesthetic for eye, ear, and throat surgery. In the South, however, the legend grew up that it stimulated defiance and retribution among blacks. According to drug historian David Musto, anecdotes told of superhuman strength, cunning, and efficiency resulting from cocaine. The drug was even believed to improve pistol marksmanship, and blacks under its influence were said to be unaffected by lightweight .32-caliber bullets, causing southern police departments to switch to .38s.

In 1962, the NYPD, working with federal drug agents, scored a much-celebrated triumph over the "French connection"—a chain of distribution in which Turkish opium was shipped to Corsica, refined in Marseilles, and imported into the United States. The team of detectives who broke the case became the core of an elite narcotics squad known as the Special Investigating Unit, where, in due course, Bob Leuci was assigned. Narcs on the take didn't make monthly collections as plainclothesmen did. They pocketed their money in the form of "scores": sometimes an arrested drug dealer would explicitly offer a bribe in return for his release or some form of artfully staged leniency. More often, even that formality was bypassed: the cops would simply relieve a dealer of his money and drugs and take most of it for themselves, vouchering a plausible minimum as contraband or prisoner's property. The drugs came in handy as a means of compensating informants; a few detectives took the process a step further, reselling some of what they had seized. Leuci and his fellow "princes of the city"—as they came to be known through a book and movie that gave a somewhat fuller picture of the state of the war on drugs than the more popular *French Connection* book-and-movie package—were celebrated as heroes even as many of them acquired luxury cars, pricey suburban homes, and long suede and leather coats, in which they bore a more than passing resemblance to the drug dealers they had, to all intents and purposes, become.

After the Knapp commission came into being, David Durk nudged Bob Leuci into delivering the testimony that carried the inquiry from the familiar territory of gambling into the unfamiliar territory of drugs. Leuci, like Bill Phillips and several other members of this latest generation of implicated cops, wound up wearing a wire and acting as an undercover agent against ex-colleagues and superiors—another practice that set the Knapp scandal apart. Months of double agentry left him with what *Life* magazine called a "racing stripe" across his rib cage—the result of the repeated application and removal of strips of adhesive tape that held a microphone to his chest. For a time, his prosecutor handlers tried to present him as a reluctant money-grubber in the mold set by Max Schmittberger (with Lincoln Steffens's assistance); eventually Leuci was compelled to acknowledge an embarrassing degree of eager involvement. Nevertheless, more than fifty cops out of a unit that had never numbered more than eighty were eventually transferred, dismissed, or indicted; several more, including the commander of the unit, avoided arrest by cooperating with the inquiry, while two detectives committed suicide before their cases came to trial.

In 1974, a sixty-seven-year-old Democratic politician from Brooklyn named Abe Beame became mayor. The previous year, Lindsay had passed over Chief Inspector Codd for commissioner in favor of a younger Pat Murphy favorite, Chief of Patrol Don Cawley. A fervent believer in the principle of seniority, Beame recalled Codd from retirement to be his police commissioner. But while no one could ever accuse Codd of fostering a climate of innovation, a number of Murphy's anticorruption policies endured. Uniformed cops were discouraged from contact with drug dealers, saloonkeepers, and other so-called corruption hazards. The Inspectional Services Bureau—Murphy's beefed-up version of Internal Affairs—was placed under a fanatical chief, John Guido, and the detective and vice units remained relatively clean.

Another, more conspicuous, legacy of the Lindsay years was the Bauhaus-style edifice—redolent of the sixties—that became police headquarters at the end of 1973. A conveniently brief stroll away from City Hall, it was a fourteen-story maze of offices that matched the increasingly bureaucratic temperament of the institution. Officially, it was One Police Plaza, which got shortened to 1PP, and then transmogrified, by many cops, to "the puzzle palace."

Fear remained the leitmotif of the department. The bosses worried about the misdeeds of cops; the rank and file, for the first time, about unemployment. In June 1975, struggling with the accumulated burden of years of fiscal mismanagement, New York was unable to meet its payroll. The following month, the city began the layoff of fifty thousand employees, including five thousand police officers. Beame and his political supporters might have avoided this extreme step—if they had wanted to. But the decision to include cops in the layoff program was seen by some as a useful scare tactic in the effort to get the feds to cough up the money the city needed to avert bankruptcy: it was "federal dollars or federal troops," Governor Hugh Carey argued.

Unfortunately for the police, Washington called the city's bluff. (FORD TO CITY: DROP DEAD was how the *Daily News* reported the president's response.) By now there was no turning back, not with the other city unions—mainstays of Beame's political base—watching carefully to make sure the cops took their hit. In a single year, the strength of the NYPD fell from over 31,000 to less than 26,000. In the end, the city got the federal loan guarantees it was after only by ceding control of its finances to a board of bankers and other private citizens. For the last two years of his term, Mayor Beame was a figurehead with roughly the same power as the leader of a banana republic occupied by U.S. Marines.

The layoffs were a terrible blow to an institution long seen as a bastion of job security. Even in the Depression, cops had not been fired; and now, unlike then, crime was soaring. By 1972, murders were running at an annual rate of twenty-two per hundred thousand citizens—triple the rate of a few years earlier. Between 1966 (the first year the figures for other crimes had been kept accurately) and the beginning of the 1970s, the number of reported robberies had risen from twenty-three thousand to nearly ninety thousand a year. To the citizenry, the police were looking less and less credible as a source of protection.

With the rank and file increasingly focused on questions of pay and job security, the Patrolmen's Benevolent Association moved to the fore. The union president was an in-your-face cop whose idea for avoiding layoffs was to go on TV waving his revolver and pointing to his empty holster as a symbol of the city's impending defenselessness. Many rank-and-file cops were feeling equally contentious. Mimicking other city employees whose wages had been frozen, off-duty officers staged angry public protests in 1976, picketing Commissioner Codd's house in Queens, blocking traffic on the Upper East Side, and urinating on the lawn of the mayor's official residence, Gracie Mansion. The police had clearly learned something about demonstration tactics from their experiences on the other side of the barricades.

When Muhammad Ali and Ken Norton met for the heavyweight championship at Yankee Stadium that September, a mob of militant cops showed up, hoping to get some free worldwide publicity. It turned into a night of horror. Fifteen hundred off-duty cops roamed about like high school kids at a pep rally, shouting, among other slogans, "Beame is a shrimp" and "Codd is a fish." Three high-ranking chiefs were knocked down and slugged by protesting underlings as they alighted from their official vehicle. In the melee, the chief of the department lost a valuable diamond ring. The four hundred on-duty officers gave their fellow unionists a wide berth. Kids from the area began snatching the jewelry of the arriving glitterati. In charge of the police detail was Assistant Chief Anthony Bouza, the Bronx borough commander. Casting about for a fall guy afterward, headquarters' gaze quickly settled on Bouza. A cop given to quoting Melville and Sartre, he explained that the jewelry snatchers were "feral children" who had "impinged on the consciousness" of "middle- and upper-class Americans." Then he bowed to the inevitable and resigned to take a job as deputy chief of the New York City Transit Police.

Mayor Beame's last year in office, 1977, was a flurry of disasters. A serial killer dubbed Son of Sam by the press began shooting down women (and sometimes their male escorts) in the streets. It took the police eight months and four separate incidents to notice a pattern and set up a task force to investigate. Another four months—and three more shootings, bringing the overall tally to five dead and six wounded—passed without an arrest. When the killer was finally caught a year after his spree had begun, it was more the result of luck than great detective work. On his last shooting in July 1977, he left his white Ford Galaxy parked at a fire hydrant on a Brooklyn street and got a ticket. At about the same time, some Yonkers inhabitants became suspicious of a neighbor and reported him to the NYPD. Brooklyn detectives noted that the traffic ticket checked to a Yonkers resident. A squad of police officers went to the home of twenty-four-year-old David Berkowitz, spotted his car with a rifle inside, and waited for him to appear. When he came out of his building, Berkowitz was carrying a manila envelope that held a .44-caliber gun, which by then had killed six people and wounded seven. "Okay," he said, "you got me."

That same "Summer of Sam," a power failure caused a citywide blackout. During a similar episode in 1965, the mood of New Yorkers had been upbeat—according to legend, an abnormally high number of babies were born nine months later. This time mobs looted stores with little interference from the scaled-down police force. And now that many of the city's cops lived fifty miles from their commands, mobilizing extra manpower was a difficult business. Congressman Ed Koch, a candidate for mayor, had the presence of mind to declare that *he* would have summoned the National Guard. Koch won and appointed a well-spoken lawyer named Robert McGuire as police commissioner. With no new hires, the strength of the force continued to fall, reaching twenty-two thousand officers by 1980, or approximately 30 percent fewer than there had been six years earlier. The crime rate went in the opposite direction: serious crime had gone up nearly 40 percent since 1974.

Bobby Evers, a former army paratrooper who was working in construction when the NYPD accepted him in 1973, was one of the many cops who had the misfortune to join the department at the beginning of one of its bleakest eras. In the early seventies, the job seemed to be defined by the corruption scandal and the fiscal crisis. Over the next two decades, things went from bad to worse. Evers started out in the Nineteenth Precinct, on the Upper East Side of Manhattan. At the outset of his career, he would recall, there was a sizable cadre of veteran cops, including a few thirty-year men, from whom he learned tips he would later pass on to another generation of rookies. One was to use a small wad of paper to plug up a keyhole, thus enabling a woman who had been threatened by an errant boyfriend or spouse to sleep safely. Another was to ask the radio dispatcher to replay the description of a crime suspect for the benefit of an angry citizen who believed he had been stopped for no good reason. In the Nineteenth Precinct and, later, the Seventy-first, in the Crown Heights area of Brooklyn, Evers would adhere to another practice he had been taught as a rookie: keeping the windows rolled down, regardless of the weather, as a means of staying alert.

As time passed, however, it seemed to Evers that savvy, dedicated older cops became more of a rarity. Many of the younger ones who, in the normal course of things, might have been expected to become knowing graybeards were developing a more callous attitude toward the job: since the city had broken faith with them, they reasoned, they owed nothing back. Evers saw cops race through their careers. The thinking was: first put in your time, then find some undemanding job in the private sector that, with the pension check as supplement, would mean a cushy retirement. "Twenty and out" became the unofficial department mantra.

Fueling the cynicism of the rank and file was the belief that the bosses were out to get them. And in many cases, they were. From headquarters rained down a series of "Thou shalt not"s, based, it seems, on the premise that cops were untrustworthy by nature. One element of the program, as many in the uniformed force understood it, was to lay off drug arrests. "Every working cop knew that if you were involved in too many drug collars, the police department would put your name on a list," Evers recalled. As a result, gambling and narcotics joints operated with impunity in Crown Heights, offering up a few empty boxes of cereal in their windows in a feeble effort to pass themselves off as grocery stores. "Thou shalt not police" was the message that many cops took away from the various directives.

"The only organization I've ever seen that comes close to the police department is Mother Russia," Evers liked to say. (He was of Lithuanian descent; the name had been shortened from Evaskovitch.) "We have our own trial room where you can get hung. We have our own gulags. We have our own group of psychiatrists that'll find you nuts."

Evers's philosophy of policing was not to let his feelings for the organization cloud his feelings for the job. As a PBA delegate for twelve years, he stood ready to go to the mat with his superiors over, say, the denial of overtime compensation that cops were rightfully entitled to. But he was no less disdainful of cops who would go through a tour of duty taking two or three radio calls while others took fifteen or twenty. During the crack epidemic of the 1980s, he and his longtime partner, Tommy Goldsmith (who had a distinguished police career of his own), spent hours one day looking for a missing infant whose mother had left him in the care of a neighbor with a history of drug use. Evers decided to check out every crack den he knew. They eventually traced the baby to a crack den in an adjacent precinct, and Evers advised the sentry in front that they had the place surrounded—this was pure bravado. "Bring the baby out immediately or else everybody's getting busted," he commanded. The child was delivered safe and sound.

The dark mood of the NYPD also infected its brethren of the transit and housing police; those departments, too, suffered budget and personnel cuts, and their morale, which had never been very high, plummeted. Patrolling the sunless, dank, noisy underground subway system or the depressing public housing complexes was not something that many people yearned to do, and it took someone with rare inner reserves of determination to care about such a job in the atmosphere of the times.

Jack Maple joined the transit police as an eighteen-year-old civilian aide in 1970. Three years later, he was made a patrolman and posted to Brooklyn, riding trains and patrolling platforms. During his first year of service, Maple came across a man swinging a four-foot-long iron pipe and chasing another cop on a subway platform. Rushing to his fellow officer's assistance, Maple was hit over the head and sank down. The suspect stood over him, preparing to swing again. Maple managed to fire five rounds before blacking out. A third cop converging on the scene also fired, and the suspect fell dead. The transit police never told the officers whose bullet was the fatal one.

A year later, while working a plainclothes anticrime detail, Maple tried to arrest a drug dealer; in the ensuing struggle, the dealer grabbed his gun away and fired two shots so close to the cop's face that his cheek was burned by the muzzle flash. Maple managed to get his hand on the gun, squeeze the trigger, and wound the dealer. This kind of case spelled trouble. Maple had followed the perp from the subway up into a public park. The department tended to regard its officers as guards; as such, they were not supposed to concern themselves with events that transpired outside the agency's area of jurisdiction. Most transit cops could live with this limitation. Maple couldn't. He made a habit of following suspicious characters from the subway into the streets, keeping them under observation, and arresting them, in some cases, for crimes committed in the great outdoors. Complaints were made. Soon the transit police Internal Affairs Unit began following Maple around. On one memorable occasion, an internal affairs man stood by, taking notes, while Maple rolled on the ground trying to put handcuffs on a mugger.

Maple, like Evers, sensed that most of the city's police work was being done by a relatively small cadre of cops. In court, he kept seeing the same group of city, transit, and housing officers—a sort of corporal's guard responsible for a big share of all the arrests. And for their efforts, it seemed, they often became the target of suspicion. Arrests, of course, meant overtime, which had to be compensated at time and a half. The city was very reluctant to pay overtime, and what little there was, in the view of one of Maple's superiors, should be spread around. To the list of Maple's sins was thus added that of "taking money away from other cops."

The dedication of some cops was amazing. The NYPD's citywide Anti-crime Unit was one of the most dangerous assignments on the force. Its officers, in plainclothes and unmarked cars, patrolled high-crime areas looking for gun toters and stickup men. Bobby Gallagher had a knack for telling by the way somebody walked whether he was armed. Many a street criminal with a gun in his belt would make a constant subconscious effort to keep it from falling out. Spotting a likely suspect, Gallagher and his partner did not leap out of their car with their own weapons in hand; that could have led them into shooting an innocent person or fighting a gun battle in which their slow-firing .38-caliber revolvers would be matched against nine-millimeter semi-automatics. Instead, they would unobtrusively move in until Gallagher was close enough to place his hand over the suspect's weapon, making it impossible for him to draw it. During his seventeen years of service, Gallagher made 1,200 loaded-gun arrests and received 210 citations. In 1984 Governor Mario Cuomo named him New York State police officer of the year. But he ended up in a homicide unit where he was mostly expected to write reports. Like a number of other conspicuously active cops in the seventies and eighties, Gallagher bailed out of the department early, starting a private security firm in 1986.

After his promotion to detective in 1980, Jack Maple decided on a change of lifestyle. Five feet, seven inches tall and stocky, he bore the nickname, at the time, of "Fatso." Now he went on a diet, cutting ten inches from his waistline, and bought three designer suits. In place of Fatso there appeared a Damon Runyon character with derby hat, bow tie, and white shoes. He began hanging out at the plush Waldorf and Plaza Hotel bars. Before his sojourn was over, he had mortgaged his home to borrow $28,000, which, by his own account, he "quickly converted into bottles of Dom Perignon and Broadway shows." A youthful marriage had also ended, and the new Maple squired many a glamorous woman before his money ran out and they did, as well. A profile in *New York* magazine described Maple as "the cop who loved the Oak Bar," referring to a fashionable watering hole at the Plaza.

Maple's assigned area, the Times Square subway complex, resembled a Casbah. Hordes of prostitutes and three-card-monte men waited to fleece tourists and the bridge-and-tunnel crowd from New Jersey. Muggers were attracted to Forty-second Street, or, as they called it, the "Deuce." Maple continued his practice of following the bad guys out of the subway. Sometimes he would mount a stakeout near a store that sold holsters and gun paraphernalia; somebody who patronized such a place, Maple reasoned, was more likely than the average Joe to be carrying a gun. On occasion, his instincts were validated by an arrest. In 1985, Maple made sergeant and was put in charge of a decoy squad. The unit was composed of cops made up to look like stiffs—bait for muggers—and backup cops who sought to blend in with the street population. On New Year's Eve, when the ball dropped in Times Square, Maple and his crew would mingle in the dense crowds until they spotted a "wolfpack," a team of robbers preparing to move in on a victim. Just as they were about to strike, the cops would jump them, and there would be a wild melee, sometimes requiring a cavalry charge by the mounted police to help make the arrests. Maple became the subject of another *New York* magazine story, this one entitled "Hunting the Wolfpacks." More than once, suspected muggers would be found carrying a picture of Maple and his crew, cut out of the article.

By the mid-1980s, drugs were plainly the biggest problem facing the NYPD, and a profound change had taken place in the drug trade. The Italians, the dominant force as recently as the late 1960s, were receding in importance. The business had become decentralized, with a number of other groups entering the lists, peddling not only heroin but also South American cocaine. Black gangsters took advantage of the more open nature of the business to stake out their claim. Not too many years earlier, the highest a black man could go in organized crime had been to obtain a ghetto franchise from the Mafia. Even the celebrated Ellsworth "Bumpy" Johnson, Harlem's number one gangster from the 1940s through the '60s, was just a lieutenant of the Genovese family. One of his '70s successors, Frank "Peewee" Matthews, was running a multi-million-dollar East Coast cocaine and heroin empire while still in his twenties. Although he started as an underling of the Gambinos, Matthews became powerful enough to tell them to back off. When he was arrested in 1973, he posted bail and disappeared with $20 million.

With so many new players in the game, old rules were forgotten. The excesses of the Prohibition Era had taught the stalwarts of traditional organized crime that widespread killing was wasteful and likely to bring down the wrath of the government. The new kids on the block had yet to learn this valuable lesson. Not only would they kill a rival; sometimes they would compel him to watch his wife being disemboweled. On occasion, they took out the victim's children as well. The term *Colombian necktie* came into use in New York City to describe a form of murder in which a person's throat was cut and his tongue pulled down so that it dangled through the slit.

If police history had been destined to repeat itself, conditions in the NYPD's vice units should have gradually returned to normal now that the Knapp commission was fading from memory. They didn't. In the years that followed, the brass and the vastly expanded vice squad known as the Organized Crime Control Bureau generally stayed straight. The kids in the patrol cars were the ones who succumbed. Set down in ghetto precincts where drug dealing looked almost as monotonously normal as gambling in the blue-collar neighborhoods the cops came from, they were less likely to see the penalties than the rewards: money enough to buy a comfortable house and a fancy car while they were young enough to enjoy it. Most cops resisted the lures of the drug trade, but even among the straight ones there was a widespread readiness to observe the "blue wall of silence"—the rule against informing on crooked brethren.

Henry Winter was appointed to the force in 1974, at age twenty-two. Laid off the following year, he headed out to Colorado, where he briefly became a deputy sheriff. After the NYPD recalled him in 1978, Winter eventually landed in the Seventy-seventh Precinct, in Bedford Stuyvesant. There he hooked up with a group of young cops who were shaking down drug dealers and, before too long, selling drugs themselves. When a radio-car crew wanted to summon the other members of the ring to raid a dealer's apartment in quest of drugs and money, the call went out for the "buddy boys" to respond, giving

Winter's group a nickname. Most of their activity took place on the midnight shift, when supervision was traditionally slack; at any rate, no one in the precinct professed to have noticed anything amiss. Headquarters was equally oblivious. Young minority drug lords were simply not on the One Police Plaza radar; nor was the notion of uniformed patrolmen pocketing large sums of illicit money—an unknown phenomenon when the top brass were young. It fell to the special prosecutor for criminal justice (an office that came into being after the Knapp investigation) to act. In 1985, his agents took Henry Winter into custody and convinced him and his partner to wear a wire, entrapping others in return for a ticket out of jail. Eventually thirteen police officers were arrested; another killed himself. A few years later, Winter would do the same. Meanwhile, logic suggested that if such a ring was operating in one precinct, headquarters might do well to look elsewhere for the same pattern of behavior. The special prosecutor, Joe Hynes, helpfully supplied the department with a list of ten ghetto precincts where drugs flourished and dealers had complained of police shakedowns. His warning went pretty much ignored.

The situation grew dramatically worse with the advent of crack in 1985. This easily ingested cocaine derivative was a junkie's delight, potent and cheap. It was also a dealer's dream. A kilo could be purchased for as little as $20,000, melted down, and sold for several times that amount. The only other piece of equipment needed to go into business was a firearm. "Anyone bold enough to shoot a gun qualifies as an entrepreneur," one prosecutor remarked. The lure of BMWs, Mercedes-Benzes, and glittering jewelry was too much for many young men to resist. Drug gangs developed out of sports teams and music groups. A typical crew was overseen by a gang lieutenant or subboss, with each member assigned a specific function. The "lookout," who might be a thirteen- or fourteen-year-old working for a hundred dollars a day, sounded a warning whenever he spotted the cops. The "hawker" hustled buyers: "Do you smoke, sir?" was a common opening line. If someone responded positively, a "steerer" took him to the "seller," who filled the buyer's order with goods from the "stasher," often a female concealing the goods under her clothes. To avoid being caught with marked bills passed by an undercover cop, a "messenger" laundered the payment through a nearby storekeeper, who got a percentage for his trouble. Watching over the crew was a gunman who stood ready to deal with rival gangs or disgruntled customers. It was not unusual for buyers to come back and complain about the quality of the merchandise. Sometimes they would flash a gun for emphasis, and the homicide squad would eventually be called in. Even simple customer complaints against inefficient service could keep homicide busy. One steerer put a customer ahead of another in the line of buyers; the passed-over customer shot the customer who had received preferential placement. The steerer was fired for her incompetence.

The new recruits brought street-gang methods to the drug business: shoot first and shoot often was the rule. Yet they were, in many cases, little more than children. "Just think," a detective said of a youth suspected of committing four homicides and engaging in a machine-gun battle with police. "One of these days, he will be old enough to drink."

In the late 1970s, a group of young men calling themselves the Vigilantes began robbing and killing drug dealers in upper Manhattan. They told the neighborhood that they were getting rid of the dealers, but they wound up installing their own team instead. The new leader came out of the local music business, and many of his gang members had been part of his singing group. By the early '80s, the Vigilantes numbered thirty members and two dozen associates. In their shamelessness and fearlessness, they adopted olive-green military outfits with black boots, and, as a sign of their status, members wore hatchets on chains around their necks: silver for soldiers and gold for lieutenants and above. A special homicide investigation unit in the office of New York County District Attorney Morgenthau was created after the killing of a witness scheduled to testify for the state at the murder trial of one of the gang members. The unit eventually put a number of the Vigilantes in prison on sentences of twenty-five to life.

The murder figures zoomed on up, as gangs all over the city began to struggle for control of the crack trade. In 1985, the city recorded 1,384 homicides; in 1986, 1,582; in 1987, 1,672; virtually the entire increase could be attributed to drug-related killings, which, over the course of the decade, rose from approximately 20 percent to 40 percent of the city's murders. All around the town, inner-city neighborhoods took on the quality of free-fire zones. Since the gang members typically went about in flak jackets, the prescribed tactic for a hit man was to "kill 'em in the head"—that is, walk up close and blow the victim's head off. Another tactic was to spray a street corner, which had the effect, often, of not only killing the intended target but wounding or killing five or ten bystanders. Such an outcome was viewed, by some of the perpetrators, as a useful way of indicating who was in charge of the streets thereabouts. Children were often hit, and a terrible new phrase crept into the jargon of the street: gunned-down innocents were "mushrooms" because they popped up underfoot. (According to some commentators, the term came from the mushroom in a Super Mario Brothers Nintendo game.) Nursery schools in some parts of the city began teaching children to drop down flat when they heard a popping noise; those who performed properly were rewarded with a treat.

The police were way behind the curve. There were only two gangs in the city, one headquarters boss told a national-magazine reporter at a time when two hundred might have been closer to the mark. Because the drug gangs did not have the well-defined structure and permanence of Mafia families, they were hard to situate on an organization chart. So, for many cops, they did not exist. Yet the gangs killed more people in a year than the Mafia did in twenty. The news media, too, was slow to grasp what was happening. If the Gambinos and the Luccheses had been at war, there would have been headlines.

Beginning on New Year's Day 1988, a seventeen-year-old East Harlem crack addict named Leslie Torres killed five people and wounded six others in the space of eight days. He had no previous record. Crack, according to Torres, made him "feel like God." If such a rampage had taken place a few blocks farther south, in the chic regions of the Upper East Side, media attention and police action would have been instantaneous. Because it was confined to the barrio of East Harlem, it went largely unnoticed.

In the 1970s, the Genovese family had put one of its black lieutenants, "Pop" Freeman, in charge of drug operations in southeast Queens. In 1978, he retired at age seventy, bequeathing his franchise to Ron "Bumps" Bassett, who cut out the Mafia and began dealing directly with Colombian suppliers. Bassett created a distribution network that stretched up and down the East Coast, until a federal indictment in Baltimore forced him to turn South Jamaica over to Lorenzo "Fat Cat" Nichols. In 1985, a New York State parole officer filed papers to send Nichols back to prison after his arrest in a narcotics raid. In retaliation, Nichols ordered his lieutenant, a Rastafarian named Howard "Pappy" Mason, to have the parole officer, Brian Rooney, killed. Mason delegated the task to an underling. Lured into an ambush, Rooney was shot to pieces while he sat in his car. In Nichols's world, it sometimes took far less provocation to trigger murder. Fat Cat sponsored a summer basketball tournament called the Supremes Night Invitational Fastbreak Festival, or SNIFF. During a game in which the teams were playing for $50,000 in prize money, a referee—a popular former college basketball coach—made a controversial call; as the crowd watched, he was beaten to death by a dealer who jumped from the stands. In 1987, a sixty-one-year-old taxicab dispatcher named Mildred Green witnessed a murder committed by Nichols's gang and testified secretly before a grand jury. Information leaked, and she, too, was hit.

Fat Cat and Pappy eventually went too far. In November 1987, a Guyanese immigrant named Arjune (he had no other name) called the police to report crack dealing on his corner. The cops arrived and arrested one of the local gang members; but some of his henchmen, hanging around, heard police-radio transmissions that identified Arjune's house as the source of the tip. At four-thirty the next morning, the house was firebombed. The fearless Arjune accompanied cops on a tour of the neighborhood and spotted one of the bombers, who was duly arrested. Ten minutes after he returned home, two more Molotov cocktails were thrown at his house. Fearing another Mildred Green situation, the 103rd Precinct commander ordered round-the-clock protection: a "fixer" known as "the Inwood post" was established; it consisted of a one-man patrol car stationed at 107th Avenue and Inwood Street. A lone cop was, of course, a sitting duck if anyone had a strong desire to get him out of the way. In the past, however, organized crime had hesitated to do such a thing. (While many of the events in the movie *The Godfather* had a factual basis, the murder of a New York City police captain by Michael Corleone did not. Lieutenant Petrosino's assassination had occurred in Sicily.)

Shortly before three-thirty in the morning on February 25, 1988, a 911 operator received a report of a police officer shot at 107th Avenue and Inwood Street. As cars responded, a precinct patrol sergeant came on the radio twice to nervously query "Is the Inwood post on the air?" There was no answer. Several police cars reached the scene simultaneously, and officers peered into a parked patrol car. Its inside was coated with a red mist, and a uniformed police officer sat in the front seat with the top of his head blown off. The dead man was a twenty-two-year-old rookie, Eddie Byrne. A bunch of local drug dealers had done what the mafiosi had never dared do: assassinate a police officer.

At last, the drug gangs became worthy of general attention. Federal agents and local police mounted major drives, which, among other things, led to the imprisonment of Nichols, Mason, and their cohorts. (In 1992, federal prosecutors indicted and convicted four men in the murder of Parole Officer Rooney, seven years earlier.) Vice President George Bush, soon to be elected president, appeared at a rally in Queens, where he accepted a replica of the murdered officer's badge from his father. The drug wars were the lead item on the six o'clock news, and City Hall itself was threatened. In the 1980s, a high-profile crusading prosecutor appeared on the scene in the person of Rudy Giuliani. A native New Yorker, he had practiced law in a prestigious firm, served in high positions in the Justice Department in Washington, and, as U.S. attorney for the Southern District of New York, won convictions against a cast of criminal characters that included Wall Street bankers and brokers, Mafia bosses, and corrupt political leaders. Eddie Byrne's brother was one of his assistants. It was no secret that Giuliani intended to run for mayor. If the NYPD and the Koch administration could not control drugs and crime, Giuliani looked like a man who could.

Koch's original police commissioner, Bob McGuire, had moved on. His replacement, Ben Ward, was the first African-American to occupy the post. (Just a few months prior to appointing Ward, Mayor Koch had been resound-ingly booed while testifying at a congressional subcommittee hearing on police brutality in Harlem.) Ward was a well-credentialed cop who had a law degree and had served as deputy commissioner for community affairs under Pat Murphy before being named the state's commissioner of corrections.

The NYPD's options were limited. It did not have enough beat cops or community contacts to mobilize the public against the street gangs—things had gone too far for that, in any case. Ward and his advisers thus fell back on the customary device of forming special squads, known, in this case, as tactical narcotic teams (TNT for short), to cleanse the affected neighborhoods by making large numbers of arrests. In the not too distant past, this would have been a simpler affair: as recently as the 1950s, the police could have cleared the streets by sweeping down nightly and filing loitering or disorderly charges against everyone hanging around a suspected drug location. Since the '60s, though, the courts had frowned on undiscriminating law enforcement of this sort. It became necessary, therefore, for the NYPD to follow the "buy and bust" approach. An undercover cop would buy drugs with marked money, and a backup team would make the arrest. Of course, major felony arrests of this sort could easily overwhelm the courts and jail facilities; perhaps the high command didn't foresee a need to continue the campaign that long. But if anyone imagined that a whirlwind series of roundups reported on nightly television would be sufficient to force the drug gangs off the streets, that certainly did not happen. In devising the TNT plan, police strategists had failed to consider an important factor. Vacancies in the bottom rungs of the drug gangs could easily be filled with other young men anxious to make enough money for the good life. When TNT cleaned up one neighborhood and departed for another, the boss dealers would simply find replacements for their arrested underlings. Thus, the TNT initiative actually had the effect of increasing the number of people employed in the drug business, even as it brought the criminal justice system to the edge of collapse.

The chief judge of New York State declared an emergency in the court system, shifting judges from civil trials (always important in the commercial capital of the United States) to criminal ones. The jail system began to bulge at the seams with drug arrestees, so the city bought barges to house the overflow. Prison hulks had not been used in New York since the departure of the British after the revolution.

And crime continued to rise. In 1989, the city recorded over 1,900 murders, up nearly 40 percent in four years. Along with the drug busts that got featured coverage on the evening news, there were yet more pictures of dead bodies. TNT had not solved the problem. In a broader sense, the post-Knapp police department was unable to cope with the crime, the drugs, and the violence that had spread across the city in the 1970s and '80s. It was equally caught off guard by the new drug-related police corruption. Many of the police brass were demoralized by what they saw as the city's general downward spiral. Their careers had begun in the early postwar years, when New York City was the rich capital of the world, not a charity case living on the federal dole. Second- and third-generation cops many of them, they had been reared to look upon the police job as a source of lifetime security. It no longer was. New York, in the eyes of many police commanders, had become a Third World city where crime could not be suppressed, only contained. As one high-ranking chief told an interviewer in 1976, "There were blocks in the city so bad—where rocks were thrown off roofs at the cops—that the Department simply did not send anyone into them; they stationed patrol cars at either end instead." It was not the way the NYPD had traditionally handled tough beats, those that cops of yesteryear had referred to as "battle rows."

15

"Dave, Do Something!"

Buried in any number of file cabinets, desk drawers, and closets of the postmillennial NYPD is a 112-page booklet that made the rounds in January 1991. It is a remarkable document—a rare attempt to think about the past and future of a profession inclined to live in the moment. That inclination, in fact, was part of what the authors—a team of police officials and consultants answering to Police Commissioner Lee Brown—hoped to change. In a few years, they declared, the department would no longer be an "incident-responding bureaucracy." Instead of lurching from emergency to emergency, officers would get to know their beats: in the world of community policing, as Brown and his strategists depicted it, every neighborhood would "have one or more police officers" familiar with "its people, their concerns, the crime problem, the make-up of the blocks, the crises of daily living and the support systems available to help people live better." Community police officers, unlike plain old police officers, would be problem solvers. Working with local residents and businesspeople, they would zero in on the chronic conditions that put neighborhoods on edge—a park taken over by drug dealers, for example. Once a problem came to their notice, they would "assume responsibility" for its solution.

In New York, as in other cities, community-policing enthusiasts had a habit of getting so caught up in the community part that they forgot the police part. At times, the institution they described sounded less like a police force than a team of all-purpose ombudspeople who would be out attending meetings, massaging hurt feelings, and fixing everything that needed fixing. Community policing could be vague. It could be grandiose. It could be insufferably warm and fuzzy. It was all too easy to dismiss as—in the words of Darryl Gates, the hard-nosed chief of the Los Angeles Police Department—"a bunch of cops grinning at people and patting kids on the heads and handing out lollipops." It was many things to many people, perhaps because, at bottom, it was less a blueprint for what policing should be than a critique of what it had become.

In the 1920s, the cities of the western United States, which had grown up in the auto age, put most of their policemen into cars. Eastern cities, by contrast, continued to see patrol cars primarily as backup for foot patrol or as a way of countering automobile-borne bandits. Into the early 1950s, most precincts maintained only two or three radio motor patrol cars, or RMPs, as they were known. Then, gradually, the RMP took over policing in the East as well.

Even in dense areas where traffic was slow, a car had advantages. It was a good place to put things like flashlights, first-aid kids, and complaint forms, which could be a pain to carry around. It could serve as a temporary ambulance or office. And, of course, it had a radio—a compelling advantage during the many decades that passed before portable radios became lightweight and reliable enough to bring footmen into the same kind of tight communications as RMP cops.

In the early days of policing, citizens who needed help had to go out and physically find the police, either on the beat or at the precinct. By the middle decades of the twentieth century, the telephone had eliminated that stage of the process. And by the late 1960s, New York, like other cities, had a 911 emergency number, enabling citizens (at least in theory) to get through to the police right away. Between 911 and the police radio system, the police were seemingly in a position to get to the scene of any crime within minutes—swiftly enough, in many cases, to apprehend the perpetrators. Since motorized officers covered more territory than foot cops, more criminals would see them, and thus, it was theorized, be deterred from committing crimes in the first place.

The new emphasis on cars could be presented, then, as a benefit to the public. But it also held a powerful appeal for police managers. Foot cops were difficult to monitor; they tended to hang around "gossiping" with people—an activity now seen as a waste of time, at best, and an invitation to corruption, at worst. In any event, it was hard to know exactly what a foot cop was doing. With the advent of radio cars, police patrol could be organized on a sort of factory model: the radio run, or "job," became the defining unit of a patrolman's work (as was the "case" for detectives). Police supervisors could keep close track of where their officers were and what they were doing, much as factory supervisors kept track of workers on an assembly line. Management now had a vast body of data to record, file, and analyze in the cause of improved efficiency.

Professional policing and motorized policing—the two ideas went pretty much hand in hand, and they dominated the field nationally from the 1930s through the '70s. Then they ran into resistance. The professional police officer, skeptics began to point out, was likely to be a disengaged police officer. Professional policing rewarded an officer's knowledge of procedures, not his knowledge of the city or community. By the riot era of the 1960s, cops—once familiar figures in inner-city neighborhoods—were strangers to most people. To compound matters, the police in some cities were increasingly likely to live in the suburbs, and, like other suburbanites, they viewed many of the people they had left behind with fear or scorn. The police car itself was a barrier. For a citizen with a problem, a patrol car was not as easy to approach as an officer on foot. This was even more true when cops rolled their windows up, as they sometimes did, to stay warm in winter or (if the car was air-conditioned) cool in summer. Since radio-car officers generally worked in pairs, they spent a lot of time talking to each other.

In the minority neighborhoods of New York and other cities, the police were often perceived as a mechanized army of occupation, an image troubling to many people inside as well as outside the profession. After stepping down as John Lindsay's police commissioner in 1973, Pat Murphy became president of the Police Foundation. Bankrolled by the Ford Foundation, this Washington-based think tank emerged as the liberal alternative to an older group with a more standard law-and-order line—the International Association of Chiefs of Police, or IACP. The Police Foundation sponsored research that challenged some of the basic tenets of professional policing, such as rapid response.

At a heady moment in the 1930s, police managers had looked forward to a day when, with fast enough cars and smooth enough communications, it might be possible to surround virtually any criminal before he could escape. The problems with this idea become painfully obvious with a 1975 Police Foundation study, conducted in Kansas City: the average crime victim or witness, it turned out, waited half an hour before calling the police, if, indeed, such a call was ever placed. Suddenly, the notion of response time—one of the key measurements of police performance for as long as anyone could remember—didn't seem quite so critical. The deterrent value of patrol was another idea that withered under scrutiny. Radio cars passing back and forth through a neighborhood had no detectable effect on crime, according to a second (and more attention-getting) Kansas City study.

In turning away from foot patrol, the profession also turned away from the low-level complaints that had been the footman's forte: the gang hanging out on the street corner, for example. The judiciary, meanwhile, was throwing out antiloitering laws and setting new limits on the police power to stop and search. But as much as the police liked to complain about being "handcuffed" by the courts, most police managers were happy to get out of the messy and problematic business of dealing with low-level disorder. The time saved, they told themselves, could be better applied to fighting serious crime.

And yet, in city after city, the heyday of professional policing had also been a period of rising crime. Was it possible that the police, by de-emphasizing what they saw as minor crime, had somehow contributed to the growth of major crime? The political scientist James Q. Wilson, who taught at Harvard University (and served on the board of the Police Foundation), thought it was possible. In an influential 1982 article for *Atlantic Monthly*, Wilson and a researcher named George Kelling argued that the police had all but decriminalized such things as graffiti, loud music, aggressive drunkenness, and urinating in public. The neglect of these problems, Wilson and Kelling contended, caused law-abiding people to cower or hole up indoors, creating conditions in which criminals felt freer to commit crimes of all kinds. The "broken-windows theory," as it came to be known (by analogy with the way a broken window, if left unfixed, seemed to encourage acts of vandalism), dovetailed with ideas articulated two decades earlier by the urbanologist Jane Jacobs. In her book *The Death and Life of Great American Cities*, Jacobs portrayed the police as subsidiary partners in the enterprise of crime control; the first line of defense, according to Jacobs, was a critical mass of confident and engaged citizens actively monitoring the scene.

Spurred by all this new thinking and questioning, cities around the country devised programs that were meant to put the police in closer touch with neighborhoods. One such experiment occurred in Newark, New Jersey, whose police director, Hubert Williams, eventually succeeded Murphy as the Police Foundation's president. Another got under way in Houston, Texas, under the leadership of Police Chief Lee Brown, who would move on to New York after the election of Mayor David Dinkins in November 1989.

By the late 1980s, many New Yorkers were tired of Ed Koch's confrontational brand of politics. The dissatisfaction was crystallized by an ugly racial murder on the eve of the Democratic primary. In August 1989, a used-car ad drew a group of young black men into the heavily white Bensonhurst section of Brooklyn, where a mob of young whites attacked them. One of the black youngsters, Yusuf Hawkins, was shot to death.

Mayor Koch, over the course of his three terms as mayor, had made a point of going to community meetings in neighborhoods where he was not popular, and the reaction had often prompted his police guards to suggest that he leave by a back exit. He had steadfastly refused. It was Koch's proud boast that he always departed as he arrived, with his head held high—and by the same route. But when he went to the Brooklyn wake of Yusuf Hawkins he had to leave by a side door and TV news shows broadcast pictures of the mayor's limousine racing backward to escape an angry crowd. In September 1989, the city teetered on the edge of racial disorder. In the Democratic primary that month, Dinkins defeated Koch. He went on to edge Rudy Giuliani in the general election that November.

New York's first African-American mayor was a soft-spoken, courtly gentleman. His police commissioner, Dr. Lee Patrick Brown, was cut from similar cloth, and both were easygoing, cautious, and careful by nature. A native of Oklahoma, raised in the San Joaquin Valley of California, Brown had been a college-football lineman, then a cop in San Jose, ultimately rising to the rank of sergeant. After earning a doctorate in criminology from the University of California at Berkeley, he had served as the appointed sheriff of Multnomah County, in suburban Portland, Oregon, and later as the police chief of Atlanta and then Houston. Widely regarded as an innovative administrator, Brown also had close ties to the conservative leadership of the IACP, which, shortly before he came to New York, had elected him as the first black president in the organization's ninety-seven-year history. His workday began shortly after dawn with a half hour of meditation. His avowed heroes were Jesus, Gandhi, and Martin Luther King Jr.

The NYPD, under Commissioner Ben Ward, had already launched a modest community-policing program, assigning a sergeant and a team of ten to twelve officers to each of sixty-four of the city's seventy-five precincts. Brown's intentions, he revealed in May 1990, were far more ambitious: he proposed to convert the entire force to the new approach. To provide the level of in-depth neighborhood patrol and citizen service that he had in mind, Brown added, the force would need another five thousand officers to go with the twenty-six thousand it already possessed.

New York City, at the time, was in the grip of a severe economic recession, dating back to a stock-market plunge in the fall of 1987. Under pressure from the financial community to cut services across the board, Mayor Dinkins was certainly in no mood to spend a huge sum of money on the police. But his attitude soon changed.

As Dinkins entered office, the crack epidemic was peaking, and so was the violence that went with it. In the summer of 1990, a series of high-profile homicides made headlines around the world: an assistant district attorney was killed by a stray bullet outside a Bronx courthouse; a media executive was shot dead at a public phone across from his apartment in Greenwich Village (his own phone was out of order); a tourist from Utah was stabbed to death in front of his parents in a Midtown subway station; a nine-year-old girl was shot as she slept in her parents' car after a family trip to an amusement park; a three-year-old was shot while asleep at home, when a person or persons unknown pumped eighteen bullets through the steel door of his family's apartment; a nine-month-old died in his walker, yet another victim of a blast of gunfire through an apartment door. More than forty children were killed by random gunfire in inner-city neighborhoods in the first six months of the year.

Crime had been a hot political issue in New York for a quarter of a century. In 1990, the public perception changed from "It's bad and we should do something about it" to "It's out of control and nothing is being done about it." In a number of different surveys, a majority of New Yorkers expressed a longing for some other place of residence. The news media, in characteristically dramatic fashion, began to portray a city perched on the edge of collapse. DAVE, DO SOMETHING! screamed a headline in the *New York Post.*

Dinkins did something. To stem the crisis, he made a heavy investment of political as well as financial capital. Brown would get the five thousand new cops he had asked for. The city would, at the same time, underwrite an array of counseling, education, employment, and drug-intervention programs aimed at the young. Dinkins's initiative, which went by the name Safe Streets, struck many political commentators as impossibly expensive. But with the support of his fellow Democrat Governor Mario Cuomo, he sold it to the legislature and the city council, which, between them, enacted a set of dedicated taxes to pay for the plan. The heavy emphasis on law enforcement went against Dinkins's liberal grain. Still, he could console himself that he was building a different police force as well as a bigger one. Under the philosophy of community policing, Dinkins told reporters, a patrolman would be in a position to gently chastise a youngster out too late by telling him, "Jamaal, go home." (Dinkins had a grandson named Jamaal.)

By early 1991, the crack epidemic had crested, crime had declined slightly, and the public's attention was no longer riveted. This reduced sense of urgency suited the police commissioner. Brown, not one to shake things up, saw community policing as a long-term enterprise. He was also an outsider, of course—the first imported police commissioner since the ill-fated Howard Leary in 1966. (Leary had been brought in to implement the civilian review board, as Brown was going to implement community policing.) Although his commitment to reform was more earnest than Leary's, Brown, too, was a stranger to the department, and, like Leary (who had maintained a residence in Philadelphia), he never completely bonded with New York. Nor did he accommodate himself to its impatient rhythm. Brown, who had a good deal of higher education under his belt, took an academic approach to the problem of implementing the new philosophy of policing. He organized seminars where the top brass were addressed by professors. Brown himself spent a lot of time at symposiums and conferences, frequently in other cities. Some cops took to referring to him as "Out of Town Brown."

Community policing had its successes. In one Brooklyn neighborhood, crack dealers had overrun a vest-pocket park, causing the elderly to shun its benches and the parents of small children to avoid its swings and seesaws. A community-policing officer chose a novel strategy to combat the dealers. He persuaded local residents to keep an eye on the park and call whenever they saw a dealer hiding drugs. He would visit the park as often as six times a day in order to confiscate the stashes. The effect wasn't just to hurt the dealers economically but to put them in some jeopardy with their superiors, since they had to explain how they had come to lose their wares without being arrested. In response, some dealers began to keep the drugs on their persons, but that practice made them vulnerable to arrest for more than just loitering. Before long, they left the park altogether.

More than a thousand civilians were enrolled in a block-watch program in one Manhattan precinct. One hundred forty of them volunteered to act as drug busters—callers registered to report drug activity anonymously. Responding to complaints about a drug dealer who had threatened the residents of one local apartment building, the beat cop began slipping his business card under doors, asking people to contact him anonymously, which some did. The dealer was soon identified, found to be an illegal subletter, and evicted.

Given enough time, perhaps, the community-policing idea might have worked its way into the NYPD culture. In the event, however, it never progressed beyond a pilot program consisting of a handful of specially trained, and mostly younger, cops in each precinct. The bulk of the force, already on the job, learned little about the initiative beyond a few announcements amid the hurried confusion of roll call. The community-policing cops continued to be known by the name the plan had been given under Ward, CPOP (for Community Patrol Officer Program), which made them sound ridiculous. Many regular cops called them "See-Moms" instead of "C-POPs."

In an effort to raise their status, Brown and his commanders began giving out awards to officers for "the success they achieved in making a neighborhood a better place." At an honors ceremony in October 1991, the commissioner began by bestowing a cop-of-the-month award on a captain who had saved a man's life by shooting and killing the assailant who had been holding him hostage at knifepoint. This was the sort of police work that had traditionally been honored on such occasions. The second award, however, went to a Staten Island patrolman who had saved . . . twenty-five wedding dresses. As the department explained it, he was being recognized, in the first place, for calming the angry customers of a bridal shop that had closed without notice, and then for mediating between them and the store owner. To Brown, this "act of compassion and initiative" was the very epitome of "problem-solving policing." To many radio-car cops, the juxtaposition of the wedding-dress caper and the hostage taking came as a shock. "He won it for *that*?" one incredulous cop asked a reporter for the *Times*.

The general public, however, was inclined to withhold judgment on community policing—and on the Dinkins administration in general—until a hot summer night in 1991, when the city was struck by one of those events that turn the police into an "incident-responding bureaucracy," whether they like it or not. Early on the evening of August 19, a police car sped through the center of Brooklyn, clearing the way for a VIP in a chauffeur-driven sedan. Heading west on President Street, the two cars made it across Utica Avenue, a major bus route and shopping boulevard, before the light turned red. A third vehicle, a weather-beaten station wagon, did not. Struggling to keep up, it struck a car going north on Utica, spun out of control, and careened into two seven-year-old children on the crowded sidewalk.

Four men eventually stumbled out of the station wagon and onto the corner of President and Utica. They were dressed in dark suits and top hats—an odd costume for August, but a familiar one to inhabitants of the neighborhood known originally as Crow Hill (when freed slaves settled there in the early 1800s) and more recently as Crown Heights. They were Lubavitchers—Hasidic Jews who had emigrated en masse from eastern Europe after World War II.

The Lubavitchers were one of three population groups who converged on the area in the 1950s and '60s. The others were African-Americans, many of them part of the great exodus from the South, and immigrants from the Caribbean. As the newcomers moved in, an older population of Irish, Italians, and Jews moved out. In the 1960s, the spiritual leader of the Lubavitchers, the Grand Rebbe Menachem Schneerson, felt it necessary to tell his followers that Jewish law barred flight from the neighborhood. By 1991, the roughly fifteen thousand members of the sect (about 10 percent of the neighborhood's residents) were virtually the only whites remaining.

The four men in the station wagon were the rebbe's guard detail that night. They had been accompanying him home from his weekly visit to the graves of his wife and his father-in-law, the rebbe before him. Security was a sensitive issue in Crown Heights. Jews frequently complained to the police and the mayor's office about crime committed by blacks. Blacks, in turn, argued that the Lubavitchers, a small minority, got undue privileges and attention from the city. The local police precinct, the Seventy-first, was accustomed to assigning a pair of radio cars to sit semipermanently in front of the Lubavitchers' stately headquarters at 770 Eastern Parkway. (The protection had originally been ordered in response to threats from a rival Jewish sect.) A police car patrolled the ritual baths of the Hasidic women, and police escorts were routine when the rebbe traveled by car—a service demanded by the Lubavitchers on the grounds that he was a worldwide religious leader, comparable in stature to the pope.

At the accident scene, Yosef Lifsh, the driver, sought to join a group of bystanders in attempting to extricate the children from underneath the car. He was quickly disabused of that idea when others in the crowd attacked him. One of the passengers began to call 911 on a portable phone, and he, too, was assaulted.

Five minutes had passed when the first police car reached the scene. One look and Officers Mark Hoppe and John Marinos realized that this was no ordinary accident. After radioing for assistance and directing onlookers to move back, they joined the effort to rescue the children, Gavin and Angela Cato, who were cousins. Officers Nona Capace and Richard Colonna, arriving a few minutes later, looked after the Hasidim. An ambulance was on hand now, belonging to the Lubavitchers' privately funded, volunteer rescue service, Hatzoloh. Officer Capace quietly instructed the Hatzoloh crew to remove the Hasidic men. They didn't really need the medical attention—she just wanted them out of harm's way. A few more minutes passed before city ambulances arrived and took the children to Kings County Hospital. Angela Cato recovered. Gavin Cato was pronounced dead on arrival.

The first police units radioed for additional help, and by 9:00 P.M. about twenty officers were on the scene, trying to fill out paperwork, measure skid marks, interview witnesses, and hold back the angry throng. Word of the incident, and rumors about it, were spreading rapidly. The Hatzoloh ambulance crew was said to have refused to transport the black children. After an argument with the police, Gavin Cato's father claimed that an officer had pushed him; that story, too, would be widely repeated. It was one of those hot nights in the inner city when the streets are everybody's living room, and the flood-lights set up to help a police accident-investigation unit do its work drew still more people to the corner. When rocks were thrown at the police, they called for more reinforcements. Nearby residents, meanwhile, phoned 911 to report a riot. The situation got so bad that, before long, officers had to withdraw from the area. For the next hour and a half the crowds continued to gather at the site of the accident.

Around 11:00 P.M., a tall, bald black man mounted the hood of a car. "Do you feel what I feel?" he exhorted his listeners. "Do you feel the pain? What are you going to do about it?" In response the crowd surged down the streets, throwing stones at windows and overturning cars. On Carroll Street between Brooklyn and Kingston Avenues, a thirty-two-year-old Jewish man was sur-rounded by fifteen blacks, who kicked him and struck him with bottles and rocks while chanting "Jews get out of here." Another man was beaten and robbed at the corner of Carroll and Kingston. Yankel Rosenbaum, a twenty-nine-year-old Hasidic scholar who had come to Crown Heights all the way from Australia to study under the Lubavitchers, was assaulted and stabbed four times at President and Brooklyn. A few hours after Kings County doctors had pronounced Gavin Cato dead, they did the same for Rosenbaum. It was 4:00 A.M. by the time police managed to quiet things down on the streets.

The next day, Tuesday, Hasidim and blacks both held demonstrations. Later that afternoon, the trouble started up again on President Street. Return-ing home with three small children, a Jewish woman was cornered by youths chanting "Heil Hitler!" and "Kill the Jews!" Police officers were standing nearby, she asserted later. Reaching home, she called 911. "They're breaking the windows. Utica and President, please come!" she cried. "Utica and Presi-dent, please come! They're in front of my house! Get 'em here!" Over the next few hours, she would make five more calls. Each time, she had to explain the situation all over again and answer a series of questions: How many people were outside? Had anyone been hurt? How many gunshots had been fired?

"I got a houseful of children, ma'am," she pleaded. "I am shaking. What do you want from me? Just please send the police here—it's a riot!" Hours later, her father came home and unlocked the door. It fell off its hinges: only a deadbolt lock had been holding it in place.

The police did not come for many other desperate people that night. The low-paid civilian 911 operators were not up to the task of dealing with the

influx of excited callers. One citizen had trouble getting the operator to understand that she was calling about "rocks" rather than "drugs." Another woman
phoned repeatedly about a mob that was breaking the windows of her house.
No police arrived.

On the commercial streets of Crown Heights, mobs were out looting and
burning stores, meeting little resistance from a woefully inadequate comple-
ment of police. At Sneaker King on Utica Avenue, cops stood by for hours, according to witnesses, watching kids run in and out with sneakers and jeans.
Isaac Bitton, a Jewish man coming home from work with his twelve-year-old
son, took the precaution of asking a police officer if it was safe to walk down
the block. Assured that it was, and comforted by the sight of police vans at the
two corners, he set out on his journey, only to be attacked a short distance
down the street. One of Bitton's assailants tried to hit him on the head with a
bat, missing. Another had better success with a brick. Bitton fell on top of his
son, to protect him. The mob swarmed around and tried to pull the boy out
from underneath. A man went after Bitton with a razor. In the end, he was
rescued by a black newspaper reporter who ran up and shielded him from his
attackers, screaming at them, "Stop this shit!" Only then did the police render
any assistance.

Summers had often been tense in the inner city, yet the NYPD was unpre-
pared. Many of the brass were on vacation; others were filling in for them in
an acting capacity. A number of key commanders were new in their jobs. The
last major riots to strike the city were a dim memory even for the longest-
serving veterans of the NYPD. Thus, on the first night, Brooklyn commanders
hesitated to invoke a citywide mobilization plan. The department had not
actually attempted such a thing in twenty years, and since officers would not
even have understood the radio codes necessary to set it in motion, the brass
feared mass confusion.

The riots of the 1960s were not, in any case, the most useful point of reference. The situation in Crown Heights resembled the classic "race riots" of the
nineteenth century, with one group pitted against another. The '60s riots,
by contrast, had started out as uprisings against authority, and some of the
worst violence had been the result of a heavy-handed police response. In
Crown Heights, hooligans were terrorizing innocent people. The victims
needed immediate help. It was help that the police could easily have provided.
Yet, like the prototypical generals who always stand ready to fight the last war,

the police brass seemed to be fixated on the idea of keeping their own forces under control.

On Tuesday afternoon a protest march turned ugly. Fearing injuries to police officers and civilians alike, commanders decided against an attempt to disperse the crowd. Badly outnumbered officers were pelted with rocks and bottles. Cops at the scene later recalled hearing a "white shirt" (their term for a lieutenant or higher) tell them to "retreat back to the precinct." The retreat commenced in an orderly fashion but quickly degenerated into a rout. "Everybody ran," one cop told the investigators.

Wednesday morning, in a moment of premature optimism, Mayor David Dinkins and Police Commissioner Lee Brown told reporters that the worst had passed. Then, separately, they headed off to a meeting with Crown Heights residents and community leaders at a local junior high school. Brown's limousine arrived just as a contingent of young black marchers was passing by. Spotting the commissioner, some of the youths broke away from the main body and converged on his car, pelting it with rocks. On the local police-radio frequency, cops heard something they had never heard before: a 10-13 call (an officer needs assistance) for Car 1. They responded in force, and nine cops were injured in the ensuing melee. Unlike other riot victims, Brown did not have to call more than once.

For the mayor, too, the Wednesday meeting became an eye-opening, if unplanned, tour of the combat zone. Shortly after seven o'clock he left the school and attempted to address the crowd outside through a bullhorn but was shouted down. Police intelligence officers had passed the word that there were as many as fourteen guns in the crowd. (No one suggested that their owners be relieved of their artillery.) Dinkins had been planning to walk through the streets to Gavin Cato's home—a gesture reminiscent of John Lindsay in the 1960s. His nervous aides convinced him to drop the idea. He left, as he had come, by car with a heavy police escort. As he departed, rocks and bottles were thrown at his car. When he arrived at the Cato home, an object came flying at head level between him and a deputy mayor.

One dead, roughly two hundred injured, a few dozen businesses looted or vandalized, a similar number of cars overturned or set on fire—this was the official cost of the Crown Heights riots. Emotionally, though, the damage toll was heavier. In the aftermath of the riots, New Yorkers whipped themselves into a froth of accusation and counteraccusation, which had barely begun to calm down when, a year later, a Brooklyn jury acquitted a sixteen-year-old boy, Lemrick Nelson, in the stabbing death of Yankel Rosenbaum. Now the debate began anew. To the Lubavitchers, the riots evoked the kind of horrors they had come to America to escape. David Dinkins was the city's first African-American mayor; most of the rioters were black. Upon this fact, a large edifice of speculation was constructed. People suggested that Dinkins, motivated by a bond of racial solidarity, had ordered the police not to arrest the rioters. It was a bizarre idea, indignantly denied by the mayor. But in the highly charged aftermath of the Crown Heights riots, this notion rose to the level of a near certainty among the Lubavitchers, while a number of other New Yorkers seemed to be swept up in the hunt for evidence of a no-arrest order.

The truth, as spelled out in a report commissioned by Governor Mario Cuomo, was a good deal less melodramatic, though hardly reassuring. It found no evidence of an order not to arrest rioters, yet criticized Dinkins for failing to "act in a timely and decisive manner by requiring the police department . . . to quickly restore peace and order." Police Commissioner Brown, too, had left key decisions to his subordinates. Indeed, it seemed that many of the headquarters brass had remained far from the scene, placing a heavy burden of responsibility on a group of midlevel Brooklyn commanders. Stretched thin from Monday to Wednesday nights, running back and forth from street confrontations to briefings, strategy sessions, and meetings with community leaders, they had made key errors, beginning with their decision to try to slide by with what proved to be a seriously inadequate supply of manpower.

First Deputy Commissioner Ray Kelly (a former commander of the Crown Heights precinct and a colonel in the marine reserves) was in an awkward position. His title made him the number two man in the department, but in an accommodation to a former superior of Kelly's, Brown had agreed to have the chief of the department—the number three man, in charge of all field forces—report to him directly. Hours before the Crown Heights riots began, that particular chief had retired, and no one had thought to change the arrangement; Kelly had thus been placed "out of the loop," as he put it. Yet on

Wednesday night, tired of watching events on the headquarters TV and disgusted by what he saw, Kelly "ordered" himself to the scene, stepped into the leadership vacuum, and personally directed the cops in putting down the riot.

But it was too late to save the mayor. Indeed, for Dinkins, Crown Heights seemed to set off a chain of police-related disasters, any one of them a potential career terminator. The riots were still a hot topic of discussion in 1992, when a fresh corruption scandal broke out. After the 1986 "Buddy Boys" case, some cops in Brooklyn's neighboring Seventy-fifth Precinct, angry over drug dealing by their colleagues, had been persuaded by David Durk (off the force but up to his old ways) to talk to a newspaper reporter by telephone. The first corrupt cop cited by his peers was one Michael Dowd. The department, too, had heard rumors about Dowd, but the investigation had been left largely to a single internal affairs sergeant with next to no support from above. In the absence of conclusive proof against him, the brass did the usual thing: they transferred him. Naturally, nobody was particularly glad to have such a cop around. One precinct commander placed Dowd under virtual house arrest, ordering him to sit in a chair in sight of the desk sergeant and not leave the station. Another time, he was assigned to work at a police motor pool handing out tires. Then, inexplicably—much as had happened with Charles Becker—Dowd's superiors either forgot their suspicions or bought into the notion that he had reformed. After being transferred to a precinct in the Greenpoint section of Brooklyn, Dowd was put back on patrol. A few years later, he and five other present and former New York City police officers were arrested on drug-selling charges by authorities in Suffolk County on the eastern end of Long Island. By then, Dowd rode around in a $35,000 red Corvette and owned four suburban houses, one of them valued at $300,000. In retrospect, the failure to come up with evidence of Dowd's misdeeds was inexplicable. As the columnist Mike McAlary put it, "You could indict on the house alone."

Traditionally, one of the first casualties of a great police scandal was the commissioner. The right posture for Brown, had he understood the situation and wanted to remain, would have been to express outrage and take charge, mounting a full-scale probe, flopping (demoting) top commanders, and railing against the malfeasance of those he had inherited from the previous regime. Brown was too much of a gentleman to adopt this approach. Insisting on the need for a thorough investigation, he moved slowly, defending the Internal Affairs Bureau and minimizing the dimensions of the scandal. Soon the papers were full of allegations of cover-ups and warnings of yet more revelations to come. In August, Brown announced his resignation, citing the ill health of his wife. Mrs. Brown had, in fact, been stricken with a fatal illness and wanted to return to Texas, where she would die within a year.

In New York, Brown came across as one of those nice guys who, in the proverb coined by Leo Durocher, longtime manager of the Giants and Dodgers, finish last. But as Teddy Roosevelt had shown, running the NYPD was not a fair test of anyone's executive abilities. Brown, like Roosevelt, was far from finished: he went on to serve as the nation's unofficial drug czar under President Clinton and then, in 1997, was elected mayor of Houston.

Dinkins, who had a better understanding of the way things worked in New York, did not attempt to make light of the scandal. He named Ray Kelly police commissioner and appointed another blue-ribbon panel to look into the problem of police corruption and the department's seeming inability to deal with it. In September 1993, New Yorkers listened with morbid fascination to the testimony of a succession of rogue cops. Dowd, perhaps the most gut-wrenching of the bunch, admitted to snorting cocaine in a patrol car and being on the payroll of a drug dealer (for $4,000 a week), among other criminal acts. At the scene of drug shootings, Dowd recalled, he would steal whatever he could and then graciously give the arrest to others; that way, any complaints would land on them. One time, he told a young woman whose apartment had been burglarized to call her mother in order to see if there had been any money hidden in the house for the thieves to have stolen. It turned out that her mother had left $300 in a hiding place, as the unsuspecting daughter now revealed to Officer Dowd. He proceeded to steal the money himself. The pride in his accomplishment still seemed to ring in his voice. In July 1994, Dowd was sentenced to twelve years in federal prison.

The commission—chaired by Dinkins's deputy mayor for criminal justice, Milton Mollen, a former judge—heard evidence of a similar ring of cops, known as the "Morgue Boys," operating in another Brooklyn precinct. A group of Bronx cops admitted to drug dealing, selling stolen guns, beating citizens, and engaging in forcible sex with prostitutes. Some of the precincts involved had been on the "Buddy Boys" special prosecutor's list six years earlier. When the Dowd case broke, *New York Newsday* thoughtfully published a map of police precincts that had been the subject of as-yet-unrevealed corruption charges. One precinct identified was the Thirtieth, in northern Manhattan, where, according to the paper, officers on the nightshift were shaking down drug dealers. The article was posted on the station bulletin board. Still, the shakedowns continued.

Barely had City Hall and police headquarters digested the new blow than another riot broke out in the Washington Heights section of upper Manhattan, a prime drug-dealing area. In July, three plainclothes cops in an unmarked car spotted a man who appeared to have a gun under his jacket. One officer went after him on foot while the others circled the block, hoping to trap him. Before they could get into position, however, the lone cop, Michael O'Keefe, encountered the gunman. When the officer attempted to arrest him, there was a struggle, with both men tumbling into the vestibule of an apartment building. O'Keefe radioed for help and, in the excitement, gave an incorrect location. As the battle intensified, he radioed again, giving another wrong address. His partners, unable to find him, were frantic. "Mike, where the fuck are you?" one of them cried out on the police radio for all to hear. Finally, O'Keefe came on the air with yet another wrong address, but this time he reported that he had a "perp down." The suspect had pulled a gun. O'Keefe had shot and killed him.

Wild stories swept through the neighborhood and the city. Two self-described eyewitnesses claimed to have seen the officer assault the suspect, Jose "Kiko" Garcia, twenty-four, with a radio, until he collapsed unconscious on the floor. According to their testimony, the officer stood over him and shot him at point-blank range. The media tended to accept these statements at face value. A few news stories even hinted that O'Keefe had been part of a ring of crooked cops. The next night, the Fourth of July, rocks and bottles were thrown, cars overturned, and fires set in the neighborhood. For several nights running, the riots raged on. Directing the disorder behind the scenes were some of the local drug dealers. They made sure that the riot ended before the weekend, Friday and Saturday being the busiest nights for selling drugs to kids who flocked into the area from the suburbs.

Commissioner Brown was still in office (though temporarily out of town), and the police department chose not to go public with Officer O'Keefe's desperate radio transmissions. Nor did the department reveal that the slain man had spent part of the day in the apartment of one of the alleged witnesses—an apartment where, a few months earlier, a court-authorized search had found cocaine, a loaded revolver, forty-two rounds of ammunition, and a videotape of Garcia with other men, one of them displaying cocaine. Garcia was on probation as a result of a previous conviction for attempted sale of a controlled substance, and at the time of his death was being sought on a warrant as a probation violator. It is not clear whether Mayor Dinkins was informed of these facts at the outset. In any case, he didn't just express his sympathy for the Garcia family, but in his determination to halt the disorder, went as far as to arrange for the city to pay for Garcia's burial and the family's airfare back to the Dominican Republic to attend a memorial service. Thus, to his opponents, Dinkins became the mayor who "paid for a drug dealer's funeral." And his position was made even more vulnerable when, two months later, the office of District Attorney Morgenthau released the findings of an investigation that it had conducted in partnership with the FBI. Garcia's culpability and O'Keefe's veracity were now beyond dispute. As for the two "witnesses," Morgenthau's report exposed gaping holes (as well as contradictions) in their testimony; laser-beam projections showed that they could have seen very little of the incident, in any case.

The final outburst of David Dinkins's term was staged by cops. A month after the Washington Heights affair, the mayor brought forth a bill for the creation of an all-civilian review board outside the control of the police department. In September, the PBA staged a rally of protest that was, in the judgment of most political observers, unnecessary even before it became counterproductive. To pass the proposal, the mayor needed the support of the city council, most of whose fifty-one members represented districts in the more conservative outer boroughs. Nonetheless, ten thousand officers, many accompanied by their families, assembled outside City Hall. Many cops were also angry, at the time, over the mayor's response to the Washington Heights and Crown Heights riots. Among the placards carried by demonstrators were ones reading "Dump the washroom attendant" and "Dinkins sucks." Caricatures presented the mayor with an Afro hairdo and large lips. Within a few minutes of the start of a protest march around City Hall Park, hundreds of cops broke loose from the main body, made their way through barriers, and blocked traffic on Broadway, where, laughing and chanting slogans, they surrounded cars and began rocking them back and forth. Others blocked the Brooklyn Bridge. Still another group of demonstrators surged up the steps of

City Hall, where such protests (whoever the participants) were prohibited by law. In a fracas that recalled the police riots of 1857, the police officers of the small City Hall guard detail were so heavily outnumbered that they withdrew into the building and locked the door behind them. Some of the demonstrators grabbed wooden barricades, tore them apart, and hoisted them in the air, crying "Let's take City Hall." On-duty officers who tried to get protesters down from the damaged roof of a car were booed and called "traitors" and "cheese eaters." They retreated in confusion. Commissioner Kelly, after checking out the scene, ordered an additional 250 reinforcements, and with their help succeeded in restoring order. The members of the city council had front-row seats for this brouhaha; some of them were even in a position to see their cars vandalized, and the council soon decided that a civilian review board was not such a bad idea after all. The mayor's legislation, which had been running on a fast track to nowhere, became law later that year.

It was a political victory for Dinkins, but the circumstances were difficult to square with the vision of a police force that had, as the mayor liked to claim, "reinvented itself." The corruption scandal, too, hinted at more basic problems than those that community policing seemed to have been designed to address. Community police officers, according to Brown, would "possess a whole new battery of skills"—not just problem solving but "community organizing," "interpersonal communications," and "the ability to galvanize neighborhood energies." Where in the real world were all these wonder cops going to come from? And what to do with aspiring or existing police officers who were not such paragons of multifaceted virtue? Brown and his strategists tended to skip over details of that sort. In the 1980s, the department had dropped its academic requirement to the equivalent of an eighth-grade reading level, all but abandoned physical fitness as a criterion, and delayed, curtailed, or simply forgotten to perform many of the background investigations that were supposedly an inviolable part of the process. The Mollen commission, in its final report, would gently allude to "a widespread perception . . . that virtually anyone can become a New York City police officer."

For all his troubles, David Dinkins might have been elected to a second term if his great police experiment had achieved the advertised results. But New Yorkers found the streets just as menacing at the end of Dinkins's term as at the beginning. The problem was personified in a man named Larry Hogue, whom the press dubbed the "Wild Man of Ninety-sixth Street." Hogue, who was tall and powerfully built, was receiving military disability pay as a result of being struck in the head by an airplane propeller (though not, as first reported, in Vietnam). He was a constant threatening presence at and near the intersection of Ninety-sixth Street and Broadway. On one occasion, he threw a girl in front of a moving car. Repeatedly arrested, he was just as repeatedly released by mental-health officials who deemed him "not dangerous." There seemed to be no legal basis for holding him. Not until December 1992, that is, when the story made *Sixty Minutes*. Interviewed during one of his periodic incarcerations, Hogue made it clear that he had no intention of leaving the neighborhood or changing his ways. This televised declaration of intent seemed to have a dramatic effect on the medical authorities, who suddenly decided that Hogue should remain in custody after all. But a state court judge overruled them, advancing his own diagnosis. Hogue was not mentally ill, said the judge; he had an "attitude problem."

What with one thing and another, most New Yorkers had forgotten all about community policing. But Commissioner Kelly felt a need for an assessment and assigned an assistant chief to conduct it. His report portrayed the program as a tiny make-believe police force viewed with widespread scorn by the members of the real force. Most cops, of course, were still in RMPs, where they spent the greater part of their time answering 911 calls. CPOP cops, by contrast, attended meetings and compiled thick beat books listing their neighborhood contacts. The real force operated around the clock; the community-policing cops kept banker's hours. Indeed, some of them took advantage of the flexibility of the arrangement to run personal errands and disappear for long intervals during their supposed working time. But if they seemed less than totally committed to the enterprise, the method of recruiting was partly responsible. According to the report, the promise of straight day tours with weekends off had been used as, in effect, a bribe to get cops to volunteer for the program.

For all the time they spent on outreach, the CPOP cops were not that much better known in their communities than regular cops were. In 1991, Brown had established a "model precinct" in Sunset Park, Brooklyn. Two years later, few of the local residents or businesspeople were even aware of the blessing that had been conferred on them. In a poll of five hundred civic activists in the precinct (the people most likely to know the police), only a fourth could remember any contact at all with their beat officers.

Too late to save Mayor Dinkins, the NYPD found a poster child for community policing in Officer Kevin Jett of the Fifty-second Precinct, in the North Bronx. Jett was not a "textbook cop," a reporter for the *Times* observed. He had not even read any of the department's manuals and could barely remember a brief period of community-policing instruction. Six feet, two inches tall, a former amateur boxer and a black belt in karate, he was an African-American from the same kind of street he patrolled. "I grew up in Mott Haven [the Bronx], and the mutts understand that is different from East Cupcake, Long Island," he told the *Times*. "They feel that the guys [cops] who come from there are soft." The *Times* article recounted Jett's confrontations with predators nicknamed "Cuco," "Chiselhead," "Scarface," and "Killer." The description of his beat, though, was hardly an advertisement for a safer city: at night, the *Times* reported, it "echoes with gunfire, much of it random; few here are foolish enough to sleep with their bed by a window. When the gunmen have a target, as they often do, the next morning the neighbors are out with broom and hose sweeping blood from the sidewalk."

From the cover of *The New York Times Magazine*, Officer Jett soon vaulted to the gallery of the United States Capitol Building for President Bill Clinton's State of the Union address in January 1994. At the climactic moment, Jett was invited to stand as the president hailed his work and made the case for legislation to provide another hundred thousand police officers—community police officers, of course—around the country. Bathed in glory, Jett returned to his Bronx precinct. Briefly. One of the original aims of the community-policing experiment had been to raise the status of patrol and encourage cops to stay there. Before long, however, Jett received the time-honored reward of outstanding patrolmen: he was transferred to a detective unit.

16

The Rediscovery of Crime

Lieutenant Jack Maple's first sight of his new boss was on TV. A film clip showed Bill Bratton wearing the uniform of the police force he headed in Massachusetts. To the sartorially conscious Maple, Bratton looked like a bus driver. "Who's the guy in the Ralph Kramden hat?" he asked a buddy.

Two months earlier, in January 1990, Lee Brown's appointment as police commissioner of New York City had made headlines around the country. No one paid much attention to the news that the lowly subway cops were getting a new chief. Bratton would be taking charge of a force of nearly four thousand officers—about the same number Brown had commanded in Houston, America's fourth-largest city. In terms of status, however, the job was invisible; and next to the well-traveled Brown, Bratton's background seemed provincial. Brown had held top police jobs in Oregon, Georgia, and Texas; the high point of Bratton's career had been his reign as chief of the Metropolitan District Commission police, who kept the peace along a ribbon of parks and highways in suburban Boston. While Brown had a Ph.D. from Berkeley, Bratton had a bachelor's degree—earned in a special program for cops—from a local commuter college.

He grew up in a working-class, Irish-Catholic family in Dorchester. His father toiled in a chrome-plating shop by day and at the post office by night—full-time jobs both of them. The family ate supper at four-thirty in the afternoon, between the elder Bratton's shifts. The son had spent his whole life in Boston, except for a three-year stint in the army, a year of it in Vietnam. A slender man just under six feet tall with short gray-brown hair, black eyebrows, and a hawk nose, Bratton gave away his Boston origins with every syllable that came out of his mouth. When he talked about the things he hoped to accomplish in "Noo Yawk," his listeners winced.

Noo Yawk had been on Bratton's mind for years, as it happened. At the age of eight or so, he got his first look at the NYPD through a picture book, *Your Police,* which he repeatedly checked out of the library. As a teenager, after his taste in reading had matured, he came across Richard Dougherty's *The Commissioner* (the basis of the movie *Madigan,* in which Richard Widmark played a detective). Bratton was taken with Dougherty's complex psychosocial portrait of relations between the police and the political establishment. He also warmed to the book's description of a stream of white-gloved traffic cops saluting the commissioner (Henry Fonda in the movie) as he headed down Park Avenue in the morning, and to the hullabaloo that the headquarters staff made—beating their tom-toms with the message "The PC's in"—when the commissioner crossed the threshold.

After coming home from the war, Bratton worked as a telephone repairman while waiting for the next police exam. When the day came, his car, a 1966 Ford Mustang, conked out on an expressway ramp as he set out for the school where the exam was being held. With a great law-enforcement career hanging by a thread, Bratton walked back to a gas station and called his sister, who lived a couple of towns away. Wearing pajamas and floppy slippers, she rushed over in her 1960 Falcon convertible. They got there at the last possible moment.

As a young sergeant in Boston, Bratton won a medal for convincing a bank robber to surrender his gun as well as a hostage he had been holding at gunpoint. Bratton, arriving at the holdup scene, found himself standing face-to-face with the robber, over gun barrels. When more cops arrived, Bratton holstered his weapon and talked the man into surrendering. ("It's a good thing Bill could talk," one of his fellow Boston cops recalled.) The department awarded him its highest medal.

He saw more street action than many of the men and women who would occupy the top ranks of American policing in the last half of the twentieth century. But he didn't need to spend much time in the trenches to know they weren't for him. Bratton was plainly not cut out to be a patrolman, and he didn't see himself as detective material, either. He felt that he lacked the "sixth sense" that enabled the best detectives to know when a suspect was lying. Management was more in his line. "My whole career," he would say later, was "about making it to the top."

Like Bratton, Mayor Kevin White had higher ambitions, and he realized that the Boston Police Department could explode on him, as New York's had exploded on John Lindsay. In 1973, White appointed a reform commissioner, Robert DiGrazia. One night he showed up at Bratton's station in Mattapan, to address roll call. At the conclusion of his remarks, DiGrazia invited questions. One hand went up—Bratton's. "How do you get out of here?" he asked. There was stunned silence, followed by laughter. But DiGrazia made a mental note of his badge number and did some inquiring. Two weeks later, Bratton was transferred to Brighton, a mostly white, middle-class area known, in Boston P.D. parlance, as a "Bonton district." Its comforts included paid details that brought in extra income—something Bratton needed at the time, since he was recently divorced and financially responsible for a small child. His career progressed nicely after that, from patrolman to sergeant to lieutenant in charge of a widely ballyhooed community-policing initiative.

In the late 1970s, Bratton hooked up with a group of academics who held court at Harvard's Kennedy School of Government. Through his academic contacts, Bratton became an avid consumer of the literature of corporate motivation. Police departments were punishment-centered bureaucracies prone to issuing rules and orders—and more don'ts than dos. In the private sector, as Bratton learned, this style of administration was losing favor. In a seminar with top business executives, he could talk the latest management-analysis lingo. But he could turn around and address a roll call in a very different vocabulary. In that setting, he would begin by complimenting the cops on their good work, making sure to cite a few recent cases that had been well handled. Then Bratton would tell a story illustrating some problem that had surfaced and pointing up the need for a higher standard of performance. His manner was that of a loving father gently chastising his son: "I know you haven't noticed that Mom has been carrying those heavy groceries, but from now on I'm sure you will help her out."

Bratton's street career had left him with a strong distaste for bosses who steered clear of volatile situations lest something go wrong and they share the blame. "When I was working District Fourteen, we had a major broo-ha in one of the public parks, and every cop in the district was there," he recalled.

"There were two sergeants back in the station, and we were calling for P.S."— patrol supervisors—"and neither one of those bastards would come out. They were two cowards hiding at the stationhouse. We had a lot of them like that in Boston. They didn't want to see anything."

In 1980, after just ten years on the job, the thirty-three-year-old Bratton was made the number two man in the Boston P.D. Although his civil-service rank was that of a mere lieutenant, he seemed poised to move on up to the top. Then, during a 1982 interview with *Boston* magazine, Bratton guilelessly mentioned his hope of becoming commissioner someday, "be it one year or four."

"The guy acts like I'm already cold in my chair," the incumbent commissioner, Joe Jordan, told an aide. A few months later, Bratton was bumped into a peripheral job. He decided to bail out of the Boston P.D. in order to run the police force responsible for Boston's rapid-transit system, the MBTA. Next he went to the MDC, then to New York.

He was not a mayoral appointee. Bratton answered to the New York City Transit Authority, itself a unit of a quasi-governmental agency known as the Metropolitan Transportation Authority, whose chairman, Robert Kiley, had held the same post at the MBTA. For over thirty years, the city and state government had debated the idea of folding the subway police force into the city force. The NYPD itself had flip-flopped on the issue several times. In the latest flip, the department had decided it wanted the transit cops. But Kiley was equally sure he didn't want to lose them, for the police loomed large in his plans for the subway system.

As long as anyone could remember, holding the fare down had been a sine qua non of political success in the city, regardless of political party. In that spirit, one generation of elected leaders after another had skimped on basic maintenance of the subway system, leading to steady declines in patronage. In the 1980s, the MTA tried to break the cycle by spending billions of dollars on new subway cars and the overhaul of stations, tracks, and switches. Still, the public perception of the system remained negative. Surveys were duly conducted. The public, it turned out, was not unappreciative of the improvements made to the infrastructure; it was put off, however, by problems that had gone unaddressed: rowdy teenagers, boom box radios, aggressive panhandling, and homeless people sleeping in cars and stations. Bratton, who had been indoctrinated into the broken-windows theory at Harvard, was determined to do something about these so-called quality-of-life offenses. First, though, he set out to motivate his cops.

There was a certain amount of consternation in the upper echelons of the Transit Authority when, early in his tenure, Bratton expressed a desire to make transit cops the "best dressed" in the city. Toward that end, he provided them with a black British "commando sweater," which, one skeptical reporter noted, wasn't "much different from a regular dark blue sweater, except that it has shoulder patches and little holes in the front to pin a badge on." Soon the transit police became the first local law-enforcement officers to be equipped with nine-millimeter semiautomatic pistols—something that NYPD cops had been seeking for years but that were, like so much else in that department, being studied. Everybody from Mayor Dinkins and Police Commissioner Brown to *The New York Times* agreed that a .38 special ought to be sufficient unto any cop's needs. For Bratton, however, the issue was simple. He put himself in the shoes of his officers, who thought: the bad guys have them; we don't.

Soon after his arrival, the new chief made a nocturnal inspection of his troops. He found one of them slouched against the wall of a station smoking a cigarette. The average police executive, beholding such a shabby representative of the profession, would have taken his name and given him a tongue-lashing. But Bratton was determined not to follow Teddy Roosevelt's example of scoring points at the rank and file's expense. He asked the cop what his post was. "This is it," he replied, explaining that he was under orders to spend his entire tour of duty in that one spot, protecting the token booth and deterring fare beaters—a mission that transit cops disdained, considering it beneath them.

Fare beating was, in fact, a management priority at the time. While there had always been people who jumped the turnstiles without paying, the 1980s had seen the rise of a new breed of "coin suckers," who would whisk paying customers in through half-cocked turnstiles and remove their partially deposited tokens by literally sucking them up out of the slots. Usually there were no police present, and the tollbooth clerk's only recourse was a feeble shout of "Pay your fare!" Beyond the lost revenue, which ran into the hundreds of millions of dollars annually, the coin suckers and turnstile jumpers contributed to the feeling of a system that was out of control, and they were a huge source of annoyance to their fellow—paying—passengers.

So the Transit Authority wanted something done, and in the quasi-military world of the police, the authority's wish would normally have been the chief's command. But Bratton, Vietnam veteran that he was, did not want to be put in the position of issuing orders likely to be greeted with scorn. For a policy to be effective, he believed, it had to be embraced by the rank and file. Since cops didn't consider fare-beating enforcement to be police work, he would hire private guards to do the job instead.

In that decision, however, he failed to reckon with the transit police union. Boredom or no boredom, the union rushed to the defense of its turf; and again Bratton listened. Fare-beating enforcement would remain a police job, he agreed, but cops would go about it differently. Instead of being deployed in uniform to act as scarecrows, they would descend on a station as a team, and in plainclothes, with the aim not of deterring fare beaters but of catching them in the act. And instead of putting them through the booking process, which meant an average time in custody of twenty-four hours, Bratton had a city bus converted into a mobile booking office—a "bust bus." That way, the arrestees could be released with a summons in an hour or two. Many, of course, failed to keep their court dates, but, as Bratton reasoned, they could expect to be locked up, at least briefly, if they got caught again.

If the fare-beating problem was delicate, the homelessness question was a moral as well as legal nightmare. In the past, the Transit Authority had swerved back and forth between doing nothing and doing ugly things like having its maintenance crews use high-pressure hoses to clear homeless people out of stations. Now the police began telling people, homeless and otherwise, that they couldn't lie sprawled across a subway seat or camp in the tunnels the tracks ran through, where, as Bratton noted, several dozen people were run over or electrocuted every year. Still, even this softened approach did not impress many civil libertarians or advocates for the homeless. It didn't go down very well with Jack Maple, either.

In Maple's mind, being a cop meant going after criminals, not rousting homeless people. The broken-windows theory did not impress him. "Rapists and killers," Maple would later observe, "don't head for another town when they see that graffiti is disappearing from the subway." Now the commander of the department's central robbery squad, Maple was an obsessive student of crime and a fount of ideas for dealing with it. He had quarreled with a series of superiors over their (in his view) weak-kneed anticrime commitment. From where he sat, the quality-of-lifers represented yet another step in the wrong direction. Never lacking in chutzpah, Maple composed a sweeping anticrime memo and gave it to Chief of Detectives Mike O'Connor, who passed it along to Bratton. To Maple's surprise, Bratton read his memo and wanted to discuss it. Bratton, Maple, and O'Connor met for breakfast, and Maple poured his heart out.

The level of subway crime in general was not high, he agreed. In fact, it added up to less than 3 percent of the city's crime. But when it came to robbery—Maple's specialty—the proportion was close to 10 percent. Between 1987 and 1990, there had been a 67 percent increase in robberies overall, and still greater increases in several troubling subcategories of robbery. One was robbery committed against Asian victims; another was "wolfpack" robbery, involving groups of anywhere from four to a dozen or more attackers.

These were especially difficult to solve because the perpetrators would move in quickly, and, as Maple put it later, often "the only thing the complainant could I.D. is the bottom of a sneaker." To make matters worse, it was traditional detective practice to consider a case closed once a single suspect had been identified. In practice, then, a pack might lose a man once in a while, but the loss was often a brief one, since the victim's testimony—usually all the evidence there was—might not be specific or solid enough to get a robbery conviction. Since law enforcement was offering no real deterrent, Maple argued, the rate of arrests added up to "acceptable losses" in the calculation of the robbers.

When Bratton decided to do something, he didn't waste any time about it. While the community-policing initiative was unfolding at a stately pace in Lee Brown's NYPD, the transit police crime program screeched out of the starting blocks. Within a matter of weeks, Maple and O'Connor launched a battery of new initiatives. They formed a decoy squad of Asian-American cops. Muggers already had to be wary of cops made up to look like rabbis, Wall Street executives, or teenagers on a date; to that list was now added the Japanese businessman dozing away on a subway train. To combat the wolfpack robberies, the transit-police brass began leaning on detectives to do what they could to convince the perps in hand to implicate their accomplices. As Maple put it, "We would debrief the little bastards, they would give up their pals, and at school the next day they would see the robbery squad come in and start pulling them out of their English classes."

A transit police warrant squad was established. In the past, the job of serving warrants that involved crime in the subways had been farmed out to the NYPD. The usual NYPD procedure was for a team of detectives to knock on a door and ask whoever answered it if the suspect was at home. If the answer was no, the cops departed, and the warrant went back in a drawer. After they left, the fugitive often came out of the closet or from under the bed and went on with his life, including his work as a mugger. Bratton took the warrants for subway robbers away from the NYPD and made it standard policy to execute them within forty-eight hours of a missed court appearance, usually at about 3:00 A.M. Instead of a pair of plainclothes cops, a squad of eight to ten uniformed cops would surround the suspect's house. The sergeant in charge would knock on the door and be told the usual: "He's not here." Rather than go away, however, the team would press for permission to enter the apartment, and frequently find the fugitive hiding within. Sometimes he would lower himself out a window or traipse across the rooftops, and the surrounding backups would head him off at the pass. If the suspect was really and truly not at home, the warrant cops went to the next most likely location—or the next twelve most likely.

Maple and his detectives painstakingly constructed a pin map of the entire subway system. They used different colored pins to indicate the tour of duty when a crime had been committed: green for daytime, red for 4:00 P.M. to midnight, black for midnight to 8:00 A.M. Different types of robberies were identified by number: No. 1 was with a gun, No. 2 with a knife, No. 3 a strong-arm robbery, and No. 4 a wolfpack. A No. 5 robbery was a form of purse snatching in which the perp stood between subway cars and, just as the train started out of a station, reached out for a victim standing on the platform.

By the summer of 1990, robberies of all five types were becoming less common, and an interesting symbiosis was emerging between Maple's anticrime initiatives and the quality-of-life campaign. To just about everyone's surprise, fare-beating enforcement was leading to a substantial number of arrests for more serious offenses. True to their criminal instincts, many robbers failed to deposit tokens as they entered the subway. One in seven fare-beating suspects turned out to be wanted for another crime; one in twenty was carrying a weapon.

Bratton's superiors, believing they were up against a problem of appearances as well as reality, were eager to publicize their success, and Bratton proved to be such an effective spokesman that the authority made him the star of a series of radio ads. Before long, his radio persona was familiar enough to inspire a parody by the talk-show host Don Imus. In the Imus version, Bratton boasted in slobbering Bostonese of a supposed pilot program of surprise visits by transit cops, at three in the morning, to recently paroled subway criminals. "We give them a little welcome-home pahty. . . . We bring cake or a box of pastry, and invite them to put on a pot of coffee. Then we chat for a while, talk about spohts, what life was like in the joint."

In April 1992, Bratton returned to the Boston P.D. as second in command, after a commission of inquiry—created in response to police mishandling of the Charles Stuart case, in which a white man shot his pregnant wife to death and blamed the deed on a fictitious black assailant—recommended sweeping changes. In July 1993, Bratton became Boston's police commissioner, only to once again follow (as *The Boston Globe* put it) "the siren song of ambition from Boston to Manhattan" six months later.

Rudy Giuliani was the mayor now. The swashbuckling former federal prosecutor intended to run his administration hands-on, after the fashion of Fiorello La Guardia. New Yorkers generally remember La Guardia (if they remember him at all) reading the Sunday comics on the radio during a newspaper strike; but he spent a lot of time reading the riot act to his commissioners. Even Lew Valentine got complaining memos from the mayor about "stupid" reports emanating from the police commissioner's office. Sometimes the memos came accompanied by a mayoral threat to take over the department.

Giuliani, coming away from one of his first conversations with *his* police commissioner, had the uncomfortable feeling that Bratton was someone who might have difficulty remembering (as an aide put it) "which of them had been elected by the people." Members of the Giuliani administration (other than the mayor himself) were supposed to speak to the press as little as possible; they were to avoid statements likely to call personal attention to themselves or raise public expectations. With one exception, they got the message. The exception was Bratton.

"We will fight for every house in the city," he declared in a flight of Churchillian rhetoric at his swearing-in. "We will fight for every street. We will fight for every block. And we will win." (Watching the speech back in Boston, some of his former aides remembered that he had used the same words at his swearing-in there, the previous year.) Scarcely a week after his appointment, Bratton was on page 1 of the *News* promising, I'LL END THE FEAR. Aides to the mayor began to worry about the Giuliani-Bratton chemistry.

One of Bratton's first tasks was to deal with the fallout from the Mollen commission investigation. In mid-April, it got out that at least a dozen cops at a precinct in upper Harlem—dubbed the "Dirty Thirty"—had been providing paid protection to local drug dealers, and beating and robbing those who were slow to appreciate the need for such arrangements. The usual drill for a modern police commissioner was to call a press conference at headquarters, denounce the cops who had actually been charged, heap praise on the remaining 99 percent of the force, and wait for the story to go away. Instead, Bratton showed up at the precinct along with the arrest team, personally collected the shields of two of the accused, and announced that their badge numbers would be permanently retired, so no cops would ever have to wear them again. At the next morning's roll call, Bratton gave a stunned group of the arrested officers' coworkers a talking-to. They could expect a lot of ugly looks from the citizenry, he advised them. And with reason: some of them had in all likelihood committed the same crimes: "We're probably not going to be able to get all of you—that's unfortunate," Bratton said. Others, he added, had surely known what was happening and had kept the knowledge to themselves. "I've been disappointed—being quite frank—that more did not come forward," he said. "We need to think carefully about that."

Bratton was not the first commissioner to come down hard on crooked cops. Unlike Pat Murphy, though, he did not intend to be remembered mainly as a corruption fighter. "It's a plate I've been given in New York," he told a reporter. "It's here, and I'm going to have to deal with it. But it's not something I'm going to be fixated on." To underscore that point, he went out of his way to issue statements of support for cops who, in his judgment, had been wrongly accused, and he seemed to take an almost eager delight in denouncing those he saw an antipolice, including the Civilian Complaint Review Board's investigators ("not high-quality people") and the lawyer for an undercover transit policeman shot by an NYPD officer ("an ambulance chaser"). Unlike other "reform" commissioners, Bratton proved to be popular with the rank and file. Of course, he gave them what many had long wanted:

the freedom to go out and be cops; to arrest criminals, not drive past them; and to investigate cases, not just write reports on them.

In one respect—the wholesale turnover of top commanders—Bratton followed the postscandal pattern. He promoted one-star chief John Timoney to four-star chief of department (and later first deputy commissioner). One-star chief Lou Anemone was made three-star chief of the patrol force (later succeeding Timoney). Both were hard-charging bosses from the younger generation of commanders. Workaholic, one-star chief Pat Kelleher was put in charge of "reengineering the organization"—that is, questioning all aspects of its operations. Kelleher, too, would move up rapidly. Bratton's deputy commissioner for public relations was John Miller, former TV news reporter who had started his career at age fifteen, concealing his youth with a giant fedora pulled down over his ears and an unlit cigar clenched in his teeth. In recent years, he had been the media's expert on organized crime, known for his expansive coverage of the doings of the colorful "godfather" John Gotti.

And, of course, there was Maple, who had gone with Bratton to Boston and now came back with him to New York, to occupy the newly created post of deputy commissioner for crime-control strategies. Maple's prominence would have drawn comment even if he had been a great diplomat, which he wasn't. Bringing a transit police lieutenant into the top ranks of the NYPD was like making a coast guard lieutenant a three-star admiral in the navy. But when Bratton and Maple began to hold major headquarters meetings about crime, Chief Timoney noted the novelty of the subject matter. There had been meetings about corruption, he recalled. There had been meetings about demonstrations. There had been meetings about practically everything *but* crime.

The centerpiece of Maple's new program was an institution that became known as Comp Stat (short for computer-generated comparative statistics). Prior to Bratton, the crime numbers had often been months behind. Now they came out weekly. At intervals of four to six weeks, an entire police borough command, led by the two-star chief in charge along with his inspectors, captains, and other key players, and accompanied by commanding officers of special units in the area such as detectives and narcotics, would be assembled in the command center, or "war room," on the eighth floor of One Police Plaza. Meetings would convene at 7:00 A.M.—not an hour of great activity at headquarters in years gone by. Commanders would be questioned on the crime conditions in their particular areas of jurisdiction. In the room long tables, lit by green lamps, were set up in a horseshoe, facing a lectern. Sitting opposite the lectern in a central position were Deputy Commissioner Maple and Chief of Department Anemone. A high-tech console flashed maps and graphs on overhead video screens. Commanders were called to the rostrum to make their presentation, then grilled with frequent reference to the map. Crime by crime, sector by sector, a precinct would be scoured by laser pointer.

It was a new experience for the bosses, and many fumbled and stumbled. Some were obviously unacquainted with the most basic facts about crime in their areas. A precinct commander might be asked, for example, why his burglary rate was up. If he said he didn't know, he was in trouble. Who was committing the burglaries? Had the captain perhaps noticed a concentration of daytime burglaries around a large public high school? To emphasize the point, the laser beam would sweep over the locations under discussion, like an accusing finger. Did he not infer any relationship between the burglaries and the high school? Had the captain talked to the precinct detective squad lieutenant, or the local narcotics and youth division supervisors? After some hesitation, he would say that he had. Since these gentlemen (or ladies) were in the room, Anemone would ask them to join the captain at the podium and explain their collective plan. Within a moment, it would became apparent that they had not consulted on the problem. Anemone would bore in on them like a shark. "Who owns this?" he would ask, meaning, who took responsibility for the problem? The silence that often followed suggested that no one did. A detective lieutenant might then explain that he had prepared a report on the case. Anemone would sharply remind him that reports don't solve anything. Maple's contribution, on one occasion, was to flash a Pinocchio image on the screen, using his laser beam to make the nose grow as a chief struggled through his confused explanation. Some victims blew up; a few virtually lost their commands on the spot. Some left the room and went straight to the pension office. Those who kept their wits might fall back on the old excuse "I need more cops." Anemone's reply would be "How many?" To a captain, fifty might sound like a nice impossible figure. Headquarters, he would tell himself, would never transfer that many cops in one fell swoop. "You got 'em," Anemone would say. And very soon, fifty officers would be on their way to the troubled area. (Anemone could afford to be so generous because of the hiring binge that had originated with David Dinkins—but no one ever mentioned him.) A month or so later, when the commanding officer returned, it would behoove him to be able to show that he was now on top of the burglary situation—of the entire crime situation—in his precinct. If he couldn't, he would be told to put in his papers.

In Comp Stat, Bratton's corporate-management training converged with Maple's maniacal knowledge of crime patterns and statistics. After six months of the new methods, many of the carryover commanders were gone, and their replacements knew what was expected of them. In the past, orders had always filtered down from above through a lengthy chain of command from police commissioner to chief of department to chief of patrol, and so on down to precinct commander. The chief of detectives or the head of the Narcotics Bureau were people precinct commanders read about in newspapers but rarely met. Now they were all sitting together for hours at a stretch. A whole generation of new and younger commanders was being developed at Comp Stat. A captain learned to acknowledge serious problems up front and to spell out the steps that he or, increasingly often, she had taken. The next time around, she would recount the success that had been achieved, in numbers of arrests. Junior commanders like Deputy Inspector Joe Dunne, a burly mustachioed reincarnation of a nineteenth-century precinct commander, quickly mastered the system. In his Brooklyn command, the crime-and-scandal-ridden Seventy-fifth Precinct, murders fell from 125 (the year before he took over) to 45 (two years later). Meanwhile, Dunne shot up to two-star chief. (By 1999, he was the four-star chief of department.) This was not rocket science: at any corporate sales meeting, a division manager would be expected to know his sales figures, the characteristics of his market, and how he intended to increase his share. But it was all new to the NYPD.

Rank-and-file cops, of course, could not be told to put in their papers, nor did they care much about statistics. Transfers were also not much of a threat to them—at least not to cops already assigned to high-crime precincts in the Bronx or Brooklyn. The thinking was, "Where can they send me?" Yet if crime and disorder were going to be brought under control, more than a handful of cops had to pitch in. In Queens, where three out of ten New Yorkers live, 28 percent of the patrol force had not made an arrest in the first six months of 1994. Maple, who formulated his strategies on the basis of his studies of military history, derided them as "conscientious objectors." Bratton's team came out with a series of anticrime strategies dealing with guns, drugs, car theft, and so on. Each strategy had a number and a color-coded booklet. In retrospect, some of the ideas might seem obvious: "Just Ask" posters, for example, reminding patrol officers and detectives of a new, department-wide effort to question suspects more persistently and ask everyone arrested with a gun where he had gotten it. "Now any time a gun arrest is made, we're called in to debrief the suspect," a robbery-squad detective noted. "Nine times out of ten, you won't get anything. But it's worth it for that one time."

Under the doctrine of community policing, the beat cop had been responsible for solving all of a neighborhood's problems. Bratton dropped this pretense. While he continued the program itself (without expanding its scale), the precinct captain became the repository of power and responsibility. To emphasize the point, Bratton abolished the division level of command (which had fallen between the precinct and the borough), and the Comp Stat meetings brought precinct commanders into regular face-to-face contact with the top brass.

Maple was something of a latter-day Thomas Byrnes. Although the rules prevented him from being made chief of detectives, he functioned as if he held that post. He had Byrnes's shrewdness and self-confidence; he was similarly adept at using statistics to measure performance; most of all, he believed in the importance of detectives in fighting crime. At the beginning of the Bratton era, the department's detectives averaged six collars a year; the only cases that interested some of them, according to Maple, were the ones likely to lead to a book deal. Since Pat Murphy's day, police commissioners had downplayed the importance of the Detective Bureau. Often it had been placed under commanders who had never been detectives themselves. Yet all the while, the number of investigators had continued to grow. In Murphy's day, the bureau—which included eight hundred narcotics investigators—had constituted about 10 percent of the department's personnel. By the time Bratton took over, the Detective Bureau and the equally large Organized Crime Control Bureau accounted, between them, for nearly 20 percent of the force.

Crime, meanwhile, had been internationalized by the ease and speed of travel and communications. The modern NYPD was confronted with offenses committed by perpetrators sitting at computer terminals thousands of miles away. To investigate such cases required a new degree of sophistication. With DNA testing—the fingerprint-dusting of the twenty-first century—

crimes could be solved years after they had occurred; in effect, there was no longer such a thing as an unsolved case. Yet as Maple was wont to complain, many a detective could be found sitting on a barstool bragging about the big case he was working on—while squandering the critical first few days of the investigation. Narcotics detectives were in the habit of leaving work at 7:00 P.M., and many took weekends off, even as the drug dealers went into high gear.

Detectives had jealously guarded their sources of information from one another since the days of Jacob Hays. In a city where 40 percent of the annual two thousand murders were drug-related, it might have seemed useful for homicide (part of the Detective Bureau) and narcotics (part of the Organized Crime Control Bureau) to confer about someone like, say, a gunman known on the streets as Freddy Krueger. A hit man for drug dealers, Krueger had a body count to his credit greater than his namesake in the movie *Nightmare on Elm Street*: in the first seven months of 1992, Krueger had murdered seven people and, by rumor, taken a hand in the murder of twenty-five others. Yet the Detective Bureau knew nothing about him. In the midst of his murder spree, he was arrested in the Bronx for pulling a gun on somebody. He gave a false name. Since his record indicated that he had never been arrested before, Krueger was released after signing a form; he hadn't even been required to post bail, thanks to a previous round of criminal justice reforms. Six months later, he was caught near the George Washington Bridge carrying a nine-millimeter. This time, he gave his real name, Francisco Medina. Again his record was clean, and again he was let go, pending trial. The only investigative unit in New York City with any information on Krueger and his operations was the small homicide investigating squad working out of the office of Manhattan D.A. Robert Morgenthau. For years, with only fitful help from the NYPD, Morgenthau's team of detectives had been going after the drug syndicates. Krueger was finally captured in the Dominican Republic, after committing a murder there.

Even before Bratton and Giuliani had come along, the crime rate had been falling, gently. Now it plunged. In 1994, New York saw a 12 percent reduction in reported crime, followed by 16 and 14 percent drops in the next two years. Questions were raised about the accuracy of the official statistics; the questions were pretty much put to rest by the figures for murder, traditionally the most accurately reported (and least manipulable) of crimes. The number of murders fell from nearly two thousand in 1993 to less than a thousand in 1996. Crime, it was true, was also dropping in some other cities, perhaps reflecting a widespread reaction against the ravages of crack cocaine, whose popularity seemed to have crested around 1990. But the national trend, as New York City officials were quick to point out, was not nearly as dramatic or sustained as the local one; nationally, the volume of crime dropped 5 percent between 1993 and 1996; in New York City, it fell 35 percent. The New York figures, all by themselves, accounted for one-third of the nation's decrease.

It was the kind of trend that people could *see*—and *hear*. In neighborhoods once controlled by gangs and drug dealers, fearful homebodies took to the streets again, and longtime neighbors got acquainted for the first time. New Yorkers accustomed to the sound of gunfire on summer nights discovered a new, sleep-inducing quiet. Even scholars who had long doubted the ability of the police to have much effect on crime found themselves shifting ground. "I think I am experiencing a foxhole conversion," said one early doubter, Franklin Zimring, a criminologist on the faculty of the University of California at Berkeley.

What some people took to calling the "New York miracle" was, of course, also a political miracle. Historically, crime had been a big problem at times, and a less big problem at other times; but it had never been anything but a problem. Now, suddenly, the relative absence of crime had become something for the city's leaders to take credit for. But who deserved the credit?

Even if Bratton had hidden from the news media, he would have attracted attention. And he didn't hide. He was on TV constantly, and often found in other places not frequented by the police commissioners of the past. With his third wife, a lawyer who was carving out a new career for herself as a TV commentator (on the O. J. Simpson case, among other topics), he had taken an apartment on Central Park South—a street long associated with wealth and celebrity. Late of an evening, Bratton, Maple, and their crew would gather at an Upper East Side in-joint called Elaine's. Sometimes they would convene an anticrime strategy session at their table, and a movie star would lean over to offer advice.

From City Hall came a succession of private warnings and edicts involving the police brass's dealings with the press. Headquarters would go through the motions of obeying these directives. But Bratton's attitude, to judge by the results, seemed to resemble that of Admiral Nelson toward his superiors' attempts to rein him in during the Napoleonic Wars. Once, when Nelson didn't like the flag signals he was seeing, he switched his telescope to his blind eye and went ahead and fought the battle his way. Bratton's efforts at compliance were not sufficient, at any rate, to keep his face from landing on the cover of *Time* magazine in January 1996. (The fate of Commissioner Kennedy in 1961 ought to have warned him against cultivating coverage in that particular publication.) Nor did they keep him from mentioning, during a TV appearance, his hope of reviving the old police parade after a lapse of more than sixty years. A peculiar confluence of scheduling considerations, Bratton added, seemed to require the planned procession to occur on his own birthday. (The mayor swiftly vetoed the idea, citing the expense.)

When it came to actual matters of policy, Bratton could not complain of a lack of mayoral support. Not a few superior officers, angry at the goings-over they had received from Anemone and Maple, spoke to elected officials, who carried word of their unhappiness to City Hall. Police bosses were influential people in New York; any previous mayor (except La Guardia) would have told the commissioner to cut out the rough stuff. Giuliani, who believed in that sort of management, ignored the protests. He even managed to get the Transit Police merged into the NYPD, by the simple means of threatening to cut off the city's subsidies. (Bratton, in a reversal of his previous position, now supported the merger. The NYPD just hadn't had the right leadership before, he explained.) There seemed to be only one serious area of open disagreement between the two men: public relations. But that one topic alone was enough to sour the relationship from beginning to ignominious end.

Things came to a climax toward the end of 1995, when word reached City Hall of a $300,000 deal that Bratton had signed for a how-we-slashed-crime book. The mayor's people took him to task for not clearing the arrangement with them; now that they knew of it, the city's Corporation Counsel launched a formal investigation of what were described as possible conflicts of interest. Bratton had also become the subject of a second inquiry—into what a mayoral spokesman called "vacation trips paid for by millionaires to such places as Palm Beach, Colorado, and Notre Dame for a football game."

The commissioner's term was nearing its official end. This was largely a formality, as mayors had demonstrated for a century by appointing new commissioners whenever they chose. As a legal matter, however, reappointment was required, and the Giuliani administration let it be known that the two probes would have to run their courses before the mayor could even consider another term for Bratton. In March 1996, Bratton resigned, and Maple went with him. When Giuliani failed to appoint John Timoney as Bratton's successor, he quit, too, getting off a public blast at the mayor and his choice for PC—Fire Commissioner Howard Safir, who had been a federal narcotics agent and the chief fugitive-hunter for the U.S. Marshal's Service.

In an echo of Thomas Byrnes's departure a century earlier, there were New Yorkers who expected the miracle to evaporate once Bratton left. But crime continued to fall, the number of murders to 983 in 1996, and 770 in 1997. In 1998, the city recorded 633 murders—less than a third of the level of the early 1990s, and indeed the lowest figure in thirty-five years. (Chicago, with not quite 40 percent of New York's population, had 703 murders that year.) In 1999, however, murder was up 6 percent, and the trend continued into 2000.

Over the course of his three years in the job, Bratton had spoken freely and often about the life he envisioned for himself after he stepped down. What he had in mind, he indicated, was a job as CEO of a major corporation. One thing was for sure: he wouldn't go the route of so many commissioners before him and become another "Joe Blow security director." To the delight of his critics, the job he wound up taking was a management post with a security-services firm. He soon moved on to a similar executive position with another company before leaving to become a freelance consultant.

In at least one sense, Bratton's departure could be said to have been well timed. In August 1997, a Brooklyn cop named Justin Volpe was assaulted after responding to a brawl outside an East Flatbush nightclub. Volpe arrested a thirty-two-year-old Haitian immigrant named Abner Louima in the mistaken belief that Louima had punched him in the head. Later that night, while processing the arrest at the Seventieth Precinct stationhouse, Volpe took Louima to the rest room, where he rammed a wooden broomstick into the defenseless man's rectum. Indicted and convicted on federal civil-rights charges, Volpe was eventually sentenced to thirty years' imprisonment; three other officers were also convicted in the case.

Until the summer of 1997, the NYPD had been riding high—acclaimed locally, nationally, and even globally for the "miracle" of cutting the crime rate in half. Then, as had often happened in the past, its image began to deteriorate. The Louima case was a police commissioner's nightmare, and it was only the first of several for Bratton's successor. In February 1999, four members of the citywide Street Crime Unit decided to investigate what they saw as the suspicious behavior of twenty-two-year-old Amadou Diallo, who was standing near the entrance of an apartment building in the Soundview section of the Bronx. As they approached, Diallo reached into his pocket and removed an object that at least one of the officers took for a gun. It turned out to be a wallet. The young man holding it was a hardworking and religiously devout immigrant from Guinea, in West Africa, who made his living as a street peddler and shared an apartment in the building with three roommates. By the time the cops learned these facts, he was dead. Of the forty-one shots they had fired at him, nineteen had struck their mark.

The case revealed a chasm of difference in the worldview of many cops, on the one hand, and many citizens, especially blacks and Hispanics, on the other. The police had joined in the general revulsion over the Louima episode; by contrast, most cops saw Amadou Diallo's death as a terrible accident—one that "could happen to any of us," a plainclothesman told a reporter for the *Times*. Mayor Giuliani described it as an aberration. In fact, the number of people killed by officers of the NYPD had fallen from an average of thirty in the first years of the decade to nineteen by 1998. (The following year, it declined to a modern low of eleven.) And by bringing about a precipitous drop in the number of shootings in general, Giuliani argued, he and the police department had saved the lives of countless black and Hispanic New Yorkers.

But many blacks and Hispanics—and whites, too—were not comforted by the mayor's line of reasoning, which he spelled out with his customary prosecutorial vehemence. The death of an innocent and law-abiding young man at the hands of the police might not be an everyday event, but the incident stirred an outpouring of testimony about people who, it seemed, hadn't found it necessary to do much beyond being young black males in order to become the objects of police action. Although Commissioner Safir ordered changes in the Street Crime Unit (even putting its members back in uniform, briefly), neither he nor his boss acknowledged a major problem, and they vigorously defended the decision two years earlier to triple the size of the unit from 138 to 438 officers.

The motivation for doing so had been plain enough. Getting guns off the street was widely regarded as one of the surest ways of cutting crime. In 1997, when the Street Crime Unit was expanded, its members seized 1,139 guns—a 59 percent increase over the previous year. But even within the unit itself, there had been some uneasiness about the speed and scale of the expansion. Its commander at the time, Deputy Inspector Richard Savage, had gone so far as to resign over the issue, fearing the loss of what he later described as a vital "intimacy of training and supervision" with the influx of so many young and inexperienced officers.

The four officers involved in Diallo's death were both young and inexperienced (the senior-most of them, Sean Carroll, had less than a year of street duty with the unit), and they had never worked as a team until that night, when a shortage of cars brought them together. And the fact that all four were white lent an appearance of validity to the argument of many police critics that such a thing would never have happened on, say, the Upper East Side of Manhattan. Out of all the cops in Street Crime, in fact, only 3 percent were black. Commissioner Safir, who admitted to some dismay on this score, recalled asking an African-American chief to "make his best efforts to increase the number of minorities in Street Crime." The chief, defending his admittedly unsuccessful attempt to do so, raised a whole new set of troubling questions. Such units, he suggested, had consistently been more attractive to white than nonwhite officers; in the expansion process, Street Crime had relied on its existing members as de facto recruiters, and "if you . . . start with an overwhelmingly white unit, that's what you end up with."

The cops involved in the Diallo incident would argue that they had good reason, and every legal right, to check him out. Officer Carroll would recall seeing Diallo "peek out" of the doorway and then "slink back." To many New Yorkers, this sounded like slender grounds for sizing someone up as a likely criminal. Critics wondered aloud whether some of Diallo's "suspiciousness" might have been attributable to his discomfort or fear on seeing four strange men drive up; he might have removed his wallet, it was theorized, intending to produce identification, or to turn over his money, mistaking the cops for robbers. As vociferously as the police department and the mayor defended the cops, critics denounced them. Neither side seemed to see something that the Diallo incident itself and similar controversies over the years made clear—that there was no firm and settled body of law or departmental doctrine to guide the police in such encounters. And with crime going down and the number of Street Crime cops going up, the forces of supply and demand suggested, as a practical matter, that the definition of suspicious conduct might be getting looser.

The case inspired a series of angry demonstrations in which former mayor David Dinkins, among many others, was arrested. When the Bronx district attorney indicted the four policemen on second-degree murder charges, the defense commissioned a poll. Roughly 80 percent of the borough's inhabitants, it showed, could not fathom a justification for such a barrage of police bullets. In response to a motion that the officers' lawyers filed without much optimism, a New York State appellate court decided to move the trial out of the city, raising parallels with another notorious case—the beating of Rodney King, in which four Los Angeles cops had been exonerated by a suburban jury. The Reverend Al Sharpton, one of the Diallo protest leaders, railed against what he called "judicial apartheid." The defense had, in fact, proposed suburban Westchester County as an alternate venue. But the appeals court moved the trial to Albany instead; and though the state capital would once have been a very odd place for accused cops to go in search of sympathetic treatment, that was where a jury of eight whites and four blacks acquitted the four officers on all charges in February 2000.

Within a few weeks of the verdict, two more unarmed black men were shot to death by undercover narcotics police, setting off a new round of protests. As they had often done in the past, critics and supporters of the police divided into hard-line camps. The theme, on one side, was a police force that had gotten out of control, and the need for new and tighter rules, enforced by an outside monitoring agency. The other side warned about cops being "handcuffed" and discouraged from doing their jobs. Giuliani—by now immersed in a heated campaign for the United States Senate against First Lady Hillary Rodham Clinton—struck back hard at his critics, even going so far as to release one of the dead men's juvenile arrest records.

But there was opportunity as well as danger in the air. For as long as anyone could remember, basic questions of police strategy and deployment had been quietly decided at headquarters or City Hall or, in the absence of guidance from those power centers, in squad rooms and radio cars. The Diallo case had created the stirrings of a call for a public airing of these formerly low-profile matters. Such a conversation would be a profound change, but it would take place against a background of unusually broad support for the police department, even among minorities. What they wanted from the police, polls consistently found, were two things: protection and respect. (In a 1999 poll of black New York City residents, commissioned by the U.S. Department of Justice, 77 percent of those surveyed expressed general approval of the department's performance.) While overseeing the prosecution of the Louima case, Zachary Carter, the United States attorney for the Eastern District of New York, had initiated an investigation of the department's handling of citizen complaints, leading to an attempt to negotiate new mechanisms for ensuring a proper response. Such guarantees were necessary, Carter argued, precisely because of the high value that many minority residents placed on the services provided by the police. "It is in the inner city, where the victimization rates are highest," he pointed out, "that the police are most needed."

Studies in several cities suggested that when people were treated with obvious courtesy and fairness, even the experience of being stopped and checked out by the police could leave a favorable impression. Looking at these issues in the 1980s, criminal-justice scholars at the State University of New York at Albany had made the interesting discovery that some of the NYPD cops regarded most highly by their peers had a knack for defusing potentially violent situations. The implications seemed obvious: maybe their methods could be studied and taught. If the NYPD could manage, by such means, to improve its relations with African-Americans and Hispanics, it would only be repeating a process that had taken place with a succession of other population groups over the years—a logical if very belated development. "The relationship between the police and inner-city residents," Carter observed, "is a love affair waiting to happen."

A Note on Place-Names

In the late 1800s, New York City consisted of the island of Manhattan and, to the north, a piece of the mainland area known as the Bronx. To the west of Manhattan, across the Hudson River, is the state of New Jersey. To the south, out in the harbor, is Staten Island, historically and geographically more a part of New Jersey than New York. Across the East River (which is really a tidal channel) from Manhattan lies the western portion of Long Island, including Brooklyn and Queens, which, along with Staten Island, became boroughs, or political subdivisions of Greater New York City, in 1898.

Boroughs are geographically identical with a county (a subdivision of the state). Bronx and Queens counties have the same names as the boroughs. Manhattan is New York County, Brooklyn is Kings County, and Staten Island is Richmond County.

New York City has seventy-six police precincts, but their numbers run as high as 123. The discrepancy reflects a gradual process of consolidation since pre-automobile days, when cops had to walk from their stationhouses to their posts. Precincts are important local institutions, and it has never been easy to close one. The present number is only nine fewer than existed half a century ago.

Precinct numbers have changed many times over the years. Whenever possible, we have tried to give the geographic location of a precinct instead of, or along with, its number. In most cities, a precinct (or district or division, depending on the local parlance) would be referred to as the Twenty-first or as Precinct Twenty-one. In New York, cops speak of the two-one. But we use the more conventional form.

335

Sources

NEW YORK CITY POLICE

Books, Dissertations, and Oral Histories:

Alexander, James I. *Blue Coats: Black Skin: The Black Experience in the New York City Police Department Since 1891.* New York: Exposition Press, 1978.

Astor, Gerald. *The New York Cops.* New York: Charles Scribner & Sons, 1971.

Battle, Samuel. Interview. Columbia Oral History Collection, Butler Library, Columbia University, New York.

Bloch, Eugene. *Famous Detectives.* New York: Doubleday, 1967.

Bouza, Anthony V. *Bronx Beat: Reflections of a Police Commander.* Chicago: Office of International Criminal Justice, 1990.

———. *Police Intelligence: The Operations of an Investigative Unit.* New York: AMS Press, 1976.

Bratton, William, with Peter Knobler. *Turnaround: How America's Top Cop Reversed the Crime Epidemic.* New York: Random House, 1998.

Costello, Augustine. *Our Police Protectors.* 1885. Reprint, Montclair, N.J.: Patterson Smith, 1972.

Carey, Arthur C. *Memoirs of a Murder Man.* Garden City, N.Y.: Doubleday, Doran & Co., 1930.

Collins, Frederick L. *Homicide Squad: Adventures of a Headquarters Old Timer.* New York: G. P. Putnam's Sons, 1944.

Daley, Robert. *Prince of the City.* New York: Houghton Mifflin, 1978.

———. *Target Blue.* New York: Delacorte Press, 1973.

Fiaschetti, Michael. *You Gotta Be Rough: The Adventures of Detective Fiaschetti of the Italian Squad as Told to Prosper Buranelli.* Garden City, N.Y.: Doubleday, Doran & Co., 1930.

Gelb, Barbara, *Varnished Brass.* New York: G. P. Putnam's Sons. 1983.

Jeffers, H. Paul. *Commissioner Roosevelt: The Story of Theodore Roosevelt and the New York City Police, 1895–1897.* New York: John Wiley & Sons, 1994.

Lardner, James. *Crusader: The Hell-Raising Police Career of Detective David Durk.* New York: Random House, 1996.

Limpus, Lowell M. *Honest Cop, Lewis J. Valentine; Being a Chronicle of the Commissioner's Thirty-six Years in the New York Police Department.* New York: E. P. Dutton, 1939.

Maas, Peter. *Serpico.* New York: Viking Press, 1973.

McAdoo, William. *Guarding a Great City.* New York: Harper & Bros., 1906.

McAlary, Mike. *Buddy Boys.* New York: Jove, 1991.

———. *Cop Shot.* New York: Jove, 1992.

———. *Good Cop, Bad Cop.* New York: Pocket Books, 1994.

McAllister, Robert. *The Kind of Guy I Am.* London: Hammond and Hammond, 1959.

McDonald, Brian. *My Father's Gun: One Family, Three Badges, One Hundred Years in the NYPD.* New York: Dutton, 1999.

McElroy, Jerome et al. *Community Policing: The CPOP in New York.* Newbury Park, Calif.: Sage Publishers, 1993.

Maple, Jack, with Chris Mitchell. *The Crime Fighter: Putting the Bad Guys Out of Business.* New York: Doubleday, 1999.

Miller, Wilbur R. *Cops and Bobbies: Police Authority in New York and London, 1830–1870.* Chicago: University of Chicago Press, 1977.

Morris, Edmund. *The Rise of Theodore Roosevelt.* New York: Coward, McCann, and Geoghegan, 1979.

Murphy, Patrick, with Thomas Plate. *Commissioner: A View from the Top of American Law Enforcement.* New York: Simon & Schuster, 1977.

Neiderhoffer, Arthur. *Behind the Shield: Police in Urban Society.* New York: Doubleday, 1967.

Petacco, Arrigo. *Joe Petrosino.* Trans. Charles Lam Markmann. New York: Macmillan, 1974.

Reardon, James. *The Sweet Life of Jimmy Riley.* New York: Wyndam Books, 1980.

Reynolds, Quentin. *Headquarters.* New York: Harper, 1955.

Richardson, James F. *The New York Police: Colonial Times to 1901.* New York: Oxford University Press, 1970.

Silverman, Eli. *NYPD Battles Crime: Innovative Strategies in Policing.* Boston: Northeastern University Press, 1999.

Thale, Christopher. *Civilizing New York City: Police Patrol 1880–1935.* Doctoral dissertation, University of Chicago, 1995.

Tunney, Thomas J. *Throttled! The Detection of the German and Anarchist Bomb Plotters, by Inspector Thomas J. Tunney . . . as Told to Paul Merrick Hollister.* Boston: Small, Maynard & Company, 1919.

Van Every, Edward. *Sins of New York as "Exposed" by the Police Gazette.* New York: Frederick A. Stokes Co., 1930.

Valentine, Lewis J. *Nightstick.* New York: Dial, 1947.

Wallander, Arthur. Interview. Columbia Oral History Collection, Butler Library, Columbia University, New York.

Walling, George. *Recollections of a New York Chief of Police.* 1887. Reprint, Montclair, N.J.: Patterson Smith, 1972.

Whalen, Grover. *Mr. New York: The Autobiography of Grover Whalen.* New York: G. P. Putnam's Sons, 1955.

Willemse, Cornelius. *Behind the Green Lights.* New York: Alfred A. Knopf, 1931.

———. *A Cop Remembers.* New York: E. P. Dutton, 1933.

Woods, Arthur. *Policeman and Public.* New Haven, Conn.: Yale University Press 1919; Montclair, N.J.: Patterson Smith, 1975.

Articles:

Alexander, Jack. "Profile: Commissioner Lewis J. Valentine." *The New Yorker,* 3, 10, and 17 October 1936.

Bayley, David H., and James Garofalo. "Patrol Officer Effectiveness in Managing Conflict During Police Citizen Encounters," in *Report of the New York State Commission on Criminal Justice and Use of Force,* 1987.

Bingham, Theodore A. "How to Give New York the Best Police Force in the World." *North American Review* (May 1908).

———. "Foreign Criminals in New York." *North American Review* 188 (September 1908).

Byrnes, Thomas. "How to Protect a City from Crime." *North American Review,* July 1894.

Critchley, T. A. "Peel, Rowan and Mayne: The British Model of Urban Police." In *Pioneers in Policing,* P. J. Stead, ed. Montclair, N.J.: Patterson Smith, 1977.

Denlinger, Sutherland. "Old Hays—There Was a Cop." Six-part series, *New York World Telegram,* 1–6 March 1937.

Kempton, Murray. "The Cop as Idealist." *Harper's,* March 1962.

Mackaye, Milton. "Profile: Commissioner Edward Mulrooney." *The New Yorker,* 24 October 1931.

"New York's Police Chieftains." *Harper's Weekly,* 23 April 1892.

"Nineteen Thousand Cops." *Fortune,* July 1939.

Perelman, S. J. "Don't Blame Inspector Byrnes." Introduction to Thomas Byrnes, *Professional Criminals of America.* New York: Chelsea House, 1969.

Sayre, Joel. "Profile: John Broderick." *The New Yorker,* 26 December 1931.

———. "Profile: John Cordes." *The New Yorker,* 5 and 12 September 1953.

Schlesinger, Arthur, Jr. "The Business of Crime." Introduction to Thomas Byrnes, *Professional Criminals of America.* New York: Chelsea House, 1969.

"Strong Arm of the Law" (cover story, Commissioner Stephen P. Kennedy). *Time,* 7 July 1958.

Thompson, Craig. "New York's Communist Cop." *The Saturday Evening Post,* 20 March 1954.

Werner, M. R. "Profile: Dr. Parkhurst." *The New Yorker,* 19 and 26 November 1955.

Wheatley, Richard. "The New York Police Department." *Harper's New Monthly Magazine,* March 1887.

Wilson, James Q., and George Kelling. "Broken Windows: The Police and Neighborhood Safety." *Atlantic Monthly,* March 1982, 29–38.

POLICE IN GENERAL

Fogelson, Robert M. *Big City Police.* Cambridge, Mass.: Harvard University Press, 1977.

Fosdick, Raymond. *American Police Systems.* 1920. Reprint, Montclair, N.J.: Patterson Smith, 1969.

Fuld, Leonhard F. *Police Administration: A Critical Study of Police Organizations in the United States and Abroad.* New York: G. P. Putnam's Sons, 1909.

Goldstein, Herman. *Problem-Oriented Policing.* New York: McGraw Hill, 1990.

Graper, Elmer D. *American Police Administration.* 1921. Reprint, Montclair, N.J.: Patterson Smith, 1969.

Monkkonen, Eric. *Police in Urban America 1860–1920.* New York: Cambridge University Press, 1981.

Reppetto, Thomas A. *The Blue Parade.* New York: Macmillan–Free Press, 1978.

Sherman, Lawrence. *Scandal and Reform: Controlling Police Corruption.* Berkeley: University of California Press, 1978.

Smith, Bruce. *Police Systems in the United States.* 2nd rev. ed. 1949. Reprint, New York: Harper, 1960.

Sparrow, Malcolm K., Mark H. Moore, and David M. Kennedy. *Beyond 911: A New Era for Policing.* New York: Basic Books, 1990.

Stead, Phillip J. *Pioneers in Policing.* Montclair, N.J.: Patterson Smith, 1977.

Walker, Samuel. *A Critical History of Police Reform: The Emergence of Professionalism.* Lexington, Mass.: Lexington Books, 1977.

CRIME AND CRIMINALS

Books, Monographs, and Articles:

Adler, Polly. *A House Is Not a Home.* New York: Rinehart and Co., Inc., 1953.

Asbury, Herbert. *The Gangs of New York.* New York: Knopf, 1927; New York Paragon, 1990.

Cohen, Patricia Cline. *The Murder of Helen Jewett: The Life and Death of a Prostitute in Nineteenth-Century New York.* Alfred A. Knopf, 1998.

Gosch, Martin A., and Richard Hammer. *The Last Testament of Lucky Luciano.* New York: Dell Publishing, 1974.

Johnson, David R. *Policing the Urban Underworld: The Impact of Crime on the Development of the American Police, 1800–1887.* Philadelphia: Temple University Press, 1979.

Joselit, Jenna Weissman. *Our Gang: Jewish Crime and the New York Jewish Community, 1900–1940.* Bloomington, Ind.: University of Indiana Press, 1983.

Karmen, Andrew. "Murders in New York City." In *Crime and Justice in New York City*, ed. Andrew Karmen. New York: McGraw-Hill, 1998.

Katcher, Leo. *The Big Bankroll: The Life and Times of Arnold Rothstein.* New Rochelle, N.Y.: Arlington House, 1958.

Kelling, George C., and Catherine M. Coles. *Fixing Broken Windows: Restoring Order and Reducing Crime in Our Communities.* New York: The Free Press, 1996.

Kneeland, George J. *Commercialized Prostitution in New York City.* 1917. Reprint, Montclair, N.J.: Patterson Smith, 1969.

Landau, Henry. *The Enemy Within.* New York: G. P. Putnam's Sons, 1937.

Lardner, John. "The Martyrdom of Bill the Butcher." *The New Yorker,* 20 and 27 March 1954.

Logan, Andy. *Against the Evidence: The Becker-Rosenthal Affair.* New York: McCall Publishing Co., 1970.

Matsell, George W. *Vocabulum, or the Rogue's Lexicon.* New York: G. W. Matsell, 1859.

Musto, David F. *The American Disease: Origins of Narcotics Control.* Expanded ed. New York: Oxford University Press, 1987.

O'Connor, Richard. *Courtroom Warrior: The Combative Career of William Travers Jerome.* Boston: Little, Brown, 1963.

Paul, Raymond. *Who Murdered Mary Rogers?* Englewood Cliffs, N.J.: Prentice-Hall, 1971.

Peterson, Virgil W. *The Mob: 200 Years of Organized Crime in New York.* Ottawa, Ill.: Greenhill Publishers, 1983.

Root, Jonathan. *One Night in July.* New York: Coward-McCann, 1961.

Roth, Andrew. *Infamous Manhattan: A Colorful Walking Tour of New York's Most Notorious Crime Sites.* New York: Carol Publishing Group, 1996.

Rovere, Richard H. *Howe & Hummel: Their True and Scandalous History.* New York: Farrar, Straus, Giroux 1947.

Srebnick, Amy G. *The Mysterious Death of Mary Rogers: Sex and Culture in Nineteenth-Century New York.* New York: Oxford University Press, 1995.

Sutton, Willie, with Edward Linn. *Where the Money Was.* New York: Viking Press, 1976.

Sutton, Willie, with Quentin Reynolds. *I, Willie Sutton.* New York: Farrar, Straus, and Young, 1953.

Talbert, Roy, Jr. *Negative Intelligence: The Army and the American Left, 1917–1941.* Jackson, Miss.: University Press of Mississippi, 1991.

Train, Arthur. *From the District Attorney's Office.* New York: Charles Scribner's Sons, 1939.

Vona, Daniel. "Organized Crime in New York City: Its History and Current Rackets." In *Crime and Justice in New York City*, ed. Andrew Karmen. New York: McGraw-Hill, 1998.

Wallace, Irving. *The Fabulous Originals: Lives of Extraordinary People Who Inspired Memorable Characters in Fiction.* New York: Alfred A. Knopf, 1954.

Waller, George. *The Story of the Lindbergh Case.* New York: Dial, 1961.

Wilentz, Sean. *Crime, Poverty and the Streets of New York City: The Diary of William H. Bell, 1850–1851.* Manuscript. New York Historical Society.

Witcover, Jules. *Sabotage at Black Tom.* Chapel Hill, N.C.: Algonquin Books, 1989.

Wolf, George, with Joseph DiMona. *Frank Costello: Prime Minister of the Underworld.* New York: Bantam Books, 1975.

NEW YORK CITY LIFE

Books:

Benfey, Christopher. *The Double Life of Stephen Crane.* New York: Alfred A. Knopf, 1992.

Bernstein, Iver. *The New York City Draft Riots: Their Significance for American Society and Politics in the Age of the Civil War.* New York: Oxford University Press, 1990.

Broun, Heywood, and Margaret Leech. *Anthony Comstock: Roundsman of the Lord.* New York: Boni Liveright, 1927.

Bruce, Robert V. *1877: Year of Violence.* Chicago: Quadrangle Edition, 1970.

Buckley, Peter G. *To the Opera House: Culture and Society in New York City, 1820–1860.* Unpublished dissertation. SUNY, Stony Brook, 1984.

Burrows, Edwin G., and Mike Wallace. *Gotham: A History of New York City to 1898.* New York: Oxford University Press, 1999.

Capeci, Dominic. *The Harlem Riot of 1943.* Philadelphia: Temple University Press, 1977.

Cook, Adrian. *The Armies of the Streets: The New York City Draft Riots of 1863.* Lexington: University of Kentucky Press, 1974.

Crane, Stephen. *The New York City Sketches of Stephen Crane.* Ed. R. W. Stallman and E. R. Hagemann. New York: New York University Press, 1966.

Crouthamel, James L. *Bennett's New York Herald and the Rise of the Penny Press.* Syracuse, N.Y.: Syracuse University Press, 1989.

Curran, Henry H. *Pillar to Post.* New York: Scribner, 1941.

Ernst, Robert. *Immigrant Life in New York City, 1825–1863.* New York: Octagon Books, 1979.

Fermer, Douglas, *James Gordon Bennett and the New York Herald.* Royal Historical Society. 1986.

Foster, George G. *New York by Gas-Light.* Berkeley: University of California Press, 1990.

Fowler, Gene. *Beau James: The Life and Times of Jimmy Walker.* New York: Viking, 1949.

Gardiner, Alexander. *Canfield.* Garden City, N.Y.: Doubleday, 1930.

Garrett, Charles. *The LaGuardia Years: Machine and Reform Politics in New York City.* New Brunswick, N.J.: Rutgers University Press, 1961.

Gilfoyle, Timothy. *City of Eros: New York Prostitution and the Commercialization of Sex, 1790–1820.* New York: W.W. Norton, 1992.

Goldman, Emma. *Living My Life.* 1931. Reprint, New York: Da Capo Press, 1970.

Gottehrer, Barry. *Mayor's Man: One Man's Struggle to Save Our Cities.* New York: Doubleday and Co., 1975.

Handlin, Oscar. *Al Smith and His America.* Boston: Little, Brown, 1958.

Headley, Joel Tyler. *The Great Riots of New York, 1712 to 1873; including a full and complete account of the four days' draft riot of 1863.* New York: E. B. Treat, 1873.

Heckscher, August, with Phyllis Robinson. *When La Guardia Was Mayor: New York's Legendary Years.* New York: W.W. Norton and Co., 1978.

Hone, Philip. *Diary.* Vol. 1. New York: Dodd, Mead, 1889.

Jaffe, Steven H. *The Rise of the Urban Newspaper Reporter in New York City, 1800–1850.* Doctoral dissertation, Harvard University, 1985.

Kahn, E. J. *The World of Swope.* New York: Simon & Schuster, 1965.

Kessner, Thomas. *Fiorello H. La Guardia and the Making of Modern New York.* New York: McGraw-Hill, 1989.

Koch, Edward I., with William Rauch. *Mayor.* New York: Simon & Schuster, 1984.

Lewinson, Edwin R. *John Purroy Mitchel: The Boy Mayor of New York.* New York: Astra Books, 1965.

Longstreet, Stephen. *City on Two Rivers: Profiles of New York—Yesterday and Today.* New York: Hawthorn Books, 1975.

Lossing, Benson J. *History of New York City.* New York: G. E. Perine, 1884.

Maeder, Jay, ed. *Big Town, Big Time: A New York Epic.* New York: Daily News Books, 1999.

Mitgang, Herbert. *The Man Who Rode the Tiger: The Life and Times of Judge Samuel Seabury.* Philadelphia: Lippincott, 1963.

———. *Once Upon a Time in New York: Jimmy Walker, Franklin Roosevelt, and the Last Great Battle of the Jazz Age.* New York: The Free Press, 2000.

Morris, Lloyd. *Incredible New York, High Life and Low Life from 1850 to 1950.* Syracuse, N.Y.: Syracuse University Press, 1951.

Mott, Frank Luther. *American Journalism: A History, 1690–1960.* New York: Macmillan, 1962.

Moss, Frank. *American Metropolis.* 3 vols. New York: Peter F. Collier, 1897.

Nadel, Stanley. *Little Germany: Ethnicity, Religion, and Class in New York City 1845–80.* Urbana: University of Illinois Press, 1990.

Nevins, Allen, and John Krouthead. *The Greater City: New York, 1898–1948.* New York: Columbia University Press, 1948.

Newfield, Jack, and Wayne Barrett. *City for Sale: Ed Koch and the Betrayal of New York.* New York: Harper & Row, 1988.

O'Dwyer, William. *Beyond the Golden Door.* Ed. Paul O'Dwyer. Jamaica, N.Y.: St. John's University Press, 1987.

Patterson, Jerry E. *The City of New York. A History Illustrated from the Collections of the Museum of the City of New York.* New York: Harry N. Abrams, 1978.

Pleasant, Samuel A. *Fernando Wood of New York.* New York: Columbia University Press, 1948.

Pray, Isaac Clark. *Memoirs of James Gordon Bennett and His Times.* New York: Stringer and Townsend, 1855.

Riis, Jacob A. *The Making of an American.* New York: Macmillian, 1901.

———. *How the Other Half Lives.* 1890. Reprint, New York: Hill and Wang, 1957.

Sante, Luc. *Low Life: Lures and Snares of Old New York.* New York: Vintage Books, 1992.

Sayre, Wallace, and Herbert Kaufman. *Governing New York City.* New York: Russell Sage Foundation, 1960.

Scheiner, Seth M. *Negro Mecca: A History of the Negro in New York City, 1865–1920.* New York: New York University Press, 1965.

Seitz, Don C. *The James Gordon Bennetts, Father and Son, Proprietors of the New York Herald.* Indianapolis: Bobbs-Merrill, 1928.

Shapiro, Fred C., and James W. Sullivan. *Race Riots, New York, 1964.* New York: Thomas Y. Crowell Company, 1964.

Smith, Mortimer Brewster. *William Jay Gaynor, Mayor of New York.* Chicago: H. Regnery Co., 1951.

Spann, Edward K., *The New Metropolis: New York City, 1840–1857.* New York: Columbia University Press, 1981.

Stallman, R. W. *Stephen Crane, A Biography.* New York: George Braziller, 1968.

Steffens, Lincoln. *The Autobiography of Lincoln Steffens.* New York: Harcourt, Brace, 1931.

Still, Bayrd. *Mirror for Gotham: New York as Seen by Contemporaries from Dutch Days to the Present.* New York: New York University Press, 1956.

Stoddard, Lothrop. *Master of Manhattan: The Life of Richard Croker.* New York: Longmans Green, 1931.

Stokes, I. N. Phelps. *The Iconography of Manhattan Island, 1498–1909.* New York: Arno Press, 1967.

Stott, Richard B. *Workers in the Metropolis: Class, Ethnicity, and Youth in Antebellum New York City.* Ithaca, N.Y.: Cornell University Press, 1990.

Strong, George Templeton. *Diary.* Vols. 1 and 2. Ed. Allen Nevins and Milton H. Thomas. New York: Macmillan Publishing Co., Inc., 1952.

Sullivan, Mark. *Our Times: America at the Birth of the Twentieth Century.* Abridged edition. Ed. Dan Rather. New York: Scribner, 1996.

Syrett, Harold C., ed. *The Gentleman and the Tiger: The Autobiography of George B. McClellan, Jr.* Philadelphia: J.B. Lippincott Co., 1956.

Taylor, Robert. *The Diary of Robert Taylor.* New York Public Library, Manuscript Collection.

Thomas, Lately. *The Mayor Who Mastered New York: The Life and Opinions of William J. Gaynor.* New York: Morrow, 1969.

Tocqueville, Alexis de. *Democracy in America.* 1835. Reprint, New York: Alfred A. Knopf, 1945.

Walsh, George. *Gentleman Jimmy Walker.* New York: Praeger, 1974.

Werner, M. R. *Tammany Hall.* 1932. Reprint New York: Greenwood Press, 1968.

———. *It Happened in New York.* New York: Coward-McCann, 1957.

CRIMINAL JUSTICE REPORTS AND DOCUMENTS

Report and Proceedings of the Senate Committee Appointed to Investigate the Police Department of the City of New York. 5 vols., 1895 (Lexow Committee).

New York Assembly. *Final Report of Special Committee to Investigate the Public Offices and Departments of the City of New York.* 5 vols., 1900 (Mazet Committee).

Report of the Special Committee of the Board of Aldermen of the City of New York to Investigate the Police Department (Curran Committee), 1913.

The Investigation of the Magistrates Courts in the First Judicial Department and Attorneys thereof, Final Report of Samuel Seabury Referee. 1932.

Wiretapping in New York City, Volume V of The Minutes and Testimony of the Joint Legislative Committee to Investigate the Public Service Commissioners. Albany, 1916.

Report of the Commission to Investigate Allegations of Police Corruption and the City's Anti-Corruption Procedures (Knapp Commission), 1974.

Report of the Commission to Investigate Allegations of Police Corruption and the Anti-Corruption Procedures of the Police Department (Mollen Commission), 1994.

Statement of Robert M. Morgenthau, District Attorney of New York County and Accompanying Letter to Police Commissioner Raymond W. Kelly. Re: The Fatal Shooting of Jose Garcia by Officer Michael O'Keefe, September 10, 1992.

Mayor's Committee on Management. The New York City Police Survey (Bruce Smith Report). New York: Institute of Public Administration, 1952.

Mayor's Advisory Committee on Police Management and Personnel Policy. Final Report. 3 vols., 1987.

Task Force on New York City Police Community Relations. Report to the Mayor. March 1998.

Girgenti, Richard H. A Report to the Governor on the Disturbances in Crown Heights. Vol. 1. An Assessment of the City's Preparedness and Response to Civil Disorder. 1993.

Kelling, George C., et al. The Kansas City Preventive Patrol Experiment: A Summary Report. Washington, D.C.: Police Foundation, 1974.

Pate, Tony, et al. Police Response Time: Its Determinants and Effects. Washington, D.C.: Police Foundation, 1976.

———. Reducing Fear of Crime in Houston and Newark: A Summary Report. Washington, D.C.: Police Foundation, 1986.

New York City Police Department. Policing New York City in the 1990s: The Strategy for Community Policing. January 1991.

New York Police Department. Strategy #1: Getting Guns Off the Streets of New York. 1994.

———. Strategy #2: Reclaiming the Public Spaces of New York. 1994.

———. Annual Reports. 1909 to date.

———. Magazine Spring 3100. 1930 to date.

CHAPTER 1: A CRY FROM THE BOTTOM OF THE HUDSON

Police: Costello, *Our Police Protectors;* Critchley, "Peel, Rowan and Mayne"; Denlinger, "Old Hays"; Richardson, *The New York Police.*

Crime and Criminals: Cohen, *The Murder of Helen Jewett;* Paul, *Who Murdered Mary Rogers?;* Peterson, *Mob;* Srebnick, *The Mysterious Death of Mary Rogers;* Taylor, Diary; Wallace, *The Fabulous Originals.*

New York City Life: Burrows and Wallace, *Gotham;* Gilfoyle, *City of Eros;* Longstreet, *City on Two Rivers;* Moss, *American Metropolis;* Sante, *Low Life;* Tocqueville, *Democracy in America.*

James Gordon Bennett and the Penny Press: Fermer, *James Gordon Bennett;* Jaffe, *The Rise of the Urban Newspaper Reporter.* Mott, *American Journalism;* Pray, *Memoirs of James Gordon Bennett;* Seitz, *The James Gordon Bennetts.*

CHAPTER 2: "I MIGHT AS WELL CARRY A CLUB"

Police: Costello, *Our Police Protectors;* Miller, *Cops and Bobbies;* Richardson, *The New York Police.*

Accounts of Career of George Walling:
Walling, *Recollections of a New York Police Chief;* "The Police in New Hands," *The New York Times,* June 10, 1885; Obituary, *The New York Times,* January 5, 1892; Career Retrospective, *The New York Times,* January 31, 1892.

Crime and Criminals:
Asbury, *Gangs of New York;* Bell, *The Diary of William H Bell.*

New York City Life:
Bernstein, *The New York City Draft Riots;* Buckley, *Astor Place Riots;* Burrows and Wallace, *Gotham;* Cook, *Armies of the Streets;* Morris, *Incredible New York;* Moss, *American Metropolis;* Pleasant, *Fernando Wood of New York.*

CHAPTER 3: THE FINEST

Police: Costello, *Our Police Protectors;* Richardson, *The New York Police;* Thale, *Civilizing New York City;* Walling, *Recollections of a New York Chief of Police;* Wheatley, "The New York Police Department"; Willemse, *Behind the Green Lights;* Willemse, *A Cop Remembers.*

Riots of the 1870s:
Bernstein, *The New York City Draft Riots;* Bruce, *1877: Year of Violence;*

Costello, *Our Police Protectors;* Headley, *The Great Riots of New York, 1712 to 1873; The New York Times,* July 26, 1877.

New York City Life:
Burrows and Wallace, *Gotham;* Morris, *Incredible New York;* Riis, *The Making of an American;* Steffens, *The Autobiography of Lincoln Steffens.*

On Colonel Ellsworth and his Zouaves:
Catton, Bruce. *This Hallowed Ground.* New York: Washington Square Press, 1956.

CHAPTER 4: THE GREAT DETECTIVE

Inspector Byrnes and His Detective Bureau:
Costello, *Our Police Protectors;* Riis, *Making of an American;* Steffens, *The Autobiography of Lincoln Steffens;* Schlesinger, "The Business of Crime"; Perelman, "Don't Blame Inspector Byrnes"; "New York's Police Chieftains," *Harper's;* William Inglis, "Celebrities at Home: Thomas F. Byrnes," *Harper's Weekly,* November 13, 1908; Obituary, *The New York Times,* May 8, 1910; "Inspector Byrnes, A Super Detective," *The New York Times,* May 25, 1931.

Crime and Criminals:
Asbury, *The Gangs of New York;* Byrnes, *Professional Criminals of America;* Carey, *Memoirs of a Murder Man;* Collins, *Homicide Squad;* Peterson, *Mob;* Walling, *Recollections of a New York Chief of Police;* Byrnes, "How to Protect a City from Crime."

CHAPTER 5: "DOWN WITH THE POLICE"

Police: Richardson, *The New York Police.*

Crime and Criminals:
O'Connor, *Courtroom Warrior;* Rovere, *Howe & Hummel;* Train, *From the District Attorney's Office;* Report: Lexow Committee, esp. testimony of Capt. Schmittberger, (5311–5384), Inspector Williams (5431–5578), & Supt. Byrnes (5709–58).

New York City Life:
Broun, *Anthony Comstock;* Gardiner, *Canfield;* Riis, *How the Other Half Lives;* Riis, *The Making of an American;* Steffens, *The Autobiography of Lincoln Steffens;* Stoddard, *Master of Manhattan;* Werner, *Tammany Hall.*

The Parkhurst Crusade:
Fowler, Dorothy G. *City Church: The First Presbyterian Church in the City of New York, 1716–1976.* New York:

First Presbyterian Church, 1981; Parkhurst, Charles H. *Our Fight with Tammany.* New York: Charles Scribner's Sons, 1895; Werner, *It Happened in New York.*

CHAPTER 6: THE GLORIOUS RETREAT

Police: Richardson, *The New York Police;* Willemse, *Behind the Green Lights;* Willemse, *A Cop Remembers;* Report: Mazet Committee.

Roosevelt as Police Commissioner: Jeffers, *Commissioner Roosevelt;* Morris, *The Rise of Theodore Roosevelt;* Riis, *The Making of an American;* Roosevelt, Theodore, *Autobiography;* Steffens, *The Autobiography of Lincoln Steffens.*

New York Life: Burrows and Wallace, *Gotham;* Crane, *New York City Sketches of Stephen Crane;* Gardiner, *Canfield;* O'Connor, *Courtroom Warrior;* Morris, *Incredible New York;* Moss, *American Metropolis;* Stallman. *Stephen Crane, A Biography.*

CHAPTER 7: "SO MANY RACES UP AGAINST YOU"

Police: Alexander, *Blue Coats: Black Skin;* Battle, Oral history; Bingham, "How to Give New York

the Best Police Force in the World"; Bingham, "Foreign Criminals"; Carey, *Memoirs of a Murder Man;* Fiaschetti, *You Gotta Be Rough;* McAdoo, *Guarding a Great City;* McDonald, *My Father's Gun.*

On Max Schmittberger: White, Frank Marshall. "The Chief Inspector." *The New York Times,* March 14, 1909; Riis, *The Making of an American;* Steffens, *The Autobiography of Lincoln Steffens;* "Schmittberger Is Made an Inspector." *The New York Times.* March 3, 1903; Obituary. *The New York Times.* November 2, 1917.

On Joseph Petrosino: Bloch, *Famous Detectives;* City of New York Parks and Recreation Department, *Lt. Joseph Petrosino Park Naming Ceremony,* May 29, 1987; Petacco, *Joe Petrosino.*

Crime and Criminals: Asbury, *The Gangs of New York;* Joselit, *Our Gang;* Peterson, *Mob.*

New York City Life: Scheiner, *Negro Mecca;* Syrett, *The Gentleman and the Tiger.*

CHAPTER 8: "JUST A LITTLE LIEUTENANT"

Police: McAdoo, *Guarding a Great City;* Willemse,

Behind the Green Lights; Willemse, *A Cop Remembers;* Report: Board of Aldermen (Curran Committee).

Crime and Criminals: Asbury, *The Gangs of New York;* Peterson, *Mob.*

Becker-Rosenthal: Benfey, *The Double Life of Stephen Crane;* Logan, *Against the Evidence;* Root, *One Night in July;* Stallman, *Stephen Crane.*

New York City Life: Curran, *Pillar to Post;* Kahn, *The World of Swope;* Smith, *William Jay Gaynor;* Syrett, *The Gentleman and the Tiger;* Thomas, *The Mayor Who Mastered New York.*

CHAPTER 9: THE NYPD GOES TO WAR

Police: Bouza, *Police Intelligence;* McAllister, *The Kind of Guy I Am;* Tunney, *Throttled!;* Woods, *Policeman and Public.*

Espionage, Sabotage, and Subversion: Goldman, *Living My Life;* Landau, *The Enemy Within;* Talbert, *Negative Intelligence;* Thompson, "New York's Communist Cop"; Witcover, *Sabotage at Black Tom.*

New York City Life: Lewinson, *John Purroy*

Mitchel; Sullivan, *Our Times.*

CHAPTER 10: SHOOFLY

Police: Limpus, *Honest Cop, Lewis J. Valentine;* Valentine, *Nightstick;* Whalen, *Mr. New York;* Willemse, *Behind the Green Lights;* Willemse, *A Cop Remembers;* Mackaye, "Mulrooney Profile" *(The New Yorker);* Alexander, "Valentine Profile" *(The New Yorker);* Fortune, "Nineteen Thousand Cops."

Crime and Criminals: Adler, *A House Is Not a Home;* Gosch and Hammer, *The Last Testament of Lucky Luciano;* Katcher, *The Big Bankroll;* Peterson, *Mob;* Wolf, *Frank Costello.*

New York City Life: Fowler, *Beau James;* Garrett, *The La Guardia Years;* Handlin, *Al Smith and His America;* Heckscher, *When La Guardia Was Mayor;* Kessner, *Fiorello H. La Guardia and the Making of Modern New York;* Mitgang, *The Man Who Rode the Tiger;* Mitgang, *Once Upon a Time in New York;* Walsh, *Gentleman Jimmy Walker; Investigation of the Magistrates Courts* (Seabury Report).

CHAPTER 11: THE CELEBRITY COPS

Police: Carey, *Memoirs of a Murder Man;* McAllister, *The Kind of Guy I Am;* Reynolds, *Headquarters;* Sayre, "Broderick Profile"; Sayre, "Cordes Profile"; Valentine, *Nightstick;* Willemse, *Behind the Green Lights;* Willemse, *A Cop Remembers;* Report: Wiretapping in New York City.

Crime and Criminals: Gosch and Hammer, *The Last Testament of Lucky Luciano;* Katcher, *The Big Bankroll;* Sutton, *Where the Money Was;* Sutton, *I, Willie Sutton;* Waller, *The Story of the Lindbergh Case.*

New York City Life: Kessner, *Fiorello H. La Guardia and the Making of Modern New York;* Morris, *Incredible New York.*

CHAPTER 12: BATTLE IN THE LEAD

Police: Alexander, *Blue Coats: Black Skin;* Battle, Oral history; Bouza, *Bronx Beat;* Valentine, *Nightstick.*

New York City Life: Capeci, *The Harlem Riot of 1943; Daily News, Big Town, Big Time;* Gottehrer, *Mayor's Man;* Kessner, *Fiorello H. La Guardia and the Making*

of Modern New York; Scheiner, *Negro Mecca;* Shapiro, *Race Riots, New York, 1964.*

CHAPTER 13: ON THE PAD

Police: Daley, *Prince of the City;* Daley, *Target Blue;* Lardner, *Crusader;* Maas, *Serpico;* Murphy, *Commissioner;* Neiderhoffer, *Behind the Shield;* Reardon, *Jimmy Riley; Time,* "Strong Arm of the Law"; Kempton, "The Cop as Idealist"; *New York City Police Survey* (Bruce Smith Report); Report: Knapp Commission.

Crime and Criminals: Peterson, *Mob.*

New York City Life: Gottehrer, *Mayor's Man;* Maeder, *Big Town, Big Time.*

On Mayor O'Dwyer: O'Dwyer, *Beyond the Golden Door;* MacKaye, Milton. "The Ex-Cop Who Runs New York." *The Saturday Evening Post,* May 31, 1947; Oursler, Fulton. "The Remarkable Story of William O'Dwyer." *The Reader's Digest,* May 1952.

CHAPTER 14: TWENTY AND OUT

Police: Bouza, *Bronx Beat;* Daley, *Prince of the City;* Gelb, *Varnished Brass;*

McAlary, *Buddy Boys;*
McAlary, *Cop Shot;*
Maple, *The Crime Fighter;*
Mayor's Committee: Police
Management. *Final Report.*

Crime and Criminals:
Vona, "Organized
Crime in New York";
New York Newsday, "Deadly
Gangs," 4 Part Series,
September 13–16, 1987.

New York City Life:
Koch, *Mayor;* Newfield,
City for Sale.

CHAPTER 15: "DAVE, DO
SOMETHING!"

Police: Goldstein, *Problem-
Oriented Policing;* Kelling
and Coles, *Fixing Broken
Windows;* McAlary, *Good
Cop, Bad Cop;* McElroy,
Community Policing;

Murphy, *Commissioner;*
Sparrow, *Beyond 911;*
Norman, Michael. "One
Cop, Eight Square Blocks,"
The New York Times,
December 12, 1993
(profile of Officer Kevin
Jett); Wilson and Kelling,
"Broken Windows; *The
Kansas City Preventive
Patrol Experiment; Police
Response Time; Reducing
Fear of Crime in Houston
and Newark; Report to the
Governor on Crown Heights*
(Girgenti report); *Policing
New York City in the 1990s;*
Mollen Commission
Report; Statement of
Robert M. Morgenthau.

CHAPTER 16: THE
REDISCOVERY OF CRIME

Police: Bayley and
Garofalo, "Patrol Officer

Effectiveness in
Managing Conflict";
Bratton, *Turnaround;*
Alice McQuillan,
"High-Powered Cops
Target Guns," *The
Daily News,* October 11,
1998; Maple, *The
Crime Fighter;* Silverman,
*NYPD Battles Crime;
Report to the Mayor,*
March 1998; *Strategy #1:
Getting Guns Off the
Streets; Strategy #2:
Reclaiming the Public
Spaces.*

Crime and Criminals:
Fox, Butterfield.
"Crime Fighting's
About Face." *The
New York Times,*
January 19, 1997;
Karmen, "Murders in
New York City."

Acknowledgments

We enjoyed writing this book, so we're grateful to Sarah Chalfant, Andrew Wylie, and Liza Walworth of the Wylie Agency for making it possible. Our editor, Jack Macrae, ably kept our eyes on the ball. We also thank Katy Hope, David Koral, and many helpful others at Henry Holt.

In our account of the last half-century or so, we benefitted from the recollections of Jerome Belson, Anthony Bouza, William Bratton, Charles Connolly, James Curran, Robert Evers, Sanford Garelik, Robert Hair, Jack Maple, Robert McKenna, Frank McLoughlin, Milton Mollen, Patrick Murphy, Michael O'Connor, Samuel Sherrid, and others who preferred not to be cited. For sharing with us their extensive research on police deaths, we are grateful to Michael Bosak and John Reilly.

For the excellent service that we received from a number of research institutions and archives of one sort or another, we thank Robert Engel, Nicole Wells, and the librarians of the New-York Historical Society; Eileen Morales and Elizabeth Ellis of the Museum of the City of New York; Director James O'Keefe and librarian Ina Liebholtz of the New York City Police Academy; Kenneth Cobb of the Municipal Archives; Vice President Mary Rothlein of the John Jay College of Criminal Justice and Larry Sullivan and the staff of the Lloyd G. Sealy Library; Angela Troisi, Eric Meskauskas, and Faigi Rosenthal of *The Daily News;* and Linda Amster and Dennis Laurie of *The New York Times.*

Among the many authors of previous books and articles involving the NYPD are a few who have served us particularly well. Augustine Costello's 1885 history and the overlapping memoirs of George Walling (on which Costello appears to have been an uncredited collaborator) are wonderful troves of information. James Richardson's history of the nineteenth-century department sets a high standard of thoughtfulness and reliability. Anyone who writes about the Helen Jewett case owes a large debt to Patricia Cline Cohen's superior book on the subject. And like all chroniclers of the police and the underside of New York in the late 1800s, we are very glad that Jacob Riis was there and paying such close and generous-hearted attention.

Our research on the vital, but little-known, role of the NYPD during World War I was considerably aided and abetted by Henry Landau's 1937 *The Enemy Within*. The author, a former British intelligence officer, was part of the team that gathered evidence on wartime sabotage for the lawsuit against the German government. Jules Witcover's account of the Black Tom explosion was also invaluable.

Virgil Peterson's voluminous and carefully documented book on the New York mob makes it clear why this onetime FBI agent, who went on to head the Chicago Crime Commission, was long considered the country's leading expert on organized crime.

The chapter on the Detective Bureau in its heyday would be much less rich if Joel Sayre had not written his splendid two-part *New Yorker* profile of Johnny Cordes. This chapter also draws on Quentin Reynolds's "Headquarters," itself based heavily on the recollections of Detective Frank Phillips.

Research assistance to the authors was provided by Christa Carnegie, Thelma Collado, and Theresa Wang. James Bock, Steven Jaffe, Daniel Czitrom, Brendan Koerner, and Roslyn Schloss read and improved various pieces of the book-in-progress. Thank you all.

Tom Reppetto wishes to thank Gary Beller, chairman of the board of directors of the Citizens Crime Commission of New York City, and the members of the board's executive committee for granting him release time to work on this book. (All statements in it, however, reflect the views of the authors and not necessarily those of the commission.) James Lardner thanks Sarah Rimer and Jim Impoco; they'll understand why.

We could never have assembled the illustrations without the great generosity and savvy of Natasha Lunn.

Index